HOMELANDS, HARLEM *and* HOLLYWOOD

HOMELANDS, HARLEM *and* HOLLYWOOD

SOUTH AFRICAN CULTURE AND THE WORLD BEYOND

ROB NIXON

ROUTLEDGE • NEW YORK AND LONDON

Published in 1994 by
Routledge
29 West 35 Street
New York, NY 10001

Published in Great Britain in 1994 by
Routledge
11 New Fetter Lane
London EC4P 4EE

Library of Congress Cataloging-in-Publication Data
Nixon, Rob
    Homelands, Harlem and Hollywood: South African Culture and the
    World Beyond / Rob Nixon.
       p.   cm.
    Includes index.
    ISBN 0-415-90860-4   ISBN 0-415-90861-2 (pbk.)
    1. Apartheid in mass media. 2. South Africa—Foreign public
    opinion.   3. South Africa—Relations—United States.   4. United
    States—Relations—South Africa.   5. South Africa—Civilization—
    20th century.   I. Title.
DT1757.N59   1994   93-47906
070.4'49306'0968—dc20   CIP

British Library Cataloguing-in-Publication Data also Available.

for Anne and my parents

CONTENTS

ACKNOWLEDGMENTS

IN WRITING THIS BOOK, I have benefited greatly from the stimulation, encouragement, criticisms, and curiosity of friends and acquaintances. I wish to thank all who have given of their time to read portions of the manuscript, respond to queries, or engage with me over the issues at stake. Particular thanks go to Michelle Adler, Homi Bhabha, Elleke Boehmer, Hazel Carby, Neville Choonoo, Ann Douglas, Liz Gunner, Carolyn Hamilton, Clifford Hill, Jean Howard, Qadri Ismail, Donald McRae, Shula Marks, Frank Meintjies, Gerry Mofokeng, Aamir Mufti, Njabulo Ndebele, Pitika Ntuli, Sarah Nuttall, Dan O'Meara, Kenneth Parker, Benita Parry, Daniel Riesenfeld, Edward Said, Hilary Sapire, Tessa Spargo, and Patricia Wald.

I owe a special debt to my students and colleagues at Columbia: their intellectual companionship and intellectual provocations created an invaluable context for the emergence of this book. I would like to extend my thanks as well to David Blake at the Institute of Commonwealth Studies, London; Sandy Rowoldt at the Cory Library, Rhodes University, Grahamstown; and Brenda Sharp at the National Film, Video and Sound Archives, Pretoria. Without their expertise, innovative suggestions, and good humor this would have been a very different book. Whatever oversights or errors of judgment it contains remain, however, my own.

Sections of *Homelands, Harlem and Hollywood* first appeared in *South Atlantic Quarterly, Social Text, the Village Voice,* and *Transition.* I greatly value the support that I have received from the editorial staff at *Transition* and the Voice Literary Supplement, especially the friendship and editorial cunning of Henry Finder, Scott Malcomson, and M. Mark.

E. Ann Kaplan and Michael Sprinker at the Humanities Institute, SUNY Stony Brook, helped provide a stimulating environment during an early phase of this project. In its closing stages, the book benefited from the knowledgeable and meticulous attention of Neill Bogan, Stewart Cauley, Bill Germano, and Eric Zinner at Routledge. I thank them all.

I wish to acknowledge the generous support of the SSCR-MacArthur Peace and Security Program which enabled me, among other things, to research and write the final sections of the manuscript. The time that the award opened up proved invaluable; but more than that, the SSRC-MacArthur program has given me access to the exemplary forms of interdisciplinary community that it stimulates and sustains.

I was most fortunate to arrive at the Institute of Commonwealth Studies at a time when Shula Marks held the directorship. Her unsurpassed knowledge of South African history is remarkable in and of itself. What was even more extraordinary was her ability to generate, in a slenderly funded and administratively beleaguered institution, a spirit of intellectual passion, rigor, and munificence. I wish to thank her for her friendship and for the many forms of support she has made available to me.

As always, my greatest debt—one that in its variety and depth defies description—is to Anne.

*There's a certain
amount of traveling
in a dream deferred*

—Langston Hughes,
  "Montage of a Dream Deferred"

1 INTRODUCTION

HOMELANDS, HARLEM AND HOLLYWOOD spans the period from apartheid's implementation in 1948 to South Africa's first democratic elections in 1994. The book is centrally concerned with the diverse ties between South African culture and the world beyond its borders. No other post-World War II struggle for decolonization has been so fully globalized; no other has magnetized so many people across such various national divides, or imbued them with such a resilient sense of common cause. An abiding irony thus animates the ensuing chapters: an ideology dedicated to the sundering of communities set in motion vast transnational processes of incorporation—the divestment campaign, and the boycotts of culture, sport, trade, oil, and military hardware. Shared opposition to apartheid played, moreover, an indispensable role in binding unstable international organizations like the United Nations, the Organization of African

Unity, and the Non-Aligned Movement; at times it almost served as their *raison d'etre*.

In 1966, Robert Kennedy began an address to the University of Cape Town with these words:

> I come here this evening because of my deep interest and affection for a land settled by the Dutch in the mid-seventeenth century, then taken over by the British, and at last independent, a land in which the native inhabitants were at first subdued but relations with whom remain a problem to this day, a land which was once the importer of slaves and now must struggle to wipe out the last traces of that form of bondage.[1]

"I refer, of course," Kennedy concluded, "to the United States of America." Kennedy's words capture the intense yet ambiguous ties between South Africa and the U.S.A., two frontier colonies notorious for racial injustice—the one with a black majority of some 35 million, the other with a black minority of almost identical proportions. In a 1981 lecture on "South Africa in the American Mind," the president of the Carnegie Corporation, Alan Pifer, reminded another South African audience that "we Americans have a psychological affinity with your country."[2] Pifer's "we," however, papers over vast differences among Americans in their imaginative responses to apartheid. That much was made manifest by two other American judgments of South Africa that same year.

In 1981, Ronald Reagan, seeking to bolster his policy of "constructive engagement," entreated Americans to look understandingly at South Africa's racial problems "based on our own experience in our own land."[3] June Jordan felt differently:

> I used to imagine South Africa somewhere hidden as deep as the most unspeakable fears that I knew as a child. I used to think it must be a rather small hole of howling white savagery. It would not be beautiful or large or bright or able to grow peaches on a tree that someone would water and cultivate, day by day. South Africa used to seem so far away. Then it came home to me. It began to signify the meaning of white hatred here. That was what the sheets and the suits and the ties covered up, not very well. That was what the cowardly guys calling me names from their speeding truck wanted to happen to me, to all of me: to my people. That was what would happen to me if I walked around the corner into the wrong neighborhood. That was Birmingham. That was Brooklyn.[4]

Such transcultural echoes have reverberated with great emotional force across the Atlantic divide. If black Americans dubbed the Bronx "New York's Johannesburg" and Chicago "Joburg by the Lake," black South Africans christened the Johannesburg community of Sophiatown "the Chicago of South

Africa" and "Little Harlem."[5]

The mutual fascination between America and South Africa has expressed itself in a myriad of cultural transfigurations that have entered literature, music, television, film, photography, art, and theater on both sides of the ocean. In the book that follows, I trace the creative possibilities and dilemmas that have arisen from the refracted images that South Africans and Americans have produced of each other. I consider how Nelson Mandela came to be apotheosized as a trans-Atlantic Messiah; how the "Sun City" music video reanimated the American divestment campaign; how Hollywood movies about South Africa muted the radicalism of the freedom struggle, rendering it more palatable to American liberals; how Verwoerd demonized American TV as a foreign pestilence on a par with poison gas and the atom bomb; and how Sophiatown writers converted Harlem culture into a cosmopolitan resource that helped contest apartheid's revocation of black claims on the city.

If South Africans and Americans have imagined each other in ways that reflect a vexed sense of half-shared histories, this has sometimes led to an illusory sense of mutual intelligibility. Throughout this book, I have tracked not just the lines of cross-cultural allegiance but the barriers, the slippages, the places where the path peters out. The inevitably partial character of the connections becomes particularly manifest in the unstable zone of ethnic and racial discourse: the terms black, African, "colored," nonracial, multiethnic, multicultural, pluralist, and minority have quite different valences and implications in the U.S.A. and South Africa.

No inquiry into the diverse ties between South African culture and the outside world can afford, however, to restrict itself to American affinities. Larger issues, wider links are at stake. As the British critic Paul Gilroy reminds us, one of the most tormenting questions of our age is how to "act locally yet think globally."[6] Over several decades and in the most diverse international circumstances, non South African artists and activists have converted apartheid into a concern that has bridged local need and global awareness. This book is stationed in those border zones where foreigners have reconceived the idea of apartheid and its overthrow under the transforming pressures of their own dreads and dreams. In the chapters that follow, I explore the alliances of anger that apartheid has provoked; I explore, too, how the prospect of South Africa's emancipation has served as a reservoir—to adapt Cornel West's phrase—of "audacious hope."[7]

It is equally crucial, moreover, to consider transculturation in the other direction. How have South Africans reacted to the internationalizing of their struggle? How inventively have they raided other literatures, films, music, and oral history for consolation and inspiration? To what degree has the regime acted against foreign and local resistance by pathologizing "alien" cultures as polluting or subversive?

Any such inquiry must tackle the critical role of culture in bounding and binding the nation. Rival appeals to cultural tradition have played a decisive role in South Africans' fractious efforts to fortify their claims to "true" nationhood—whether these be cast in racial, ethnic, or nonracial terms. These rancorous contests over the lineaments of national belonging have entailed myriad projections and counter-projections of the lineaments of national exclusion. Thus the deeply cultural question of who is accommodated and who is left unhoused by the nation has become indissociable from competing visions of how to define cultural difference—as white or black, English or Indian, Xhosa or Tswana, Inkatha or ANC, cosmopolitan or rural, European or African.

Culture's centrality to the showdown, under apartheid, over national belonging is brutally illustrated by the fate of the bantustans or "homelands." From the regime's standpoint, Transkei, Ciskei, Bophuthatswana, Venda *et al* amounted to foreign nation-states whose territorial boundaries marked impermeable cultural divides. In rationalizing the creation of these human dumping grounds, the regime mounted deterministic arguments premised on what Neal Ascherson has called, in another context, the notion of the "cultural chromosome."[8] Such state efforts to commandeer culture in order to bludgeon into shape nations whose imputed "naturalness" was culturally sanctified, gives a vicious twist to June Jordan's remark that "everybody needs a home so at least you can have some place to leave which is where most folks will say you must be coming from."[9] Through the invention of the "homelands," millions of Africans were reconceived as foreigners and told they came from places that, prior to their forced removal there, they had never been.

Once such people had been deported as culturally certifiable foreigners, they could then be reimported on strictly controlled grounds as labor units. Nationalist Party spokesmen conceded as much: "they are only supplying a commodity, the commodity of labour...it is labour we are importing and not labourers as individuals."[10]

Faced with the life-threatening consequences of such ethno-cultural straitjacketing, many black South Africans affirmed their right to more complex, mobile, and expansive identities. They drew on the precedents and resources of neighboring and distant cultures with an eclecticism that defied all ethnic cultural moulds. Along with a smattering of whites, black South Africans became active in setting up alternative cultural bodies within the country's borders, as well as in mounting sporting and cultural boycotts internationally. They thereby challenged head-on the official image of who gets to represent the nation and how that nation is culturally configured.

Apartheid became, across the world, popularly associated with fixity—with a refusal to "move with the times" and, more precisely, with attempts to petrify racial and ethnic identities in a condition of timeless purity and physical isolation.[11] Officially, the bantustan system was premised on the notion not of stasis but of ethnic cultural nations becoming more like themselves, i.e. on the spurious argument that in isolation they would grow toward greater authenticity. In practice, the system, even judged by its own bizarre terms, allowed for no development at all. Yet the regime's efforts to hold culturally circumscribed races and ethnicities—often at gunpoint—to the most punishingly phantasmagoric standards of authenticity, required and provoked tumultuous upheavals. The fixities of apartheid unleashed wave upon wave of forced removals and illicit border crossings, military invaders and migrant laborers, along with a sprawling diaspora of guerillas, refugees, and exiles who had to piece together the most ironically hybrid identities on foreign shores. Thus an ideological obsession with "pure" belonging—in league with a racist capitalism—became a profound source of displacement and rootlessness. Those who have survived these dislocating imperatives bear witness to what Raymond Williams called "the infinite resilience, even deviousness, with which people have managed to persist in profoundly unfavourable conditions."[12] As I argue in my chapter on the remarkable refugee writer, Bessie Head, inventive courage can transform "deviousness" from an affliction into a cross-border resource.

Apartheid's reputation as an anomalous aberration has sometimes encouraged—particularly in the cultural sphere—an intellectual isolationism that cannot do justice to the scale or variety of such transmigrations. Too often, considerations of South African culture occur in conditions of spatial and temporal quarantine: apartheid is scrutinized both as a case apart and as an anachronism, a throwback to the crude racism of another age. In this book, I depart from that tendency by insisting on the wider links between the discourses of absolute rupture, authenticity, racial purity, and ethnic nationalism on the one hand and, on the other, the idioms of cosmopolitanism, transculturation, hybridity, and internationalism.

The 1990s have given a new clarity to the force of these broader ties. For so long, South Africa and the Eastern bloc combined to shape our prevailing image of both cultural persecution and *ecriture engage*. Despite their ideological antipathy, anti-apartheid and anti-communist writers became bracketed in the West as emissaries of extremity whose presence was at once disquieting and reassuring. This improbable coupling warned liberal Westerners of the fragility of their own freedoms while paradoxically often reaffirming such audiences' cosy self-content.

But in the ideologically ragged interregna of the 90s, artists from neither South Africa nor the former communist bloc can expect to claim that role again.

If the monstrous divisions of Berlin and apartheid left a deep imprint on the post-war moral and imaginative order, the demise of the former Soviet bloc and apartheid's terminal phase have again overlapped in ways that have altered, quite profoundly, our image of the temper of the times.

In both regions, the rhetoric of endings has been accompanied by upward spiralling political expectations amidst plummeting material circumstances. As I suggest in my closing chapters, the abrupt disturbance of core discourses of modernity—progress and multi-ethnic nationalism, Marxism and revolution, communism and anti-communism—has left a profound sense of disorientation and has provoked emotional surges between inflated dreams and bitter foreboding.

Since 1990, South Africa has no longer been amenable to the imagination in the familiar ways. During this period of wavering promise and grim disquiet, many of the traditional preoccupations of the society have gone into retreat: the obsessions, for instance, with the malign devotions of increasingly idle censors, with revolution, exile, and the communist-anti-communist agon. The country's racial inequities have in no sense ended, yet the cleanly etched lines of the apartheid-anti-apartheid conflict have given way to more diffuse—and often less distinctive—forms of social change. Consequently, we have witnessed a shift in the current decade from a perception of South Africa as isolated from world tendencies to a common view of it as just one symptom in the global gallery of disasters and flickering hopes that has characterized the recessionary aftermath of the Cold War.

Well before the Cold War's demise, the Czech social scientist, Milan Hroch, observed that "where an old regime disintegrates, where old social relations have become unstable, amid the rise of general insecurity, belonging to a common language and culture may become the only certainty in society, the only value beyond ambiguity and doubt."[13] In the 1990s, Hroch's words have assumed a premonitory force unimaginable at the time of their issuance. In my final chapters I track the increased salience of culture as both a prize and weapon of conflict amid the rampant insecurities of South Africa and parts of the former Eastern bloc. Drawing on current debates over the cultural reinventions of ethnic identity, I explore the resurgence of cultural and territorial claims couched in the idiom of the myth-encrusted past.

However, we should be wary of pigeon-holing the "new" violence as a uniformly atavistic revival of blood-hatreds. To do so risks obscuring other, less resonant aspects of the feuding: the armaments and psychological legacy of the Cold War, particularly among disoriented military men who were formerly buoyed up by now defunct or diminished enemies; the reluctance of dying orders to forsake power; the brutal stand-offs between rival groups desperate to align themselves with newly powerful words, above all "democracy."

In South Africa and the Eastern bloc, "democracy" has become the Pied Piper of political discourse, drawing in its train a rag-tag of the most unlikely, incommensurate followers. Through overnight feats of ideological cross-dressing, apartheid apparatchiks, communist party chiefs, and sundry other impromptu democrats have suddenly joined the jig of political respectability. The hustling in the 1990s for the right to incarnate "true" democracy has created wracking dilemmas for those who, at great cost, have historically embraced democratic values. As author and critic, Njabulo Ndebele, has observed, the South African regime

> has appropriated many of the ideals of the liberation movement. One effect of such appropriation is to reduce the capacity of those ideas to inspire a visionary optimism among the oppressed. If these ideals can be espoused by everyone, including the nationalist government, then they enter into the hurly-burly of day-to-day politics where they can be stripped of their dignity. The potential result is that a moral and visionary desert is being cultivated precisely at a time when vision and morality are needed.[14]

Thus, one might add, any consideration of culture's role in the improvisation of genealogical claims should be seen in tandem with the impulse on the far right, in parts of the de Klerk administration, and in Inkatha, "to hang on to the dead end of 'white' history for as long as possible."[15]

Ndebele's alarm over the encroaching "moral and visionary desert" should be seen in not just national but international terms. For the aftermath of the Cold War has witnessed the waning of stark, polar politics within and beyond South Africa. Apartheid and the idea of its revolutionary overturning are just two of the many post-WWII verities—the dreams and the demonologies—that have been radically disturbed by the collapse of the Eastern bloc. With the discrediting of communism and anti-communism, South Africans have had to adjust to the loss of a principal paradigm for rationalizing apartheid and a principal paradigm for opposing it. Thus, the 1990s have begun the attenuation of South Africa's distinctive place as one of the great galvanizing issues of the post-War age. For most of that era the notion of apartheid was relentlessly translated into international terms—because it contravened the global impulse toward decolonization, desecrated memories of the Holocaust, and offended the spirit of the Civil Rights Movement. Against the background of these three definitive experiences of our age, the idea of apartheid and its overthrow helped set the compass of human suffering and the compass of human hope.

part one

THE AMERICAN CONNECTION

1

HARLEM, HOLLYWOOD, AND THE SOPHIATOWN RENAISSANCE

Ag, why do you dish out that stuff, man?…Tribal music! Tribal history! Chiefs! We don't care about chiefs! Give us jazz and film stars, man! We want Duke Ellington, Satchmo, and hot dames! Yes, brother, anything American.

—Unnamed African man in conversation with the incoming editor of *Drum*, Johannesburg, 1951

ONE DRIZZLY DAWN in February 1955, 80 trucks and 2000 armed police descended on Sophiatown, a Johannesburg suburb, and drove off with the first consignment of people to be evicted. By 1960, the state-enforced hemorrhaging of Sophia had bled it of its last inhabitants. In the process, the regime obliterated the most diverse and culturally innovative community South Africa had known, compelling most of its black homeowners to become renters in a distant, soulless, segregated township called, with typical euphemism, Meadowlands. On the spot where they killed Sophia, a white suburb was raised up and christened Triomf—Afrikaans for Triumph.

The destruction of Sophiatown remains the country's most symbolically charged memory of forced removal, a policy that from the mid-fifties onwards would uproot 3.5 million people. As Sophia's chroniclers—Bloke Modisane,

Can Themba, Nat Nakasa, Lewis Nkosi, Todd Matshikiza, Es'kia Mphahlele, and Don Mattera among them—passionately recount, Sophiatown was more than just a place. It came to name an era and a departed style of life. Modisane, Sophia's most plangent elegist, recalls it as "perhaps the most perfect experiment in non-racial community living"—an approximate perfection to be sure but by South African standards a symbol of hope in practice.[1] The legacy of Sophia defies simple resolution. It is a sign of apartheid at its most calamitous, yet also a guiding memory of possibility—a gravestone that doubles as a beacon.

Sophia, or Kofifi as the locals knew it, lingers in South African argot as short-hand for 50s cultural brio—for the journalists and fiction writers, the shebeen queens presiding over speakeasies, and the jazz artists and gangsters who revered style, especially style that borrowed amply from Hollywood. As the apartheid regime refined its scheme for racial labeling, American clothes and records spoke with the fine arrogance of other styles of being. Giant finned cars became voguish, as did movie slang, Woodrow hats, Florsheim shoes, and clothes labeled Palm Beach, Palm Dale, and Magregor; Dorothy Dandridge, Sidney Poitier, Humphrey Bogart, James Cagney and Richard Widmark all became idols.[2]

As a foreign influence on Sophiatown culture, America did not pass unrivalled: one feels throughout the literature of that place and era the strong tug of the writers' almost uniformly English, mission school education. But the idea of America had a distinctively populist prestige and an impact that was diffuse and multiform. It was manifest in Themba's enthusiasm for "the township transmigrations of American slang"; in Matshikiza's double-life as a hard-boiled journalist and pianist for the Harlem Swingsters; in the dapper image of Nkosi dancing through the traffic, a copy of *Go Tell it on the Mountain* wedged beneath his arm; and in Mattera's early life, poring over *Up From Slavery* and *Native Son*, but also modelling his look on a celluloid conception of a Chicago gangster.[3] In short, if English culture was associated principally with liberal efforts to distill a black middle class, much of the American culture available to Sophiatowners enjoyed a more scattered, cross-class appeal.

Above all, it was swing, the blues, and jazz—Count Basie, Dizzy Gillespie, Bessie Smith, Charlie Parker, Duke Ellington, Satchmo—that took root and inspired, helping South Africa's most scintillating performers—Miriam Makeba, Dolly Rathebe, Hugh Masekela, and Abdullah Ibrahim—grow cosmopolitan in Sophia. As Todd Matshikiza testified, some of the mission-educated musicians had internalized a disdain for African forms. Yet ironically, it was the African undertones in Ellington and Count Basie that increased their appeal to South African performers. Peter Rezant, for instance, recalls how "I liked Duke Ellington; I liked his music because it always had that African sound, that sound of a fellow coming across the veld playing this concertina underneath his blanket, repeating this thing for a long time and also humming there: hmmm-mm, ummmmmmmm."[4] Thus certain local performers who felt ambivalent about African music found it more alluring and acceptable when it returned in a transmuted, transatlantic guise.

The American affinities of this powerful sphere of Sophiatown culture have been richly documented by David Coplan in his *In Township Tonight! South Africa's Black City Music and Theatre*.[5] As Coplan makes clear, Sophiatown's musical renaissance was already flourishing in the 40s and to some extent predated the literary heyday to which I wish principally to attend.

If America provided an immense stimulus, Sophia's own cultural resourcefulness prevented craven imitation. Foreign tones enriched everything from *kwela* music to popular journalism, but what emerged was finally and characteristically Sophia. "The fabulous decade," Nkosi called the Sophiatown of the 50s, with all the euphoric nostalgia of an exile.[6] It was, by most standards, a grim fabulousness, lightened in retrospect by the political gloom that shrouded the South African 60s. Dougmore Boetie, ever alert to Sophia's contradictions, remembered it as "a black heaven glowing with sparks of hell."[7] Likewise, when Themba, the era's most barbed journalist, celebrated his community's "swarming, cacophonous, strutting, brawling, vibrating life" he carefully added his amazement at people's talent for surviving against all odds.[8] For all its adversities, Sophia seemed to offer a self-consciously new style of being amidst its defiantly urban jumble of ethnicities and classes and its unique concentration of artistic as well as criminal ingenuity. The ghetto's writers, at a loss for local precedents, reached abroad for illustrious analogues. Thus Sophiatown became imaginatively recast as "the little Paris of the Transvaal," or more often, as a halfway house between the Harlem of the renaissance and the Chicago of the silver screen.[9]

LITTLE HARLEM

What was the force of the ties between two communities 8,000 miles and three decades distant, between Nkosi's "fabulous decade" and Arna Bontemps's "foretaste of paradise"?[10] The broad if loose affinities between Sophiatown and Harlem were a matter of sensibility and social circumstance. The two worlds— in so many ways disparate—were yoked through a mixture of influence and analogy, inevitably partial and unevenly felt, but impassioned none the less. The imaginative common ground is perhaps best conveyed obliquely through Ralph Ellison's evocation of the blues—"an impulse to keep the painful details and episodes of a brutal experience alive in one's aching consciousness, to finger its jagged grain, and to transcend it, not by the consolation of philosophy but by squeezing from it a near-tragic, near-comic lyricism."[11]

Sophiatown's flowering during the 50s was only graced *ex post facto* with the appellation "renaissance." But that retrospective designation implicitly acknowledged Harlem as a powerful half-precedent for the kind of precarious, bruised transcendence that Sophia's artists achieved amidst the traumas of apartheid.[12] It was thus scarcely surprising that long after their community's dismemberment, several Sophiatown writers would make the pilgrimage to Harlem. Nakasa

Fig. 1: The *Drum* office. H. Nxumalo, C. Motsisi, E. Mphahlele, C. Themba, Ntsipi, A. Maimane, Xashima, Choho, B. Gosani. On floor, Mtetwa, Eyantyi. (Jurgen Schadeburg)

recalls how he bore with him a mental map of his destination gleaned from Langston Hughes short stories and Baldwin essays; he anticipated a place that might have passed for a Johannesburg ghetto.[13]

But the associations were not merely imaginative; they sprang from particular social affinities. Both Harlem and Sophiatown experienced a cultural upsurge in the aftermath of black migration toward the inevitably unsteady promise of urban employment during an era of growing industrialization. In the American South and South Africa, severe drought, crop failure, and generally deteriorating rural conditions became further spurs to rural exodus.[14] In the U.S., World War I served as a major catalyst for industrial growth and for the accompanying black influx into northern cities, while in South Africa World War II quickened a similar migration. As Arnold Rampersad has observed, "every major American war from the Revolution to Vietnam…has led to a material advance in the freedom of black Americans."[15] Equally, the aftermath of such wars has often sharpened disillusionment among black workers who had replaced departing white soldiers or responded to rising industrial output. For, along with all female workers, they have typically found themselves in the frontline of firings during post-war declines. Black soldiers returning from military service have often voiced anger over their unrewarded patriotism, as they readjust to disenfranchisement in a white supremacist society.

This pattern after World War I has long been acknowledged as a critical element in the genesis of the Harlem Renaissance.[16] However, comparable circumstances prevailed in post-World War II South Africa, as sacked black workers and demobbed soldiers took particular umbrage at Prime Minister Jan Smuts's two-faced stance on human rights. The war had transformed Smuts into a global leader, a leading architect of the new world order; yet he failed to give any local substance to his high-flown international principles. The war efforts of black South Africans on the battlefront and in industry left them no closer to the prospect of job security or the vote.

Within three years of the war's end, the Smuts regime had been ousted and replaced by the main party of Afrikaner nationalism, a change which over the course of the 50s profoundly jeopardized the status of urban Africans, most dramatically in Sophiatown. If African-Americans had found themselves in 1919 in a recessionary climate replete with Southern lynchings, race riots, and racial scapegoating, black South Africans faced, after 1948, a far more vicious backlash. Over the course of the next decade, the National Party would extend and fortify the country's already formidable battery of racist legislation.

Nkosi, writing as a member of the generation which came of age after World War Two, recalls how

> we were not, by any means, prepared to forgive the indecent readiness with which our immediate elders were prepared to believe that after this history of war and pillage white people meant well by us, and that given time they would soon accord us equal say in the running of the country's affairs. Not only had our elders apparently believed this patent hoax, but during the Second World War they had allowed themselves to be pressed into service under the impression that they were helping win freedom and democracy for *us*! This seemed to us incredible stupidity.[17]

Nkosi and the rest of the post-World War II Sophiatown set exuded, like their Harlem predecessors, a spirit of defiant self-reliance and would not be bullied into forsaking their city foothold. *Drum* magazine, the principal outlet for

Sophia writing, projected an expressly cosmopolitan target audience—"the new African cut adrift from the tribal reserve—urbanised, eager, fast-talking and brash."[18]

The writing of the "New African" was suffused with an iconoclastic, anti-"tribal" energy. But it was not always able to obscure its melancholy severance from the past. What Mphahlele and company craved was an affirming precedent: in Harlem literature some of them recognized a world that was black and urban, spoke of the trauma and promise of displacement, and defeated all "tribal" categories. At a time when the very idea of belonging to the city was coming under increasing legislative pressure, the Harlem Renaissance helped emergent South African writers fortify their claim. In short, their affiliation with a bold city strain of African-American writing became, to adapt an apartheid term, a tonic form of "unlawful association."

Such links were based in most cases upon little more than scattered, chance reading; or, as J.U. Jacobs has argued, upon the infusion of jazz and blues into Sophia's literary idiom.[19] Langston Hughes, however, offered a more direct line of influence through his association with *Drum* magazine which featured his work on several occasions in the 50s. In 1954, Hughes served as a judge for *Drum's* annual short story competition and that same year sent copies of *The Weary Blues* and *The Ways of White Folks* to Mphahlele, a gesture that set in motion both a literary influence and a durable friendship.[20] Mattera and the *Drum* columnist, Casey Motsitsi, also felt the allure of Hughes's prose, particularly, in Motsitsi's case, the Hughes of *Simple Speaks His Mind*.[21]

The "New Negro," whose advent Alain Locke had heralded in his eponymous anthology of 1925, was clearly a major forebear of the "New African."[22] As Tim Couzens has observed, it was H.I.E. Dhlomo, a South African writer steeped in Harlem literature and conversant with Locke's volume, who first voiced the idea of the New African in 1945.[23] Others followed: Peter Abrahams's autobiography, *Tell Freedom*, which appeared in 1954, records his ecstasy of recognition upon discovering Locke's anthology.[24]

Locke's introduction to that volume brimmed with optimism in its portrait of the "New Negro" as iconoclastic, independent, and ineradicably cosmopolitan; a figure, in every sense, on the move. Sophia's writers, for related reasons, typically denounced state-enforced ethnic designations as immobilizing and viewed "tribal" categories as impediments to the engine of African progress. Most of the urban literati counterposed such "tribalism" to the modernity they claimed, a protean affirmation that involved distancing themselves from the rural past, often with the full force of renunciation. (This is not to suggest that their response to the urban-rural divide was wholly uniform. Matshikiza, for one, was less estranged from rural traditions and less dismissive of them than

Themba and Nkosi).

Locke's vision of "New Negro" cosmopolitanism encompassed more than the desire to "recapture contact with the scattered peoples of African derivation"; but that ambition stood as a definitive component.[25] An African internationalist dimension was apparent, too, in the spirit of hope voiced by Mphahlele when he recalls the 50s as "a highly optimistic period…a decade of real idealism" in South Africa.[26] News of the stirrings of decolonization in East, West, and North Africa peppered the pages of *Drum*, as did tales of African-American achievement—chiefly told through star billings like Joe Louis, Sidney Poitier, Dorothy Dandridge, and Louis Armstrong. A tone of vicarious pride typically infused such features.

If Sophiatown proved almost as critical to the profile of the "New African" as Harlem had to the "New Negro," this was not least for reasons of property. Alongside two neighboring communities, Sophia was set apart from the great bulk of urban South Africa by Africans' retention of the right to own property, a prerogative that elsewhere had been abrogated. Thus a unique depth of material belonging grounded Sophiatown culture's elaborate explorations of identity and voice. In short, the community's cultural achievements were indissociable from its ability to feel, in Themba's phrase, "house-proud."[27]

In a Miriam Tlali novel one character reflects back on "[our] beloved Sophiatown. As students we used to refer to it proudly as the 'center of the metropolis.'…[It was home to] the best musicians, scholars, educationists, singers, artists, doctors, lawyers, and clergymen."[28] Her comment underscores the unparalleled concentration of professionals who dwelled in Sophia and became emblematically central to ideas of racial pride and uplift. However, even more dramatically than in Harlem, these strata, though symbolically powerful, constituted a decided minority. For the great bulk of Sophiatowners were working class or lumpens for whom property ownership remained an abstract prospect.

Sophia thus possessed a small but—by South Africa's dire standards—significant and influential black middle class. In numbers, wealth, or education, it never approached the strength exhibited by the equivalent class during the Harlem Renaissance. However, the Sophiatown writers who belonged to this relatively elite stratum within the community faced more acute versions of many of the dilemmas that had confronted their African American predecessors. How, from the teetering liminality of their artistic aeries, were they to engage with the social needs of the broadly impoverished urban populace below? What stance were they to assume toward the mass movements of the day? Could—or should—their art aspire to enhance racial uplift? How best might they respond to the white cultural ethos that held sway in the bastions of artistic advancement—through emulation, assimilation, prudent accommodation, or separatism?

The Sophiatown set remained, on balance, not much closer to the populist politics of their time than most Harlem writers had been to the Garveyism of the 20s. The South Africans' detachment was less acute by the end of the 50s, as the ANC-led Congress Movement gathered force and *Drum* magazine devoted increasing coverage to the momentous events of the time.[29] But despite *Drum*'s broadly sympathetic reporting of resistance politics, the majority of Sophia's writers remained politically unattached. Certainly, Sophiatown literature seems decidedly remote from organized resistance politics when compared with the Black Consciousness outpourings of the 70s, and with the creative upsurge during the 1980s which was closely linked to a burgeoning populist politics.

A writer's distance from mass politics does not, however, necessarily imply an adherence to art for art's sake. Sophiatown authors often envisioned culture as an immense surrogate force for social change. Nkosi spoke of "a surge of optimism...that art might yet crack the wall of apartheid."[30] Modisane voiced the view, pervasive on both black and white liberal sides of the fence, that "if South Africa could not be subverted politically, then perhaps culturally and socially the whites could be seduced into realising that integration was a sane policy...."[31] Such utterances were infused with a kindred cultural idealism to that advanced by Locke, James Weldon Johnson, Charles Johnson, and Jessie Fauset, among others, during the Harlem Renaissance. James Weldon Johnson, one recalls, proclaimed in 1928 that "through his artistic efforts the Negro is smashing" racial barriers "faster than he has ever done through any other method," while for Locke "the only safeguard for mass relations in the future must be provided in the carefully maintained contacts of the enlightened minorities of both race groups," with artists in the vanguard of the enlightened.[32] Charles Johnson intoned that literature had "always been a great liaison between races" and offered significant hope in the enterprise of racial reconciliation.[33]

These paired inclinations—to remain distant from organized politics and to flatter art's powers of social transformation—were not universal in either renaissance. One thinks, for instance, of the complex figure of Claude McKay, a theoretical radical who never fully engaged with populist politics. During the Sophiatown era, most though not all writers kept their distance from the ANC and the Congress Movement. Alfred Hutchinson, however, was one of the accused in the protracted Treason Trial of the mid-fifties, while Mphahlele joined the ANC in 1955.[34]

Despite such exceptions, there was an unmistakeable leaning among writers during the heydays of Harlem and Sophiatown toward a leeriness of organized

arg pols + art

politics and a belief in art's healing possibilities. Given such common tendencies, it is scarcely surprising that related criticisms have been leveled against leading figures of both eras. In an influential estimation of the Harlem Renaissance, David Levering Lewis has found some of Locke's views "irresponsibly delusional"[35] and argued that

> [The Talented Tenth] might have tried to pursue a path that more nearly corresponded to the political and institutional needs and aspirations of the masses of Afro-Americans….The architects of the Renaissance believed in ultimate victory through the maximizing of the exceptional.[36]

In the South African context, critics like Nick Visser, David Maughan-Brown, and Kelwyn Sole have assailed Sophiatown as a literary renaissance that failed, principally on grounds of elitism, naivete, political disengagement, and misplaced cultural idealism.[37] *failure*

Some of these charges are unanswerable. However, the putatively 20/20 vision of hindsight can generate its own myopic anachronisms. We should not allow the glaring limitations of both Harlem and Sophia's cultural flowerings to skew our sense of the options available at the time. It is, for example, easy to exaggerate writers' snobbery by idealizing the mass movements from which they kept their distance. While most Harlem writers had little truck with Garveyism, Garveyism itself was deeply flawed, beset, in its own fashion, by sentimentality, elitism, and corruption. The ANC of the early 50s was also, though to a lesser degree, a somewhat dissatisfactory and residually elitist body. (Later in the decade, when it became more populist, the ANC garnered some support from certain *Drum* writers.) If the Sophiatown set were prone to overrate culture's political potency, the ANC exhibited the opposite failing: it largely declined to take culture seriously, an attitude that would scarcely have encouraged writers to become more directly engaged.[38] Thus, the glaring defects of vision among the literary elites in both 20s Harlem and 50s Sophiatown should not obscure the shortcomings in the mass movements available at the time.

The phrase "literary elites" is itself only ambiguously apposite. Given the power of racist institutions to block advancement at every turn, most Harlem and Sophiatown writers enjoyed a precarious or evanescent sense of material privilege. Moreover, social stratification occurred in circumstances where the middle classes enjoyed very limited possibilities of keeping the working and underclass at a physical remove—another feature of Harlem life that was exaggerated in Sophiatown. As Paul Gready has observed in a fine essay on the period, "Sophiatown lacked a geography of class. One could not choose one's neighbours, and the wealthy Mabuzas, Xumas, and Rathebes lived alongside the poor and wretched. It was possible to live, or create the illusion of living, in all layers of society at once."[39] This unsteady mix of immersion and elevation suffused much of the liveliest literature of the time, nowhere more so than in the work of Themba who epitomized such ghetto brinkmanship. As one *Drum* editor testified, Themba "combined a taste for Euripides and Blake with a restless life of intrigue and action in the streets and backyards of Sophiatown."[40] While he remained distant from mass politics, such a writer could never assume a purely abstract relation to the urban underclass.[41]

More disturbing than the ambiguous class limitations of Sophia's literary renaissance was its relentless machismo: the atmosphere was airlessly male and sometimes misogynistic. The sexual politics of *Drum* writing swung between the merely retrograde and (in the case of Themba and Nkosi) the deeply dismal. The general tenor of the magazine's advertising, letters, and advice columns ratified and disseminated such attitudes. What is striking, however, is not just the aggressive mixture of paternalism, misogyny, and the absence of female writing—all pervasive features of South African life during the 50s—but the new, distinctive forms that the assault took.[42] In an acute analysis of this dimension of *Drum*, Dorothy Driver has argued that in embracing an urban modernity the magazine promulgated "an ideology of domesticity, whose aim was the establishment of a consumer-oriented nuclear family, headed by the husband and father and hospitable to female authority only in its carefully controlled domestic forms." The weakening hold of rural patriarchal traditions on city dwellers meant that social hierarchies and conventions of courtship had to be reinvented. What emerges in Driver's account are profoundly altered relations between black male anxiety and female subjection. On the one hand, *Drum* advocated Western romantic love as a prestigious marker of modernity; on the other, romance incurred for men the threat of "financial debt as they strove to 'earn' modern women" under the crippling conditions of apartheid. Thus the "new" woman found herself increasingly bombarded with the trappings and standards of Western beauty, while being projected as a threat to the urban man's virility and a drain on his pocket. *Drum* became complicit in a wider effort to contain the "menace" and desirability of women within an ideology of domesticity. In the process, the public sphere was cast as inviolably masculine while the private sphere was feminized—notwithstanding the fact that most urban black women held jobs in the public domain.[43]

INTER-RACIAL MASQUERADE, THE WHITE HAND, AND THE JUNGLE TRACK

The fate of any cultural renaissance is likely to depend, in large measure, on its ability to shield its iconoclasts from a deforming dependency on inimical institutions. If, during Harlem's high era, it proved immensely difficult for African-American artists to sustain institutional self-reliance, in Sophiatown thirty years later the obstacles to such an achievement were far more daunting. In both cases, if to differing degrees, writers found themselves overly preoccupied with the task of negotiating their way round, under, or through white institutions that remained the dominant arbiters of cultural worth.

The Sophiatown Renaissance displayed a local variant of that two-step danced between those whom Zora Neale Hurston sardonically dubbed the Niggerati and the Negrotarians; that is, between dutiful Harlem artists and their motley white patrons and sympathizers. The dance of allure and repulsion required, on the part of Sophia's aspirant writers and musicians, some elaborate shimmying. Masquerade and mimicry, camouflage and persiflage, patronage and paternalism all marked the black-and-white embrace.[44]

Even more strikingly than in Harlem, Sophiatown's interracial entanglements depended on the special relations that developed between the black and Jewish middle classes. Whatever limited contact—be it activist or bohemian—occurred between Sophia and the bastions of white ease was conducted largely between these two groups. Despite their tiny population, South African Jews predominated in white radical and liberal circles—in the Communist Party, for instance, as well as in theatrical, musical, and publishing circles. As whites, South Africa's Jews were the bearers of immense privilege and held a number of the most powerful positions in mining and industry. Yet they also carried a local history of discrimination. The electoral victory of the National Party in 1948 sharpened Jewish fears, for Afrikaner nationalists in the 30s and 40s had repeatedly condemned Jews as decadent, unassimilable cosmopolitans and had demanded, on occasion, their deportation. Given the scale of black artists' institutional disempowerment, Jewish contacts held out the prospect of a promising if highly ambiguous resource. The regime's assault on black urban land rights only intensified the projected value of such a rapprochement: for black artists who ridiculed the "dead end" of an enforced "jungle track," Jewish bohemians offered one of the liveliest sources of cosmopolitan culture.[45]

If 125th Street was Manhattan's most resonant divide, Johannesburg had its own version of sorts: the "color bar," as the strip of veld was called separating Sophia from the staid white suburb of Westdene. Vaulting the "color bar" over weekends became a source of *frisson* and some genuine, if largely one-sided, risk. Mphahlele, in interview, has likened this sudden enthusiasm for breaching the line to the white vogue for Harlem flings in the late 20s.[46] At the beginning of the 50s, few whites ventured into Sophia's *shebeens* (speakeasies); by mid-decade it had become—among a limited set of liberals, radicals, and their European and American visitors—a trendy pastime.[47]

Two Jewish Johannesburgers who frequented Sophia—novelist Nadine Gordimer and Phillip Stein, a bookseller friend of Modisane's—recall how white liberals at the time zealously invoked E.M. Forster's injunction, "only connect."[48] Had *A Passage to India* not *Howard's End* been prescribed at the local university, the irony would surely have become manifest: Forster's early idealism about goodwill was far less apposite under apartheid than his later reflections on liberalism's wretchedly inadequate bridging of colonist and colonized.

The 1959 jazz opera, *King Kong*, typified the problems that dogged well-meaning but somewhat delusory Sophiatown efforts at devising art with an interracial luster. Based on the tragic life of the heavyweight boxing champ, Ezekiel "King Kong" Dhlamini, the jazz opera was pitched as "a show-piece of black-white unity of purpose."[49] The producer, Leon Gluckman, crowed that "any white person who has seen the show will think twice now before he pushes an African out of the way on a street corner. It's not politics, but a question of human relations."[50] *King Kong* would prove that, despite their adverse circumstances, "Africans are capable of cultural achievements equal to any the whites can show."[51]

With a score by *Drum* writer and composer Matshikiza, *King Kong* was billed as a work of innovative syncretism blending "jazz heard on Gramophone records, radio hit tunes, film music" and "the older fabric of "tribal" rhythms and work songs."[52] Some of the performers, notably, Miriam Makeba and ten- year-old penny whistler, Lemmy Mabaso, proved spectacular. However, the division of labor remained profoundly racialized: the actors, musicians, and dancers were overwhelmingly black, while the producer, director, and lyricist were all white. The distribution of responsibilities showed and *King Kong* remained primarily a blockbuster for white audiences.

Gordimer's Sophiatown novel, *A World With Strangers*, which appeared in 1958, a year before *King Kong*, offers an uncanny, anticipatory gloss on just such floundering collaborations. With icy skepticism, the character Steven Sithole remarks that a particular jazz-opera, jointly conceived by a Sophiatown musician and his suburban counterpart, resembles "more a white man's idea of what a black man would write, and a black man's idea of what a white man would expect him to write, than the fusion of a black man's and a white man's world of imagination."[53]

Some Sophiatown writers adhered to their own variant of the liberal hope that, in combination, friendship and high culture might crack the barriers thrown up by apartheid. Their attitude bears comparison with that of Harlem liberals like White and Locke. *The New Negro*, as Rampersad has noted, had white readers as its principal target: "Through the display of black sensitivity, intelligence, and artistic versatility, it was believed, whites would come to a new understanding of the humanity of African-Americans and help to accelerate social change."[54]

But for Sophia's authors the psychological toll of such inter-racial outreach was immense. Mphahlele recalls how his hunger for acceptance by white publications left him snared in a double-bind: when whites rejected his work he felt the bitterness of discrimination, when they accepted it, he feared he was being patronized.[55] As Nkosi observes, "the European presence in us contributed to a feeling of self-consciousness; a desire to be judged and rewarded by our European critics."[56] And that desire, in turn, sometimes skewed their sense of audience.

Modisane's mordantly lyrical autobiography, *Blame Me on History*, offers the most affecting account of a generation's inner division and unsettled cultural loyalties. Unlike Mongane Wally Serote, Njabulo Ndebele, Mafika Gwala, and most black writers who came of age during the 70s, the Sophia group inherited from their mission-school education a sweet tooth for the culture and values of white liberalism. It is a historical and class oddity of Modisane's writing that his renditions of Johannesburg ghetto life are flavored with comparative allusions to Victor Hugo, Dickens, *The Inferno*, *Paradise Lost*, *Dr. Faustus*, Plato, and *The Bible*.

Modisane saw through the risible attempts of a paper-thin black middle class to pitch gentility against racism. Yet he was half-in-love with their conviction "that a gentleman does not raise his voice in loud protest: he persuades, makes accommodations, accepts compromises, binds himself to the honour of a gentleman's agreement."[57] Nor did he quite lose his fondness for their high-culture style.

Like many mission-educated black intellectuals, Modisane found himself stretched between the wider community he inhabited and the narrow world of Big-C Culture that he coveted and from which, as apartheid tightened, he was increasingly barred. He, and literati like him, felt wracked by the pressure to broker between Sophiatown's cultural life and the often exoticizing tendencies of whites who controlled publishing and the media.[58] Torn apart by incompatible expectations, Modisane remained unable to forgo either life: "I am the eternal alien between two worlds; the Africans call me a "Situation," by Western standards I am uneducated."[59] Themba had another word for this liminal condition: "crepuscular," the twilight fate of being "caught in the characterless world of belonging nowhere."[60]

A "Situation" was argot for any comparatively educated African, anyone possessing the qualifications to apply for positions advertised under "Situations Vacant" in the columns of the white press. For an African to possess "advanced education" usually meant, in the straitened circumstances of 50s South Africa, no more than that he or she had completed high school. In contrast to the Harlem Renaissance, the Sophiatown Renaissance could draw on almost no university educated artists and intellectuals.

As part of his brinkmanship, Modisane honed a colossal talent for smooth yet impassioned scorn. Much of it he directed at liberals whose culture he envied while despairing of the individuals who possessed it. On the efforts of white and black socialites to douse apartheid with suburban tea, he writes:

> I remember that I used to become overpowered by a sense of self-consciousness. I felt that I was a curiosity at most of those tea parties. I was a piece of rare Africana; subjected to such illuminations like: "I've never met an intelligent African before—I mean an African who is actually articulate." Most of them were visibly struggling with the word "African" which was almost always one beat too late.[61]

Simultaneously exoticized and patronized, the Sophiatown set had to cope with a distant version of the parlor primitivism that characterized many of the contacts between Harlem and white Manhattan. Harlem writers and cultural brokers as varied as Zora Neale Hurston, Langston Hughes, Nella Larsen and Locke were impelled as a matter of survival—and sometimes, as a matter of sport—to refine the arts of dissembling.[62] As Shula Marks has observed of contacts across interracial faultlines, inattentiveness to the work of masking can lead historical interpreters to mistake "quiescence for acquiescence."[63] Baker has argued that a command of "the minstrel mask by blacks constitutes a primary move in [the advent of that] Afro-American discursive modernism" which was the Harlem Renaissance's distinguishing achievement.[64] Under his own more arduous circumstances, Modisane reinvented the mask both as a literary trope and a way of life. "The African," he declared, "needs to be a master in the art of chicanery" and become adept at donning the "canvas smile."[65] "Africans have discovered—and this by way of self-protection—that the white South African is hopelessly and fanatically susceptible to flattery, a weapon which the Africans use with vicious enthusiasm to express their sincerest contempt."[66] Elsewhere, he speaks of how the stratagem of masking allowed him to play "the eternal actor in a make-believe world of tinsel reality, revealing the face, the profile which photographed the best…"[67]

By now a rich and voluminous literature has emerged around the issues of masking and mimicry, a body of critical work by, among others, Frantz Fanon, James Baldwin, Steve Biko, Henry Louis Gates, Hazel Carby, Homi Bhabha, Luce Irigaray, Houston Baker, and Shula Marks. The insights of this literature ought always, however, to be measured against conditions that are unavoidably local and immensely variable in the possibilities they allow.

Otherwise the risk arises of sentimentalizing masquerade by abstracting it into a unitary phenomenon that is inherently, if ambiguously, empowering. Modisane's position illustrates this risk lucidly: under apartheid he had far less room to manoeuver behind masks than did, say, Hughes in Harlem. Faced with claustral options, Modisane came to experience an asphyxiating convergence between his performed self-effacement and a deeper defacement: "I have no face," he concluded, "I have no name, my whole existence slithers behind a mask called Bloke."[68]

The struggle to emerge from under the immense weight of white institutions—formidable enough in Harlem—was, in Sophiatown, almost unimaginably more taxing. Nkosi spoke of the white minority's "near total hegemony" in the cultural sphere through "their roles as academics, as critics, as anthologists and impresarios, as gallery owners and publishers, and as consultants of those who owned virtually all the means of cultural production."[69] Harlem at its cultural zenith had been relatively wealthier, endowed with a larger black middle class and with better educated cultural brokers. Enablers with the status and connections of James Weldon Johnson, the Harvard and Oxford educated Locke, Fauset, and Walter White were inconceivable in Sophia's cultural circles. There were, moreover, proportionately many more African-Americans at college, as lecturers and students, than black South Africans. (In combination, these restrictive circumstances ensured that the Sophiatown Renaissance never begat the full range of genres: it bore little that was noteworthy by way of theater, poetry, or novels. Its central literary achievements lay in autobiography, short fiction, and the essay). Furthermore, South Africa's smattering of college-educated Africans—including, at the time, young leaders like Nelson Mandela, Walter Sisulu, and Oliver Tambo—were understandably more drawn to the political than the artistic sphere as, compared to the Harlem of the 20s, there was a better organized and broader populist movement for progressive change.[70]

Harlem's writers enjoyed access to a range of outlets for their work—among them, *Opportunity*, *The Crisis*, and *American Mercury*. The Sophiatown set were, by contrast, forced into an almost unchallenged reliance on a single publication, *Drum*, which dwarfed all others as an influence on the style of the period. At its inception in 1951, *African Drum* (as it was then known) was suffused with an ideology of white trusteeship. It was larded with Christian pieties and was condescendingly rural in many of its assumptions. It featured a series called "Know Yourselves" about different "tribal" identities and a column by a white ethnomusicologist, "Music of the Tribes."[71] In the first issue, an installment of Alan Paton's novel, *Cry, the Beloved Country*, could be found flush against Countee Cullen's celebrated poem, "Heritage":

What is Africa to me:
Copper sun or scarlet sea,
Jungle star or jungle track
Strong bronzed men, or regal black,
Women from whose loins I sprang
When the birds of Eden sang?[72]

The juxtaposition of *Cry, the Beloved Country* and "Heritage" is revealing of *African Drum*'s inclinations. On the one hand, Cullen's poem did alert black South Africans to new affinities, prompting, for example, this response from a Mr. Zondi:

> Sir, Not until I read your magazine and read that beautiful poem by an American negro had I known that the American negroes still long for Africa. I had thought that, Americanised and mechanised, they were thankful to be oblivious of the "Dark, Dark Continent."[73]

On the other hand, the Christian primitivism of Cullen's poem is tinged with pastoral yearning and with the pathos of what Paton calls the "broken tribe."[74] Cullen's lost African Eden may have been a diasporic abstraction, while Paton's Eden found expression in the rolling hills and "tribal" integrity of precolonial Natal, but together their work offered up a nostalgic duet for an African identity set in an irreducibly rural past. In the context of South Africa in 1951, the tragic pastoral tones of these otherwise divergent works were consistent with the political project of resurrecting that chimera, the "unspoiled" African.[75]

Cry, the Beloved Country played a singular role in shaping an international understanding of apartheid and achieved, in addition, a particular local significance for the Sophiatown Renaissance. The reasons for the book's impact were manifold: its unsurpassed reach as a literary influence on global perceptions of South African racism; the coincidence of its publication in 1948 with the advent of Afrikaner nationalist rule and official apartheid; its incarnation of a missionary ethos of white trusteeship; and its emergence as a cardinal counter-text for the Sophiatown set—it was the book they wrote against.

Paton's novel stands as the only blockbuster in the annals of anti-apartheid literature. For decades it was canonized in school curricula from Kansas to Karachi, and it has outsold every other South African literary work. Especially in the U.S.A., multi-media attention amplified the novel's influence. A cinematic adaptation, starring Sidney Poitier, appeared in 1951(and premiered in South Africa at Johannesburg's Harlem Cinema); Felicia Komai produced a version in verse drama; *Life* ran a cover story on "Paton and his Beloved Country," and Kurt Weill and Maxwell Anderson collaborated on a Broadway adaptation that ran for 273 performances—the "musical tragedy," *Lost in the Stars.*[76]

The novel and its spinoffs helped propel South Africa's racial injustices into the international headlines during the late 40s and early 50s. As many of the Sophiatown set began writing in precisely those years, they found Paton everywhere before them. In the absence of sustaining literary progenitors, they tended to approach *Cry, the Beloved Country* as a negative forebear, a book that clarified their sense of where it was they were not coming from. Modisane, Nkosi, Themba, Nakasa, and Mphahlele all inveighed against Paton for demonizing city life and adopted his leading man, Rev. Stephen Kumalo, as an anti-hero who incarnated the unctuous religiosity, the deference, and the urban incompetence that were antithetical to all they professed.[77]

Paton's plot revolves around an urban rescue mission. Kumalo, a Zulu parson, leaves his tranquil rural parish in search of lost family who have been sucked into the cesspool of Johannesburg, a place of confused identities and mongrel values. The Rev. Kumalo, whose quest takes him to Sophiatown, finds that his brother has become a political "agitator," his sister has "sunk" into prostitution, and his son Absolom is headed for the gallows after murdering an upstanding white reformist. Returning to his rural parish, Kumalo despairs both of city life and of the prospect of racial justice. However, his spirits are boosted by the forgiveness extended to him by the white father of the murdered man—a sleight-of-hand on Paton's part, in the individualistic spirit of "only connect."

Nkosi gave voice to his generation's rejection of Kumalo on the grounds that

> we, the young, suspected that the priest was a cunning expression of white liberal sentiment. Paton's generosity of spirit, his courageous plea for racial justice…were not of course in question. What was in question was Paton's method, his fictional control of African character which produced an ultimate absurdity like Stephen Kumalo: an embodiment of all the pieties, trepidations and humilities we the young had begun to despise with such a consuming passion….In Stephen Kumalo we thought we saw, then, another Uncle Tom secretly finding his way into our midst by rural train via Ixopo and Carisbrooke, covered with the dust of the humble and the lowly, speaking in the measured cadences of a Biblical tongue, which was scarcely recognisable to us.[78]

Mphahlele added his lament: Kumalo's stations of the cross suggested that "patient, Christ-like suffering on the part of the black man can move the adamant heart of the white man to philanthropic deeds that will bring the black man hope."[79]

Paton's liberal variant of a trusteeship ideology has to be seen against the contest between a paternalistic English handclasp and the white fist of Afrikaner nationalism, both of them, though in different ways, devastatingly destructive. Ironically, *Cry, the Beloved Country* appeared in the very year when the electoral victory by Afrikaner nationalists had sounded the deathknell of the paternalism that the book incarnated. Written prior to the advent of full-blooded apartheid, the novel was thus an anachronism at birth.[80] Between 1949 and 1959, the new regime assailed black claims on the cities and strove to unscramble the cultural and ethnic mixes that proliferated there. The Prohibition of Mixed Marriages Act, the Immorality Amendment Act, the Population Registration Act, the Group Areas Act, the Prevention of Illegal Squatting Act, the Bantu Education Act, the Preservation of Separate Amenities Act, the Natives Resettlement Act, the Group Areas Development Act, and the Bantu Self-Government Act all eroded the rights of urban blacks while deepening their resolve to stay.

Under such circumstances, Paton's categorical divide between urban degeneration and rural regeneration offered little consolation. Although his assault on South African racism rankled with the new regime, many of the terms of his attack were compatible with the Afrikaner nationalist onslaught against urban Africans as corrupt, impure, and "detribalized." Urbanization was indeed, for many Africans, a saga of bewilderment and loss; but it also held out prospects of relative economic advancement and cultural excitement. Above all, as Sophia's writers insisted, cosmopolitan identities could not be unravelled by herding people into overcrowded lands or forcing them to suffer the destitution of black labor on white farms. In short, airy dreams of a pure return to more "authentic" identities risked reinforcing the National Party's efforts to "fossilize" Africans— as Themba put it—"into tribal inventions."[81]

Drum, a revamped version of *African Drum*, came to play a powerful role in the symbolic resistance to such fossilization. It amplified the voices of a defiantly impure cosmopolitanism, projecting an urban look and ethos, and confirming the professional classes in their attachment to the city. Ten months after *African Drum*'s inception in 1951, the publication—which was losing money—began to break with the "tribal" focus that the serializing of *Cry, the Beloved Country* had epitomized. A new editor, the Oxford educated Englishman, Anthony Sampson, strove to give the magazine a more urban tilt: he jettisoned "Know Yourselves" and "Music for the Tribes," and ditched the epithet "African" from the title, evidently to signal a more internationalist pulse.[82] Sampson appears to have heeded the advice proffered by the likes of boxing promoter, Job Rathebe. The problem with the old *African Drum*, Rathebe averred, was that "it's got the white hand on it.... *Drum*'s what white men want Africans to be, not what they are. We're trying to get away from our tribal history just as fast as we can. We don't want *Drum* to remind us."[83]

Sampson expeditiously appointed an all-African team of reporters: one result was a less anthropological prose, fast-paced and irreverent.

In features and fiction alike, *Drum*'s accent fell on sex, sport and crime, on the ills but also the (mostly male) thrills of city life. However, *Drum*'s obsessive probing into gangsterism and alcoholism were not pitched as arguments against the city per se and were offset by African success stories. Some of those profiled

Fig. 2: Nathan Dambuza Mdelele, leader of Sophiatown's famous Manhattan Brothers. (Jurgen Schadeburg)

were local, like Sophia's own Dr. Xuma, a leading activist in the campaign against forced removal; but inevitably, given the frailty of South Africa's black professional classes, *Drum* plundered many of its images of upward mobility from African-America. Duke Ellington, Louis Armstrong, Althea Gibson, and Joe Louis all received star treatment, alongside features like "High Life in Harlem,"

"Negro University" (on Howard), and a regular column, "Negro Notes From USA."

Drum's advocacy of New African values jarred with apartheid policy: National Party strategists saw not New Africans but lamentable "black Englishmen," overeducated upstarts, corrupted and corrupting, who had defied their racial station.[84] While *Drum* was scarcely a dissident forum, it gave symbolic sustenance to urban identities that could not be reduced to the negative plight of "detribalization." Moreover, while the magazine spurned a party political line, it did carry exposés of forced removals, apartheid prisons, and the near slave conditions on some Transvaal farms. After beginning tentatively, *Drum* afforded increasing coverage to the volatile—if as yet nonviolent—political campaigns against the National Party's battery of prohibitive legislation.

However, *Drum*'s role in shifting the parameters of black middle class identity was fraught with ambiguity, not least because, though written by black men, the magazine remained throughout the 50s white-owned and edited. Without it, few among the Sophiatown set would have acquired the self-assurance or experience to become writers; but the apprenticeship that *Drum* allowed was hedged about by stylistic and imaginative constraints. As one commentator observed of the early years of the Harlem Renaissance, "the white presence... hovered over the world of art and literature like a benevolent censor, politely but pervasively setting the outer limits of its creative boundaries."[85]

At *Drum*, that hovering presence took the quintessentially South African form of mining money. Jim Bailey, the magazine's proprietor, was the heir to a fortune made off gold. According to Arthur Maimane, the *Drum* staff "was discouraged from writing about the mines....It was Bailey's children's inheritance."[86] Mphahlele concurs: "in shaping the magazine the white hand was very strong, in particular from Bailey behind the scenes. He had a strong desire to avoid confrontational material."[87] (Such charges call to mind Zora Neale Hurston's lamentation—in her fine essay, "What White Publishers Won't Print"—that the white literary world remained stubbornly resistant to vast swathes of African-American life).[88] In short, Bailey's sensitivity about mining stories and conflict, together with the *Drum* writers' own non-militant inclinations, their isolation from migrant labor, and their almost exclusive masculinity created a broad hiatus in the spread of the magazine's concerns.

The *Drum* writers found themselves disfigured by the tug-of-war between English capital and Afrikaner ethnic nationalism for control over black culture. Modisane and company belonged to the last generation of black intellectuals to be imbued with a liberal education at church schools like St. Peter's, the "Eton of Sophiatown." As such, they epitomized the class of "black Englishmen" that Verwoerd so loathed and sought to throttle with his Bantu Education Act of

1953. Everything *Drum* represented defied Verwoerd's grim edict that "The Natives will be taught from childhood to realise that equality with Europeans is not for them.... There is no place for him [the "Bantu"] above the level of certain forms of labour."[89] Against such a brutal backcloth, *Drum* can be seen to showcase the refusal of a defiant elite to shut down its talents and aspirations. Yet the scope and character of their defiance remained crimped by the very educational system they sought to defend, producing as it had, a narrow, overly dependent, and Eurocentric buffer class. Thus Bailey's magazine helped, in a myriad of important ways, consolidate an urban look and outlook but it could never quite do so outside of a subtly censorious paternalism.

HOLLYWOOD HOODS

As oppressive legislation mounted during the 50s, black South Africans found themselves facing not just the habitual denial of their citizenship but the virtual foreclosure of the law-abiding life. An urban African could enter, with no effort at all, a life of lawlessness; legality was, under the circumstances, the more taxing status to maintain.[90] Commenting on these deteriorating conditions, Modisane concluded that

> because [white South Africans] had been educated into an acceptance of the primacy of law and order, they did not—unlike their reflections in the Southern States of America—mob themselves into a lynching pack; perhaps it was that they held a dependable reliance on the banditry of the law to adequately proximate their murderous anger.[91]

Many black South Africans answered their imposed illegality by embracing an outlaw image.[92] For most *Drum* writers, the contest between daring outlaws and the "banditry of the law" became a symbolic fixation. They wrote tirelessly about illicit speakeasies, forbidden multiracial sex, knife-happy *tsotsis*, passing, and black forays into whites-only churches. Adopting a debonair lawlessness as both a way of life and a writing style, they turned to their beloved Hollywood for ways of dressing up their defiance in criminal chic and of announcing, in the process, their irrevocable urbanness.

Hollywood offered a mixture of transport and recognition; a reprieve from apartheid's suffocating prohibitions but also entry into a land of celluloid gangsters that could confirm and inspire South Africa's criminalized non-citizenry in their shadow-lives beyond the pale. The synthetic lure of Hollywood's crepuscular glitter pervaded Sophiatown culture. Modisane dubbed his modest dwelling "Sunset Boulevard"; Maimane, who dressed in detail like a Hollywood journalist, renamed himself J. Arthur Maimane, after J. Arthur Rank;[93] a whole gallery of murderers—Durango Kid, Lefty, Styles, Gunner Martin, Boston Blackie—filched their crime-names from the movies.[94] Of Hollywood's Sophiatown hits—Howard Hawks's *Scarface*, Mervyn Le Roy's *Little Caesar*, Stanley Kramer's *The Defiant Ones*, and Joseph Mankiewicz's *No Way Out* among them—William Keighley's *Street With No Name* ranked as undisputed favorite. Starring Richard Widmark as gang boss Stiles, it drew such a cult following that local youths boosted their street cred by imitating Widmark's overcoated, Benzedrine-sniffing, apple-munching cool.[95] When Sampson took over the editorship of *Drum*, Themba maintained that unless he saw *Street With No Name* he would fail to understand his readership.[96] Sampson's viewing of the movie in lively Sophiatown company confirmed Themba's impression.

The *tsotsi* or gangster stood as a critical bridging figure between the criminal underworld of Hollywood fantasy and Sophiatown street-life. *Tsotsis* understood with a visceral force the culture of ingenious illegality; they were urban frontiersfolk who survived by staying not within the law but just beyond its grasp. It was they who were principally responsible for giving American style and slang a local subcultural look and accent. Paradoxically, the gangsters' adaptations of foreign style rendered black urban culture all the more inimitable and thereby indisputably indigenous. This achievement was of crucial symbolic import in an age when apartheid officialdom ruthlessly assailed cultural amalgams as deviations from an always rural authenticity.

Kort Boy, a Humphrey Bogart fan and Sophia's most notorious *tsotsi*, testifies to the detailed appropriation of American modes. The founder in 1947 of a gang called the Americans, he credits MGM with his initial schooling in knifework.[97] Kort Boy recalls how his gang "used to wear American clothes, like Palm Beach, Palm Dale, Magregor shirts, Magregor trousers, Florsheims, Stetson hats,…but I used to specialise in a straw hat like Frank Sinatra."[98] His followers displayed a trademark partiality for Chevrolet Bel Airs and Cadillac coupes.

So astronomical was unemployment among Johannesburg's black youth during the 40s and 50s that, as Clive Glaser has observed, the majority of young men were involved (if to varying degrees) with *tsotsi* culture.[99] They occupied that middle terrain between survival and active resistance where the boundaries are seldom clearly drawn. As *tsotsis* disdained the ethos of civility, nonviolence, Christianity, and the work ethic that lay at the heart of ANC support, *tsotsis* could—in an equivocal, anarchic sense—be considered more radical than Sophia's political leaders.[100] They might, on occasion, throw their weight behind ANC orchestrated protests, but their tactics tended to be unpredictable and ill-disciplined. Their opportunism and predations on the black community made them a menace. Yet if *tsotsis* terrorized their overwhelmingly black victims, they also won an ambiguous respect in Sophia, not least among some *Drum* writers, who admired their swaggering culture of ingenuity, their unqualified attachment to the city, and their rare ability to instill dread among whites who were otherwise virtually unassailable.[101] Answering "white arrogance with black arrogance," the indisputably urban mien of the *tsotsi* reaffirmed for Nkosi, Nakasa, Themba, and Modisane their own passionate, polemical resistance to rural belonging.[102] As Huddleston testified,

> the *tsotsi* I know best has never set foot in the country....The only life he knows is the life of the town. The only standards he recognises are those provided by an urban, industrialised society. He would be as much a stranger in the *kraals* of Zululand as I would be in Tibet.[103]

The term *tsotsi* itself entered local parlance in the 40s as a corruption of the American idiom, "zoot suit."[104] The gangsters were thus named because they favored narrow trousers; so narrow, in fact, that they sometimes resorted to vaselining their legs in order to ease on the trousers. The *tsotsis'* magpie pilferings from Hollywood extended to movie diction. *Tsotsitaal* (gangster speak) is an Afrikaans-based patois with a larding of English and vernacular languages, notably Zulu, Xhosa, and Sotho. (The precise composition of this patois can vary considerably from neighborhood to neighborhood, let alone from city to city). Sophia gangs embellished their lingo with punchlines from *Street With No Name* and other cult movies: "Remember, guys, I'm de brains of dis outfit"; "Take some bucks, go buy you some nice clothes. I like my boys to look smart."[105] On occasion, such catch phrases filtered into the idiom of political protest. After seeing *Summarkand*, Sophiatown's graffiti artists found a local portent in the line "He Who Comes to *Summarkand* Shall Himself be Destroyed." The words resurfaced on the doomed walls of the ghetto as "He Who Comes to Destroy Sophiatown Shall Himself Be Destroyed."[106]

Writers like Themba and Matshikiza prided themselves on their command of *tstotsitaal*, sometimes invoking it (with evident exaggeration) as a mark of their classlessness. The look and slang of *tsotsis* and Hollywood hoods combined to help Themba and Co. project an image of chic recklessness, allowing them to keep in play the perks of professional status and the perks of disreputability. Nkosi pictures Themba as

> the supreme intellectual *tsotsi*...in the words of the blues singer, "raising hell in the neighbourhood." The neighbourhood in which he raised hell was that sombre, fearful community of the intellect so hideously terrorized by the political regime in South Africa.[107]

Certainly, in the increasingly airless excitement of 50s Sophiatown, these "intellectual *tsotsis*" developed a deathrow disregard for journalistic risk. They lived and wrote tough; they crusaded against drabness and injustice; they daubed corrosive cynicism on everything that cramped them, a cynicism that Themba, for one, applied with equal liberality to himself.

Yet the metaphoric appropriation of *tsotsidom* and Hollywood was not without its complications. Given their distance from organized politics, some *Drum* writers were seduced by the melodrama of illegality in the limited theaters of the bedroom and the *shebeen*. At times they exaggerated the power of acts of reckless disregard—the flouting of prohibition laws, say, or the pursuit of the white women they dubbed "ivory towers"—to strike a blow against racial domination.

The question of the political efficacy of *tsotsis* and "intellectual *tsotsis*" needs to be separated from the rather different issue of their morality. During the 50s, white fears of Hollywood's improbity reinforced white projections of blacks and the city as dragging each other down in a mutually damaging, degenerate embrace.[108] Apartheid bureaucrats did their best to limit black exposure to films that might be interpreted as subverting white authority. Mrs. F. Creswell, a member of the Board of Censors, exemplified this attitude: in 1956 she announced that the Board maintained a "determined front" to exclude from South Africa any films where "Red Indians are shown as good fellows and the White man as a crook, because of the bad influence they would have on Natives."[109]

As Glaser recounts, one concerned citizen—symptomatically, a doctor—wrote into the Johannesburg *Star* in 1954 warning of film's incitement to felony: "We are helping feed the fires of crime by our indifference to what is a canker in our society—the showing of crime films to the less educated class of our population."[110] The head of the city's Non-European Affairs Department, W.J.P. Carr, offered some brisk reassurance: in such films, the enforcers of the law routinely triumphed over the outlaws. Given Hollywood's predilection for casting cops and upright men in heroic roles, crime movies could not possibly pose a threat to society's moral fibre.[111]

Carr's response is fascinatingly wrongheaded. He had evidently not heard audiences at Sophia's Odin Cinema barrack the FBI as they closed in on Richard Widmark.[112] His error relates directly to the caveat that Robert Stam and Louise Spence issue in their pathbreaking essay, "Colonialism, Racism, and Representation." Stam and Spence warn against overemphasizing the narrative impetus of a film in the quest to assess its freedom from or complicity in racism.[113] To do so, they argue, is to deny the complexities of viewers' patterns of identification and thereby the potential for what Manthia Diawara, in a related piece, calls "resisting spectatorship."[114]

*complexity of
spectator resistance*

To judge from the atmosphere at Sophia's Odin and Balansky's Cinemas, from the idolatry of Widmark, from the passion with which *tsotsis* would imitate a gangster's limp or lisp, and from the craze for Bogart and Sinatra slouch hats; to judge from all these signs there were ample young male Sophiatowners who energetically resisted the moral resolution of Hollywood gangster movies.[115]

Nkosi and Modisane—an inveterate cinemaphile who portrayed himself as "literally raised inside the cinema"—were both alert to the tensions between identifying along racial, class, and gender lines on the one hand, and with the moral drive of the plot on the other.[116] The complexity of spectator resistance is suggested by their diametrically opposed responses to Westerns. Clearly, in most gangster movies, white actors embodied both good and evil whereas in Westerns the divide was persistently racialized. Nkosi recalls resisting cowboy plots in a manner that squares with the *tsotsis'* attraction to the gangster underdog. In his words,

> I definitely identified with the weak…people who were unarmed. Not because they were particularly black, or because I knew anything about Indian culture versus white culture, but simply because they were unarmed and I saw the same forces ranged against them, the same technologies ranged against them, that seemed to be in play in my own particular situation….It is possible that the color element also came into it.[117]

Yet according to Modisane, as children he and his friends followed the thrust of Western narratives, foreclosing the possibility of solidarity among the colonized. Modisane recounts how as lads playing on the frontier between Sophia and an adjoining white suburb, "The mud pool was the Wild West of America or the dark interior of Africa; and to us, out there in the pool, the white boys were the Red Indians and we were the cowboys." Interestingly, he acknowledges that "the symbols were undoubtedly reversed in the white camp."[118]

The dearth of women writers in the Sophiatown era has left us with inadequate testimony as to how female spectators positioned themselves in relation to Hollywood's male frames. One surmises that their identification would have been complicated not only by the rampant masculinity of gangster and cowboy movies but by the quite different cultures of illegality among Sophiatown's women and men. While young *tsotsis* were the principal male embodiments of anti-authoritarianism, among women, the spirit of self-empowering lawlessness was conveyed principally by older not younger women—by the beer-brewers and *shebeen* queens (like Modisane's mother) who controlled the speakeasy trade under prohibition.[119] It may have been that much harder for such mature women to find in Hollywood ratification, however oblique, for their particular style of profitable dissidence.

Indeed, our grasp of Sophia's appropriations of film are limited by imbalances in testimony, and above all, by our excessive dependence on the recollections of *Drum* writers. Mattera's autobiography, *Memory is the Weapon*, first published in 1987, helps to some degree crack open this virtual monopoly, by offering a street level angle on the impact of American on *tsotsi* culture.[120] *Memory is the Weapon* chronicles Mattera's metamorphosis from abandoned child into street hood and his stint in prison on a murder charge of which he was later acquitted. Focused on the 50s, his testament only hints at the poet-activist to come, the man who would spend most of the 70s banned and under house arrest, and who would turn belatedly to writing.

Mattera was a cinemaphile. However, unlike the "intellectual *tsotsis*" his relation to the underworld was more than metaphoric. Although he acknowledges some cultural crossover between writers and gangsters, he is insistent on its limits: "We were in the streets, and they were in the desks. We used to call such people 'situations'."[121] While Themba and Co. sallied forth against the establishment from the relative safety of their bylines, Mattera led the Vultures, one of Sophia's bloodiest teen gangs, against the Berliners, Americans, and Russians in combat over turf—World War II and Cold War reruns, South African style.

Mattera—who worked for a time as an usher at the Odin Cinema—drew the name for his gang from the movie, *Where No Vultures Fly*.[122] It was from such films, too, that he drew his English. Most *Drum* writers were steeped in the formal English of the mission schools, adding an overlay of *tsotsi* patois for its social and stylistic cachet; but for Mattera, the street corner brew of *tsotsitaal* and movie English served as his *metier*.[123]

Thus Hollywood's fulgent shadows fell rather differently across the lives of Modisane and Mattera. The former, looking back at his own fiction, remarks how "my heroes were social maladjusts in a society where heroism is measured by acts of defiance against law and order."[124] If Hollywood affected Modisane's characterizations, Mattera was forced to plunder the movies more squarely for self-characterization. Yet both efforts bespeak their authors' groping for role models, for inadmissible fantasies that could prop up turf claims, whether to gangland or, more fundamentally, to the right to think and feel with the full force of a cosmopolitan belonging.

CONCLUSION

As a community of hope in the face of hardening tyranny, Sophiatown symbolized the refusal of city blacks to jettison their urban amalgams and become retribalized in distant townships or rural dumping grounds. The persistence of Sophia rankled with the regime because it was one of the last areas where city blacks could legitimately own property; it had emerged, moreover, as an ANC stronghold. Sophia sheltered black, mixed-race, Chinese, Indian, and even some white South Africans, challenging Verwoerd's chromatically pure dreams.

In terms of ethnic purity, Mattera exemplifies some of the beautifully hopeless cases. At the turn of the century, his Italian grandfather had jumped ship in Cape Town and married a South African of Dutch-Xhosa-Griqua extraction; to confound things further, Mattera's mother was Tswana.[125] One August day in 1955, he and his schoolmates were lined up in a government courtyard for official ethnic classification. To improve the chances of an "upward" rating, names were invented freely, in immigrant fashion: Khumalo became Cummings, Mokwena gave way to McKwenna. Yet these "immigrants" had never budged from their native land. That day Mattera acquired the inflicted identity of "colored." He came to imagine himself for the first time as "colored," he declares, through the dual experience of ethnic designation and forced removal.[126]

Nakasa's jumbled ancestry further dramatises the inventive rigidities of apartheid classification. Remarking on the absurdity of any attempt to return him to a true ethnicity, Nakasa observed:

> I am supposed to be a Pondo, but I don't even know the language of that tribe. I was brought up in a Zulu-speaking home, my mother being a Zulu. Yet I can no longer think in Zulu....I am just not a tribesman, whether I like it or not. I am, inescapably, a part of the city slums, the factory machines and our beloved shebeens.[127]

How, in the tangle of Sophiatown, could anyone sort out essence of Zulu from essence of Tswana, or Sotho from Xhosa, as apartheid bureaucracy demanded? Vast numbers of Sophiatowners possessed no earthly connection with the rural regions that, by decade's end, Verwoerd had inventively designated as their "homelands." But the regime insisted that blacks would only be tolerated in the city as renters and temporary sojourners with no permanent claim on urban residence. The face of Sophia mocked apartheid, so it had to be destroyed.

The Harlem Renaissance had spun into decline by the early 30s, with racial tensions worsening and the Depression magnifying the ghetto's miseries. Political debate had grown increasingly polarized with an upswing in communist and anti-communist rhetoric; many writers followed the turn to the left. Insistent desperation further eroded the ethos of inter-racial liberalism. Times were inclement for belletristic bridge-builders, and widespread abjection accentuated the improbability of literature—especially literature that disdained to be propagandistic—contributing to racial uplift. The 1935 riots incarnated the insurrectionary mood, as a racial assault on a Puerto Rican youth triggered thousands of Harlemites to avenge themselves on white property. The savage response from the police left three African-Americans dead, scores more injured and jailed.[128]

If the Harlem Renaissance waned rapidly, the Sophiatown Renaissance suffered a far more sudden and harrowing eclipse. By 1960, Sophiatown had been razed in its entirety as the regime sought to grind into oblivion the idea and spirit of black urban belonging. That same year, a further act of immense brutality destroyed the reformist hopes, the interracial outreach, and the spirit of nonviolent protest that had marked much of the fifties. On 21 March 1960 police at Sharpeville fired on unarmed protesters, killing 69 people and wounding 180, most of them shot in the back. South African politics took a sudden leftward and rightward surge: Verwoerd outlawed the ANC and PAC whose leaders in turn went underground or into exile, where they launched the armed struggle for freedom. The criss-crossing ideologies of communism and national liberation both gained adherents, although anti-apartheid forces were severely outgunned and outmaneuvered throughout the state crackdown. In short, the Sharpeville massacre and its aftermath ensured that the fifties would be seen as the swan song years of South African liberalism; for the next three decades, it would remain frail and feeble voiced.

Inside South Africa, the 1960s were inclement times for literature, especially literature that sought to remain obliquely political. Much of the decade's richest writing—including the autobiographies of the exiled Sophiatown set—was penned abroad. In 1966, South African literature became, in effect, white by decree. A new statute banned the past and any future work of 46 writers, almost all of them black. Ironically, the regime issued the ban under the Suppression of Communism Act, although most of the authors had been determinedly liberal.[129] The names Modisane, Themba, Nakasa, Nkosi, Matshikiza, and Mphahlele all appeared on the list. Not content with the material bulldozing of Sophia, Verwoerd had summoned his censors for a second blitzing in an effort to raze the place from record and memory.

Nakasa threw himself from a New York skyscraper; Arthur Nortje apparently killed himself in Oxford; Themba committed what amounted to alcoholic suicide in Swaziland. Modisane and the others lived on, doubly burdened by the isolation of exile and the knowledge that their books could be neither owned nor read inside South Africa. Nor, indeed, could anything the authors said be quoted. "What is the use," one of them asked, "if the people you write about don't read what you're writing?"[130] Very few of the Sophiatown diaspora could find the energy to produce thereafter.

Nakasa's gravestone stands in New York's Ferncliff cemetery near the burial site of Malcolm X, an uncanny presentiment of the coming turn in South African politics.[131] For between Nakasa's era and the next great literary upsurge, the Black Consciousness outpourings of the 70s, stands the formidable figure of Steve Biko. Biko helped release into politics that blocked anger which, in Sophiatown, too often imploded or petered out in the cul-de-sac heroism of prodigious drinking. *Blame Me on History* and Themba's *The Will to Die* serve as the clearest statements of the historical need for Biko and Black Consciousness, as this cry of exasperation from Themba suggests:

> The whole atmosphere is charged with the whiteman's general disapproval; and where he does not have a law for it, he certainly has a grimace that cows you. This is the burden of the whiteman's crime against my personality that negatives all the brilliance of intellect and the genuine funds of goodwill so many individuals have. The whole bloody ethos still asphyxiates me.... Leave us some area in time and experience where we may be true to ourselves. It is so exhausting to have to be in reaction all the time.[132]

Biko played a seminal role in delivering black South Africans from the politics of reaction and the enervating compact with liberalism.[133] Certainly, no writer of the Sophiatown era could have announced with Biko's self-assurance: "Black culture...implies freedom on our part to innovate without recourse to white values."[134]

The outlawing of Sophiatown literature left young Black Consciousness authors facing a variant of the Sophiatown predicament: how to write unsupported by forerunners or, more precisely, by access to their efforts.[135] When the 70s set did gain a belated, piecemeal familiarity with Themba and company, their judgements tended to be harsh, as in Mongane Serote's reproach of Nakasa:

> Nat tommed. He tommed while we were rat-racing for survival; he had the time and energy to say to us, 'There must be humans on the other side of the fence; it is only we who haven't learned how to talk.'... His achievements as an artist were loudly applauded by the liberals, and that was the flame, Nat being the moth....Poor Nat, he died still believing that he was a non-white.[136]

The spirit of Serote's rebuke calls to mind Richard Wright's broad brush dismissal in 1937 of his Harlem antecedents—"prim and decorous ambassadors who went a-begging to white America."[137] If each renaissance was subsequently assailed by more militant writers, the analogy has decided limits. For the *ex post facto* coherence of the Harlem Renaissance contained within it the greater diversity of voices, some of whom were critical of black middle class obeisance to white values. Hurston, for one, disdained the Niggerati taste for theater which sees "a creature with a white head and Negro feet strut[ting] the metropolitan boards."[138] And none of the Sophiatown set's pronouncements could match the celebrated defiance of Hughes in "The Negro Artist and the Racial Mountain"—not just his impatience with the black middle class for "aping things white," but his sanguine insistence that

> We younger Negro artists who create now intend to express our dark-skinned selves without fear or shame. If white people are pleased we are glad. If they are not, it doesn't matter....If colored people are pleased we are glad. If they are not, their displeasure doesn't matter either. We build our temples for tomorrow, strong as we know how, and we stand on top of the mountain, free within ourselves.[139]

The objections of Wright and Serote do, however, illustrate a common tendency: the force with which each renaissance has engaged, through quarrel or inspiration, those who followed. Each new wave of writers feels the pressure to reinvent Harlem and Sophia according to its own needs and circumstances. If Black Consciousness writers constructed from Sophiatown a parable of the perils of liberal communion, the prevailing spirit of populist nonracialism in the 80s was more conducive to sympathetic rereadings. Thus, as part of a wider enthusiasm for 50s retro, Sophiatown became the subject of several emotionally powerful, though not always uncritical, revivals.[140]

Questioning the received view of the Harlem Renaissance as a failure, Houston Baker has urged us to weigh its political shortcomings against its discursive legacy; to take, that is, a longer view of what he calls the "deformation of mastery" and the "mastery of form."[141] In estimations of the Sophiatown set, a similar balancing act is required. Part of the difficulty in arriving at such a judgment comes from accumulative, grandiose projections of the *Drum* writers as the "voice of an era." They were no such thing. Their impact on the discursive possibilities in South Africa was marked by profound limitations of class, and above all, of gender. Moreover, their distaste for state-imposed rural identities led many of the Sophiatown set to overreact with an often uninformed disparagement of rural experience per se. Thus their new syntheses brought about new exclusions, their innovative eloquence fresh silences.

To refuse a univocal reading of Sophiatown writing as either categorical progress or regress allows for a more complex sense of its discursive legacy. A member of the ANC Youth League, A.P. Mda, could simultaneously lament the "spineless liberalistic philosophy" of a publication like *Drum* while acknowledging that it helped imbue "vast sections of our people" with a feeling of self-importance: "The monthly journals and pictorials have served in no small way to destroy the sense of inferiority and futility which have eaten into the very vitals of our national life, generation after generation."[142] Similarly, despite his reservations about *Drum*'s politics, Mphahlele credits it with marking the arrival of "a certain stage of articulation, which hadn't been there before."[143]

Forced removals reduced Sophiatown to rubble in all but memory, and its writers were strewn across the globe. Yet its literature helped fortify urban identities that were incontestable achievements well past petitioning. For whatever infirmities it manifested, Sophiatown writing did possess the full weight of belonging. It gave a solidity to the language and iconography of that outlaw condition, that "unnatural" pairing, the urban African. Through the force of their insistent "Here to Stay" *Drum* writers challenged the apartheid project of shrinking black city dwellers into "temporary sojourners." When Sophiatowners sided with the cultural elan and demonic crush of the city against "tribalized" rural dumping grounds, they were backing not just a vision of the right to belong but of the right to do so in the fullness of their diversity.

Much of the ballast for this cosmopolitan dream came from abroad, above all, from the Americas of Harlem and Hollywood. In the process of reworking America for their own ends, Sophia's artists left a resounding testament to the hazards and value of staying the cosmopolitan course under conditions where "mixing" had become demonized as an aberration. As Mattera recalls, "in Sophiatown nobody looked at the colour of your skin. It was who you were that counted.... In another time Sophiatown will be reborn. Not the Sophiatown of the slum, but the Sophiatown of the idea, the ethic."[144]

THE DEVIL IN THE BLACK BOX
The Idea of America and the
Outlawing of TV

There is nothing to prohibit television as long as the set is not used.

—Dr. Albert Hertzog, Minister of Posts and Telegraphs, *Hansard*, 1963

The absence of a native liberation movement in South Africa is equivalent, very nearly, to the enforced absence of television in South Africa.

—Prof. James Burnam, *National Review*, 1966

SOUTH AFRICA'S TOTAL BAN ON TV prior to 1976 ranks as the most drastic act of cultural protectionism in the history of the medium. The ban also stands as the most extensive act of preemptive censorship by a regime notorious for curbing free speech. The outlawing of TV went far beyond the familiar state measures of removing from circulation—often in advance of their issuance—a writer's books, a politician's words, or an organization's publications. For by proscribing TV altogether the National Party anathematized an entire technology.

The South African ban on TV bears directly on some of the most pressing concerns in cultural studies today, not least the relationship between two striking intellectual developments of the past decade: the resurgent interest in nationalism and the ascent of media studies. Despite the media's critical role in generating, consolidating, and disseminating images of national belonging, it is typically driven to the margins of nationalist theorizing or omitted altogether. Among the recent surge of influential studies of nationalism, only Benedict Anderson affords the media any prominence in proposing that print capitalism acted as an indispensable catalyst for modern nationalism.[1] Anderson's emphasis on the bonds between communications technology and national community notwithstanding, he remains, as Philip Schlesinger has observed, oddly indifferent to the impact of post-Gutenberg technologies on the invention and circulation of rival visions of the nation.[2] One should add that in a rare comment on non-print media Anderson briskly concludes that in the late twentieth century "advances in communications technology, especially radio and television, give print allies [in consolidating the nation] unavailable a century ago."[3] However, as I argue in this chapter, the relationship among print, radio, and TV cannot be reduced to such supplementary simplicities. Certainly, the apartheid ban on TV turns Anderson's supposition on its head: the Nationalist Party's antipathy to the medium derived in part from the belief that TV would erode, not fortify, print and radio as agents of ethnic nationalist cohesion.

The South African state's resistance to TV raises other intriguing questions, among them, whether cultural imperialism can be adequately represented in terms of power relations between nation-states. Cultural imperialism has conventionally been theorized as a stronger state's cultural domination of a weaker one, but such an approach typically ignores contests over cultural power within the weaker state. This is a particularly telling oversight in the South African instance, where the regime's prodigious reinventions of national and ethnic cultures for the purposes of internal domination complicate simple theories of TV as a conduit of foreign, notably American, cultural imperialism.

Because Afrikaner nationalists were fearful of admitting TV not just into the nation but into the home as a national microcosm, their arguments against the technology dramatize the gendered construction of the boundaries between private and public spheres. In addition, the fierce debates over the consequences of installing TV help expose the racial and gender underpinnings of technological narratives of modernization and progress. South African proponents of TV extolled the technology as an agent and badge of progress, while TV's opponents envisaged it as the instigator of a Gadarene rush to cultural suicide. However, it becomes apparent that these reversible narratives of advancement and degeneration were both expressly premised on racialized visions of progress and regress.

TV TOXINS AND CULTURAL IMPURITY

TV had been glimpsed at Johannesburg's Empire Exhibition in 1936—the year the medium was launched in Britain and just four years after its experimental introduction in parts of the USA.[4] Yet there was to be a lag of four decades between that first Johannesburg sighting and the inauguration of a South African TV service. As early as 1949 the Broadcast Amendment Act had placed control of TV under the aegis of the South African Broadcasting Corporation; but such was the National Party's resistance to the medium that this remained an interminably abstract responsibility.[5] By the time SATV finally went on the air in 1976, over 130 nations could boast a prior service. By that stage, South Africa had become TV's final frontier in the industrialized world.

Apartheid's chief architect, Prime Minister Hendrik Verwoerd, urged that TV be regarded with the same circumspection as poison gas and the atom bomb.[6] Other Afrikaner nationalists continued in this vein, fondly invoking a German physicist's judgment that "while the atom bomb kills the body, television destroys the soul."[7] Dr. Albert Hertzog, the cabinet minister responsible for media affairs, convicted the telly in its absence of being nothing more than "spiritual opium and spiritual *dagga*"(*ganga*).[8] Hertzog fulminated against "that agent of super-hypnotism," "that evil black box; sickly, mawkish, sentimentalistic, and leading to dangerous liberalistic tendencies."[9] With a pharmacological flourish, Hertzog attested before parliament that "inside the pill [of TV] there is the bitter poison which will ultimately mean the downfall of civilizations."[10]

What enabled TV to incarnate, from the 1950s through to the early 70s, menace of such proportions? Because the technology is so imbued with the idea of America, Afrikaner arguments against TV throw into relief the uneasy relationship between apartheid ideologues and those specters of American culture that haunted their imaginings. Verwoerd, speaking in 1960, warned that "the effect on our cultural life, particularly of the largely American influences which would go hand in hand with television, is not a matter that one can treat lightly."[11] Such anxieties gathered intensity during the 1960s as the peace movement, anti-war protests, feminism, rock and roll, student uprisings, flower power, Satanism, and the Civil Rights Movement could all be projected as degenerate contagions that TV would transmit. The Civil Rights campaign induced particular anxiety. A parliamentary group sent to study American TV warned that programs were choked with "integration propaganda"; the technology, it was believed, would pander to those whom W.W.B. Eiselen had dubbed "the apostles of assimilation."[12] Thus, as one member of parliament later declared, the medium threatened to "denationalize South Africans and Americanize them."[13]

However, the threat from America cannot be seen in isolation. It was superimposed on the old conflict between British imperialists and Afrikaner ethnic nationalists in their quest for control over the country's mineral resources, black inhabitants, and cultures. Afrikaner nationalists found confirmation for their historical animosity toward their former overlords in the decadence of Twiggy and the Beatles. More damaging than such moral dissolution, however, was the British version of "integration propaganda." Hertzog observed with distaste that "friends of mine who recently returned from Britain tell me one cannot see a programme which does not show Black and White living together; where they are not continually propagating a mixture of the two races."[14]

The Nationalists' perception of America and Britain as a joint threat was complemented by the less predictable projection of the West and "Russia" as partners in the subversion of "the South African way of life." The regime repeatedly maintained that TV would simultaneously further the aims of communism and American-style monopoly capitalism, both inimical to ethnic nationalist identities. This fear of a dual capitalist-communist onslaught was in turn premised on a residual Afrikaner conviction that the internationalisms of capitalism and communism existed in a symbiotic relationship, and that neither was compatible with Afrikaner self-preservation.

Thus the Nationalists resisted TV in large part because they believed it would become an uncontrollable conduit for foreign ideologies—a composite brew of communism, liberal humanism, African liberation, and (in keeping with that strong strain of Afrikaner anti-Semitism) "international money power."[15] However, the regime vindicated its resistance to TV on the grounds not just of external threats but of internal ones as well. It demonized the technology as an agent of *cultural fusion* during an era when the regime was hellbent on enforcing *cultural fission* by implementing its bantustan ideology. This scheme, aimed at dispersing African resistance and controlling African labor, was premised on the reinvention of territorially and culturally discrete ethnic national identities. Against this backdrop, the regime can be seen to have opposed TV less because it was thought to corrupt individual morality than because it was deemed hostile to the "authenticity" of these national constructs. TV was feared as an agent of cultural imperialism but also, through its association with American "melting pot" ideology, as an agent of cultural miscegenation. Hence, Verwoerd's party condemned TV as dangerously denationalizing and incompatible with the apartheid blueprint for segregating communities along purported ethnic nationalist lines.

PREEMPTIVE CENSORSHIP AND CULTURAL IMPERIALISM

Afrikaner nationalists were not alone in implicating TV in the spread of moral turpitude. But their assaults should be distinguished on several grounds from the censorious protestations of, say, Mary Whitehouse in Britain or Phyllis Schlafly in the USA. In Britain and America, as in most countries, critiques of TV's purported debasement of national morality gathered force only *after* the technology's inception. Governments ordinarily admitted TV as soon as it was deemed affordable. While the degree of government control varied from one society to the next, the medium was by and large accepted as one more modern convenience—there was no long, suspicious hiatus separating invention from implementation. Hence, in most countries only after TV's installation did controversies flourish over its impact on everything from family dynamics and national identity to sleeping habits and living-room decor. Under apartheid, this scenario was played in reverse: a quarter of a century before TV showed its face, the regime flooded the country with advance warnings about the social chaos that this alien would unleash.

The prominence of rationalized fantasy in preemptive censorship makes it particularly suggestive material for an analysis of nationalism. Censorship, like nationalism, seeks to articulate group identity around a set of exclusions. To narrate and depict who we are inevitably entails narratives and depictions of who it is that we are not. In other words, censorship and nationalism intersect in so far as they both set the parameters of community by dividing the admissible from the inadmissible, the values, products, and people who belong from those deemed unassimilable and alien. Afrikaner nationalists' protracted, byzantine justifications of the TV ban thus give unusual focus to their intellectual and administrative efforts to reconceive the categories of community—be they ethnic, racial, or national.

The Nationalist regime assailed the forms of belonging available to South Africans with unusual violence. In turn, it represented the preemptive ban on TV as an honorable effort to safeguard the sovereignty of such brutally reinvented groups. Together these developments unsettle some of our deepest suppositions about cultural imperialism, given that in the post-World War II era the discourse of cultural imperialism has taken shape around four abiding assumptions: that it is principally of American provenance; that its main conduits are the moving images of TV and Hollywood; that the critique of cultural imperialism is typically a leftist idiom; and that the appropriate unit of analysis is the nation state, cultural imperialism arising when the institutions, products, and values of a powerful nation state threaten those of a smaller or more vulnerable one.

The history of TV's absence under apartheid bears out the first and second of these assumptions: the South African regime did see America as a leading source of cultural imperialism and TV as its principal manifestation. However, the South African experience throws the remaining two suppositions into question. If, in the post-World War II era, the anti-imperialist cry against *le defi americain* has typically emanated from within a Marxist-socialist spectrum ranging from Herbert Schiller and Fidel Castro to Jack Laing and Ariel Dorfman, under apartheid this cry was taken up by the far right. The South

African case, moreover, disturbs the common assumption behind theories of cultural imperialism, that national culture and the nation-state are coterminous. The shortcomings of this assumption can be understood in terms of the trajectory of this strain of theory.[16] When the discourse of cultural imperialism reached its apex during the 60s and 70s, the anti-capitalism of cultural imperialist theorizing was often wedded to a romantic view of the internal coherence of "Third World" nation-states. This limitation was exacerbated by the fact that theories of cultural imperialism were often based on studies of the USA's cultural impact on Latin American nation states. Most of these states exhibit greater religious, ethnic, and linguistic cohesion than almost all their African and most of their Asian equivalents.

The assumed sanctity of the nation-state as *the* legitimate unit of cultural self-regulation cannot account for circumstances where people give precedence to the invented international "kinships" of religion (Catholicism, say, or Islam) or of cross-border ethnicity (Kurds, Somalis, Armenians) over the invented "kinships" of nation-state nationalism. Neither can it account for the contest among national cultures within the nation-state—a point of acute relevance to understanding right wing South African critiques of American cultural imperialism. Such charges highlight the difficulty of explaining, via a cultural imperialist paradigm, circumstances where an ethnic micronationalism like Afrikanerdom seizes state power and invokes the principle of national cultural sovereignty against the putative predations of a foreign national culture. To reduce this scenario, in the South African instance, to a clash between a muscular American imperialism and a weaker Afrikaner nationalism is to ignore the complex relations between international and intranational discrepancies in cultural power.

Left and right wing critiques of media imperialism—like those articulated by Herbert Schiller on one ideological flank and by the Afrikaner politician, J.A. Marais, on the other—share some significant common ground. That much is suggested, for instance, by Marais's warning of the "deadly enmity" between TV's commercialism and national culture and by Schiller's assertion that "Television as it operates today is a mortal enemy of national identity. As a market-driven industry, TV practically guarantees the destruction of national identity."[17] Schiller and Marais are both prone to downplay the complexities of mediation, assuming an instrumental vision of TV's impact whereby reception gets glossed as imposition. Moreover, both critics give priority to the nation as a unit of cultural belonging and present national culture as an absolute condition. There is no accommodation of the possibility that, as Stuart Hall has suggested, culture may simultaneously become more global and more local through what he calls a "double-helical movement."[18] That is, neither critic acknowledges that the internationalizing of culture may produce not simple homogenization but new melds expressive of a shifting sense of cultural belonging that may nonetheless retain a national component. Finally, both Schiller and Marais repudiate American TV on grounds of anti-imperialism in tandem with anti-capitalism. Thus, from both ends of the political spectrum, monopoly capital and TV are represented as collaborative solvents of national and ethnic bonds, the result being economic integration and cultural homogenization.

However, Marais and like-minded Afrikaners pressed their hostility toward TV's internationalism one step further than Schiller. Besides projecting monopoly capitalism and TV as denationalizing forces they assailed TV's affinity with communist internationalism and liberalism. Indeed, among the more vocal Afrikaner opponents of the medium, it became an article of faith that TV, like monopoly capitalism, communism, and liberalism, promotes sameness.[19] One prominent Afrikaner portrayed TV as

> a mighty instrument for the wiping out of all spiritual, cultural, and national differences among our diverse population groups. In practice, it will appear to be not only an effective agent of spiritual-cultural conformity and integration, but eventually also lead to the ideals and goals of the international liberalism and communism of our day, namely a simultaneously switched on herd and a socialist society.[20]

TV, the ultimate agent of cloning, thus came to be cast as an emissary of a Janus-faced Soviet-American challenge to the integrity of Afrikaner nationalism and, beyond that, to the segregated authenticity of all South Africa's pututative ethnic nations.

During the era when the TV imbroglio reached its apogee, the intransigent Dr. Piet Meyer wielded considerable institutional clout. It was he who came to voice the most paranoid Nationalist fear of a Hydra-headed internationalism. In 1959, the year of his appointment as chairman of the South African Broadcasting Corporation, Meyer published a book on the evolution and destiny of Afrikaner nationalism in which he sketched a veritable Niagara of international forces threatening to inundate Afrikanerdom: "Russian and Chinese communism, India imperialism, Eastern, Middle Eastern and North African Mohammedanism, West European liberalism, American capitalistic sentimentalism, and fervent anti-white Bantu animism in Africa."[21]

This sense of well nigh universal engulfment should not, however, leave the impression that anti-imperialist objections to TV were enunciated only in the name of safeguarding Afrikaner nationalism. The groups depicted as vulnerable to TV's corrosive influence were subject to shifts in historical and ideological emphasis: they included, at one time or another, the Afrikaner nation, the white nation, the white race, the Bantu nation, a constellation of ethnic groups advancing toward self-governing nationhood, Western civilization, Christian Western civilization, and the family. This profusion of threatened identities suggests the contradictions within the rhetorical repertoire of a racist nationalism. The regime vindicated its animosity toward TV by sliding among the registers of ethnic nationalist solidarity, national racial solidarity, religious solidarity, and pluralism. The pluralist objection to TV operated through what may be termed the racism of cultural tolerance—that is, a racism whose preservationist discourse allows it to operate without the explicit enunciation of races.[22] Hertzog exemplified the "respectfulness" of cultural racism when he complained that TV would discriminate against South Africa's "Bantu" cultures who would lack access to the medium. "It is typical of this side of the House[the National Party]," he asserted, "that we grant the Black man what we grant ourselves."[23]

In the most contradictory of their arguments against TV, Meyer and Hertzog reverted to what Wilhelm Reich has termed "national internationalism," the process whereby an ultranationalism ordinarily hostile to international solidarities annoints itself defender of an imaginary transnational community—in this case, the "white race" or Christian Western Civilization.[24]

Despite these inconsistencies in the regime's case against TV, the overriding objection remained relatively constant: that TV's magnetic pull towards central domination would produce what was sometimes termed "integration," at other times, "denationalization." As the Nationalists were at pains to point out, the setting up of TV is far more costly than radio or newspaper initiatives. It has therefore tended—particularly pre-cable—to generate more heavily centralized services than other media. In addition, the steep costs of production are apt to render national TV services more reliant on foreign—typically American—programming. The South African regime could use these tendencies to vindicate its claim that the technology would advance an American assimilationist ideology that would jeopardize innate cultural differences—be they between Afrikaners and English, black and white, or (particularly after the Promotion of Bantu Self-Government Bill of 1959) among a variety of state promoted ethnic national groups.

Foreign commentators on the ban have sometimes expressed bafflement at the National Party's reluctance to harness TV's propaganda potential. As one bemused British observer put it, "tyrants do not fear television; they use it."[25] However, South Africa during the late fifties and sixties was no orthodox tyranny. The Nationalists maintained that TV's centralized, internationalist tendencies ran counter to their program of political domination through the proliferation, not the containment, of ethnic nationalist differences.

A TROJAN HORSE IN THE LIVING ROOM: THE SUBVERSION OF DOMESTIC SPACE

"If the home is to become a non-stop movie house, God help the home."[26] Thus spoke Orson Welles in 1955. Albert Hertzog, who took over South Africa's media ministry three years later, concurred. Hertzog warned that anarchy would unfold if his compatriots admitted "a little bioscope[cinema] into the lounge."[27] "We must not forget," he continued, "that television is only a miniature bioscope which is being carried into the house and over which parents have no control."[28]

"Carried into the house": it was this invasiveness of TV, its transgression of the boundaries between public and private, masculine and feminine, production and reproduction, wage labor and domesticity that made it such a magnet for moral debate. As Lynn Spigel has documented, with the spread of the technology in 50s America came a profusion of contradictory notions about its repercussions: TV was reputed to "enhance family solidarity" or, in that 50s neologism, promote "togetherness."[29] It could help keep problem children at home, yet putatively caused tantrums, cancer, and, among obsessive viewers, a hitherto unknown condition called "bugeye."[30]

Almost as relentlessly as Americans, white South Africans were inundated with theories about the ethical, educational, and biological impact of TV on family life. However, unlike Americans, South Africans lacked access to the technology; they thus had no experience against which to measure such speculation. The result was a free for all fantasia of effects, a wild mixture of rumor, pathology, and quarter-baked accounts of half-baked foreign research. Politicians and "experts" projected TV as the cure-all for the ailing "Western" family or, more commonly, as the end of familial civilization. One of the medium's most vocal advocates in South Africa maintained that "nothing has helped so much as television to re-create family life. Family life in the twentieth century was gradually being broken up. Television has brought the family together again."[31] Hertzog veered to the other extreme: TV, he believed, was "the greatest destroyer of family life in the Western world."[32]

Hertzog was not alone in this conviction. From Afrikaner newspaper editorials, the letters columns, the radio, and parliamentary speeches, one can piece together a doomsday scenario in which TV overturns all the hierarchies that discipline family life. The Nationalists erected their fantasy of the disintegrating home on the sands of technological determinism and racial behaviorism. What emerges is a sorry scene of domestic anarchy: under TV's spell, men grow effeminate, women become addictive consumers and bad mothers, sons and daughters degenerate, servants become idlers and rapists, watchdogs lose their bark, and nobody does the housework.[33]

Warning of TV's corrosive impact on Western civilization, Meyer preached that "the most serious and dangerous challenge facing Christian Afrikaners in South Africa today is that of liberalism and communism. Liberals want to make men and women equal, they are trying to make men effeminate and women manly."[34] This fear of TV as an innately equalizing technology resurfaces in several guises: the medium levels not only the natural, divinely sanctioned rankings of gender, but the sacred hierarchies of generation and race as well.

TV would unman the master of the house and assert its alien authority in his stead. The technology "turns men into another kind of being…it would cause absolute chaos to South African life."[35] In the topsy-turvy world of TV effects, adult debasement is matched by the denaturing of children: according to J.J. Engelbrecht, under TV's sway "children are forced into premature adulthood. This is characterized by spiritual confusion and a lack of confidence in adulthood, as well as. . . an unwillingness to become an adult."[36] Another parliamentarian maintained that "for the first five years, both husband and wife…become slaves to television," a view reiterated by Verwoerd.[37] The insistent metaphor of techno-slavery reinforced the idea that TV would not merely violate home life, it would overturn the domestic hierarchies, elevating servants and children while debasing white adults.

A concerned correspondent cautioned in a Transvaal newspaper that

> Just as the alcoholic says with every glass: just the one, then I'm going home so we will say: just the one program, then I will go to sleep. And while the servants enjoy the programs during the day, the wife will be at work so as to help pay for the new "must have."[38]

Thus TV drives the wife from the home into the unnatural business of female wage labor, prompting her to forsake her spiritual responsibilities in pursuit of material gratification. This scene of familial abandonment is compounded by the unattended servants who, instead of ordering the house, lapse into idleness.

Nor, according to Hertzog's variant of this tale of domestic degeneration, is the regime restored upon the wife's return. Hertzog offered up this admonitory fable to parliament:

> It is afternoon and the Bantu house-boy is in the living room cleaning the carpet. Someone has left the television set on. The house-boy looks up at the screen, sees a chorus line of white girls in scanty costumes. Suddenly, seized by lust, he runs upstairs and rapes the madam.[39]

In his Pavlovian nightmare, Hertzog depicts three forces as triggering this sexual-political "native uprising": a lapse in white vigilance, TV's infusion of profane values into the home, and black depravity. This and kindred TV horror stories of domestic and national ruin placed particular store on the collaborative threat posed by the two enemies stationed within the home—the alien (generally American) culture transmitted by TV, and the black servant, figured as an overly literal receiver of alien signals, and regarded with a mixture of dependency and mistrust.[40]

Opponents of TV invoked the figure of the Trojan Horse in seeking to convey this threat of subversion from within.[41] Once the TV set, an apparently benign oddity, had been wheeled through the portals of the white home, it would disgorge, under cover of night, hostile forces that would destroy the volksmoral—the moral fibre of the nation—from within. Crucial for this argument was a vision of TV as a promiscuous technology, not just in sexual terms, but in the sense that it advanced cultural miscegenation. Television's failure to respect what, for most Afrikaner Nationalists, were innate, divinely ordained cultural differences, made the technology a volatile presence in the white home where "incompatible" races worked in close physical proximity.

On returning from the USA, a prominent South African writer testified that American TV was "98 per cent a school for crime."[42] While Nationalists claimed "indisputable proof that it promotes juvenile delinquency," they expressed particular distress over TV's impact on blacks of all ages.[43] "You cannot possibly use cowboy films or crime films," Hertzog admonished, "because you must remember that those films may be seen by our Native population."[44] For J.C. Otto, TV's "pathological partiality for the Black man" exacerbated this threat:

> What happened in regard to the Freedom Riders in the U.S.A.? There the television cameramen came along to photograph everything. There too the Black man was represented as being the oppressed and ultimately emerged as heroes. The overseas money magnates have used television as a deadly weapon to undermine the moral and spiritual resilience of the White man.[45]

Leading spokesmen for the ban agreed that British TV was undesirable, but not quite as depraved as its American cousin.[46] The critical difference lay in the floods of advertizing that inundated the American viewer. The same force that drove the housewife to abandon the home for the lure of wage labor threatened to wash away the inner sanctum of the family beneath the tides of capitalist desire. In a tirade against media advertising, W.C. du Plessis warned parliament of the spiritual dangers of the impulse to commodify time, a tendency whose endpoint would be a tragic compact of Mephistopholean dimensions:

> The Lord gave us eternity, gratis and free. We are now busy dividing it up in quarter hours, ten-minute and five-minute periods, and we sell time. One of these days we will take a mortgage on eternity and give our soul as secu-

rity for that mortgage. I am warning against the consequences of this type of broadcast on our family life and on our social life.[47]

Hertzog, too, opined that

> the effect of television is more intensive than in the case of a cinema because you are in a more intimate relationship with it; you sit in a darkened room close to the television set. It makes a deep impression upon you with the result that television is an excellent advertising medium.[48]

By providing blueprints for crime, inducing techno-slavery, heroizing "the Black man," and serving as the long arm of international capitalism, TV would progressively weaken the bonds of home and, beyond that, of the nation.

In some spheres, like language, Afrikaner culture was projected as the vulnerable target of such assaults; in others, it was the broader category of white culture.[49] Certainly, by the 1960s, Nationalists were apt to speak of TV's threat to the white rather than the exclusively Afrikaner home. Yet even in this period, Nationalists' pathological anxieties about white domestic disintegration bear the mark of a massive Afrikaner investment, earlier in the century, in the moral authority of an idealized *volksmoeder* (mother of the nation). Indeed, the Nationalist flattery of TV's imperial powers cannot be understood apart from the historical construction of the Afrikaner home as an anti-imperial redoubt. It is against this backdrop that TV's threatened surrogacy for the white mother—the prospect of a "glass teat"—unleashed such violent fantasies.[50]

If the myths of ethnic nationalist identity are typically premised on an idealized past, they also frequently depend on an idealized mother as emblem and guarantor of continuity with that past. Thus women, above all maternal women, are repeatedly cast in symbolically conservative, atavistic roles. Elsabe Brink and Isobel Hofmeyr have both argued that the construct of the *volksmoeder* played a vital part in the imaginative labor of papering over the divisions among the class-riven groups who came to be projected as the Afrikaner nation.[51] As one nationalist ideologue put it, "The moral life of a nation is controlled by the women, and by the women can we measure the moral condition of the people."[52] A version of this mythical upholder of the national ethos resurfaced in the TV apparitions of the 50s and 60s: under TV's spell, the *volksmoeder* would defile the spiritual cradle of the nation by granting the values of entertainment, commercialism, and individual selfishness precedence over the religious and educational responsibilities of the *volk*'s self-sacrificial female ideal.

Afrikaner alarm over TV's imagined onslaught was partly a fear of historical regression, of losing to British and American imperialists the cultural, political, and economic clout that Afrikaners had significantly extended since rising to power in 1948. The Afrikaner obsession with foreign cultural swamping, particularly Anglicization, had been accentuated between the world wars in response to the proliferation of cinemas—a trial run, of a sort, for their TV anxieties. In 1919, Hofmeyr notes, the magazine *Huisgenoot* lashed out at the mish-mash of foreign commodities that was later christened and condemned as *bioskoopbeskawing* (bioscope or cinema culture).[53] The attack in *Huisgenoot* admits a sense of the power and longevity of cultural imperialist discourse among Afrikaner nationalists. The magazine warned that

> A foreign culture is ensconced in powerful fortresses and citadels. With every new delivery by sea thousands of cheap English books are distributed throughout the country....Our biggest daily papers, the cinemas, the school system, the language of our courts, the shops with their fashions and merchandise, the furniture in our houses are all bastions and agents of a foreign culture which claims for itself the right to overrun and conquer the world.[54]

However, no embattled Afrikaner could have imagined in 1919 quite how imperial lounge furniture could become.

LANGUAGE IMPERIALISM AND THE ADVOCACY OF RADIO

In 1929, a professor active in the Afrikaans language movement reasoned that "Providence would not have given us a language if we ought not to have had one, otherwise the whole world would have been populated with Britons."[55] To many Afrikaners some thirty years later, TV threatened—if not to populate the world with Britons—at least to flood the world with English. In their unease Afrikaners were not alone: from Wales to Quebec, from Tanzania to Malaysia to France, the rise of TV amplified anxieties about the yoke of Anglicization.

One need not subscribe to a genetic vision of the nation to grasp the force and appeal of Samuel Johnson's conception of languages as "the pedigree of nations."[56] So many other claims frequently hang on the prestige and status of a language: if the language, as centerpiece of a national cultural identity, is weakened, that may hasten other forms of decline. It may readily enfeeble, for instance, land or educational claims—to regional autonomy or to schooling in pupils' mother tongue.

Afrikaner opponents of TV shared with cultural nationalists elsewhere an unease at the technology's linguistic repercussions, but their anxieties took an unusually acute form. There are several reasons for this: the shallow history of Afrikaans as a recognized language; raw memories of English language domination; and the Calvinist perception of the nation as not merely a natural but a sacred unit of belonging. During the first quarter of the twentieth century,

Afrikaners controlled almost no public institutions: South Africa's courts of law, schools, universities, media, and civil service were all heavily weighted against their culture and language. Indeed, for most of its historical course, the progenitors of Afrikaans were little more than a dispersed and derided series of *patois*, the "kitchen languages" of women and servants. The tongue was belittled in English and Dutch institutions, and pupils often brutalized for speaking it at school.[57] Not until 1925 was Afrikaans enshrined as an official language.

As Hofmeyr has documented, the petit bourgeois intellectuals who ultimately secured the legitimacy of Afrikaans, did so by developing a network of newspapers, magazines, and presses which conferred on the language the coherence, influence, and dignity of print.[58] The development of the Afrikaans language thus stands as a powerful illustration of Benedict Anderson's insistence on the ties between the rise of modern nationalism and the ascent of print culture.[59] Linguistic consolidation was critical for the popular transmission of the idea of a nation blessed with an organic coherence. The claim to possess a discrete language became crucial to the creation of an imaginary national continuity, which in turn provided a symbolic base from which to mobilize against English and black bastions of power. In a paradox typical of the nationalist invention of tradition, Afrikaans was held to be a new, "virile" language and simultaneously as evidence of the nation's longevity. Thus, the efforts by petty bourgeois Afrikaners to stabilize and disseminate the language represented an early, integral phase of a wider effort to reconstrue an unstable, internally fractured spread of classes and interests as a unique, indivisible nation.[60]

The crucial phase of "building a nation from words" occurred in the first quarter of the century and culminated in the elevation of Afrikaans to official language status in 1925.[61] However, it was during the 1930s and 40s that the brokers of Afrikaner nationalism—Meyer, Hertzog, and Verwoerd among them—labored most effectively to institutionalize the idea of the Afrikaner nation as a monolithic, divinely ordained community whose origins and destiny transcended class, regional, and gender divides. The ideological labor of manufacturing this cultural and economic nationalism entailed disengaging white Afrikaans speakers from organizations in which they mixed with the English or blacks. Afrikaners were persuaded and cajoled into identifying instead with ethnic nationalist trade unions, banks, cultural bodies, schools, and churches. Thus, for someone like Meyer, the fear of Anglicization was not an isolated fear of linguistic subjection; Anglicization also "involved the sacrifice of Afrikaner Christian nationalism…for English egalitarian liberalism and economic capitalism."[62]

Amidst their general accusations that TV obliterated proud national distinctions, Hertzog, Marais, Meyer, Otto et al reserved a special concern for the technology's impact on press and radio services. Their anxiety arose largely from the perception that TV acted as an agent of language imperialism and would thus jeopardize other media upon which the survival of the Afrikaners' language—and by extension their Christian national culture—depended. Hertzog and company feared that TV would reverse many of the gains that Afrikaans had made in its unequal battle against English. The technology threatened do so first, by eroding the advertising base on which Afrikaans newspapers depended, and second, by extending the authority of English, given that the majority of programs would be imported from the USA and Britain. Thus the TV debates helped reanimate anti-imperialist anxieties, as Afrikaner nationalists foresaw a showdown against that old enemy duo, the English language and foreign controlled monopoly capital.

If Afrikaner nationalists reserved a special anxiety for the fate of their press, their campaign to obstruct TV was equally marked by a relentless advocacy of radio. After Hertzog appointed the ultranationalist Meyer as chairman of the South African Broadcasting Corporation in 1959, radio became conscripted for the promotion of the Afrikaans language and Afrikaner cultural nationalism. When Meyer maintained that "radio distinguishes itself [from TV] by the fact that it does not enslave and does not *want* to enslave the human spirit" he was not just implying that TV is remorselessly addictive.[63] The motif of slavery set off powerful historical reverberations: by implication, TV threatened to reverse the course of Afrikaner national destiny, returning the *volk*, its language, and culture to the thrall of those British imperialists in whose concentration camps 28,000 Afrikaners had died during the Anglo-Boer War and under whose domination they had long smarted. In short, Meyer and company attacked TV as a launching pad for imperialist assaults on Afrikaner self-determination, while lauding radio for its susceptibility to ethnic nationalist control. Radio found favor, moreover, because it could respond cheaply and flexibly to the great variety of languages which, in the divine scheme of things, served as the surest markers of those irrefutable national differences on which apartheid ideology depended.[64]

NATIONALISM AGAINST IMPERIALISM

During his first speech as Prime Minister in 1958, Verwoerd gazed back at Afrikaner history and proclaimed that "this has indeed been the basis of our struggle all these years: nationalism against imperialism."[65] Television was not, on this occasion, the subject of his address, but the historical, philosophical, and religious vision that informed Verwoerd's claim was fundamental to his regime's newly vehement rejection of the technology.

There had been mumbling objections to TV since the early 50s. However, the rise to power in 1958-59 of the ultra-right troika of Verwoerd, Hertzog, and Meyer lifted the decibels of the debate. Between them, Verwoerd as Prime Minister, Hertzog as Minister of Posts and Telegraphs, and Meyer as head of the South African Broadcasting Corporation, commanded the heights of South Africa's media policy. They pronounced more volubly and more frequently against TV, stressing its incompatibility with their obsessive schemes to subjugate, disperse, and disown South Africa's black majority by parcelling them out into rural bantustans.

Television's three most powerful adversaries under apartheid had all been prominent activists and spokesmen during the 1930s and 40s for an embattled Afrikaner nationalism that had taken shape, to a considerable degree, around an anti-imperialist project.[66] One discerns a substantial (if inevitably incomplete) overlap between the arguments that Verwoerd, Meyer, and Hertzog mounted against fusion, integration, imperialism, communism, internationalism, and secularism in the 30s and 40s and the case they would later mount against TV.

All three held leadership positions in the Broederbond, the neo-Masonic brotherhood that played—particularly during Verwoerd's term—a decisive role in reformulating Afrikaner ideals and infusing them into state policy. Of the three men, it was Hertzog who, from 1958 to 1968, used his authority as Minister of Posts and Telegraphs to become TV's most publicly adamantine antagonist. Hertzog's opponents derided him as a Mad Hatter, a Mother Grundy, Chief of the Luddites, and King Canute, for seeking to beat back the tides of technology.[67] However, Meyer, Hertzog's ideological henchman from the mid 30s, may ultimately have been the more decisive figure behind the scenes in the entangled histories of Afrikaner nationalism and telephobia. For almost half a century—between 1933 and 1981— Meyer exercized an influence in Afrikaner cultural institutions unsurpassed in reach or duration.[68] The 1960s, the critical decade of the TV controversy, was the highwater mark of his power, as he simultaneously commanded the South African Broadcasting Corporation and the Broederbond.[69]

Like Hertzog, Verwoerd, and other Broederbonders hostile to TV, Meyer emerged, in the 1930s, as a leading proponent of what Dunbar Moodie has termed neo-Fichteanism.[70] From the perspective of the TV debates, one of the most salient articulations of neo-Fichteanism is found in Dr. Nico Diederichs's 1935 tract, *Nationalism as World-View and its Relationship to Internationalism*.[71] As Diederichs's title suggests, he was intent on theorizing the interface between ethnic nationalist and international identities—the flashpoint issue of the TV debates. Shortly after the publication of *Nationalism as World View*, Meyer came out publicly in defense of Diederichs's ideas, many of which were echoed in Meyer's early tracts, like *The Struggle of the Afrikaner Worker* (1941), as well as in later writings like *Trek Further* (1959) and *The Spiritual Crisis of the West* (1966), which appeared during the peak years of the TV furor.[72]

Diederichs ventured that international culture was innately degenerate as it violated the Creator's partition of the species into distinctive nations. Moreover, internationalism was marred by a materialism that prevented humans from achieving self-realization, a spiritual impulse that could only be satisfied through the spiritual form of national culture, the divinely ordained marker of difference. "Any effort to obliterate national differences," Diederichs intoned, "thus means more than collision with God's natural law. It also means an effort to shirk a divinely established duty or task."[73] In these terms, individual freedom could only be achieved through the higher freedom of the nation—indeed, the individual was a more abstract, insubstantial entity than the nation.[74]

Neo-Fichtean conceptions of the nation came to be adjusted through their intellectual and institutional fusion with Kuyperian Calvinism as well as through the competing needs and definitions of the Afrikaner nationalist project. Nonetheless, certain neo-Fichtean assumptions about national identity were carried forward into the 60s by cultural conservatives like Meyer and Hertzog. Their anti-imperialist ardor arose not just from a fear of external domination but from a philosophical conviction that the nation—as bounded by culture and language—constituted a sacred unit of difference. Meyer's assertion that "it is definitely certain that Godlessness is more prevalent among bilingual people than among monolinguals," surely marked the nadir of such thinking.[75] SACRED

Television was thus condemned as a profane technology not merely in the loose sense that it trafficked in swear words, nakedness, and blasphemy; it was more fundamentally profane in its enmity toward the nation as an institution sanctified by heaven. The medium transgressed the divine matrix of differences by stimulating intercultural (i.e. international) mixing, and by setting the needs, freedoms, and desires of the commodity-crazed individual above those of the nation. Diederichs had spoken of the Creation as God's endorsement of "the multiplicity and diversity of nations, languages, and cultures," evidence of his aversion to "deadly uniformity."[76] *Verkramptes*[arch-conservatives] like Meyer, Hertzog, and Marais fell back on a related argument in the 60s, when they opposed not just racial mixing, but the dilution of Afrikaners' ethnic identity through increasing cultural, political, and economic collaboration with English South Africans and foreigners.[77] Opposition to TV as a conduit for "deadly uniformity" should thus be seen as just one facet of a broader struggle against national "dilution" in all its varieties—through liberal individualism, racial mixing, communism, imperialism, monopoly capitalism, commercialism, and the cosmopolitanism of English South Africans and the Jewish and Indian diasporas.

The subject of TV often occasioned a detailed cataloguing of the Afrikaner nation's projected imperial enemies. In such listings, the Soviet Union and the West—above all, America and Britain—were characteristically fused into a composite antagonist. The Nationalists perceived Western liberals as the shock troops of Soviet communism: their combined advance would be accelerated by TV's pinko technology.[78] As Dr. J.C. Otto explained to parliament in 1966,

> liberalists, communists and leftists all use TV to influence people. In many programmes the white man is presented as a bad person, as the suppressor and exploiter of the black man. The white man is depicted as the person causing misery and frustration for the black man.[79]

When, in August 1969, a *Washington Post* editorial advocated that South Africa adopt TV as a way of modernizing its racial attitudes, Jaap Marais responded fiercely in *Hoofstad*: "Do not install a TV service. South Africa is not open to Russian or American controlled propaganda. That way the people will not be abandoned to the forces of commercialization."[80]

The reference to commercialization offers a clue to the deeper historical reasons for the National Party's twinning of "Russia" and America as enemies. During the decade-and-a-half prior to their ascent to power in 1948, Afrikaner nationalists repeatedly articulated the *volk*'s destiny in anti-imperial terms that isolated as the leading enemies of Afrikaaner unity communism and foreign controlled monopoly capital, the term "foreign" here being stretched to include English-speaking South Africans.[81] Communism and monopoly capitalism were jointly condemned for abetting imperialist internationalism. For communists, so the argument went, the international working class served as the decisive imagined community, in line with Marx's notion that the workers have no fatherland. Concomitantly, under international capitalism, imperial corporations wrenched people from their national moorings, violating the nation by propagating commercial individualism. As Dan O'Meara has cogently argued, during this formative phase of Afrikaner nationalism, hostility was directed toward international monopoly capitalism and seldom towards capitalism per se: indeed, the rise of an ethnic nationalist capitalism was central to the consolidation and empowerment of the Afrikaner nation.[82]

The fear of both communism and monopoly capital suffused the militant Christian National Socialism of Meyer's Ossewa Brandwag pamphlets during the early 1940s, in which he labored to dissuade Afrikaans workers from identifying with class over *volk* in the battle with the monopoly capitalists who dominated the South African economy.[83] During the pre-War era, Afrikaners had coined the term Hoggenheimer—a derogatory corruption of Oppenheimer, the family name of South Africa's most powerful mining magnates—in carica- turing a composite Jewish-English capitalist imperialism. During the TV controversy, Hertzog and his henchmen dusted off the hoary specter of Hoggenheimer as a warning against those who were insufficiently fearful of the medium. Thus when Harry Oppenheimer appealed for TV in 1964, Hertzog swiftly intervened, warning, with barely veiled anti-Semitism, that "the over- seas money power has used TV as such a deadly weapon to undermine the morale of the white man and even to destroy great empires within fifteen years, that Mr. Oppenheimer and his friends will do anything to use it here."[84]

Hertzog's assault on Oppenheimer exemplifies the slippage between the con- tention that TV would subvert the Afrikaner nation and the quite different claim that it would abrogate white South Africa. Clearly some of the projected threats to Afrikaners could not apply to English South Africans, above all, the linguistic threat. In this way, TV's assailants cast English South Africans in contradictory roles as Afrikaners' cultural and economic enemies whom TV would fortify, and as Afrikaners' racial allies whom TV would undermine. This contradiction dogged the efforts of anti-TV crusaders to reconcile their perceptions of TV as a national and a racial threat. (Indeed, on occasion, they would portray the tech- nology as menacing something called the "white nation.")[85] A related tension emerged in the attacks on America, which was sometimes charged with having imperial designs on South Africa, at other times charged with lax complicity— hastened by commerical TV—in the decline of the "white race" and Western civilization.[86]

During the 60s, this hostility toward America and Britain was redoubled by the perception of both countries as rapidly degenerating. The National Party persisted in outlawing TV largely because it was thought to transmit all the "con- tagions" of 60s counter-culture, the endpoint of which would be racial integration and national disintegration. The continuities between these alleged effects of TV and the "disease" of racial mixing were driven home metaphori- cally: the figuring of TV became indissociable from what one MP called the "deadly germs of integration and the even more deadly germs of equality and assimilation."[87] TV was a "pestilence and a plague" which would, it was feared, "contaminate children."[88] It was, moreover, the duty of government to immunize citizens against the "TV virus."[89] Accumulatively in these polemics, the nation- alist alarm over "foreign transmissions" acquired an overdetermined force, as the discourse of media technology dovetailed with the racialized discourse of epidemiology.

Meyer, in a flash of hubris, suggested in 1965 that America had fallen so deep into degeneracy that Afrikaner nationalism ought to take over as interim custo-

dian of Western values. Persuaded that the Afrikaners exhibited "the strongest
Western nationalism, in the world today," Meyer reasoned that an Afrikaner-
led South Africa could offer the West

> the lead in the racial struggle of the present and the future. South Africa
> will make a decisive contribution to the consolidation of the entire West
> as a white world united in its struggle against the joint forces of the yellow
> and black races of the earth. When America reaches this level of maturity in
> the emergent world period, overcoming the transitional sickness and taking
> over the leadership of the whole white world, the West will be very
> favourably placed to win the racial struggle on a global scale.[90]

Having condemned TV on the grounds that it is ineluctably international,
Meyer ends up urging international action in defense of Afrikaner nationalism,
white South Africa, the "white race," and Western civilization. He thus sides
with the cross-border identities that he elsewhere claims are the products and
agents of imperialist domination, be it communist, liberal humanist, or monopoly capitalist. Meyer's arguments are rife with the contradictions of nationalist
internationalism, whereby the more virulently xenophobic a nationalism
becomes the more it aligns itself imaginatively with the transcendent constructs
of "the race."

During the TV brouhaha, the regime's appeals to racial solidarity repeatedly
contradicted its efforts to vindicate the ban by distinguishing between the right-
ful claims of national sovereignty and the illegitimacy of internationalism. Such
contradictions became doubly acute once the bantustan system gained impetus during the 1960s. With the imposition of this system, anti-TV crusaders
could fortify their case by making it sound less self-interested: TV would not
merely threaten the national sovereignty of Afrikaners but the multiple sovereignties of all South Africa's kaleidoscopic "ethnic nations." Thus even Hertzog,
who elsewhere proposed that TV would induce racial degeneration, maintained
that the technology would be prejudicial towards blacks, as its costiliness would
leave their diverse national cultures underrepresented.[91] Similarly, an official
advertisement placed in *The Times* in 1970 declared that

> within the borders of South Africa there are more different nations, more
> different races, creeds and colours than in any other country. The main
> task of the South African Broadcasting Corporation is to provide an enrich-
> ing, ennobling service to all, differing[sic] from one another with respect to
> language and cultural identity.[92]

Thus the bantustan system allowed *verkramptes* to justify their resistance to TV
by parading the kind of sensitivities to difference that would scarcely seem

incongruous in a contemporary American manifesto of multiculturalism.

Beaumont Schoeman's article, "TV: a Powerful Medium of Integration," exemplifies this sophistical style of reasoning; it illustrates, too, how quickly the paternalism of bantustan multiculturalism reverted to brazen racism. Schoeman maintained that

> [TV] doesn't respect differences and stresses uniformity. It breaks and loosens up cultures, it sweeps aside borders and eats away at the values of communities. The propagandists call it a powerful agent of democratization which is a sweet-sounding equivalent of calling it an agent of homogenization....There is no more powerful medium for dismantling the population groups' sense of identity. Nor is there a more effective instrument for the furtherance of integration.[93]

"Integration" here swivels Schoeman's argument away from a defense of multiple, parallel community identities toward a binary, hierarchical vision of racial decline. Once TV had created cloned humanoids and with them a culture of the lowest common denominator, Schoeman continued, the technology would inevitably "drag the spiritual standards of the whites down to the level of the nonwhites."[94]

Through the giddy success of *Understanding Media* (1964), Marshall McLuhan helped transform popular perceptions of electronic communications well into the seventies. His views only entrenched National Party fears that TV would subvert state efforts to disperse black South Africans into atomized ethnic "homelands." McLuhan, one recalls, maintained that

> as electrically contracted, the globe is no more than a village. It is this implosive factor that alters the position of the Negro, the teen-ager, and some other groups. They can no longer be *contained*, in the political sense of limited association. They are now *involved* in our lives, as we in theirs, thanks to the electric media.[95]

For a regime determined to *contain* the African nationalist threat by reinventing "pure" Xhosa villages in Transkei, Zulu villages in KwaZulu, Ndebele villages in KwaNdebele and so forth across a succession of ethnically "authentic" bantustans, McLuhan's vision of TV as productive of a "global village" represented the most dire form of technological dystopianism.[96]

TV, RADIO AND THE THREAT OF AFRICAN DECOLONIZATION

The white South African dispute over TV occurred under the long shadow of African decolonization stretching down from the north. In 1959, two years after Ghana's independence, a Nationalist Party MP voiced the fear that African nationalism would become "the monster which may still perhaps destroy all the best things in Africa."[97] As independence movements gathered momentum across the continent, South African adversaries of TV began to fantasize about an alliance between a "monstrous" African nationalism and the "Devil's box," a pairing that threatened to become the tag-team champions of calamity.[98]

The projected threat posed by the TV-African nationalist duo has to be seen in terms of both South African and foreign liberation movements. Among TV's adversaries, Africa's decolonization triggered a familiar set of alarm bells about the encroachment of internationalist, communist, and liberal humanist values. The regime feared, moreover, that the newly independent states would invade South African air-waves and foment unrest among black South Africans by means of alien, insurrectionary ideologies. To have countenanced TV's introduction would, in these terms, have increased black South Africans' vulnerability to cross-border broadcasts.

Yet radio proved to be the more immediate threat. As early as 1952, Hertzog had warned that the cheap short wave radios, the so-called Saucepan Specials, that pervaded British colonies gave Africans access to Radio Moscow propaganda.[99] By 1958, the Nationalists were expressing outright alarm at the proliferation of hostile radio stations as African states gained their independence. That year, Ghana followed Egypt's and Ethiopia's example in setting up a radio transmitter that could penetrate South African air-waves. As Lebona Mosia et al have observed, the Ghanaian station gave as its *raison d'etre* "the liberation and unity of the entire African continent."[100] Radio Tanzania also assumed a particularly engaged role, and by 1968 was hosting broadcasts by eight liberation movements, the ANC and PAC among them.

By 1961, Nationalist anxieties about media invasion had reached fever pitch. Hertzog fulminated against the powerful propaganda stations that were "waging a cold war against the whites in Africa."[101] These attacks, he intoned, were emanating from Radio Accra, Radio Leopoldville, Radio Cairo, as well as from Peking, Moscow, Morocco, Nigeria, Damascus, and the Sudan. Nationalist concern over such broadcasts was quickened by the sudden, radical turn taken by the South African liberation movements in the wake of the 1960 Sharpeville massacre. Within months of the massacre, both the ANC and the PAC had been declared unlawful organizations; the ANC and South African Communist Party's response was to create a military wing and take up arms against the state.[102]

When the subject of TV's introduction was raised in parliament that year, Hertzog and Basie Coetzee insisted that the money would be far better spent on "Bantu" radio stations so as to counter foreign radio offensives.[103] "The Bantu," in Coetzee's words, "is subject to the most harmful and the most scandalous propaganda...which is nothing else than an attempt to incite the Bantu against the white man in this country."[104] That very year, Radio Bantu was launched.

Radio Bantu, which eventually broadcast in nine African languages, was introduced as the principal media wing of the bantustan system. Its official aim was "to serve the seven Bantu peoples of the country, according to the nature, needs and character of each, and, by encouraging language consciousness among each of the Bantu peoples, to strengthen national consciousness."[105] Hertzog and Co. perceived Radio Bantu as TV's antithesis. Television would putatively denationalize Xhosas, Zulus, Tswanas, Venda etc., generating the kind of wider, unruly solidarities that could fuel black revolt. Radio Bantu, on the other hand, was immune to the poison of overseas influence and would hopefully fracture African nationalism by inculcating more localized ethnic nationalist identities. Radio Bantu strove, in addition, to seduce black listeners away from foreign broadcasts. Indeed, more than seduction was involved: the regime beamed out Radio Bantu on a low range, high frequency system and made available cheap FM radios which were incapable of receiving broadcasts from abroad.

National Party anxieties about African nationalism and American TV were not as discrete as one might have supposed. As I proposed in the previous chapter, the U.S.A. became, for many urban black South Africans, a leading source of cosmopolitan values, reaffirming their attachments to an internationalized urban culture at the very time when the regime sought to disqualify them from city residence and thrust upon them essentialist ethnic identities. The TV variant of this cosmopolitanism was, from the Nationalist Party's perspective, associated with the nation busting ideology of consumerist individualism. In the late fifties and early sixties, Hertzog and Co. feared that TV would ignite the fires of consumerist demand in an explosive atmosphere where political demands, inside the country and across the continent, were on the rise. Thus, the regime's hostility to America as a major source of cosmopolitan values was compounded by its animosity toward the American advertizing ethos, which, it imagined, would spark discontent in the tinder-dry atmosphere of decolonization.[106]

In apartheid logic, advertizing culture was like decolonization in so far as it encouraged the twin evils of envy and egalitarianism. In banning closed circuit TV from trade fairs, Hertzog explained that it was necessary "to prevent too many people from becoming attached to what they were not allowed to possess."[107] Tom de Koning, an academic "expert" on communications, extrapolated that "the greatest effect on the blacks [of commercial TV] will be the raising of their cultural aspirations. They will see other blacks with cars, houses, and so on and ask, "Why can't I have that?" In a real sense there will be a westernisation of blacks because of television. And their political claims will escalate as a result."[108]

Such voices never explained how black material discontent fostered by capitalist advertizing was to be channelled into the revolutionary, overwhelmingly anti-capitalist liberation struggle.[109] Nonetheless, the Nationalist line of reasoning allowed for a sweeping condemnation of all purported egalitarianisms, be they driven by corporate capitalism, or, in the case of African decolonization, inspired by liberal humanism, socialism, or communism. The regime sought to counter these imagined egalitarian threats by quarantining black South Africans from foreign influence, by dispersing them into "authentic nations," and by pulverizing all dissent. The ban on TV can thus be seen as one of a variety of measures intended to defuse African nationalism.

In one of the more overblown estimations of TV's powers, an American professor, James Burnham, ventured in the *National Review* in 1966 that "the absence of a native liberation movement in South Africa is equivalent, very nearly, to the enforced absence of television."[110] (It is perhaps not surprising that on this point, the American author of *The Suicide of the West* and the South African author of *The Spiritual Crisis of the West*, Meyer, agreed). Burnham measured South Africa's success in keeping TV and black revolt at bay against America's failure to do so:

> What is "the civil rights movement," what could it be, apart from the media? The Montgomery bus strike that began its history, the march on Selma that brought it top billing, would have been nothing but a local bus strike and a local marching if it were not for the media; nothing would have constituted them part of a "movement" of historical significance.[111]

At the time of Burnham's attack on American TV for purportedly granting black revolt renown, encouragement, and cohesion, South Africa's liberation movement was in the doldrums. Between 1963 and 1972 a vicious state crackdown in every sphere overwhelmed the dissolute forces of black resistance. But if, as Burnham declared, TV was an inestimable ally of insurrection, surely black South Africans would have been clamoring for its installation so as to advance their fortunes? Yet nothing of the sort occurred. TV was never remotely a priority of the liberation movement; indeed, for the entire duration of the ban, black South Africans played virtually no part in the altercations.

South Africa was crippled by a desperately uneven access to older, more basic criteria of modernity than TV—like electricity, for one. In the mid-sixties, only 1.5 percent of black homes were electrified. Thus the call to remedy South Africa's backwardness by introducing TV would have meant, for the most part, widening the technological gulf between blacks and whites. For this reason, although the ANC was committed to introducing TV, they were unlikely to make it a policy priority. Instead, like the National Party—indeed, like most African governments and resistance movements—the ANC saw radio as the principal media battlefield. After a brief, quashed attempt to launch Radio Freedom inside South Africa, the organization began broadcasting regularly from abroad in 1969. Radio Freedom's resources were meager, its results uncertain, but it did proffer a radical alternative to the divisive impulse of Radio Bantu.

THE CLAMOR FOR TV AND THE RACIALIZING OF MODERNITY

I have suggested that South Africa's rulers quarantined the country from TV principally because they perceived it as an agent of national dissolution, cultural fusion, and racial integration. However, the Nationalists sought to bolster their cause by marshalling scientific arguments. As early as 1953, they contended that the pace of technological change meant that any hasty adoption of TV would result in a superannuated system. In the admonitory words of the Minister of Post and Telegraphs, "We do not know what science may discover tomorrow or the day after."[112] Nationalist spokesmen continued to urge technological caution throughout the fifties and sixties. Yet such warnings could be invoked *ad infinitum*. As one proponent of TV remarked caustically:

> if that argument is valid then films should never have been allowed into South Africa before the development of the sound track for films in 1929; then it was also a bad economic investment for anybody to buy a model T Ford before World War I because there was the possibility of automatic transmission after World War II.[113]

As this comment indicates, Nationalist animosity toward TV did not go unchallenged—the regime's opponents often criticized its technological recalcitrance. Yet the technological objections to the Nationalist stance brought in train other more intricate arguments—about the nature of progress, modernity, civilization, racial, and national identity. Indeed, South Africa's inter-white wrangling over TV reveals with uncommon clarity the danger of taking nationalism's often atavistic iconography at its own estimation. By the same token, it reveals how those who oppose a "backward looking" nationalism in the name of an enlightened modernity may continue to propagate a transnational vision of advancement in which whites remain cast as the "race" of progress.

By 1953, a strong pro-TV lobby had emerged, principally among white English speaking South Africans whose case was advanced by the United Party and English language sectors of the press. The raucous parliamentary exchanges that ensued between TV's opponents and advocates made it apparent that more was at stake than TV's compatibility with apartheid definitions of national-cultural sovereignty. Accumulatively, the TV imbroglio developed into an intense contest over the criteria of civilization and modernity in which the racializing of both concepts was barely concealed. For the Nationalist spokesmen and Afrikaans press, civilization's continuance required TV's exclusion; for the United Party and English press the resistance to TV was a resistance to civilization itself. Would TV induce degeneration or was its absence a mark of backwardness?

This conflict stemmed in part from divergent conceptions of national identity. Unlike Afrikaners, English speaking whites never developed a strong ethnic nationalism and, for reasons of language, culture, and class, their sense of projected community tended to be more accommodating of international, particularly British and American, elements. On the basis of these foreign cultural and economic entanglements, they were sometimes assailed by Afrikaner nationalists for their flawed patriotism—they were not "true" South Africans, but "a section of a nation overseas," a bridgehead for alien interests.[114] This accusation resurfaced insistently over the course of the TV fracas.

The disparity between English South Africans' economic preeminence and their relative weakness in the corridors of political power gave them every reason to favor TV as a potential capitalist and cultural ally. If the National Party's claim that it shielded black cultures from the cosmopolitan solvent of TV was manipulative and self-serving, so, too, was the United Party's obsessive linkage between TV and progressive civilization. The UP, its media backers, and corporate allies could thereby portray themselves as the beleaguered representatives of enlightened modernity trying to free South Africa from the backward gaze of a "primitive" Afrikaner nationalism. Yet the United Party (and the corporate interests aligned with it) were profoundly conservative. During the height of the TV debates, the UP supported the banning of the ANC and PAC, the introduction of detention without trial, and opposed "one person, one vote."[115] Thus the safe technological terrain of TV enabled a group that benefited from and (in all important spheres) advocated apartheid, to portray itself as the standard-bearer of a progressive modernity.

During the drawn-out campaign for TV, the United Party's attachment to technological definitions not just of modernity but of civilization assumed all the predictability of a mantra. The UP and white English Press disclosed a persistent anxiety about South Africa's possible disqualification from the inner circle of civilized, modern nations. TV thus became a threshold issue: lacking this paramount marker of technological modernity South Africa risked banishment from the club of the truly civilized. To outlaw TV was "to fail to keep up with civilised countries throughout the world."[116] In 1962, a United Party parliamentarian lamented that "we are one of the only civilized communities in the world today that does not have TV;" eight years later, a fellow party member could add, with heightened alarm, that "of all nations in the world we are now the most backward" with regard to TV.[117]

A pro-TV editor insisted in 1969 that "to debate the desirability of television today is as sensible as to argue the merits and demerits of the internal combustion engine. It is an essential part of civilised living."[118] His complaint merged appeals to rationality, standards of civilization, and the inexorable thrust of scientific advancement. From this perspective, to resist a technological innovation of TV's magnitude was to throw gravel in the engine of progress. Thus the UP could present their openness to the technology as a triumph of forward looking commonsense over the "flat earthists" who had driven South Africa into "the age of the water bucket, the ox wagon and the TV *tokoloshe*."[119] Yet the UP's projection of themselves as outriders of progress and rationality was premised on a conception of both Afrikaner and African cultures as antiquated and mired in irrationality. Indeed, the phrase "TV *tokoloshe*" (a Zulu or Xhosa evil spirit) implies that the regressive Nationalists viewed technology through the narrow prism of African superstition rather than the wide windows of Western reason.

Despite its standing as Africa's industrial leviathan, South Africa was only the 23rd African country to accept TV—in the wake of such economic minnows as Uganda, Zambia, and Ethiopia.[120] The UP's principal response to this disparity was to cry shame that South Africa should be "left behind by countries like Rhodesia, India, Nigeria, even Ghana."[121] Accumulatively, in the context of Third World decolonization, the UP's insistence on the "shame" of South Africa's inability to flaunt such an icon of technological progress took on an explicitly racial dimension.

It was Senator Crook who exposed this tendency most clearly, when he insisted that

> it is in the country's interest and that of the people of South Africa that we should have this most modern and powerful of all communications. It is in the interest of South Africa and in the interest of the prestige and good name of South Africa that we should not be bracketed with the most backward peoples of the world such as the Eskimos who have not got television.[122]

The sudden guest appearance of the Eskimos exemplifies the tendency within the UP and English press to racialize technology when invoking it as a litmus test for civilization, modernity, and progress. In colonial thought, the Eskimos, no less than the "Bushmen," the Pygmies, and the Zulus, have long been cast in the risible role of "civilization's" racial-technological antithesis. Progress, in these terms, is an ethnic procession.

Thus, while the motor car and ox-wagon proved serviceable metaphors for progress and regress during the parliamentary stand-offs over TV, they should not seduce one into taking the UP at its own symbolic estimation. English South Africans (and others in the UP) were prone to fixate on TV as a surrogate barometer of their commitment to civilized progress, yet their vision of such progress was incompatible with racial equity or other advances toward democracy.

The UP represented TV as a modern right, but their broader discourse of rights excluded the right to universal suffrage. From this contradiction flowed utterances riddled with displaced shame:

> The United Party believes that the policies of the Nationalist Government over the years in regard to television have placed South Africa in a humiliating and indefensible position in regard to other countries, and we reject the intolerance, bias and falseness of such policies.[123]

A similar mentality was at work in a 1969 newspaper editorial which intoned: "This deprivation has been deliberately imposed on the people of this country….The extent of the stultification to which South Africans have thus been subjected is practically incalculable."[124] Deprivation and stultification here referred not to the fallout of apartheid but to the consequences of no TV.

The 1966 (all-white) elections marked the apogee of such thinking, as the UP centered their campaign on the decoy question of "Want TV? Vote UP." (Government supporters responded by doctoring their opponents' electoral posters to "Want TB? Vote UP," bringing it into line with their vision of TV as a viral technology.)[125] For the great bulk of South Africans, TV was not exactly a priority on their shopping list of rights or desires.

The UP's two-faced stance on technological and political modernity was exemplified by a parliamentary speech made in 1960, soon after the Verwoerd regime had inaugurated the bantustan scheme. The speaker excoriated the regime for its "antique" position on TV and its hypocritical stand on change:

> What about this vast new experiment they are trying in the field of Native affairs, the Bantustan experiment? If you can experiment with Bantustans and with Sasol[South Africa's oil from coal plant], surely you can also experiment with TV? But that has been the type of argument used by reactionaries throughout the ages against any type of advancement. It was the reactionary's argument against the motor car.[126]

Thus, the UP, the purported party of "innovation," could shamelessly fetishize

Sasol, the motor car, TV, and the bantustans as interchangeable icons of advancement.

MAKING SPACE: THE APOLLO MOON WALK AND THE ADVENT OF TV

In 1969, the National Party appointed a commission of inquiry to investigate the relative dangers and merits of introducing TV. The commission was stacked with Broederbonders, who made up nine of its thirteen members, with Meyer in the chair.[127] Four English South African men made up the rest of the complement; no black South Africans were involved, nor—despite Afrikaner anxieties about TV's impact on the home—were any women. The report compared the organization and effects of TV in fifteen countries, the United States, Britain, Italy, Japan, and Germany among them. After nearly two years of deliberation, a conditional recommendation was issued that TV be admitted into South Africa.

What pressures prompted the National Party to agree to an inquiry in the first place? And what circumstances produced such a volte-face on the part of a regime that had been so resolutely hostile to the box? One partial answer lay in Prime Minister Vorster's sacking of Hertzog from his cabinet the year the commission was set up. Hertzog, under whose ministry the media fell, had come to personify the ultranationalist, technophobic, xenophobic, and anglophobic face of the anti-TV coalition.

Yet Hertzog's fall from power was less the root cause of a greater openness toward TV than an epiphenomenon, a symptom of deeper shifts in Afrikaner attitudes to the idea of international community which TV symbolized. Over the course of the 1960s, a breach had developed within Afrikanerdom between the *verligtes* (the "enlightened"), who argued for international outreach, and the *verkramptes* (the conservatives), led by Hertzog, who advocated the isolationist spirit that had shored up Afrikaner power since the late 1930s. Ironically, this rift within the ranks was a measure of Afrikaner nationalism's success in consolidating political power and broadening its economic base by favoring Afrikaner businesses, providing sheltered employment for unskilled Afrikaner labor in the labyrinthine apartheid bureaucracy, holding down black wages, and mounting violent, relentless assaults on black resistance. By 1964 such repression had temporarily but effectively routed mass opposition and with it enhanced South Africa's reputation among international corporations as an attractive, stable sphere for investment. During the 1960s, only Japan surpassed South Africa's rate of economic growth.[128]

In real terms black wages fell over the decade, while white wealth grew incrementally. The emergence of a powerful Afrikaner capitalist stratum altered the class composition of the *volk*, provoking clashes of interest within the alliance that had bound Afrikaner nationalism since the late 1940s. The petty bourgeois,

Transvaal based forces associated with Verwoerd, Meyer, and Hertzog began to lose ground to the more flexible capitalists who backed Vorster.[129] Compared to the *laager* politicians, the petty bourgeoisie, and small farmers, this newly confident entrepeneurial class of Afrikaners tended toward a less involuted, defensive vision of the national interest. They were profiting from and advocating expanded links with non-Afrikaner capital, be it English South African or foreign. Concomitantly, such Afrikaners were apt to see economic growth as the best guarantee of continued white domination and to consider TV as a potential asset for commerce.

Some dissenters warned that Afrikaners "were becoming too South African, too conscious of being White instead of almost exclusively aware of being Afrikaans and Afrikaans-speaking."[130] Yet such voices had become marginalized by 1969, as the increasingly muscular class of urbanized, corporate, even cosmopolitan Afrikaners proved less susceptible to the standard admonitions that TV would provoke internationalization, commercialization, imperialism, Anglicization, and secular deviations from the *volk*'s destiny of divine election. A rapprochement between Afrikaans and English capital interests on this issue was clearly signalled by the fact that in 1969 both the Afrikaanse Handels Instituut[Afrikaans Trade Institute] and the corresponding English body, the Assocation of Chambers of Commerce, urged the government to commit itself to TV.[131] In that same year, the *verkramptes*—who included seasoned opponents of TV like Hertzog and Marais—broke with the Nationalists to form the far right Herstigte Nationale Party which, however, was quickly reduced to a peripheral force. Ultimately, the tensions between white economic success and mounting world pressure on apartheid encouraged Vorster to engage in more assiduous efforts at intra- and international outreach than Verwoerd would have condoned. As Dan O'Meara put it, by the 1970s "Hoggenheimer was no longer the oppressor of the Afrikaner *volk*, but a trusted and valued partner in joint quest for profit."[132]

Over and above these changes, two extraterrestrial happenings—the Apollo 11 mission and satellite innovations—suddenly augmented the prospects of South Africa gaining TV. On 21 July 1969, Neil Armstrong strolled across the face of the moon. The event became—like TV itself—a powerful constitutive absence in white South African society. Amidst a booming economy in which Afrikaner capitalists had become increasingly enamoured of the "American way," the moon landing further tilted the balance of power away from the rejection of the U.S.A. as a culturally degenerate imperialism and toward a rival view of it as a technologically advanced world leader. In 1968, just a year before the moon landing, the American student revolts had fueled the cause of *laager* nationalists who had sought to prevent TV from spewing American decadence into South

Africa. Armstrong, Edwin Aldrin, and Michael Collins unwittingly helped turn that view around.

There was, of course, an explicitly Cold War context for the landing: astronauts 1, cosmonauts zero, a rematch after America's earlier defeat. Indeed, the event could be read not as a respite from imperialism but as the consummate act of imperialist hubris by interplanetary conquistadors bent on national glory. However, the South African media presented Apollo 11 principally as a triumph for humankind, as if on the moon the astronauts had found a third, extraterrestrial space for pure human discovery, untrammelled by the fraught dialectics between internationalism and nationalism. Whether the landing was interpreted as a defeat for communism or an apolitical triumph for the species, the media angles on the event made it unassimilable to the dominant *verkrampte* view of the U.S.A. as an anti-national, imperialist force.

Armstrong's words—"one small step for man, one giant leap for mankind"—combined two very powerful appeals: to the ideology of the family of "man," and to the ideology of the march of progress. Both applied salt to white wounds, quickening the pain of spacial ostracism from the "family" of nations and of temporal abandonment—of being "behind the times."

More dramatically than any prior event, the moon landing impressed upon people TV's power to produce the sensation of simultaneous, "global" community. This impression of supranational kinship was based not merely on the unprecedented audiences galvanized by the landing but on the transcendant images that were projected. The footage beamed into living rooms produced a moment of profound species narcissism, of the "whole" world looking up at Armstrong, Aldrin, and Collins looking down and seeing the world "whole." In that act, a moment of audiovisual idealism—TV at the zenith of its powers—fused with a moment of transcendental incorporation, the "family of man" seeing itself observed from a divine angle of vision.

Thus the moon walk allowed each watching family the illusion of participating in the unity in variety of the species. However, while the event had 800 million people around the world riveted to their TVs, South Africans were reduced to twiddling the dials on their wirelesses. For many whites—already rendered paranoid by the growing force of their exile from world affairs—South Africa's inability to partake of such a singular moment of "global" community came to seem like an exasperating, self-inflicted disinvitation. A *Rand Daily Mail* editorial captured this sense of let-down perfectly with the snappy headline "Out of this World."[133]

A journalist had once complained that Hertzog and the twentieth century seemed not to be on speaking terms.[134] The Apollo 11 mission generalized that sense of incommunicado: white South Africans had become nonparticipants in

the twentieth century. Such anxieties were exacerbated by most whites' investment in believing that they belonged on the classy side of their obsessive divides
between progress and backwardness, the modern and the "tribal," the civilized
and the uncivilized. As the drawn out wranglings over TV illustrated, the traffic
between scientific and racial calibrations of modernity had been freely licensed
under apartheid. The exclusion of white South Africans from an event that the
media billed as a scientific rite of passage into an unbounded future thus threatened both their technological self-assurance and their sense of racial superiority.

Shortly after the moon landing, the Johannesburg Planetarium offered public
screenings of the spectacle. The TV footage drew mile long queues and the
crowds—separate days for blacks and whites—were so vast that police were
called in to disperse them. Not, however, before one hundred thousand people
had witnessed the landing and—to judge from newspaper interviews—had
come away feeling, for the most part, not merely unsullied by their contact with
Hertzog's demonic box but defrauded by their exclusion from the live event.[135]

Pro-TV letters and editorials clogged the newspapers, the TV Society drew
up a petition, a successful chain letter appeal was launched, and the United Party
called for a "national" (i.e. white) referendum on the issue, claiming that the
majority—by which, again, they meant merely a majority of the white minority—now favored TV. It was pointed out that the astronauts' almost lifelong
exposure to TV had not impaired their suitability for earth shattering endeav-
ors.[136] Even Dirk Richard, a prominent hardline editor of an Afrikaans
newspaper, announced his conversion to TV.[137]

After the earlier Apollo 10 mission in 1968, the SABC had embarked on a
rearguard effort at damage control. Its annual report marvelled at how the corporation had transported the Apollo mission into "the homes and meeting
places of all people possessing radios, not only in South Africa but also in the
rest of Africa, Europe, the East and even the United States. Sharing this experience in such an intimate, and communal manner would not have been possible
through any other medium."[138] The report had proceeded to extol the "wonder
of radio":

> With the advent of TV, which is essentially a radio technique (although
> used mainly as a film medium in the intial stages) it seemed as if sound
> radio would be forced into an obscure background position in mass com-
> munications. This tendency did not last long. In recent times, sound radio
> has been moving into first position.... Radio distinguishes itself by the fact
> that it does not enslave or want to enslave the human spirit.[139]

After the much more spectacular Apollo 11 venture the following year, the
SABC was at least in a position to announce, alongside its account of the land-

ing, the appointment of a Commission of Inquiry into the "desirability or otherwise" of admitting a TV service.[140] However, the corporation persisted with the excesses of the annual eulogy to radio—by now a set-piece of the report. But it all sounded like a hymn sung in the dark. While praising the technological power of radio to bond the human race in an act of instant communion, the report maintained a studied silence over the fact that anyone anywhere had actually *observed* the Apollo II landing. Instead, it flattered radio's sensory repertoire, bestowing on it a visual capacity that rendered, by implication, TV superfluous:

> Radio brings events closer to the public and offers a *glimpse* of the drama of life. No other medium achieves this so effectively; and if there is a challenge in the Seventies, it is that radio must employ technical aids and so co-ordinate its internal organisation that it gives its audience a *view*—an intimate *view*—of the world around us....It is hoped that in building upon these foundations in the decade ahead, radio will further distinguish itself as the foremost medium for permitting an audience to *observe* history in the making. (my emphases)[141]

1969 saw a second extraterrestrial development fortify the case for TV. The increasing sophistication of satellite technology insured that as of September that year any South African family who could afford both a TV set and a R150 rooftop aluminium bowl could have international TV beamed in, circumventing the absence of a national service.[142] In *verkrampte* circles, this fresh threat set familiar alarm bells ringing. Jaap Marais warned that satellite broadcasts "will be a mighty force in the hands of the Russians and Americans. ...[T]hey will try to give greater actuality and striking power to the propaganda issuing from the platform of the UN."[143] Marais proceeded to paint a nightmare tableau:

> To form a rough image of what could happen, one must picture the events of Sharpeville and the whole international propaganda hell that came together so neatly around it, projected against South Africa in circumstances wherein the population is equipped with TV receivers through which American or Russian controlled satellites can broadcast.[144]

In an account that resurrected the old dread of a Trojan Horse in the living room, Marais issued a call for arms in this war of stealth which he considered to be doubly subversive because it went undeclared and was waged with unconventional weapons in the warzone of the psychology. "There is no more powerful instrument of persuasion," he continued,

> than TV, and a nation who can be reached by its enemies through TV

finds itself on the most dangerous battlefield imaginable, because it is forced onto the defensive and is up against an invisible enemy whom it cannot attack unless it can also direct satellite broadcasts against the enemy powers.[145]

Marais further maintained that South Africa was as psychologically ill-prepared for the introduction of TV as it was technologically ill-equipped for launching a voyage to the moon.[146] He insisted, therefore, that to launch a nationally controlled TV service as a defense against propaganda issuing from foreign satellites would be to play into the hands of the "Russians" and Americans. However, when Marais issued these opinions in September 1969, he, along with Hertzog, had recently been expelled from the National Party as part of Vorster's purge of *verkramptes*. The baton of intransigence towards TV had passed from the Nationalists to the Herstigtes. Just as Hertzog, in 1969, continued to warn that the introduction of TV would spell the end of the white race, so too, Marais's stance on the satellite issue was now out of kilter with reformist thinking on the issue within a realigned National Party.[147]

Nationalist cabinet ministers were no less panic stricken than Marais by the prospect of satellite broadcasts, but they recommended a contrary solution: national TV should be the first line of defense. So in an ironic *volte-face*, Nationalist leaders could now argue that the introduction of state-controlled TV was necessary for the preservation of "the South African way of life."[148] Hence, TV came to be reconceived as an anti-imperial device and an integral part of the nation's defense network. In the impassioned words of one convert, anyone who tried to withhold TV from South Africa would "be the biggest saboteur of the national defence the country has known."[149]

In short, advances in satellite technology helped reduce the contradictions between the pro-TV and anti-TV lobbies, between those who courted wider international ties and those who wished to confine community to the narrow sphere of Afrikaner nationalists or white South Africans. The appearance of the satellites allowed the Vorster regime to reverse TV policy without forsaking its polarized vision of national cultural sovereignties under threat from marauding cultural imperialists. The regime could hence introduce TV as a strategy for expanding international economic and cultural contacts, while rationalizing such an action as a protectionist measure against foreign invaders. After the commission had spent two years debating the wisdom of admitting the technology, and after a spate of further procrastinations, South African TV finally went on the air in January 1976.

3

CRY WHITE SEASON
Anti-Apartheid Heroism and the American Screen

Black consciousness seeks to produce real black people who do not regard themselves as appendages to white society.

—Steve Biko, *I Write What I Like*

1976 HAS GATHERED RENOWN as the year of the Soweto uprising, a watershed event in the history of initiatives against the apartheid state. That same year proved critical in another sense, for it began an era of increasingly intimate interaction between South African and American cultures. The scale of the 1976 revolt and the ferocity of the regime's crackdown transformed South Africa into a media concern that reached into American living rooms with unprecedented regularity. Conversely, 1976 finally saw the introduction of national television into South Africa, a long deferred development which expanded incrementally the country's exposure to the icons and narratives of American culture. Since that momentous year, the cultural border crossings between the two societies have grown in intensity to the point where the apartheid issue has been taken up in almost every genre and medium in American culture.

One of the most decisive manifestations of this cultural rapprochement was the run of big budget anti-apartheid films that appeared between 1987 and 1989—Richard Attenborough's *Cry Freedom,* Chris Menges's *A World Apart,* and Euzhan Palcy's *A Dry White Season.* The same period saw an upsurge of smaller South African-made films like Oliver Schmitz's *Mapantsula,* which gained little exposure in the U.S.A. The mass market films brought into focus an abiding dilemma in the representation of apartheid for Americans: how do you communicate the experience and values of a radical liberation struggle to a pre-dominantly liberal American audience? The question touches on fundamental issues of cinematic convention, ideological compatibility, cross-cultural com-prehension, and political efficacy.

When a cultural issue or product is exported to a new society, it is inevitably subject to refraction. The needs and concerns of the society in which it arrives become a transforming influence, so that the issue takes shape as a compromise between the prevailing history, preoccupations, and ambitions of the society of origin and those of the society with which it intersects. In the case of these anti-apartheid movies, then, it is essential to address the patterns of ideological transformation and their political ramifications. Attenborough, Menges, and Palcy all portrayed their films as interventions which sought to expand public opposition to apartheid.[1] However, their commitment to rendering their art politically serviceable presented them with a potentially tormenting choice: in directing films not just about apartheid but largely for the U.S.A., what repre-sentational adjustments would they have to make to render the South African struggle accessible to American audiences?

Given the scale and hegemony of the American communications industry, whenever there is a mass market endeavor to translate another culture's experi-ence into terms accessible to the U.S.A., American preconceptions, frames of reference, and narrative designs readily take precedence. South Africa provides an acute example of this rule of thumb as the organizations leading the libera-tion struggle have embraced ideologies that are often inaccessible, mystifying, or alienating to Americans. Whether braced by non-racial socialist, African nationalist, Black consciousness, or Marxist ideologies, virtually all of South Africa's strongest anti-apartheid organizations over the past thirty years have held radical allegiances of one form or another. The same cannot be said of opposition to apartheid within the United States, which relied centrally on a liberal constituency. The challenge of bridging cultural differences between the two societies consequently became overlaid with problems of profound ideo-logical incompatibility. This raised pressing questions. Would a big-budget film that sought to deepen American outrage over apartheid have to transform the liberation struggle into terms not merely accessible to a wide American audience but acceptable to it too? And if this did prove expedient, what might be the political cost of rearranging a radical score in a liberal key?

THE PENURY OF LIBERALISM

The dilemmas of cross-cultural representation between the U.S.A. and South Africa arise from stark differences between their prevailing political traditions. The notion of liberalism, in particular, resonates quite dissimilarly in the two societies. It is, after all, a peculiarity of American electoral politics that it should be dominated by two parties which, by the standards of most industrialized nations, are so ideologically akin. The circumstances of South African politics between 1960 and 1990 could scarcely have been more dissimilar: the principal contenders were polarized between a muscular right and a muscular left, with an emaciated liberalism in-between.[2] Only a minority of South African whites ranked as liberals; more significantly, the ideology achieved very limited purchase among the black majority, despite government and corporate efforts to establish a buffer—pro-capitalist middle class in the townships. Symptomatically, the editors of a collection on South African liberalism could not muster a single black perspective in a volume of twenty-four contributors.[3]

The anemia of South African liberalism became most manifest during the three decades between the 1960 Sharpeville massacre and the unbanning of some sixty organizations (including the ANC, the South African Communist Party, and the Pan African Congress) in 1990. However, even in the 1950s, when liberalism was stronger, relatively few non-communist whites threw in their lot with the black cause.

When white liberals expressed unease at the African National Congress's collaborative front with the communists, the ANC leader, Albert Luthuli, countered:

> All we know is that these men(sic)[the communists] come to help us. I don't deny that some might have ulterior motives, but all I am concerned about is that they came to assist me fighting racial oppression, and they have no trace of racialism or being patronizing, just no trace of it at all.[4]

Luthuli's phrasing alludes to a common complaint against South African liberalism—the *in locus parentis* tendencies of its ideology. This frequently expressed itself in a gradualist vision of change, which proposed a qualified franchise (limited to the minority of blacks possessing a set level of formal education) and advocated federalism. South African liberalism was thus habitually marred by double-speak: some of its more estimable theoretical commitments—e.g. to a multiparty parliamentary system, a free press, and an independent judiciary—were hedged about by qualifying rhetoric. Moreover, since liberals generally perceived white South African life as possessing the rudiments of democracy, liberal rhetoric has focused on extending black access to these institutions. Yet the very language of extension concealed the ethnocentric origins and exclusionary histories of such institutional structures, thereby concealing, too, their failure to reflect the priorities of the oppressed.[5]

South African liberalism's sometimes naive, sometimes self-interested efforts to tinker with the edifices of apartheid from within were matched by an emphasis on individual altruism as a force for social change—a commitment to what an E. M. Forster character once called "good will and more good will and more good will."[6] (It is not irrelevant to the South African case that Forster's liberal humanist faith in the power of human decency was irremediably damaged by his exposure to colonialism: he found that, under such circumstances, the inequities of power white anted the foundations of interracial friendship and civility. *A Passage to India* enacts the erosion of that faith.)

The credibility of liberalism as a vehicle for change took its most severe battering on 21 March 1960. Between 1912 and 1949, the ANC had sought to advance black rights primarily through constitutional means. For the subsequent eleven years inspired in part by Gandhism, black and white activists mounted successive, resourceful campaigns of passive resistance, cresting on that March day when thousands of Africans marched peacefully to police stations in the Johannesburg area in order to protest the pass laws. Despite the non-violent character of the campaign, police fired on the Sharpeville crowd, killing 69 Africans and wounding 180, most of them shot in the back. Inevitably, even African nationalists who had been influenced by liberal precepts were compelled to reconceive their struggle in revolutionary terms. As Nelson Mandela put it in 1964: "We first broke the law in a way which avoided any recourse to violence; when this form was legislated against, and the Government resorted to a show of force to crush opposition to its policies, only then did we decide to answer violence with violence."[7]

South African liberals remained intransigent on the subject of violence; despite the lessons of Sharpeville and a myriad other displays of state treachery, and despite the outlawing of the ANC and the Pan African Congress in March 1960. As liberalism's most famous advocate, Alan Paton, maintained in 1964:

> Any person who while a member of the Liberal Party plans to use violence against things or persons is not only guilty of an offence against the law, he is also guilty of grave disloyalty to the Party. …He may burn against injustices to others, and burn to set them right. He may be a zealot. He may be dedicated to his cause. But he is not a Liberal—And what is more, if he persists in his plans, he is likely to do grave damage to the whole cause of

Liberalism; how great such damage might be is at the moment impossible to predict.[8]

The liberals stance against counter-violence eroded their appeal, leaving them marooned between a recalcitrant white right and an increasingly revolutionary group of outlawed African nationalist and socialist organizations.

Liberalism in South Africa was hampered by a vast credibility problem. For three decades after the Sharpeville massacre, liberal discourse never found a home in any popular or robust political party. It became associated with a half a loaf response to the liberation struggle: with the missionary mentality of trustee-ship; with those who advocated a qualified franchise for educated blacks and would ease white guilt while maintaining white control; and with federal mod-els of a post-apartheid society, which would temper divide-and-rule strategies while preserving core areas of white privilege.[9] High profile liberals like Alan Paton and Helen Suzman limited their constituency by condemning ANC poli-cies of counter-violence as well as international sanctions.

The most powerful organizations opposing apartheid—the ANC, the PAC, the United Democratic Front, the various Black Consciousness organizations, and the Congress of South African Trade Unions—were broadly mistrustful of liberalism. Left-wing organizations and intellectuals incessantly upbraided liberals for their habit of condemning the immorality of racism while sup-pressing the historical complicity of South African capitalism in the entrenchment of apartheid. Aside from the isolated figure of Gatsha Buthelezi, no black South African leader of any standing in the 1980s could, for instance, have echoed the rhetoric of an American liberal like Andrew Young who, on a trip to South Africa, announced that "the free market sys-tem can be the greatest force for constructive change now operating anywhere in the world."[10] In a society saddled with the world's widest gap between rich and poor, and where 87 percent of the land and 95 percent of industry remained under white ownership, radical redistribution of wealth and land seemed prerequisites for political success.[11]

As Michael Dukakis's nervous electoral dance around the "L" word drama-tized, "liberal" is regularly wielded as an accusation by the American right. It is seldom a liability in the South African sense of damning you in the eyes of a politically muscular left, for in the U.S.A. liberalism has tended to connote left of center, while in South Africa it has stood as a right of center term. This trans-Atlantic ideological dissonance reverberates through the mass market anti-apartheid movies that emerged in the 80s. Attenborough's *Cry Freedom*, the first anti-apartheid movie to claim the attention of a broad audience, exemplified this discord in its most acute form.

CRY FREEDOM: THE FRAMING OF BLACK CONSCIOUSNESS

To engage the politics of *Cry Freedom*, one has to take cognizance of its historical timing. Between 1984 and the film's release in 1987, the camera assumed a sudden prominence in U.S.-South African relations. The months of October and November 1984 thrust apartheid to the forefront of the American media's preoccupations as Bishop Tutu received the Nobel Peace Prize and then, within weeks, the first of what became nationwide uprisings erupted in the Vaal Triangle. Over the next twenty-odd months, American coverage of apartheid rose to new levels as TV brought incriminating images of state violence into American homes with almost daily regularity. Organized public protest in the U.S.A. mounted across campuses, outside the South African Embassy, and in Congress, aided by the ascending visibility of Jesse Jackson, Randall Robinson, TransAfrica, Tutu, and Allan Boesak. Panicked, the Botha regime accused foreign journalists, particularly those in charge of the camers, of fomenting or deliberately staging unrest.

By the time *Cry Freedom* arrived on American screens, this situation had altered substantially. The second State of Emergency—declared in mid-86—had been followed by legislation barring TV or film recordings, drawings or other depictions of "any unrest or security action" or "any damaged or destroyed property or injured or dead persons or other visible signs of violence."[12] The camera had become demonized in the regime's eyes as an instrument of insurrection. While South African resistance during this second State of Emergency did decline, it fell nowhere near as sharply as American coverage of the crisis which, by 1987, was a ghost of what it had been a year before. Issue fatigue, the shutting down of cameras, and institutional timidity combined to drive apartheid off the small screen.

Viewed in this context, *Cry Freedom* could be seen as potentially compensatory and retaliatory, as an effort to reclaim the camera for the anti-apartheid struggle. Indeed, the movie begins with a brilliant simulation of precisely the kind of footage that had been withheld from American TV viewers: a savage police attack on the Crossroads squatter camp near Cape Town. Crowded, panoramic turbulence is, after all, Attenborough's *metier*.

Based on two books by the South African journalist Donald Woods, *Biko* and *Asking for Trouble, Cry Freedom* was billed as a movie about Steve Biko (Denzel Washington), the Black Consciousness leader murdered in police detention, and his friendship with Woods (Kevin Kline), a staid, skeptical editor of a provincial paper who is won over to the justice of Biko's cause. Before embarking on the project, Attenborough concluded that the sufferings, defiance, political ideas, and murder of a black South African leader stood no chance, on their own, of succeeding as a major movie.[13] Attenborough therefore introduced the white journalist as a bridge to a broader audience. This had two decisive consequences. First, it contradicted the fundamental premises of Biko's black consciousness philosophy. Second, it refracted a radical South African political movement through Hollywood's most durable liberal formula for dealing with the "Third World." When graced by a white visitor, preferably a male journalist-hero, obscure, squalid, tedious, and threatening "Third World" politics suddenly become adventurous and manageable—*The Year of Living Dangerously*, *The Killing Fields*, *Missing*, *Salvador*, *Under Fire*, *Cry Freedom*, and, in terms of domestic politics, *Mississippi Burning*. (I am not, of course, suggesting that the politics of all these films are identical. But in each case, if to different degrees, the mediating presence of the white outsider has ideological ramifications.)

On the surface, the convention of the innocent abroad (in Woods's case, abroad in the black townships), helps soften the edges of unfamiliar politics for a "mainstream" American audience. However, the newly educated white figure who survives to report back, his eyes now widened by calamity, becomes the emotional focus of the movie, transforming into gray background the political particulars of the culture in question. Too often, as in *Cry Freedom*, the indigenous people themselves are reduced to generic non-whites.

The use of the innocent journalist to relay information back about the "Third World" invites parallels with the relationship, in domestic dramas, between the good cop and minority communities. In each instance, the journalist or cop ventures into the place of the "other" and retrieves information about "them," a process that can entail an uneasy mixture of investigation—increasing knowledge—and surveillance—increasing control.

In the case of *Cry Freedom*, Woods's story about Biko is quickly supplanted by Woods's story about Woods, resulting in an acute case of displaced heroism. After Biko's murder, viewers are subjected to an hour-and-a-half of a South African Brady Bunch fleeing apartheid as, in a drawn out melodrama, Woods, his wife, and five kids escape South Africa. Far from commemorating Biko, *Cry Freedom* enacts Woods's supercession of that memory as the project of a radical political movement and the memory of Biko becomes subordinated to the business of proving a white lone ranger's moral mettle.[14]

The contradictory form of *Cry Freedom* entails both racial paternalism and ideological substitution. As the first of these processes is the more transparent of the two, it has provoked what has become the standard objection to Attenborough and Woods's representation of Biko's life.[15] However, the attendant transformation of the movie's ideology tends to go undiscussed. Most damagingly, Attenborough filters out the radical political discourse of the Black Consciousness Movement, replacing it with the more palatable liberal discourse of moral decency and human rights.

The hallmark of the film's liberalism is its focal commitment to the inter-racial friendship between Woods and Biko. Advertized as "the friendship that rocked the world," *Cry Freedom* locates redemptive values not in the institutions and ideologies of black resistance but in the possibility of the two men resolving their cross-racial differences. Thus, by implication, the movie suggests that the political solution to apartheid lies in a macro version of these men's microcosmic struggle to build a personal relationship that triumphs over racism and suspicion. However, instead of simply enacting Biko's values through the human drama of a friendship, Attenborough's structural commitment to that friendship betrays and obscures the very principles that Biko died for.

What might Biko have made of all this? The best clue lies in his essay "White Racism and Black Consciousness," where he writes:

> The myth of integration as propounded under the banner of the liberal ideology must be cracked and killed because it makes people believe that something is being done when in reality the artificially integrated circles are a soporific to the blacks while salving the consciences of the guilt-stricken white. It works from the false premise that, because it is difficult to bring people from different races together in this country, achievement of this is in itself a step towards the total liberation of the blacks. Nothing could be more misleading.[16]

Biko believed steadfastly that while reconciliation between blacks and whites was a distant goal, integration would not hasten apartheid's demise because the two groups would move towards each other from positions of grossly unequal power. Liberalism betrayed blacks because it obscured the fact that integration between the skewed forces of dominators and dominated would inevitably perpetuate white advantage. Ergo, tactically, blacks should withdraw from racially mixed organizations into an autonomous black political movement. "Black man(sic), you are on your own," Biko proclaimed, in a phrase that was to become the rallying cry of South African Black Consciousness.[17]

As it stands, *Cry Freedom* is no less contradictory and incongruous than a movie about Malcolm X fixated on his friendship with a white buddy. While it is historically accurate that Biko and Woods befriended each other, the image of the white journalist as custodian of Biko's memory reinforces precisely the relationship of white trusteeship that Biko abhorred and which he foresaw would compromise his vision of social transformation. As if divining, many years ahead, how Hollywood would frame his story, Biko once cautioned: "The liberals must understand...that the blacks do not need a go-between in this struggle for their own emancipation."[18]

A WORLD APART AND SOUTH AFRICAN MARXISM

Within a year of *Cry Freedom*'s appearance, a second commercial anti-apartheid movie reached the screen, the first feature to be directed by the renowned cinematographer, Chris Menges. His 1988 production, *A World Apart*, is an altogether more accomplished and coherent film than *Cry Freedom*. Set in 1963, *A World Apart* testifies to the fortitude of Ruth First, a prominent activist and writer who was harried, spied upon, detained in solitary confinement, driven into exile, and ultimately assassinated by the South African state in 1982.

However, this is by no means a conventionally commemorative movie. Both the distribution of emotion and the film's political potential are complicated by the decision to view First's activism through the eyes of her daughter, Shawn Slovo, who is thirteen years old when the movie opens and feels orphaned by her parents' devotion to the anti-apartheid cause. Slovo herself wrote the screenplay for *A World Apart*, tapping her memories of a politically disrupted family life, as well as drawing on *117 Days*, her mother's record of her detention.[19] The overwhelming presence of Slovo as writer and character turns *A World Apart* into a movie which, while inveighing against apartheid and honoring First's heroism, becomes, in addition, a gesture of catharsis, a now-adult daughter's effort to make peace with her murdered mother by working through an anger that flows from her childhood sense of abandonment in the name of the struggle.[20] Slovo's hunger for a cathartic resolution to her relationship with her mother was sharpened by the fact that their final conversation, before the letter bomb exploded, had been ill-tempered. Upon returning from her mother's funeral in Mozambique, Slovo promptly began the screenplay.

One might assume that First's race would render her a safe subject for a commercial film. Yet judging from the details about her life that Menges and Slovo suppressed, they felt obliged, almost as acutely as Attenborough, to liberalize the commitments of a celebrated South African radical in order to ratchet up the film's box-office potential. First was active in radical organizations for over thirty years. She was a member of the South African Communist Party's executive; she edited, from 1946, a weekly newspaper under the auspices of the SACP; and she unequivocally embraced the ANC's policy of violence as an indispensable counter to the institutionalized violence of South African racism. After seeking exile in Mozambique, she became a prominent adviser to the country's ruling Marxist party, FRELIMO, and it was there that she was assassinated by a letter bomb evidently mailed to her by the Botha regime. Her books included *Black Gold*, a Marxist account of Mozambican migrant labor on the South African mines, and *Olive Schreiner*, a biography (written collaboratively with *Spare Rib* editor, Ann Scott) of a founder of modern feminism. One cannot dismiss First as a deskbound Marxist abstracted from struggle—she was an activist and organizer steeped in multiple revolutionary causes in South Africa and Mozambique.[21]

For all its undeniable merits as drama, A World Apart bleaches First's life of its radicalism in a manner that summons to mind the suppression of the Rosenbergs' communist commitments in Daniel, the film based upon Doctorow's novel.[22] The only reference to First's ideology comes from a South African police officer who accuses her (or Diana Roth, as she is named in the movie) of being a "communist," until recently a rote response among apartheid's constables to anyone who disagreed, even mildly, with government policy.[23] Menges's version of First could be readily mistaken for a vaguely liberal suburban journalist, ideologically indistinguishable from Cry Freedom's Donald Woods. An American reviewer can thus scarcely be faulted for speaking of the "liberal counterparts in Cry Freedom and A World Apart."[24]

Yet First expressly rejected liberalism as a political philosophy relevant to the overthrow of apartheid. As her fellow activist, ANC lawyer Albie Sachs, intimates, liberal guilt never featured in her motives: "She was not a white fighting for the blacks, but a person fighting for her own right to live in a just society, which in the South African context meant destroying the whole system of white domination."[25] First herself puts it succinctly: "Our consciences were healthy in a society riddled with guilt."[26]

If Menges and Slovo liberalize First's commitments by keeping her Marxism under lock and key, this was clearly motivated by box office concerns.[27] So, too, according to Slovo, was the decision to suppress First's name by calling her Diana Roth: "I named the mother after Princess Diana—I figured I needed all the help I could get to make a woman who was a Communist sympathetic to western audiences."[28] Yet, in an otherwise feminist film, the decision to cloak First's identity has political ramifications. However fanciful Slovo's rationale, the lure of Diana is psychologically telling: Slovo substitutes a glamorous, aristocratic woman who achieved public fame through her marital relation to a man for a woman who was political in her own right and whose radical convictions persuaded her to refuse an ideology of social responsibility circumscribed by the family. As a consequence, Slovo and Menges squander the opportunity to inscribe First's name in international public memory, a point brought home by an American reviewer's reference to the film as celebrating "the real life character Diana Roth."[29] Ironically, First herself had to ponder the transgressive relationship between women's names and public space in her biography of the late Victorian feminist, Olive Schreiner, who published her best known book, The Story of an African Farm, under the pseudonym Ralph Iron.

Aside from the unfortunate renaming of First, A World Apart shows a readiness to acknowledge gender as an issue meriting serious political consideration.

Through its central focus on mother-daughter relations under apartheid, the film throws into relief the traditionally anguished relationship between maternity and heroism. This tension is, of course, not eccentric to South Africa, but because questions of race and class have dominated in local political campaigns, gender issues have tended to be patronized or ousted from the realm of "serious" politics. One detects, in South Africa, alarming continuities between left-wing and right-wing efforts to confine the political responsibilities of women to that of incubators of activists or patriots. As the poet, Ingrid de Kok remarks:

> I recently heard a prominent woman of great political influence express the view that feminism was a dangerous import and that it was the role of women to be "the bearers of the future citizens of South Africa." This echo horrified me, because when I was twelve I heard a Dutch Reformed minister say to a group of adolescent Afrikaans girls that "You are the future mothers of the future sons of South Africa."[30]

Patently, white South African women's experience of patriarchy cannot begin to approximate, far less deputize for, that of black women. Nonetheless, *A World Apart* plays a politically useful role in unsettling an obstinate tradition of defining women's role in the struggle as existing principally at a maternal remove from the present. Despite the fact that her husband, Joe Slovo, is prominent in both the ANC and the South African Communist Party, First represents a rare instance of a South African woman achieving a position of leadership in her own right rather than as the wife, mother, or daughter of a celebrated man. Her example thus runs contrary to a style of politics, pervasive in the "Third World," where female authority is underwritten by an absent patriarch, whether his name be Aquino, Bhutto, Chamorro, Gandhi, Mandela, or Peron.

By refracting First's radicalism through the lens of her neglected daughter, Menges risked reducing her life story to a showdown between good activism and bad motherhood; to a story, that is, of how politics unsexed her. I believe that threat is warded off by a powerful reconciliation scene between "Roth" and her daughter—"You deserved to have a mother. You do have one, just not the way you wanted"—and by the closing shots of their joint attendance at the funeral of an activist friend.

However, some male commentators have responded otherwise:

> *A World Apart* invites those who have an uncomplicated admiration for Ruth First's courage to notice the absence of a pre-occupation with her children, to speculate uncomfortably about the relationship between the personal and the political, and even to share the perception of the South African police that Ruth First was "a terrible mother."[31]

The phrase "the personal and the political" assumes, in this context, a chilling anti-feminist aspect. For there is something deeply disturbing about the ease with which an otherwise politically sympathetic reviewer can close ranks with apartheid's police, as men, against the "bad mother." Would anyone level a comparable charge against a male political detainee, by insinuating, for example, that Nelson Mandela's lifelong commitment to the struggle and his consequent imprisonment made him a "terrible father"?

A DRY WHITE SEASON AND GOOD BUDDY ACTIVISM

The appearance in 1989 of a third big budget anti-apartheid movie, Euzhan Palcy's *A Dry White Season*, added a new dimension to the liberal packaging of the South African struggle. The distributed film is shadowed by an unmade project which exemplifies the studio system's constriction of the idea of cinematic resistance to apartheid. Palcy had first sought to create "a film about South Africa entirely from the point of view of black characters."[32] However, "clearly nobody wanted to put money into a black filmmaker making a movie about blacks in South Africa. So I decided I had to find a book that would help me tell the story another way."[33] The book that furnished her with an alternative vision was the 1979 novel, *A Dry White Season*, by the liberal Afrikaans writer, Andre Brink.

The best guide to the preoccupations and tensions in Palcy's movie is the history of her source. Brink's *A Dry White Season* is a classic document of late seventies, white psychic crisis. The scale of the 1976 uprising had forced many whites to recognize, for the first time, that history was irreversibly weighted against their indefinite retention of power. White writing of the period typically responded either by fantasizing apocalyptic endgames or by scrambling a ride on the helter skelter of political change. *A Dry White Season* falls into the latter category, recounting how an Afrikaans schoolteacher, Ben Du Toit, gets jolted out of his suburban naivete by the murder of his gardener's son and by the spiral of state violence against Du Toit's and the gardener's families.

A Dry White Season emerges as a better crafted and more savvy movie than *Cry Freedom*, but they display some similar structural failings. Both chronicle the conscientizing of a white man through his friendship with a black man—Biko and *Dry White Season*'s taxi-driver, Stanley Makhaya—who schools him in black conditions under apartheid. In an analogue to the American media's style of attention, injustice exists as soon as the white man notices it, and when he does, he gets the star billing for his intrepid protest against inequity. What is at stake are the forms and origins of political agency, just as they were when Ted Koppel's South African series, during the month of the ANC's unbanning and Mandela's release, advertized itself as "*Nightline* Makes History." As if to anticipate the heroics of *Cry Freedom* and *Dry White*, Frantz Fanon once remarked sardonically on the glamorous style in which "[T]he settler makes history; his life is an epoch, an Odyssey."[34]

The novel on which Palcy's film rests give voice to Brink's sense that "the revolution I'm involved in…is a revolution in the conscience of my people"[i.e. the Afrikaners].[35] Respectable in its own terms, *Dry White Season* serves as the exhortatory fable of a liberal Afrikaner trying to rouse the conscience of his people. This vantage point governs the political action and ensures that Ben Du Toit's plight stands at the emotional center of film and novel alike.[36]

To its credit, *Dry White Season* (book and film) goes further than *Cry Freedom* in admitting a strong, multi-dimensional black character, the taxi driver, who stays the course of the film, whereas the second half of Attenborough's movie is a tale of white usurpation. And, as bell hooks points out, *Dry White Season* refreshingly overturns the Hollywood formula of killing off the black guy in order that his white buddy may live triumphant.[37] (After the police interrogator has killed Du Toit in a simulated hit-and-run, Makhaya exacts his revenge). Moreover, Palcy does doctor Brink's narrative somewhat, by excising the framing first person narrator who discovers Du Toit's diaries and pieces together his story, and by dramatically curtailing the central love interest between the schoolteacher and a liberal journalist. For all that, the taxi-driver exists primarily in a choral relationship to Du Toit, as the catalyst of his conscience, and it becomes quite difficult to square Brink's ambition to liberalize Afrikaners with the Caribbean Palcy's conviction that "as a black filmmaker I had wanted to do something about apartheid…"—particularly when one recalls her original plan for a black focused project. One has only to compare *Dry White Season* with Palcy's remarkable first film, *Sugar Cane Alley*, to recognize how distant the later, bigger movie remains from the inner dynamics of community struggle.

In defending *Dry White Season*, Palcy has sought to distinguish it from *Cry Freedom* and *A World Apart* on the grounds that her film does not shrink from including graphic torture scenes.[38] However, her preoccupation with daring to expose apartheid's horrors becomes symptomatic of her reliance on a liberal, late 70s plot. While the layer upon layer of corpses confront viewers with the poisoned fruit of South African racism, little is revealed about the culture of liberation and nothing about the major organizational agents of political change. The film's closing moments do proffer an image of resistance when the cab driver guns down the Afrikaans torturer, but at the level of strategy, significant opposition to apartheid has little to do with the isolated, retaliatory anger of the blow-'em-away sort. Makhaya's action is psychologically plausible and morally apposite, but it is scarcely a pertinent tactic for seizing the high ground.

One observes other signs of this problem. Palcy, following Brink, has Makhaya rebuke Du Toit for articulating optimism: "Hope," the taxi driver declares, "is a white man's word." Yet by the late eighties, hope had surely become more a black than a white word. The film's emphasis on victimization appears as a combined product of the more fragile condition of anti-apartheid resistance in the late seventies, Brink's liberal perspective, and studio and mass market pressures on Palcy.

As in *Cry Freedom*, much is invested in a male friendship that transcends the so-called "color bar." The brotherliness between Du Toit and Stanley, like the reconciliation of Biko and Woods, becomes the film's principal resource of hope. Both movies end up celebrating atomistic, heroic acts of white conversion and advocating personal goodwill between the black and white individuals as the motor for social change. This stance binds the two movies to a liberal American tradition of individual conscience acting alone or in two-man units. And so the microcosmic politics of the personal ends up ousting the decisive national forces—the ANC, the trade unions, the United Democratic Front, the Mass Democratic Movement, the student organizations, the End Conscription Campaign, and all the others which Mandela hailed, on his release, for having brought the struggle this far.

MAPANTSULA AND THRESHOLD RESISTANCE

For a more elaborate sense of resistance culture than Hollywood admits, one must turn to South Africa's fledgling progressive film movement and particularly to Oliver Schmitz's innovative *Mapantsula*. This 1988 film took shape as a low-budget, collaborative venture co-written by two South Africans, Schmitz and Thomas Mogotlane, with Mogotlane as lead actor and Schmitz directing. To enable them to shoot the film inside South Africa, Schmitz cloaked it as an apolitical gangster movie.[39]

The most conspicuous difference between *Mapantsula* and the films considered above derives from Schmitz's abandonment of the white liberal mediator, that iterative support for a broad American audience. The film declines to foreground white conscience as a major motor of anti-apartheid resistance. For the first time, among these movies, we have a black character as the experiential hub of an anti-apartheid story—a melancholy comment on the racial politics of the film industry. However, the hallmark of *Mapantsula*'s radicalism is its refusal to let individualized moral concerns shoulder out institutional and organizational questions strategic to the emergence of a new order. The focus on a gangster's life throws into relief three related issues critical to the direction of the struggle: the problem of distinguishing, under apartheid, between criminality and legality; the complex relations among survival, defiance, and organized resistance; and the role of the lumpenproletariat. The structure of the film suggests that the director intuited how the Manichean showdown between a tyrannical state and the long-suffering oppressed (led by a conscientized white) inevitably inflects the storyline with the rhetoric of victimization.

Mapantsula (Zulu for "thief") stages the radicalizing of a Sowetan *tsotsi* or gangster whose unbridled, self-interested rage is transformed into an affiliated political anger. At the outset, Panic, as he is known, shows equal contempt for the claims of the liberation struggle and for those who labor in menial jobs beneath white "bosses" and "madams." Then, in a twist of fortune, he gets detained in the company of trade unionists and United Democratic Front activists during a military sweep of the township. The film cuts, in an intricate series of flashbacks, between Panic's current imprisonment and his past life on the township streets. His cellmates are all UDF detainees who regard him suspiciously ("We're not criminals in here"). Yet to the state, the UDF activists are criminality incarnate, "commie-terrorists," while Panic (house-breaker, thief, assaulter, and murderer) is more valued as a prospective informer than condemned as a transgressor of the law. Police Inspector Stander batters Panic, convinced that the gangster possesses crucial information about a top trade unionist who slipped the police net when Panic was captured.

The politicizing of Panic turns on Stander's discovery that some years previous the gangster had served only six months of a murder conviction in exchange for grassing for the state. Stander can thus blackmail Panic by threatening to release this information to his UDF cellmates. Although ignorant of the trade unionist's political activities, Panic, under torture, issues a false confession. In the final scene, he must choose whether to sign—his right hand gripping a pen, his left balled into a fist—before delivering a final verdict of refusal.

From the outset, Panic is amoral. This allows the film to abstain from the reflex, polarized moralizing which often inhibits the big movies from providing incisive social commentary. By taking the risk of pointing out that South Africa's oppressed are neither automatically nor uniformly radical, Schmitz is able to focus on organizational challenges facing the resistance in the late 80s, among the most formidable of them, the challenge of integrating the vast lumpenproletariat into the struggle. Schmitz goes out on a limb by eschewing the narrow representational options Hollywood admits for black South Africans—that of the pure, powerless, tortured victim or the romanticized, saintly hero. The contrast with *Cry Freedom* is pointed: whatever the relative strengths of that film's first half, from the moment Biko appears to Woods as a blinding apparition haloed in light, the Black Consciousness leader is marked by a compensatory idealism which restricts his ability to incarnate a full, variable humanity. *Mapantsula*, by contrast, proffers a far more intimate sense of apartheid's role in the social construction of Panic's subjectivity and of the anguished options open to him among multiple forms of defiance.[40]

There is a pithy scene in *A Dry White Season* when Marlon Brando, playing the lawyer McKenzie, observes that "Justice and law are distant cousins. Here in South Africa they are not on speaking terms." If all black South Africans inhabit the alienated space between law and justice, the figure of the gangster or *tsotsi* reverberates with a special force as a symbol of illegality, particularly the illegality of urban blacks, a group which has been viewed, from an apartheid perspective, as a contradiction in terms. For decades, to be urban and black reduced one to a temporary sojourner, a labor unit floated between rural bantustans and cities on the tides of capitalist need. With the surge of racist legislation in the late 1950s and 60s, Hendrik Verwoerd and his cohorts virtually terminated "law-abiding citizen" as a viable category for urban blacks—to exist was to offend. In this context, the *tsotsi* came to represent a concentrated, if ambiguous, image of the intersection between illegality and defiance.

Many blacks responded to this imposed illegitimacy by embracing the image of the outlaw, choosing rebellious over quiescent contravention of the legal system. But the forms of revolt have varied immensely—ranging from collective ploys such as radical guerilla actions, industrial or miners' strikes, consumer and school boycotts at the one end to the atomized, opportunistic maraudings of *tsotsis* like Panic at the other. *Mapantsula* can be seen to stage one of the principal political challenges facing organized resistance in the late 80s: how to channel the capricious and often reactionary wrath of politically unaffiliated lumpen elements into more radical, organized forms of resistance.

As Don Pinnock intimates in his trenchant account of ganglife on the Cape Flats, the *tsotsi* is an ambiguous figure who inhabits the threshold of resistance and whose defiant resourcefulness can be tapped by the left or the right alike.[41] He can be regarded as a proud symbol of refusal, someone who opts out of the white-dominated system and sets up an alternative, informal mini-economy founded on violence.[42] Bloke Modisane, the Sophiatown journalist, once justified his uneasy respect for *tsotsis* in these terms: "the law is white, its legislators are white, its executive authority is white, and yet we were being criticised for not flying to the standard of the law…." Hence, he asserts, "if I had to choose between the tsotsis and the police my vote would be cast for the tsotsis."[43]

Yet, if sometimes half-admired, the *tsotsi* also instills deep fear because of his unscrupulous predations on township communities. The ambiguous status of a *tsotsi* like Panic can be read as symptomatic of the often volatile, uncertain allegiances of the lumpen as a whole. When organized resistance is surging, lumpen defiance may feed the struggle, but a combination of economic recession and a draconian clampdown (both evident under the late 80s State of Emergency) may drive many lumpen elements to pursue lives of reactionary opportunism, with the state recruiting them as vigilantes, collaborators, "instant police," provocateurs, and informers.[44] By the end of the 80s, as much as one third of the national workforce remained formally unemployed.[45]

Mapantsula, alone among these films, explores black women's layered oppression and their forms of survival. In *Cry Freedom* and *A Dry White Season*, these women, whether as domestic workers or wives, serve as a patient backdrop to the active male triumvirate of white friend, black friend, and Afrikaans torturer. And *A World Apart*, while breaking with the reflex tradition which views politics as an exclusively male drama of slug-him-or-love-him, nevertheless leaves the experience of the domestic worker in the wings. One could easily forget that domestic labor is the foremost occupation among South African women.

Mapantsula provides models of two self-sufficient women—Panic's landlady and his girlfriend, Pat, who works as a domestic. We are allowed a detailed sense, from Pat's perspective, of her abuse both by her sponging, violent boyfriend and by the white "madam" who employs her. Significantly, Pat is not simply strong in the passive resilient sense so often ascribed to black women: she throws over Panic for Duma, the trade unionist who encourages her to take legal action against the "madam" who fired her. As the movie advances, Pat's vantage point allows an exploration of the unions' radical efforts to organize domestic workers.

Schmitz is able to analyze the class and gender complexities of black life more comprehensively by shunning the liberal trope of the interracial friendship, which inevitably results in a dominant white vantage point. Moreover, the filmmaker refuses to rest his narrative on the formulae of moral condemnation which occlude or simplify fundamental economic and strategic issues. The protest march-cum-funeral which features in the mass market movies is indeed politically significant and has the added advantage of providing cinematic spectacle. But *Mapantsula* goes further than the other films in opening up a broad vision of the strategies which have empowered the resistance and begun to force the regime's hand: rent strikes, prisoners' hunger strikes, the populist actions of the UDF, and the assiduous advances of the trade union movement.

Yet *Mapantsula* was cold-shouldered by the heavily centralized distribution networks which dominate in South Africa and the U.S.A. One South African monopoly distributor did offer to disseminate the film, but only on the risible condition that it not be screened in the black townships, presumably because it was deemed inflammatory.[46] Independent screenings have since shown its popularity among township community and trade union audiences. Although the reasoning was different, the consequences were quite similar in the U.S.A. The film's failure to observe the mass market conventions of translating a radical South African narrative into a white-mediated, liberal idiom resulted in its failure to draw a major distributor. If the South African monopolists feared that blacks would identify too closely with the action, the Americans made the opposite mistake of assuming that it lacks an audience. Yet, as I can bear out from several independent screenings and discussions I have attended in New York, *Mapantsula* may offer urban African-American audiences powerful forms of identification that break with the need for a mediating friendship. The film is, after all, a political adaptation of the gangster movie, a Hollywood genre that has had an abiding impact on the styling of street culture in American ghettos and South African townships alike. Moreover, can one really dismiss as insufficiently mediated a film about the survival tactics of an outraged black underclass in a racially sundered metropolis? *Mapantsula* is set in an environment where decrepit schooling produces astronomic dropout rates; where family life is perennially undone by street violence, inflated, racially slanted imprisonments, and police bigotry; and where huge numbers eke out a tenuous survival through informal economic means. New York? Chicago? D.C.? For a sizeable American minority there exist alternative modes of identification with anti-apartheid cinema which might circumvent the imperatives of liberal framing. However, their potential tends to pass unrecognized by producers and distributors alike.

CONCLUSION

In assessing these four movies, how do we weigh the cost of the mid-Atlantic compromise between South African experience and American expectations against what may be gained from amplifying international condemnation of apartheid? On the one side stands Biko's caveat that "the biggest mistake the black world ever made was to assume that whoever opposed apartheid was an ally," on the other is the assumption—most apparent in Attenborough interviews—that box-office success is the most trustworthy barometer of a film's political seriousness.[47]

In steering this awkward course, however, we ought to avoid a pious, innocent appeal to authenticity as an alternative sole standard of worth.[48] There are two leading reasons for this. First, given the intimate overlap between value and political instrumentality in films opposing apartheid, we should retain some cross-cultural flexibility toward what might prove politically serviceable in divergent societies. (This needs to be complemented, as I have suggested in discussing *Mapantsula*, by exploring underrated, if limited, convergences between South African and American culture). Second, politically correct appeals to the "real" may disclose a sinister face, as South Africa's progressive film movement has learned all too intimately. During the eighties, the country's security police have repeatedly confiscated footage from anti-apartheid film and video makers; it was exploited as court evidence, often through devious editing and anachronistic citation. The most notorious instance of this process occurred during the protracted Delmas Trial, when the state based much of its case on five rolls of film and forty-two video and radio tapes seized from Afroscope, an affiliate of the UDF.[49] Moreover, as Harriet Gavshon chronicles, the state tracked down, detained, tortured and even murdered several people—mainly children— who testified in anti-apartheid documentaries like Sharon Sopher's *Witness to Apartheid*, CBS's *Children of Apartheid*, and the BBC's *Suffer the Children*.[50] In *Mapantsula* itself, there is an intensely disturbing moment when an interrogator seats Panic in front of a video monitor and attempts to terrorize him into identifying and incriminating participants in a funeral march. This scene can be read as a self-reflexive allegory about the hazards of documentary method and the uncertain destiny of the "real"; even perhaps, as Schmitz's coded rationale for choosing to work in feature rather than documentary.

While remaining suspicious of authenticity and mimetic adequacy as criteria of political effectiveness, I have sought to demonstrate how the terms of cross-cultural conversion in the mass market films have, for ideological reasons, designated certain forms of knowledge threatening or incommunicable. On this score, one can invoke the arguments of the distinguished South African novelist and critic, Njabulo Ndebele, against certain species of anti-apartheid literature. Ndebele contends that liberal moralism in South African culture has encouraged "an art of anticipated surfaces" which skates over the more exacting questions of social process. As he words it:

> The major commitment of such a moral ideology is the exposure of the existence of social evil with the aim of pricking the human conscience of those responsible for that evil. The result is not knowledge but indictment; …[M]oral ideology tends to ossify complex social problems into symbols which are perceived as finished forms of good or evil…[51]

Ndebele warns elsewhere of "the unintended trap of a self-evident moral advantage" which can blunt political initiatives.[52] Of the four films I have considered, only *Mapantsula* allows a developing black character whose passage through doubts, choices, and commitments brings alive the social processes and institutions that animate the resistance. Otherwise, as a rule of thumb, white characters grow towards a state of enlightenment, while black characters are ossified products, ending much as they began.

If, as Ndebele charges, anti-apartheid culture within South Africa needs to get beyond "the mere articulation of grievance"—which he reads as "the very index of powerlessness"—the question remains how this exhortation bears on anti-apartheid culture which originates abroad.[53] I would contend that in judging the mass market films we need to consider not just the dissonances between

American and South African political traditions, but also the possibility that the anti-apartheid movement in the United States, in order to extend its constituency, grew reliant on the language and imagery of victimization to a degree unthinkable in the internal resistance. This returns us to the spirit of Palcy's remark that *Dry White Season* alone showed the courage to disclose torture at its worst.

Given the constraints of time and distance, most supporters of anti-apartheid movements abroad could not be expected to follow the nuanced transformations of apartheid and the tactical adjustments of its internal opponents. When a group of South African clergy suggested in Washington in May, 1990 that only specific South African products be singled out for sanctions, dismayed American anti-apartheid groups rejected the strategy as overly subtle for their American constituency.[54] Indeed, the successful application of international pressure on South Africa has stemmed, in large part, from the ability of the American and British anti-apartheid movements to mobilize around an image of apartheid as a stable, almost timeless referent for iniquity.[55]

The historical settings of *Cry Freedom*, *A World Apart*, and *A Dry White Season* all reflected this tendency. All three strove to make an impact on late 80s apartheid, yet to do so through settings well back in time: the mid-70s, 1963, and the late 70s respectively. One might argue that this ploy shielded the films from possible erosion by current events. However, more significant I believe, is the directors' well-founded conviction that, for an international audience, any South African film exists in the undying present of apartheid and that they would thus not be viewed as period pieces.

Schmitz and Mogotlane proceeded differently, by delivering a film with a contemporary feel to it down to the nuances of circa-1988 political strategy under the specific pressures of the State of Emergency. Yet the epochal changes in South Africa and Eastern Europe from 1989 onwards quickly gave even Schmitz's 1988 film the aspect of a distant "contemporary." The turn into the 90s has sent convulsions through the verities of both apartheid and the liberation struggle: there is no plausible basis for the rhetoric of anti-communism on the one hand, nor that of revolution on the other. The most improbable cast of players—ranging from the South African Communist Party to the Nationalist regime—can be found huddled around the word "democracy." In the South African context, the term has become safely amorphous, a provisional way of bypassing the historically charged registers of socialism and liberalism.

In introducing a pivotal 1987 collection devoted to liberalism, Jeffrey Butler reflected on liberalism's tenuous authority in South Africa relative to the high standing of radical traditions. While noting liberalism's inauspicious immediate prospects, Butler suggested that the best hope for a South African liberal revival might lie in the ideology's prestige and strength abroad.[56] Indeed, by the early 90s there was little doubt that the precipitous changes in Eastern Europe had somewhat revived liberalism's fortunes in South Africa.

At much the same time as Butler but from within a tradition of left nonracialism, Ndebele reviewed relations in the late 80s between indigenous and international politico-economic traditions. Ndebele cautioned against the "humanization" of the oppressed according to the specifications of capital" and articulated an allied concern that in the shadow of international capital "the very concept of freedom has come to be standardized."[57] As South Africa proceeds beyond the sudden uncertainties of the current interregnum, the relation between Butler's and Ndebele's observations may assume a particular urgency. To what extent will largely liberal notions of freedom and democracy, strengthened by events in Eastern Europe, standardized and imported from abroad, transform the dominant currents of South African politics? And to what extent will the emergent South Africa accommodate the more radical, independently cultivated, grass-roots traditions of participatory democracy?

The jury is still out on how South Africa's radical, liberal, and conservative constituencies will adjust to each other during the 90s movement towards a post-apartheid dispensation. What seems certain is that a major shakeup of ideological alignments has begun, with repercussions for internal politics and for the image of apartheid abroad. Internally, the extreme brutality of Botha's States of Emergency and the revolutionary fervor they provoked have given way to a mood of circumspect conciliation amidst a spate of bloodshed. And while it is acknowledged that apartheid has yet to be dismantled, the international media have, since Mandela's release, submitted South Africa to a different style of attention; apartheid no longer serves with anything like the old force as a magnet for condemnation.

The political milieu that stimulated Attenborough, Menges, and Palcy to denounce apartheid through liberal, big-budget movies has receded into the past. By the same token, as South Africa glimpses the possibility of hitherto unimagined ideological accommodations, the pitch of discord between American liberalism and South African radicalism, so acute in these films, seems likely to give way to new, more modulated styles of difference.

part two

EXIT VISAS AND
NO ENTRY SIGNS

4

BORDER COUNTRY
Bessie Head's Frontline States

Oh mama mama they got me living on the frontline
Oh mama mama they got me born in the wrong time.

—Eddy Grant, "Living on the Frontline"

In those days the border was pretty much on the border of the country. Now the border goes all over the place. Sometimes straight through the middle of families. Which is, I suppose, what civil war is all about.

—James Whyle, "Sappeur Fijn and the Cow," *Force's Favourites*

BESSIE HEAD BORE THE BURDEN of a doubly illegitimate birth: in 1937 she was conceived out of wedlock and, in apartheid argot, "across the color bar." Simply by being born, she transgressed the racial and gender edicts of her society, a "deviance" that portended the torments of her later life. In her thirteenth year, Head learned that the man and woman whom she had presumed to be her parents bore no biological relation to her. That year, the South African state removed her from foster parental care and placed her in an orphanage. It was only then that Head's origins were revealed to her:

I was born on the 6th July 1937 in the Pietermaritzburg Mental Hospital. The reason for my peculiar birthplace was that my mother was white, and she had acquired me from a black man. She was judged insane, and committed to the mental hospital while pregnant.[1]

Head's mother, Bessie Amelia Emery, came from an upper-class white South African family renowned for breeding racehorses. The family's professional preoccupation with eugenics may well have compounded their deepseated racial prejudices when their daughter, on the rebound from a failed marriage, flouted racial and class taboos by entering into a sexual liaison with a black stablehand. When she fell pregnant, her parents had her locked away in the Pietermaritzburg mental asylum on grounds of "premature senile dementia."[2] Emery gave birth to Head in the asylum and, six years later, in 1943, committed suicide there. Head never met her mother, nor did she ever learn the name of her father, who fled the Emery estate without a trace.

Head was named not by her parents but by the South African state: "My mother's name was Bessie Emery and I consider it the only honour South African officials ever did me—naming me after this unknown, lovely, and unpredictable woman."[3] So at Head's christening, the distinction between private and public had already begun to dissolve, foreshadowing her almost lifelong sense of the power that the nation state wielded over the conditions of her identity.

Head once observed that her mother had been "locked up in a loony bin to save the family name."[4] Her white grandparents had endeavoured to safeguard the family name by disinheriting their errant daughter and entombing her alive in a South African mental asylum. It is one of the redeeming ironies of Head's life that the family name was saved in a quite contrary sense of the word: it was redeemed from demonic rites of purification through the writings of a "half-caste," outcast daughter.

By the age of thirteen, Head had known four sets of parents: her biological parents; the Afrikaans foster parents who, according to one version of her autobiography, adopted her as an infant only to return her a week later complaining that she "appeared to be black"; the mixed race foster parents into whose care she was then delivered; and the South African state which, acting in locus parentis, removed the young girl from the second foster parents and placed her in an orphanage as a ward of the state. Thus, from an early age, Head came to experience the family not as a natural form of belonging but as an unstable artifice, invented and reinvented in racial terms, and conditional upon the administrative designs of the nation-state.

Head's estrangements from tradition placed her under relentless pressure to improvise a sense of community and ancestry, in her life and writing alike. One critic has portrayed her novel, *A Question of Power*, as situated at the "crossroads of dispossession"—a phrase that could be readily applied to her work as a whole.[5] Yet the sheer force and variety of the dispossessions suffered by this *deracine* provoked her to pursue, with great vigor, alternative forms of belonging. The crossroads of dispossession and affiliation in Head's work are most marked in her novella, *Maru,* her autobiographical writings, her short stories, and her oral history of Serowe, the Botswanan village where she resided. To chart these junctions is to trace how, denied the solidarities of family, race, and nation, Head generated a compensatory matrix of allegiances transnationally to the Southern African region, locally to a particular village, and within that, to a community of women. Head's haunting quest for alternative, improvised

Fig. 1: Bessie Head. (George Hallet; Heinemann)

grounds for her identity generated an *oeuvre* that testifies, with singular intensity, to the inventedness of many of the most authoritative social categories—nation, family, race, and history.

The circumstances of Head's birth were not the only forms of marginality she had to contend with: as a first generation "colored," an orphan, a changeling, a refugee, a certified "madwoman," and a single mother, she led a profoundly disinherited life on almost every front. Moreover, as a so-called "colored" woman engaging with rural themes in Southern Africa, Head wrote without the sustenance of any literary lineage.

Many of the fundamental criteria for social membership—notably those of family, race, and nation—characteristically assume or invoke the authority of blood-lineage. Because Head's relationship to all these categories was so radically and traumatically liminal, she could never live the illusion of their naturalness. As such, her work offers radical insight into the contingencies underlying efforts to secure membership or exclusion from society on grounds of nature or ancestry.

Head often lamented her violent severance from the continuities that others took for granted: "I have not a single known relative on earth, no long and ancient family tree to refer to, no links with heredity."[6] This provoked a yearning for the simplest of ties—even the shape of a fingernail inherited from a grandmother, anything that would stand between her and the cavernous past. When she died in 1986 at the age of 49, Head had never met any relative other than the son whom she had conceived.

Faced with such a void, she at least had her mother's name to fall back on and carry forward. Once, when Head found herself on the brink of mental collapse, she gave voice to her mixed admiration and trepidation toward the impulsive precedent which was her mother's bequest:

> There is a terrible depth of loneliness in supposed or even evident insanity. There is more. A birth such as I had links me to her in a very deep way.... She must have been as mad and impulsive as I. ...I still say she belongs to me in a special way and that there is no world as yet for what she had done. She left me to figure it out.[7]

Head felt bonded to her mother both through the possibility of a congenital tendency toward mental illness and, more positively, through the challenge of living a transgressive life. She thus drew from her mother's name and example an equivocal security—a partial precedent in a life otherwise bereft of precedents.

THE INVENTION OF "MIXED ANCESTRY"

While the statutory definitions of so-called "coloreds" under apartheid have shifted over time, they have been persistently riven with contradictions. The state has variously sought to demarcate the category "colored" on the basis of descent, parentage, physical appearance, language preference, cultural criteria, and "general acceptance" by "the community." Even preferences for particular sports have sometimes been invoked. Of all the racial groups circumscribed by apartheid legislation, "coloreds" have been most frequently represented through layered negations. The Population Registration Act of 1950, for example, defined a "colored" as someone "who in appearance is obviously not White or Indian and who is not a member of an aboriginal race or African tribe."[8]

As an apartheid category, the label "colored" has provoked intense debate among the people so designated. The degree of its appropriation or rejection has been subject to considerable historical, regional, and class variables. As the exiled critic, Vernon February observes, after the 1976 Soweto Rebellion there was an upsurge in the tendency, particularly among younger "coloreds," to identify themselves as black—although the South African parameters of that term, too, have remained unstable.[9] In the 1980s, Allan Boesak and other prominent "colored" leaders continued to use the term selectively but began to preface it with "so-called." However, others objected to this appendage, among them Alex La Guma, formerly the ANC's representative in Havana who, together with Head, is South Africa's most distinguished mixed-race novelist. La Guma opined in 1984 that the qualifying "so-called": "Makes me feel like a so-called human, a humanoid, those things who have all the characteristics of human beings but are really artificial. Other minority people are not called 'so-called.'"[10]

The contradictions within state efforts to define "colored" South Africans in simultaneously negative and threshold terms are evident from the invocations of racial and familial idioms. "Coloreds" have been subjected both to white claims on their allegiance—as "brown Afrikaners"—and to disclaimers—as "non-whites." So, too, when whites have found it politically expedient to attempt to set "colored" and African majority interests at loggerheads, "coloreds" have become "half-brothers" and "half-sisters," "almost family." However, the imagery of partial kinship has also been used to patronize or ostracize "coloreds" as prodigal and degenerate, the embodiments of moral dissolution. This view was notoriously advanced by Sarah Gertrude Millin's 1924 novel, *God's Step-children*, a fictional polemic against miscegenation as a biological, familial, and national tragedy.[11]

Represented by South African legislation in negative and racially intermediate terms, mixed race South Africans have been especially vulnerable to administrative caprice around the issue of ancestry.[12] Yet February has quite rightly challenged Lewis Nkosi's claim that Bessie Head's "'mulatto' ancestry" accounts for her insecurity.[13] However, neither February nor Nkosi, in their otherwise limpid reflections on Head's fiction, explores her liminal relationship to the "colored" community which, for reasons of geography and gender, was never available to her as a secure ground for identity. Head was raised in a Natal missionary orphanage in a largely Indian environment, some thousand kilometers from the epicenter of "colored" culture in the Cape.[14] She moved to the Cape in 1960 at the age of twenty-three, but struggled to fit in:

> As a newcomer to the Cape, I thought I had found the ideal place for my
> mixed-race soul. But I quickly and painfully learned that if you were not

fully grounded in the colour brown, you would have to be excluded from the community's business and be ready to endure insult.[15]

Head's lack of centeredness in "the colour brown" can be ascribed in part to her geographical isolation from the "mixed race" community and in part to the fact that she was a first generation "colored" who, while victimized under apartheid on grounds of race, identified intensely with her white mother. The horrendous familial, political, and legal toll on black-white relationships meant that a high proportion of first generation "coloreds" were born outside marriage. However, given their economic and social privilege and their relative immunity from the legal consequences, white men far more frequently impregnated (and ordinarily abandoned) black women than black men did white women. Head's inverted relationship to this pattern exacerbated her difficulties in reconciling her racial and gender allegiances. As a "colored," her experience of white racism and hatred alienated her from whiteness, yet, as a woman, she felt very powerfully that her only ties to the past were through the intrepid example of her white mother, who herself had been punished for flouting racial, class, and sexual taboos.

NATIONAL AND ETHNIC DISINHERITANCE

Head's sense of familial and racial estrangement was intensified by the fact that, until the age of 42, she was also denied the moorings of nationality. Her first 27 years were spent in South Africa as a disenfranchised "colored" woman, and the next 15 in Botswana where citizenship was withheld from her, forcing her to live as a stateless refugee. Thus Head's identity was circumscribed on familial, racial, and national fronts by disinheritance, illegitimacy, and rootlessness. In the face of these circumstances, her writing and life in the Botswanan village of Serowe were distinguished by an unremitting need to reconceive herself outside the pseudo-natural matrix of familial, racial, and national traditions that formed the very grounds of her ostracism.

Head's prose is peopled largely with two types: characters whose sense of belonging is an unsettled, precarious achievement rather than a birthright and characters who risk or forfeit their inherited privileges by breaking with claustral traditions. Indeed, Head repeatedly projected forms of community and ancestry that could not be premised on the unexamined authority of inherited tradition. Her own vexed relationship to questions of origins, succession, legacies, heritages, and bloodlines left her with a deep-seated suspicion of tradition, above all national traditions, whose invented authority rests on the assumption that the nation is both natural and born of a continuous historical lineage.

Although the nation is a political and bureaucratic invention, the discourse of nationalism commonly seeks to imbue it with the natural authority of blood-lineage by representing the nation as a set of familial bonds. Etymologically, the word nation is rooted in the idea of birth. More broadly, the language of nationalism is a language of new nations being born, of motherlands, fatherlands, homelands, adopted lands, and neighboring countries. The figure of Mother of the Nation has accrued to women as diverse as Winnie Mandela, Eva Peron, and the Queen Mum. So, too, when we speak of the homecoming of exiles, their imagined destination is at once a national and a domestic space.

Feminist theorists of nationalism like Anne McClintock, Elleke Boehmer, Floya Anthias, and Nira Yuval-Davis have analyzed the contradictions between the frequent projection of the idea of the nation through a female idiom and the exclusion of women from the statutory rights available to "nationals," whose normative identity has been institutionalized as male.[16] At a rhetorical level, however, analogs between national and family ties have proved crucial to political efforts to portray the nation as a self-evident category authenticated by historical and biological continuities. This process suppresses the irrational, incoherent, and contingent dimensions to nations whose ancestry and boundaries are not emanations of an organic past but largely the products of repeated bureaucratic interventions. The administrative labor of presenting the nation as a surrogate work of nature is manifest, for instance, in the title of the American Department of Immigration and Naturalization, the body responsible for transmogrifying so-called resident "aliens" into "naturalized" Americans. Anyone who has struggled through that labyrinthine paper tunnel can testify to the perversity of construing the process of nationalization as a form of integrating people into something natural. The discourse of "undocumented immigrants" depicts much more accurately outsiders' experience of the nation as a bureaucratic, not an organic, phenomenon.

Having been rejected by her natal land and by her adopted country, Head experienced the nation first and foremost as an administrative ordeal. From 1964 to 1979, her official identity remained sandwiched between two of the world's most risible, immobilizing documents—a South African exit permit and a United Nations Refugee Travel Document—both of which denied her a national identity. The grotesquely euphemistic exit permit allowed dissident South Africans to leave the country—sans passport—with the threat of imprisonment should they ever attempt reentry.[17] The United Nations Refugee Travel Document—a document that attracts such suspicion at border posts as to be almost incriminating—was a mark of Botswana's protracted refusal to upgrade her from refugee to citizen.

When an American literary journal innocently sent Head a questionnaire about her writing habits, she remarked ruefully: "I am usually terrorized by various authorities into accounting for my existence; and filling in forms, under such circumstances, acquires a fascination all of its own."[18] As a result of the perennial, reciprocal suspicion between her and all national authorities, she approached questionnaires with the expectation not that they might ratify her identity, but that they had been devised to invalidate it. Thus for Head the nation was less an organic community than a set of administered categories that militated against her efforts to cultivate community and ancestry.

One theorist of nationalism, Philip Schlesinger, has described the nation as a

> repository, *inter alia*, of classificatory systems. It allows "us" to define ourselves against "them" understood as those beyond the boundaries of the nation. It may also reproduce distinctions between "us" and "them" at the intra-national level, in line with the *internal* structure of social divisions and relations of power and domination.[19]

Schlesinger's remarks are directly pertinent to South Africa, where the classificatory obsessions of British imperialism, inherited and transformed by Afrikaans nationalists, insured that most black South Africans lived the nation state as a brutally administered form of disinheritance. This experience of the nation state as a set of institutions destructively reinventing people by categorizing them is forcefully evoked by Don Mattera, a "mixed race" author of Head's generation. Writing of the era when apartheid bureaucrats sought to institutionalize a revamped version of the category "colored," Mattera recalls how: "A twilight people…were being conceived on the drawing board of apartheid. A hybrid species, signed, sealed and stamped into synthetic nationhood."[20]

Head's liminal status as a "mixed race" South African left her particularly resistant to the synthetic projections of the nation in categorically racial terms. Yet she might have become less resistant to the idea of the nation per se had her negative experience of the mutually reinforcing exclusions of nation and race not been repeated, disturbingly if less violently, in Botswana after she moved there in 1964. In Serowe, the village where she finally settled, she found that the inhabitants identified themselves strongly in ethnic nationalist terms as Batswana. Like many such communities, they consolidated their identity by defining themselves in opposition to certain outcast groups. The lot of the pariahs fell principally, in Serowe, to the lighter skinned "Bushmen" or "San," for whom the Batswana reserved a special term of disdain—"Masarwa"(pl. "Basarwa"). To her mortification, Head found herself cursed as a "half-caste" and "low breed" alongside the so-called "Masarwa."[21] The familiarity of the insult must have sharpened her agony, for "Boesman"/"Bushman" was a standard slur spat at "coloreds" by white South African policeman and farmers. The traumas of adoption had come full circle; the orphan whose foster parents had rejected her for appearing too black was now derided, in her adopted village, for seeming insufficiently so. Having left the racist nationalism of South Africa behind her, Head found herself in a situation where the Botswanan state refused to accept her as a national and members of her local community vilified her in racial terms.

Reading between the lines, one begins to discern the discriminatory rationale behind the bracketing of Head with the "Basarwa." From both a white colonial and a Botswana perspective, the nomadic character of the "San" or "Basarwa" militated against their claims to ownership of the land. Indeed, the abusive term "Masarwa" bears the contradictory meaning of "a person from the uninhabited country."[22] This formulation for perpetuating the cycles of dispossession is reminiscent of the catastrophic colonial designation of Palestine as "a land without a people" and Palestinians as "a people without a land." In both instances, the argument begins by designating a people as nomadic, proceeds by claiming that this precludes them from owning land, and thereby deduces that such landless people cannot, by definition, suffer dispossession. The motive for and consequence of this rationale is the accelerated dispossession of the people in question, be they Palestinians or "San."

It would thus seem that discrimination against people envisaged as "wanderers"—Jews, Romani, Palestinians, and "San"—is not confined to the West. Moreover, a related version of this prejudice is projected onto refugees as "undesirable" in their errancy. Thus the earmarking of Head as a pariah in Botswana brought together the perceptions of her as a "tribeless half-caste," as ethnically similar to the "landless Basarwa," and as a refugee. To compound matters, she bore the stigma of the single mother—a "loose" woman, anchored neither through land nor marriage to the agrarian system of property that determined social value.[23] The certification of Head as insane and her confinement in Lobatse Mental Institution in 1971 may have further exacerbated the perception of her as "wandering" and "loose"—given the mutually confirming projections in some societies of "madwomen" as "strays," and "stray" women (i.e. single ones, especially single mothers) as unhinged. Lynette Jackson's groundbreaking work on the construction of female madness in certain Southern African mental institutions is particularly suggestive in this regard.[24]

Faced with these congested projections of her as "deviant," Head could not submit to artificial divides between the pure and the impure, the authentic and the inauthentic. Nor, given her isolation, could she hope to surmount them speedily. Yet as a writer she possessed a third option: unable to find a society liberated from bigotry, she could project such a society of her own. *Maru*, which appeared in 1971, is precisely such an invention. The novel draws on Head's experiences of ostracism, but projects them towards a utopian resolution remote from her own immediate prospects.[25]

Maru's plot pivots on a racial category mistake. The two most powerful men in a Botswanan village fall in love with a newly arrived teacher, Margaret Cadmore. On account of her looks and education they assume that she is a "colored" up from South Africa. When it is disclosed that she is a "Masarwa" (i.e. "San" or "Bushman"), the social stigma against marrying such an inferior dissipates one of her suitors' passion. However, his rival, Maru, forfeits his hereditary claim to the chieftaincy, flouts tradition by wedding the outcast woman, and abandons his hidebound community.

Head once remarked that she had invested three quarters of herself in Margaret Cadmore. However, the novel revises several essential details from her own life, above all, details of racial ancestry. Head reimagines the mother of the orphaned Margaret not as an upper class white woman but as a "Masarwa." Somewhere in life, Head, the "colored" suffered discrimination on the grounds that she was bracketed with the "Masarwa"; in fiction, Margaret the "Masarwa" is initially mistaken for a "colored." Through this inversion of Head's own experience, *Maru* exposes the fickle categories on which the very possibility of racial error depends. The book as a whole anticipates an idealized community in which the bigotries of racism and ethnic nationalism are simultaneously transcended.

Given the option of passing for "colored," Cadmore defiantly reaffirms her "Masarwa" identity. So, too, in her own life, Head insisted that "There is no-one who is going to un-bushman me."[26] She sought not to fight the term of abuse but to commandeer it. In the process, she adopted the strategy common among people from denigrated groups who seek to exorcise a stigma by transforming, through appropriation, the terms of their rejection.

Head became intensely invested in *Maru*, charging on several occasions that it "ought to liberate the oppressed Bushmen here overnight."[27] Although the novella could not possibly have so grand an effect, a "Masarwa" delegation did visit Head and garland her for upholding their cause. When her hopes of winning acceptance into Serowe reached their nadir, she rebuked herself for inventing a Motswana as the redemptive figure who defects from racism:

> He[Maru] expresses my most sound and coherent views of the question of racial oppression. I twist my face in agony. Why did I give my most beautiful lines and experience to a Motswana when they all spat at me for being Coloured? Why did I do it?.... I am sick of being hated for shit and junk...[28]

Foreign reviewers of *Maru* added to the torment by carelessly granting Head membership of the very ethnic and national groups that had so vigorously rejected her. She was disturbed to read in the London *Bookseller* of "'Bessie Head, the ebullient Botswanan...' If only they knew. Here I am Bessie Head, the Bushman dog..."[29] In self-defense, she began to distance herself from the publication of *Maru*, fearing that reviewers "might say again, in error, 'Bessie Head, the Motswanan' and I shall end up in hospital again with another nervous breakdown..."[30] Taunts of racial deviancy threatened her mental balance while, in turn, her dread that she might harbor hereditary madness left her more vulnerable to charges of aberrancy.

Head's ethnic abuse at the local level converged with her bureaucratic maltreatment on the national front. The hypocrisy rankled. After all, her books had helped put Botswana on the map: *When Rain Clouds Gather* was so prized as an introduction to the country that it was routinely distributed to the stream of Peace Corps and other international aid workers who came to work in Botswana. Yet Head was left in the invidious position of being used as a Botswanan writer while being denied the security of Botswanan nationality.

There are other reasons why Head's writing eluded all national definitions. As she observed: "It has surprised me, the extent to which creative writing is often regarded, unconsciously, as a nationalistic activity. ...I have so often been referred to as 'the Botswana writer,' while in reality the Botswana personality isn't as violent as me."[31] On the one hand, the brutality of her South African upbringing set her apart from the Botswanan villagers; on the other hand, she found South Africa too hateful and too menacing to submit to literary reclamation.[32] Thus her sensibility and her subject matter were shaped on different sides of the national boundary.

Prior to leaving South Africa, Head had identified herself with Pan Africanism—an alternative allegiance to nationalism. She had been attracted to the political style of Robert Sobukwe, founder of the breakaway Pan Africanist Congress. Sobukwe, an admirer of George Padmore, had instilled in Head an imaginative identification with Africa and had helped repair her shattered sense of dignity and history. Ordinarily cynical of politicians, Head was impressed by Sobukwe's stress on reclamation of the land as the psychological and economic key to the revival of African self-sufficiency. At a time when the ANC gave greater weight to urban conditions and urban resistance, Head admired Sobukwe's insistent attention to the plight and struggles of South Africa's rural majority.[33]

However, once she moved to Botswana, Head became disillusioned with the infighting and corruption of the PAC in exile.[34] Indeed, she distanced herself from all exile politics. While still subjected to white domination, she had clung to an idealized Africa that had been proportionate to the scale and ferocity of her South African sufferings. After crossing over into Africa "proper," she discovered that Pan Africanism, which had offered a strong image of unity in the face of apartheid, retained little relevance under the quite different pressures of Botswanan village life. Head found herself among people whose experience and forms of identification were far more local than hers; they couldn't take their bearings from anything as vast and abstract as Africa.

Botswana's shallow experience of colonialism made it fallow ground for Pan Africanism which has customarily taken root in societies with a deep history of colonialism. Head's vilification as a half-caste and her unforeseen difficulties in being accepted as an African further diminished the prospect of her sustaining a Pan Africanist allegiance.[35] *A Question of Power*, her highly autobiographical novel that appeared in 1974 is in part an imaginative chronicle of her exorcism of these violent disappointments. By the end of that swirling, cathartic book, one detects the beginnings of her acquisition of new powers of belonging. Bypassed by nationalism and disaffected with Pan Africanism, she was beginning to align herself transnationally with the Southern African region and locally with the village of Serowe.

RURAL TRANSNATIONALISM AND THE REINVENTION OF COMMUNITY

Alone among the host of black South African authors exiled by apartheid, Head set the bulk of her oeuvre in her adopted locale. The work of most of the literary exiles—Bloke Modisane, Lewis Nkosi, Es'kia Mphahlele, Alex La Guma, Dennis Brutus and the others—reveals few attachments to the alien present, focusing obsessively on the imaginative recuperation of the South African past. Almost all of them wrote at a great physical distance from South Africa, having put oceans and continents between themselves and apartheid. Head's circumstances and approach were wholly different. She had avoided the standard literary routes from South Africa to Europe and North America and merely moved, in her words, "one door away from South Africa."[36] Consequently, she achieved a perspective of proximate exile in which cross-cultural differences were offset by significant continuities.

Most of South Africa's specifically literary exiles headed for those venerable magnets for bohemian diasporas—London, Paris, New York, Chicago, and Berlin. Unlike the literary set, however, most refugees and exiles from apartheid crossed over into neighboring countries, where they remained vulnerable to the predations of South Africa's regional imperial designs. For them, exile was principally a rural, not a metropolitan, plight. Thus, while Head was totally estranged from the dominant traditions of South African literary exile, her preoccupation with rural, regional experience brought her closer to the presiding traditions of South African exile per se.

Head's rural transnationalism began as an affliction which she appropriated as an allegiance. After crossing the border into the frontline state of Botswana, she became a pawn in a chess game between that country and South Africa. The Botswanans, fearing South African military intervention if the exile community expanded, refused to grant her permanent status. So for fifteen years as a refugee, she had to report weekly to the police. As pressures mounted, she began to fear that the Botswanans might certify her as insane in order to deport her to South Africa where she would be forced to reenact her mother's institutional history.[37] The specter of Sammy Peterson, a fellow refugee, exacerbated her apprehension: the Botswanans had turned him over to the South African regime, who had incarcerated him on trumped up grounds of dementia.[38] The abuse dispensed first by the South African then by the Botswanan state seeded her growing skepticism toward the grand narratives of national politics.

If Head's regional perspective began as a symptom of her viciously administered life, one of her singular achievements was to transform that regionalism into a groundbreaking literary vision. Almost all her writings are set in a Botswanan village and accumulatively they convey a powerful sense of the ceaseless border crossings of imperialists, missionaries, refugees, migrant workers, prostitutes, school children, teachers, and armies that score Southern Africa as a region.

Like her identification with the region, Head's growing allegiance to Serowe never lost its comparative edge. The complexities of this affiliation are most manifest in *Serowe: Village of the Rain Wind*, Head's oral history that appeared in 1981. *Village of the Rain Wind* offers the fullest account of her sedulous efforts to cultivate ancestry and community, dramatizing, in the process, her reliance on village and the Southern African region as complementary sites of affiliation to offset her estrangement from national and Pan Africanist identities.

From the perspective of Head's relentlessly disrupted life, the Botswanan village held a particular restorative promise. For, like most of Botswana, Serowe's history was unrepresentative of the history of Southern Africa in that it had remained relatively untrammelled by colonialism. The depth of Botswana's mineral wealth was only exposed in the 1960s and 70s and, as a mostly desert region lacking a coastline, the land contained few enticements for Europeans. Over the course of five hundred years, Portuguese, Dutch, British, French, and British explorers and colonists had remade the face of South Africa, whereas Bechuanaland (as Botswana was previously called) had been a British colony for a mere eighty years prior to independence, and even then, had only been lightly colonized. Throughout Africa, there has been a correlation between the scale of European settlement and the bloodiness of decolonization—witness the wars in Kenya, Algeria, Zimbabwe, Mozambique, Angola, and South Africa.

By such standards, Botswana had experienced a peaceful and sheltered twentieth century, a point not lost on Head as she sought a refuge from the psychic and bureaucratic violence that had undone her.

Yet for all the reasons discussed above, Head struggled to identify with Botswana at large. Instead, she focused her ambitions on Serowe, an isolated village of thirty-three thousand inhabitants where daily life was criss-crossed with indigenous traditions, some of them predating the colonial irruptions into the subcontinent. Head was encouraged in her idealism by Serowe's exiguous contact with colonialism: even among the poorest folk she recognized a resilient self-respect that she felt was far more difficult to sustain under apartheid.

Head's determination to win greater social acceptance was boosted by her experimentation with a change of genre. Compared to the solitude of composing a novel, Head's research for the oral history forced upon her a greater intimacy with the village. The process of interviewing some hundred inhabitants about their collective history became integral to her efforts to gain entry into the community through the gates of the past. Arguably, in a village where only a fraction of the population could read English, oral history allowed Head to enact her assimilation to a degree that the novel never permitted.

Head's approach to Serowe's history is redolent of Walter Benjamin's insistence that, "To articulate the past historically does not mean to recognize it 'the way it really was.' It means to seize hold of a memory as it flashes up at a moment of danger."[39] Emerging in the mid-70s from her cycles of high inner distress, racial rejection, psychological breakdown, confinement in a Botswanan mental asylum, and the strange solipsistic creativity of *A Question of Power*, Head saw local history not least as a mechanism for survival. She once remarked that "a sense of history was totally absent in me," an observation that is susceptible to layered readings.[40] Serowe promised Head a redeeming alternative to the threatening histories to which she had been exposed: familial blankness, a predestined female history of atonement for a transgressive life, and systematic racial conquest.

Head's later writings suggest that she came to view the governing forms of historical narration as symptoms and agents of colonial violence. Looking back on her South African education, she recognized how she had been denied any sense of history as a flexible resource—indeed, as anything other than an incontestable record of loss and obliteration.[41] If black South Africans labored beneath a tradition of triumphalist colonial historiography, colonialism's marginal interest in Botswana had produced a quite contrary legacy of partisan, expansive silences, as if villages like Serowe had proved so deficient in significant event as to defeat all attempts at historical rendition. As Head observed sardonically of Serowe: "There isn't anything in this village that an historian might care to write about. Dr. Livingstone passed this way, they might say."[42]

In *Village of the Rain Wind*, Head sought to offset this neglect without merely reacting to it. Struggling to piece together a rich but diffuse interview with a hundred-and-four year old man, she articulated her motives for connecting with a tradition that

> had kept no written record of [its] searches, enquiries and philosophical anguish. All that was written of this period by white historians trod roughshod over their history dismissing it as "petty, tribal wars", ...It had seemed more important that a black man should be known as a "good boy" or a "bad boy" and hurry up and down with the suitcases of his master, who was creating "real" history.[43]

With this in mind, she disturbs external, colonial standards of what constitutes event, concluding wryly: "I decided to record the irrelevant."[44]

Village of the Rain Wind thus takes shape as a remedial project that allows Head to fortify and diversify Serowe's oral records of its past while simultaneously endowing herself with a surrogate genealogy.[45] The result is a eulogy to Serowe's past that doubles as an orphan's act of affiliation.

To take up a genre of collective memory is to intervene in the parameters of group identity. All her life, Head had experienced the partialities of such collectivities from a position of exclusion. It is significant, therefore, that her efforts to influence the boundaries of Serowe through historical form stress the porousness of the village's identity, its long record of accommodating migrants, refugees, and strangers. *Village of the Rain Wind* is animated by Head's desire to chart, within Serowe's (and the Bamangwato people's) history, precedents for the values she herself upholds.[46] The history that Head fashions assumes a form that implicitly favors her claim to belong. Much of *Village of the Rain Wind*'s fascination flows from her evident investment in figures reminiscent of aspects of her own condition: the traditional storytellers, single mothers, and illegitimate children; the refugees from nineteenth-century Matabele conflicts, from the Anglo-Boer War, and from apartheid's pass laws, all of whom sought sanctuary in Serowe; the educated women straddling awkward divides; the village leaders who, dispatched across the border for their schooling, had adapted childhood memories of urban South Africa to their rural Botswanan lives. Given Head's history as an apatride extraordinaire and a champion of the "Masarwa" cause, she understandably reserves a special curiosity for those outsiders whose partial absorption into the Bamangwato people has altered the course of the culture while furnishing them with a compensatory sense of home.

Head plainly relishes an exchange with the venerable "traditional historian," Ramosamo Kebonang, whose commentary on the fraught question of origins testifies to Serowe's record of incorporation:

> "O tswa kae kae?" ("Where's your original home?")
> "South Africa," I said.
> "Well, that's all right," Ramosamo said kindly. "What we like is for all for-
> eigners to accept themselves as Mongwato and stay peacefully with us. This
> custom started from the time of our King Khama. King Khama used to be
> the lover of foreigners, both black and white. In the case of black people
> we have very large village wards in Serowe of foreign tribes. It came about
> that we cannot easily trace who is a foreigner these days. They have added
> to the Bamangwato tribe and all talk Setswana."[47]

If the presiding tone of *Village of the Rain Wind* is one of pride in a community which—to a degree unimaginable under apartheid—could set the terms
for the conduct of its own affairs, Head's cross-cultural heritage fractures her
mostly celebratory voice. The apprentice insider's claim to a slice of Bamangwato
dignity remains edged with a sense of remorse that black South Africans had
been denied such historical possibilities and had enjoyed so little respite from
dancing the colonial-anti-colonial two-step.

The regional perspective of Head's oral history makes it manifest that Serowe's
regenerative traditions of cultural syncretism are not equally available to all cultures under all circumstances. Head implies that such flexibility requires, over
and above open-mindedness, historical good fortune. Serowe's Bamangwato
people had been largely exempt from the deforming pressures of reacting against
the impositions of colonial history, colonial values, and colonial institutions.
They were thus better able to develop an easygoing eclecticism—even towards
white culture—that would have been inconceivable across most of Southern
Africa. Head's memories of colonial brutality in South Africa thus provide the
implicit backdrop for her amazement at one interlocutor's enthusiasm for
aspects of white culture: "Serowe may be the only village in Southern Africa
where a black man can say with immense dignity: 'I like some of the things the
white man brought, like iron bolts...'"[48]

Head's stance on syncretism has implications for contemporary debates on
multiculturalism as she seldom loses sight of relations of power. Her approach
suggests that the relative security of an indigenous culture is often crucial to
whether the meld proves threatening or enabling. As Head once remarked, in
Serowe every new idea "is absorbed and transformed until it emerges somewhere along the line as 'our traditional custom.' Everything is touched by 'our
traditional custom'—British Imperialism, English, Independence, new educational methods, progress, and foreigners. It all belongs."[49] But Serowe's
customary accomodations arose out of the security of its peripheral and rela-

tively fleeting subjection to colonialism, a heritage that allowed it to accommodate difference in a manner that could express, not disavow, its identity.

Such was Head's determination to belong that we can read *Village of the Rain Wind*, by turns, as a celebration of Serowe's record of cross-cultural accommodation and as a romantic projection of the author's yearnings. One senses the huge allure for Head of the idea of a society that secures its identity through flexible continuities of custom and territory rather than through the imposition of ethnic criteria. But despite her growing veneration for Serowe—replete with flourishes of romanticism—there are evident limits to Head's readiness to idealize the village whose rejection had once stung her. One hears echoes of a very personal vexation when she exposes those moments in the village history where clan ructions, failures of justice, and crimping traditions inhibited its openness to change.

BINARIES AND BEYOND

Ideally, *Village of the Rain Wind* should be read alongside *The Collector of Treasures*, the superb volume of short stories which is an offshoot of Head's research for the oral history. Between them, the two books convey her keen enjoyment of the freedom—so rare among South African writers—to engage with social issues that bypass binary forms of racial conflict. Head's impassioned sense of the vast realms of black experience—above all women's experience—that get marginalized by such Manicheanism added to the particular allure that her work held for Alice Walker, who, as an advisory editor at *Ms.*, as well as in talks, essays, and dedications, became Head's most conspicuous advocate in the U.S.[50]

Head's manifest relief at her circumvention of the white-black polarities that dominate South African literature is consistent with Walker's impatience with binary tendencies in some of the male traditions of African-American "protest literature." Remonstrating against such writing, Walker laments the way

> many of our books by "major" writers (always male) tell us little about the culture, history, future, imagination, fantasies, and so on, of black people, and a lot about isolated (often improbable) or limited encounters with a nonspecific white world.[51]

One detects in Head an allied anxiety that racial domination, through its power to compel protest, may continue to preoccupy black forms of self-definition, preventing them from setting more independent imaginative coordinates.[52]

Such sentiments have periodically surfaced in critical reflections by African-American novelists. One thinks not just of Walker, but of James Baldwin's impatience with the futile "thrust and counter-thrust" of *Native Son*, and his exasperation with those novels whose reactive rage "actually reinforces…the principles which activate the oppression they decry."[53] However, the immediate brutality of life under apartheid, together with the underdeveloped condition of South African cultural criticism, have accentuated the difficulty of diversifying away from such tendencies.

Throughout her writing life, Head's skepticism towards the dehumanizing effects of the functionalist, polarized propensities of South African literature had exacerbated her severance from tradition. Yet shortly before her death in 1986, another South African writer began to question these restrictive orthodoxies in related, though more elaborate terms. Njabulo Ndebele, South Africa's finest cultural critic and an accomplished exponent of fiction, proposed that the range of experience admitted by the main currents of South African writing has been unhealthily narrowed by the pressure on writers to display relevance, commitment, and political engagement—to write, that is, visibly in the service of national liberation.

In his tightly argued essays, collected as *The Rediscovery of the Ordinary*, Ndebele weighs the literary and political cost of the anti-apartheid imperative.[54] The predominance of accusatory politics in South African literature produces, in his view, "not knowledge but indictment" and has, paradoxically, a dehumanizing effect. Ndebele charges that the familiar panoply of victims and sellouts appear as mere ideas to be marshalled this way or that in a moral debate. Their human anonymity becomes the dialectical equivalent of the anonymity to which the oppressive system consigns millions of oppressed Africans. "Thus," Ndebele continues in terms reminiscent of Baldwin, "instead of clarifying the tragic human experience of oppression, such fiction becomes grounded in the very negation it seeks to transcend."[55] Ndebele calls for less schematic, reactive writing, writing that declines to subordinate the cultural traditions and resources of black communities to the dynamics of racial conflict.

Ndebele's controversial challenge unsettled many of the verities of the South African cultural milieu. Yet it is surely a measure of Head's marginality to the dominant purview of South African literature that Ndebele fails to mention her work as one of the most compelling precedents for so many of the qualities he advocates. The two writers share a concern that the overestimation of a narrowly-defined political relevance has produced quite specific amnesias in the literature. The pressure on writers to deliver the surface signs of heroic resistance or spectacular violence as a mark of "commitment," has, in particular, favored urban over rural experience.

Ndebele is not given to romanticizing oral culture. But he expresses perturbation at the consistent neglect, among South African writers, of peasant life. Concomitantly, he laments the failure of most fiction to avail itself of the immense narrative resources available through oral forms. The most pressing challenge, Ndebele maintains, is to "free the entire social imagination of the oppressed from the laws of perception that have characterised apartheid society."[56] This requires a widening of the circumscribed orbits of relevance through what he calls the "rediscovery of the ordinary."

I have dwelt at some length on Ndebele's ideas because, like feminism, they provide an invaluable prism through which to review the standard designation of Head as an apolitical writer.[57] The distance that Head put between herself and national liberation politics is sometimes cited as evidence of the apolitical character of her work. So, too, is her preoccupation with the "ordinary," a word that runs like a mantra through her work, acquiring an almost philosophical force. Her commitment to redeeming the ordinary was evidently commitment of the wrong, apolitical kind. Yet, what one finds in *Maru, Tales of Tenderness and Power, Serowe: Village of the Rain Wind*, and, above all, in *The Collector of Treasures*, is her gift for rediscovering the turbulent powerplays within those expanses of rural society which, from an urban perspective, may appear becalmed, bland, uneventful, immutable, and inconsequential to "real" politics.

Head's most affecting prose arises from her quickness to redeem the irrelevant, the common, the ordinary and—in the etymological sense of "earthly"—the mundane. Her approach to oral history reveals the same gift that enlivens her short story writing: the capacity to be surprised by the apparently extraneous and to detect, in the smallest shards of village life, the impress of history.

She once observed that it was Bertolt Brecht who first gave her the courage to write attentively of the insignificant and unliterary.[58] Yet at times her openness to the historical ambushes of the ordinary seems more reminiscent of Walter Benjamin. Perhaps those whom calamity has left stranded in a precarious present develop compensatory powers for discerning history in the most fragmentary of things.

Certainly, Head's devotion to the piecemeal, the marginal, and the overlooked becomes all the more powerful because it was born of necessity. Given her background, ordinariness appeared not as something which she could take for granted but as an exhausting, improbable attainment. Head's animation by the ordinary was partly a reaction against the tremendous violence of South Africa which had fallen, like a dead hand, across her imagination. In fleeing apartheid, she rejected both the imaginative priority of such extraordinary violence and the functionalist imperatives of much South African literature, both of which she rejected as dehumanizing.[59] Like Ndebele, if for somewhat different reasons, she broke with the literary tradition of the titanic clash, often staged between characters who are little more than ciphers representing self-evident moral extremes.

Head is the only black South African writer to have grown up in the city and to have transformed herself into a rural writer, in her case by crossing over into a frontline state. (Indeed, aside from the very different case of John Berger, no contemporary writer has traveled as dramatically as Head against the prevailing flow from country to city, by settling permanently in a foreign, adopted peasant community, and producing a body of fiction grounded in oral traditions). Head's reversal of the norm has encouraged the perception of her as a literary misfit rather than as a writer who anticipated the need to counter-balance South African literature's fixation with male, urban experience and with realms of spectacular conflict rather than quotidian survival.

In her literary concerns and her life alike, Head swam against the prevailing currents of black South African literary culture which flowed from country to city. Indeed, not just in literature, but in film, music, and theater, this urban drift had produced a vast body of culture around the motif popularly known as "Jim comes to Jo'burg." Her reversal of this tradition matters because it helps redress the unequal balance of urban and rural experience in the literature; but it matters, too, because it initiates a second form of redress, one that Ndebele, in urging a return to rural themes, declines to consider. For there is an inextricable link between South African literature's amnesia towards rural life and its amnesia toward the experience of women. Virtually without exception, it is the generic "Jim" who bends his way towards Jo'burg. This is broadly true regardless of whether his creators be black—like Peter Abrahams (*Mine Boy*) and Percy Mtwa (*Bopha!*) or white—Lionel Rogosin (*Come Back Africa*) and Alan Paton (*Cry the Beloved Country*).

This state of affairs results partly from gendered inequities in literacy. It stems, too, from black women's profoundly restricted access to leisure and institutional support for their writing. According to one researcher, of 140 black South African writers publishing in English between 1920 and 1988, only seven were women.[60] Yet the predominance of male urban experience is also, to some degree a consequence of the very structure of apartheid. The institution of the bantustan system for the draconian control of migratory labor resulted in proportionately many more women than men remaining in the countryside. Their ranks were swollen by the huge numbers of women—state-designated "superfluous appendages"—uprooted from the cities and other white-zoned areas and dumped in the immiserated exile of the overcrowded bantustans. In circumstances where the men were away in the city compounds for the bulk of the year or where they failed to return at all, rural women served as heads of the family and were forced to scrape a living off impossibly scarce, infertile land.

Over the past fifteen years, the lives of such rural women have begun to trickle into the literature through works like Lauretta Ngcobo's *And They Didn't Die*, Miriam Tlali's *Mihloti*, Elsa Joubert's *Poppie Nongena*, the stories of Gcina Mhlope, and the performance poetry of Nise Malange. Yet in many ways the most impressive precursor for such writing was Head's 1977 volume, *The Collector of Treasures*.[61] This may seem an unlikely claim, as Head's stories are set not in a bantustan but in a Botswanan village. Despite this displacement, however, Head conveys the cadences of rural women's lives in a manner that challenges, with unprecedented force, many of the conventional silences in South African literature.

While the dereliction of her women is less acute than that ordinarily endured in the bantustans, many of Head's concerns assume a direct, transnational relevance. Her stories are preoccupied with epidemic family breakdown, with gendered relations to the land, with tensions between peasant women's agricultural authority and their subordination to local patriarchy, and with women's crimped sense of economic and social mobility. But Head is equally engaged by the plasticity of tradition and by the intrepid women who flex its frontiers: the village's first prostitute who challenges received views on the sexual double standard and marriage ("Life"); the abused women who become husband-murderers ("The Collector of Treasures"); and the woman who conducts a clandestine affair with the village priest and advocates that post-menopausal women should take young lovers ("The Special One"). Herself born from the inconceivable, Head seems particularly drawn to women who press the limits of what is locally imaginable.

The Collector of Treasures was inspired by narrative shards left over from her research for *Serowe: Village of the Rain Wind*. The volume's genesis in oral history is manifest in Head's method, for the finest of the tales wed the emotional intensity and formal features of oral narrative to a brisk tone of journalistic matter-of-factness that seems suggestive of Head's writerly beginnings on a Johannesburg newspaper. This journalistic-oral meld is conspicuous in the three stories mentioned above, as well as "Kgotla" and "The Wind and a Boy." Collectively, they testify to Head's readiness to transfigure oral into written narrative form rather than attempting the doomed task of replicating oral features in writing. Again, in the light of Ndebele's admonitions, one can uphold *The Collector of Treasures* as an invaluable antecedent for much of what he advocates: it is a singular instance of a writer allowing rural experience both formal and thematic weight.

Although Head never returned to South Africa, she spoke of herself as having "performed a peculiar shuttling movement between two lands."[62] That phrase is best understood in light of her intimation that, while drawn to the comparative tranquility and "ordinariness" of Botswanan life, imaginatively she remained too violent for her surroundings.[63] Thus, the cross-border split between sensibility and subject matter helps account for the transnational feel to *The Collector of Treasures*. This shuttling assumes not just spacial but temporal dimensions. Head moved from brute "colonialism of a special type" under apartheid, to what, on her arrival in 1964, was the mild colonialism of the British protectorate of Bechuanaland, colonialism so muted that it had left many of the country's pre-colonial traditions relatively intact. Then, from 1966 onwards, Head lived through Bechuanaland's transformation into Botswana, a post-colonial state in official argot, yet one that fell under the long shadow of South African regional imperialism.[64] The sense of Head's passage through versions of the precolonial, colonial, and postcolonial eras—though not in that order and decidedly not in any sequence that could be read as synonymous with "progress"—insures that her later writing offers rare commentary on the porous, ambiguous frontlines among these historical divides. This quality heightens the sensation in *The Collector of Treasures* of her work as simultaneously an act of geographical and historical brinkmanship.

Indeed, Head's great triumph in *The Collector of Treasures* is the sheer range of thresholds that her stories span: between orality and literacy, village and city, the local and the national, Botswana and South Africa, the colonial, precolonial, and "postcolonial" epochs, old and new technologies, polygamy and monogamy, patriarchy and women's power, and—as someone herself routinely cast as an outlaw—those blurred boundaries between legality and illegality. All of these emerge not as simple, absolute divides, but as the objects of ceaseless, sometimes brutal, dispute. *The Collector of Treasures* sides neither with cultural preservationists nor with glib equations of change with progress. For Head's complex empathy is distributed between the newcomers or dissidents who rise up against claustral traditions and those who would shield at least some village values against the unsettling incursions of the new.

FEMINISM, MESSIANISM, AND THE POLITICS OF LAND

Head was less ambivalent toward change when it came to the status and rights of women. Her work discloses a preoccupation with the patriarchal burden shouldered by Bamangwato women—in stories like "Property," "The Collector of Treasures," "The Special One," and "The Lovers" and in the essay, "Despite Broken Bondage."[65] Yet Head dissociated herself from any suggestion that she was a feminist.[66] Moreover, as Susan Gardner has observed, Head's narrative reliance on the interventions of godlike men may diminish her appeal for many feminists.[67] Characteristically in Head's plots, "progress" depends on a man breaching conventions from a position of power, his status ensuring that his intrepid defection redraws the boundaries of tradition. In so doing, he ordinarily exercises power by relinquishing or jeopardizing his social authority. Most often, such Messianic interventions expressly ease women's lot. Head became obsessed with such redemptive men, be they historical (Khama the Great, Tshekedi Khama, Patrick van Rensburg) or figures of her own imaginative devising (as in *Maru, A Bewitched Crossroad*, "Property," and "The Deep River").

How are we to understand these apparent anomalies? Head's resistance to the label "feminist" was partly a symptom of her overadministered life and her resultant dread of being classified or boxed in. But the matter is more complex than that. Her disclaimer was surely a response, in part, to the particular variety of feminism that she was exposed to in the seventies and early eighties—an imported feminism whose concerns were primarily those of white, urban, middle class women. How could such preoccupations be reconciled with the needs of the Bamangwato peasant women around her, waging their quite distinctive battles against an agrarian patriarchy? Perhaps now, given the wider acceptance that there is no feminist orthodoxy but a range of feminisms, Head might have been more amenable to styles of feminist inquiry and activism responsive to the conditions of village women.

One should also bear in mind that for Head the position of women was indissociable from the politics of land and property. These were determined by traditions of domination that often fused elements from precolonial and colonial patriarchies. The lineage of male historical figures whom she celebrated in her writing—Khama the Great, Tshekedi Khama, Sol Plaatje, Robert Sobukwe, and Patrick van Rensburg—had one thing in common: their sense of the primacy of the politics of land and their hostility to the appropriation of land as private property. These men were all either agents or advocates of land reform even when they didn't present it specifically as a women's issue. However, in Bamangwato society, as across much of Southern Africa, women were the tillers and harvesters—a fact that Head had been dramatizing ever since her first novel, *When Rain Clouds Gather*.[68] Thus, implicit in Head's position was the recognition that for women in agrarian communities land is the decisive locus of self-government.

Head's exaltation of the men whom she called "sons of the soil" was integral to her quest to replace the hollow organisms of family, race, and nation that had betrayed her. As fundamental principles of social organization, land and soil offered the prospect of compensatory affiliations, and came to be inflected as alternative sources of lineage and belonging. Head supplemented her meager income from writing by working alongside local women in a co-operative vegetable gardening project.[69] Thus the land became the site of her labor while providing a sustaining metaphoric matrix for her work. Her prose is suffused with organic metaphors of rootedness and rootlessness, of blooming and withering, of "production under drought conditions," and of herself as a Cape Gooseberry transplanted to Serowe—all of them drawn from her intimacy with the soil. One could describe her, within the tropes that she favored, as a woman violently uprooted and shallowly transplanted, or as someone who sought to graft herself to an alien "organic" community in compensation for her severance from her family tree.

With the void of the desert behind it, the market gardening project drew life from merciless conditions, much as Head sought, through the imagination, to produce growth from her profoundly inclement circumstances. In both gardening and writing, her labor to create became integral to the exertion of belonging. Head once explained that her writing combined originality with tentativeness because she had been forced to create "new worlds out of nothing," a phrase suggestive of her association of these two regenerative activities.[70]

Head's attraction to male heroes of land rights is best illustrated by her writings on Plaatje and Khama the Great. A novelist, politician, polemicist, and historian, Plaatje was a founding member of the South African National Native Congress (later to become the ANC). He achieved renown principally through *Native Life in South Africa* (1916), his wracking account of the repercussions for Africans of the 1913 Natives' Land Act, an act which, in Head's words, "created overnight a floating landless proletariat whose labour could be used and manipulated at will, and ensured that ownership of the land had finally and securely passed into the hands of the ruling white race."[71] As Secretary of the South African Native National Congress, Plaatje participated in a delegation that traveled to England and appealed, unsuccessfully, to the British government to pressure South Africa's rulers into revoking the Land Act.

Plaatje ranks as arguably the most important South African writer on rural experience, a lapidary exception lauded by those—like Ndebele and Mbulelo Mzamane—who bemoan the urban tilt of South African literature.[72] Head's reverence for Plaatje is implicit in her short story, "Son of the Soil," but surfaces most directly in her foreword to *Native Life in South Africa*, a book that opens with this sobering reflection on the impact of the Natives' Land Act : "Awakening on Friday morning, June 20, 1913, the South African native found himself, not actually a slave, but a pariah in the land of his birth."[73] Plaatje's insistence on the bond between becoming dispossessed of one's land and being designated a pariah must have achieved a powerful autobiographical resonance for Head. The tone of her foreword to *Native Life* suggests that she esteemed Plaatje as a writer who grasped the links between identity and land and who also wrestled with issues that bore intimately on her own condition—ostracism, dispossession, forced migration, vagrancy, exile, and the idea of home.

Head once observed how "great gestures have an oceanic effect on society," flooding it with new possibilities.[74] From the perspective of her personal and historical needs, the supreme gesture of this sort came not from Plaatje but from Khama the Great, the reformist leader who ruled the Bamangwato from 1875 to 1923. Khama the Great became a monumental figure in Head's work and she never tired of reimagining him—in essays, stories, interviews, oral history, and in her final creation, *A Bewitched Crossroad*, which she called "my major obsession, the Khama novel."[75] Her imaginary romance with Khama served both as the prototype and consummation of her partiality for "great men."

Khama's triumph was that he succeeded where Plaatje was to fail. In 1895, when Cecil John Rhodes's British South Africa Company threatened to annex Bechuanaland, Khama traveled to England, protesting the seizure of land and voicing his fear that the Bamangwato would be enslaved and compelled to work in the South African mines.[76] Khama's intervention and the fortuitous failure of Rhodes' Jameson Raid against the Transvaal Republic later that year swung British opinion against Rhodes. Thus in 1896 the British Bechuanaland Protectorate came to be ruled not by the British South Africa Company but from London in a manner that enabled Khama to keep the traditional system of land tenure almost entirely intact.[77]

So the Bamangwato achieved what the African peoples of South Africa could not: control over their land, a precondition of economic and cultural independence. Indeed, Head perceives 1896 as the benchmark year in the movement toward national independence—by comparison, colonial Bechuanaland's transformation into independent Botswana in 1966 was little more than a ceremonial, nominal event. Again, Head projects property rights as the decisive barometer of self-rule in a manner that complicates conventional accounts of the nation's sequential advance from precolonial, through colonial, to post-colonial time.

In order to thwart colonial encroachments, Khama the Great had the foresight to ban the sale of land and cattle—the two principal forms of property. These measures increased the nation's control over its destiny and, as part of his package of far-reaching reforms that reconceived property and individual rights, they had specific repercussions for the status of women.

Head extolled Khama for introducing iconoclastic measures that transformed, almost overnight, the prospects for women's self-sufficiency. In 1890 Khama outlawed a number of venerable institutions, including the bride price (bogadi). But Head reserved a special admiration for two further innovations that empowered women—his decree that women could now, for the first time, inherit wealth, and his sanctioning of their right to represent themselves in the kgotla (chief's court), where previously their grievances could only be articulated through a male intermediary. Head's fascination with these two measures was surely grounded in the particulars of her own subjection. She was obsessed with heredity and vexed by the comprehensiveness of her disinheritance. So, too, her position as a "mixed race" women writer in Southern African—someone voided of a literary legacy—would have heightened her admiration for Khama's introduction of women's right to unmediated self-representation, a right that loosened their reliance on the words and voices of men.[78]

One detects in Head's portraits of these events a delight not just in the content of Khama's innovations, but in the manner of their issuance. Ideologically, Khama the Great was a twilight figure. He converted to Christianity and then proceeded to wield that Christianity against both colonial and Bamangwato institutions. His standing as a Christian convert helped him rally British philanthropists against Rhodes; the ensuing victory, in turn, guaranteed that he would retain the right to evict any missionary or settler who caused offense. Head saw Khama not just as a champion of land rights and of women, but as a self-made oddity, whose inventive eclecticism safeguarded his culture by radically transforming it.[79]

Khama the Great came to embody for Head what, to adapt Theodor Adorno's phrase, one might call "a recollection of the possible"—a resolution of past and future through the workings of expectant memory.[80] Speaking of Khama's inexhaustible allure, Head exclaimed how he had catalyzed her interest in Botswanan history: "it is fascinating because you get this grand man…oh, I love these big men! If I haven't got them, I create them!"[81] Head's obsessive flexing of her power to invent and reinvent Khama suggests a fuller psychological investment than mere historical or even political enthusiasm. Khama became, indeed, the great romance of her life.

Head's relationship with Khama—brought to fruition through the imagination—can be productively viewed from the perspective of her very different relationships to her father and mother. As a child, Head was granted some rudimentary details about her white mother—just enough to make her fear the possibility of hereditary madness and, conversely, to feel supported by her mother's transgressive daring. However, while Head could fall back on the example of her mother as a transgressive woman, her upper class whiteness restricted her usefulness as a sustaining precedent for a life of poverty dogged by racism.

If Head knew little enough about her mother, about her father she knew far less. He was black; he was a stablehand; he vanished. Head seldom speculated about him and never in any detail. Yet there is, in her sedulous creation of African saviour figures who redeem the past, more than a hint of transference. The publication in 1993 of Head's first novel, *The Cardinals*, more than thirty years after she wrote it, establishes that such male redeemers were present from the very outset of her literary career. *The Cardinals* recounts the story of the passion between a woman writer and a man whom she belatedly discovers to be her unknown father.[82] In this autobiographically-inflected incest narrative one discerns the beginnings of Head's fondness for generating men with whom to fall in love. Her mythically resonant male leads tend to serve simultaneously as fathers and lovers; they also stand, paradoxically, as the offspring of female creative desire and the catalysts of female power.

This complex process is most insistently played out through the figure of Khama the Great, who becomes the great romantic interest of Head's life while deputizing for an idealized version of her spectral father. Head projects Khama as a Messiah who promises a past of integration that can help compensate for the orphaned, first generation "colored" woman's record of abandonment and ostracism. She envisions Khama as the Father of the Nation who helped humanize the position of women, enhancing the power and liberty of the Daughters of the Nation. Khama represented "tradition" at its most accommodating: he stood, for her, as a man unafraid of mixing traditions and absorbing outsiders—like so many of her fictional characters, he risked affronting his people by transgressing the bounds of custom, in his case by marrying a Christian woman and converting to Christianity. He then caused further offence by refusing to take further wives, that is, by forsaking his hereditary prerogative to polygamy. The fortunate woman to whom this grand, munificent, transgressive, and visionary man devoted himself was none other than Elizabeta or, as she was popularly known, Mma-Bessie.[83] Need one add that this was, for Head, the name that bore her tentative sense of female continuity: it was the name she had inherited from her mother and which she in turn passed on to the presiding, autobiographical character in *A Question of Power.*

Head's imaginative investment in the history of Botswana's most powerful dynasty did not end there. A decade after Head's clandestine and scandalous birth, a much more public saga unfolded over how best to salvage the family name, a saga involving bloodlines, illegality, disinheritance, and exile. In 1948, a rancorous dispute broke out among the Bamangwato when their heir apparent, Seretse Khama, married a white Englishwoman, Ruth Williams, while studying in London. Head's comments on the ensuing conflict appear mostly in *Village of the Rain Wind*; they may be filled out from other accounts of an interracial marriage that had international repercussions.[84] Although Head does not frame her oral history of Serowe autobiographically, no one conversant with her biography can fail to hear the uncanny undertones in the details that she discloses.[85]

The marriage between Khama and Williams caused offense in multiple directions. Tshekedi, Seretse's uncle and guardian, as well as many of the most

influential Bamangwato elders, decreed the marriage to be illegal and in viola-
tion of Bamangwato custom. Seretse would be disinherited and barred from
assuming the chieftaincy. However, the Bamangwato were split over the issue
and after protracted wranglings, a kgotla admitted Seretse as the new chief in
June 1949. Tshekedi, however, dissented from this view. When Ruth Khama fell
pregnant he grew even more alarmed, proclaiming, in an eerie reversal of the
sentiments of Head's white grandparents, "The House of Khama is Seretse's
house. I want you to beget a black chief for me, not a white one."[86] Fearing that
a "mixed marriage" would not only taint the bloodline but compromise the
Bamangwato's territorial autonomy, Tshekedi drafted a pronouncement bearing the somewhat overdetermined title "European Penetration and
Miscegenation."[87] The dispute sundered the Bamangwato, several hundred of
whom Tshekedi led into voluntary exile. That exile, one of Head's interlocutors
concludes, was an event that "broke our lives."[88]

Seretse and Ruth Khama were obstructed by other, more formidable forces,
as a loose, improbable alliance developed among Tshekedi Khama, the British
Labour government, and the South African Nationalist regime. When his own
people finally granted Seretse the chieftainship in 1949, the British declined to
ratify it. One should recall that 1948 was not just the year of the Khama's marriage but the year when apartheid was first adopted as official policy by white
South Africa's newly elected Nationalist regime. At the time, Britain's Labour
government hoped to secure a monopoly on the purchase of South Africa's ura-
nium, vital for the development of the A-bomb. Fearful of alienating D.F.
Malan's Nationalists by endorsing interracial marriage just across the border,
the British government not only barred Seretse from inheriting the chieftaincy
but, in 1950, banished the couple from Bechuanaland for five years. The dispute that flared over the Khamas' persecution by the Colonial Office nearly
brought down Britain's ruling Labour Party.

Yet ultimately the controversy was resolved in favor of an ethnically flexible
conception of continuity and authenticity. It was resolved, too, in favor of a
theme that Head, perhaps inspired by the Khama saga, returned to tirelessly
in her writings: the triumph of individual love over the constraints of custom,
prejudice, and bureaucracy. After all, Seretse first couched his appeal to the
Bamangwato court in the highly unconventional terms of a personal love that
swept aside issues of property and lineage. In the end, Seretse inherited the
leadership of his people and became, two years after Head's arrival in
Botswana, the nation's first President—his white wife alongside him. In 1979,
in the ultimate breach of narrow ethnic circumscriptions of hereditary power,
the mantle of the chieftaincy passed to Ian Khama, Seretse and Ruth's "mixed
race" son.

CONCLUSION

"The circumstances of my birth," Head once wrote, "seemed to make it necessary to obliterate all traces of a family history."[89] Nothing was given to her: she lived her dream of belonging as an ongoing and always unfinished labor. Her investment in this dream hinged on a paradox. As an orphaned, uprooted, and stateless writer, she experienced a profound craving for the certainties of what she called a "whole community." Yet at the same time, she felt with the intimacy of her bones, the violence from which wholeness, sameness, origins, shared extraction, and the assurances of rooted community are born.[90]

Head's idealism amidst her congested sense of estrangement and her improvised affiliations testifies to her vision of community not as a passively transmitted set of birthrights, but as the offspring of inventive willpower. Community, in her experience, was inescapably the brainchild of imaginative remembrances and emphatic amnesias.

At a time when she faced ostracism on local and national fronts, Head expressed her resolution to belong in one of her standard familial metaphors: "[T]he best and most enduring love is that of rejection.... I'm going to bloody well adopt this country as my own, by force. I am going to take it as my own family."[91] Having lived, as a child, through the shallow, artificial genealogies produced by successive adoptions and rejections, she determined to become with a vengeance the agent of her own origins. She wrested from Serowe a surrogate history, an alternative trail of memories to that other, never wholly obliterated past of familial abandonment, racial rejection, colonial domination, and national disinheritance.

In striving to remake herself Head came to rely on another more unsettling trail of memories. Particularly during the build-up to her confinement in a Botswanan mental hospital, she feared that she was destined to recapitulate her mother's life. She was fully aware of the pathological circumstances of her mother's incarceration—they were symptomatic of what she once called "the permanent madness of reality" under apartheid.[92] Nonetheless Head found herself haunted by the possibility that her mother had transmitted to her the burden of madness.[93] As the daughter of a "stray" woman, she feared that she, too, might have to pay the ultimate price for her "errancy." Certainly, in her autobiographical writings of the late 1960s and early 70s, one senses her lurking anxiety that just as racism had pursued her to Serowe, so too, congenital madness would find her out and return her to the grip of the past.

However, as she began to cobble together a sense of belonging, so she came to project her mother's bequest of transgression in different terms. There had been, as she once put it, "no world as yet" for what her mother had done.[94] Reflecting on her own achievements, she observed: "The least I can ever say for myself is that I forcefully created for myself, under extremely hostile conditions, my ideal life. I took an obscure and almost unknown village in the Southern African bush and made it my own hallowed ground. Here, in the steadiness and peace of my own world, I could dream dreams a little ahead of the somewhat vicious clamour of revolution and the horrible stench of evil social systems."[95] Her sense here of the creativity born from isolation implies a quite different perception of "errancy." Head came to see her mother's actions increasingly less as a threat, passed down to her, of regression into insanity, than as an exhortation to audaciously invent a world adequate to such visionary error. Through her imaginative insistence that the inconceivable take its place within the orbit of the ordinary, Head was, as she recognized, dreaming in advance of her time.

Head's work was apt to project a degree of social acceptance which, in her life, she knew only as a wavering prospect. Such determined optimism quieted in her fiction the cadences of desolation that distinguished her letters. If, to the last, Head's integration into Serowe on paper remained somewhat ahead of her integration in daily life, she at least acquired a degree of allegiance and acceptance unimaginable in the 1960s and early 70s. Moreover, she had engineered for herself a spread of commitments that spanned writing as a vocation, the village, the Southern African region, and those rural women who sought a greater share of Botswana's unevenly distributed state of independence. In the process of forging these ties, Head exposed a cluster of amnesias in Southern African writing and yielded a greatly expanded sense of its prospects.

With a few notable exceptions, "coloreds" have been admitted into white South African literature mainly as shiftless, "tribeless" people burdened by their "impurity" in plots staging the relentlessly fateful repercussions of miscegenation. While Head's life and work were wrought from tragedy, neither remained merely tragic. Indeed, together they provide one of the richest anticipations of Salman Rushdie's simple but resonant remark that "notions of purity are the aberration."[96] Head made herself into what Rushdie calls a "translated person"— she was the ultimate *metissage*. For in negotiating her impacted sense of loss and her imposed sense of deviancy, she admitted a whole new range of possibilities to the phrase "mixed ancestry." Remote from racially charged determinisms, those words came to celebrate the hardwon if fitful freedom to elect and reject one's affinities and provenance.

5

APARTHEID ON THE RUN:
The South African Sports Boycott

Serious sport is…war minus the shooting.

—George Orwell "The Sporting Spirit"

To divert us from the temptations of the flesh a muddy, muscular "christianity" was employed—"healthy body, healthy mind." Wanking, however, let the side down. Let in own-goals.

—Derek Jarman, on his schooling, *Modern Nature*

FOR THE PEOPLE OF ENGLAND, 1970 nearly became the year of the locust. Early that spring, a London anti-apartheid activist, David Wilton-Godberford, made it known that he planned to wage biological warfare against the all-white South African team who were shortly to arrive for a cricket series against England.[1] Wilton-Godberford had imported desert locusts from Africa and was using them to seed a clandestine anti-apartheid breeding program at a series of undisclosed sites in north Wales. 70,000 hoppers, he calculated, would ordinarily consume 112 pounds of grass in 12 minutes; 70,000 ravenous hoppers would eat more. Warning that "the crack of a solid army of locusts feeding will sound like flames," Wilton-Godberford issued his ultimatum: if the Springbok tour went ahead, he would starve his invertebrate troops for 24 hours and unleash them—half-a-million strong—on the playing fields of England.

Wilton-Godberford's expertise lay in entomology, not theology or semiotics. For all that, the symbolic crafting of his operation was superb. The Exodus account of divine election—replete with desert plagues—has been integral to Afrikaner nationalist mythology, at times bracing arguments for white rule. There was something apposite, too, about the tone of Wilton-Godberford's threat, with its subliminal echoes of the militarism, biologism, and transcendentalism that permeate the arenas of world sport.

Operation Locust was just one facet of the Stop the Seventy Tour, arguably the most successful mass action in post-WWII British history. A brilliant ensemble of political protests orchestrated by Peter Hain, Dennis Brutus, and the Young Liberals, it forced the 1969 Springbok rugby team to retreat behind barbed wire barricades and the massed ranks of British police; it also secured the cancellation of the Springboks' cricket tour of England the following year. These actions became benchmark events in the international campaign to have apartheid's ersatz "national" teams barred from world competition.

As Wilton-Godberford's strategy suggests, the power of the sports boycott stemmed largely from its ability to grip the media by generating spectacle. It gave the liberation movement access to the passionate commitments of sports fans, a vast swathe of society largely indifferent to international politics or ignorant of the issues at stake. This allowed sport a distinctive role in the matrix of international actions—the military, nuclear, and oil bans, the divestment movement, the freezing of bank loans, and the moratoria on sporting, cultural, and academic contacts—which drew nonSouth Africans into the anti-apartheid front. Thus the boycott's role went well beyond publicizing discrimination in South African sport: it became an indispensable mechanism for training the media spotlight on apartheid per se.

From its first organized beginnings in the late 1950s, the sports ban registered some of the earliest and most sustained successes in popularizing the anti-apartheid cause abroad. In countries where the premier sports overlapped with those of South Africa—Britain, most of Africa, India, New Zealand, Pakistan, the Anglophone Caribbean, France, Ireland, Australia, Sri Lanka, Italy, and Argentina—outrage over competition against white South African teams gave vital impetus to local anti-apartheid movements. The absence of any major, nationalistic team sports common to South Africa and the U.S.A. deprived the American anti-apartheid movement of a powerful populist focus for its actions. This was a particularly unfortunate historical accident, given the visibility of African-American sporting celebrities who would surely otherwise have become a driving force in the American campaign against apartheid.

To assess the impulses behind the sports boycott is to engage with the broader political ramifications of international sport, above all, in the spheres of nationalism, race, and gender. The boycott of South Africa amounted, after all, to the most prominent, extended anti-racist campaign in the history of world sports. Arguably not since Jesse Owens ascended the Berlin Olympic podium four times against a backcloth of Nazi triumphalism has an intervention through sport had such striking political repercussions. From its inauspicious advent over thirty years ago, the boycott acquired a high profile at the United Nations and the Organization of African Unity, in the Commonwealth and the Non-

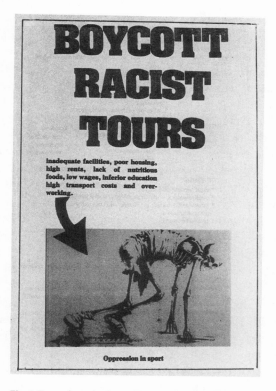

Fig. 1: Poster from the Sports Boycott. (Mayibuye Centre)

Aligned Movement, as well as at a host of international sporting bodies. Showdowns between upholders and breakers of the boycott produced incidents of national political consequence in a succession of countries—Barbados, New Zealand, Sri Lanka, England, India, Trinidad, Guyana, Australia, India, Ireland, Antigua, Wales, and France.

The ban threw into relief the preeminence of sporting agons as occasions for forging and flaunting national loyalties. Because South African "national" teams were racially exclusive, their presence on the international stage raised profound questions about the representation of nationhood. What precisely does it means for sports teams, especially male ones, to be construed as national representatives? Why has sport become such an emotive site for the engendering—and gendering—of nationalism? And to what extent do sporting events not just synecdotally "reflect" the nation but serve as a terrain on which rival versions of the nation are constructed and contested?

The controversy around apartheid in sport erupted with unusual force because it stoked one of the most ferocious controversies in the sporting world, namely, the degree to which sport should be implicated in political advocacy and retribution. In addition, the contentious bonds between sport, race, nationalism, and gender helped the boycotters gain international leverage from what might otherwise have remained a concern local to South Africans. Activists strengthened the internationalism of the ban by linking the anti-apartheid challenge to the colonial legacy of racist nationalism in the white majority nations—Britain, New Zealand, Australia, France, and Ireland—that served as white South Africa's principal sporting rivals. Thus, for example, campaigns for Aborigine and Maori land rights gained impetus from organized resistance to Springbok tours. In Britain, the Zola Budd scandal exposed the racial double standard at the heart of national immigration policy when, in 1984, the Home Office gave the Afrikaans, long distance wunderkind an inside track to British citizenship. British reporters visited Budd's Orange Free State home and cited her consumption of roast beef and Yorkshire pudding for Sunday lunch as cultural evidence of her organic Britishness.[2] In circumstances where applicants ordinarily waited 21 months, Budd was naturalized in ten days. Here again, the protests by sports boycotters over Budd's selective treatment added impetus to the wider British campaign against racist formulations of national identity.

In August 1992, Zola Pieterse (nee Budd) joined ranks with 120 other South African athletes to compete in the 25th Olympiad. South Africa had been barred from the Olympics since 1960, and the conspicuous presence of the country's first ever nonracial squad became a ceremonial marker of the boycott's termination. The ban was lifted amidst frenzied debate over the strategic wisdom of doing so. Some lauded the ANC-endorsed repeal as a shrewdly timed gesture; others challenged the decision, arguing that a political trumpcard was being squandered at a time of inadequate guarantees.

NATIONAL SPORT AND THE BODY POLITIC

International sporting contests serve, in more than one sense of the phrase, as forms of national redefinition. They are exhibitionist events imbued with the authority to recreate or simulate the nation, offering a vigorous display of a proxy body politic. This applies, above all, to male team sports which, unlike more solitary pastimes like angling or golf, are structured to provide spectacles of cooperative discipline that stage the suppression of self-interest for the collective good. Players qualify for the national side only by virtue of birth or through naturalization, that peculiar word which makes explicit the latent biologism of national teams. Unlike professional, regional, and club teams, national sides may not freely exchange players: no combination of money and talent can substitute for the fact that to represent the nation—as the etymology insists—is an expression of a birthright. The only way players can transfer their allegiances from one nation to another is by undergoing the protracted labor of naturalization—little other that a ritual rebirthing through the channels of the INS, the Home Office, or some comparable national "body."

Sporting internationals serve as occasions for national legitimation and self-scrutiny. Not for nothing are rugby, cricket, and field hockey internationals called "tests." The composition and performance of the national side readily becomes a focus for anxieties about national (or ethnic national) provenance and destiny. For if international sporting clashes raise tormenting questions about birth rights, they are equally prone to raise anxieties about the nation's prospects. National representatives—diplomats, parliamentarians, senators, military officers—typically gain authority with age, but national sporting heroes enter decline by their mid-thirties. Indeed, sport is the only significant sphere of national representation where the young reign supreme. The performance of the national side is thus commonly used as a style of clairvoyance, seeming to portend the nation's future. For it is, as Benedict Anderson reminds us, "the magic of nationalism to turn chance into destiny."[3]

In South Africa, a host of factors colluded to render sport a crucial arena of white self-esteem. The halcyon climate and the ubiquity of black domestic workers in white homes guaranteed expanses of outdoor leisure-time. Like New Zealanders and Australians, white South Africans have also harbored a special colonial animus toward British sporting teams. Afrikaners have been prone to view their prowess at the British game of rugby as sweet revenge for their imperial subjection at British hands.

Most national or ethnic nationalist groups feel economically, politically, and geographically peripheral to the centers of world power. Such nations ordinarily enjoy scant control over their destinies and are seldom afforded visibility on the world stage. Sport often offers the only arena in which nations can redress feelings of marginality and bask, however fleetingly, in the sensation of being a global force. Cameroon's triumphs over more illustrious nations in the 1990 World Cup Football typified sport's ability to bestow this surrogate sense of national power. The same applies to Western Samoa's defeat of more celebrated sides in the 1991 Rugby World Cup, to Zimbabwe's humbling of England in the 1992 Cricket World Cup and, during the Cold War era, to East Germany's spectacular performances at the Olympics. White South Africans' paranoid obsession with the sports boycott was rooted in an ethnic nationalist exasperation at being denied just such opportunities to compensate for the smallness of their population, their geographical marginality, and their political ostracism.[4]

One should note, in this regard, that the American sporting world is idiosyncratically self-contained: the year's climactic sporting events tend to be contested on an interclub not an international basis. This inward focus means that the American season does not ordinarily "climax" in international events that flaunt all the trimmings of national virility—bunting, tracksuits, and millinery in the national colors, flags, anthems, and the like. By contrast, the seasonal impetus in white South African sport—as in the great majority of societies—is toward international events. By preventing white South Africans from competing as a "nation," anti-apartheid activists deprived the sporting calendar of its principal *raison d'etre*.

In racial terms, the South African regime's insistence on segregated sports teams and leagues became symptomatic of white pathologies about the body. These surfaced in extremis around high contact sports like rugby and in swimming pool racism, with its baroque anxieties over the mingling of fluids. Colonial machismo has been exacerbated among white South African men by the militarized conditions of male bonding: for the past quarter-of-a-century, all white male school-leavers have been summoned for national conscription, a brutal rite of passage into "manliness."

White vulnerability to a sports boycott was rooted not just in the conditions of apartheid but in the character of male team sports. White sport under apartheid readily acquired a hysterical racial dimension, as segregated events became crucial sites for the forging and consolidation of white blood-brotherhoods. The structure, symbolic freight and social status of such sports generate atavistic occasions whereby men enact territorial disputes in an atmosphere of homosocial panic.[5] Particularly in North European, Anglo-Saxon, and related settler communities, sport provides men with a rare public arena for flaunting their bodies while indulging, without fear of social disgrace, in same sex bodily contact. They can touch, embrace, kiss, fondle, cradle, and mount each other, smear each other with bodily fluids, and simulate copulation, whether with teammates, Mother Earth, or the corner flag. All this is sanctioned within a carefully zoned space that has been symbolically liberated from suspicion of same sex desire.

Sporting fraternities, like military ones, rely on an aura of machismo, homophobia, and misogyny to suppress any suggestion that their intimacies are the least bit sexually ambiguous. Cheerleaders serve as guarantors of red-blooded heterosexuality—as do the idiomatic women invented through the feminizing of defeated sports teams and armies. Typically, the nation-state, national sporting authorities, and the media prevent female sports teams from becoming significant bearers of national prestige, despite their potential for doing so. It is symptomatic of this tendency that, while the anti-apartheid boycott encompassed female sports teams, they were involved in none of the decisive controversies. Thus sport is the arena in white South African society where national exhibitionism has converged most explicitly with the intimacies of same sex and same race solidarities.[6]

Under the settler-colonial conditions of apartheid, male sport's territorial agons have acquired a special urgency by embodying the consummate struggle between colonizers and colonized, the contest over the occupation, dispossession, and reclamation of land. Male team sports are, after all, little more than a series of boundary disputes staged under conditions of sanctioned violence. Under apartheid, these homosocial boundary disputes have been waged in an intensely militarized atmosphere. Because they have occurred in conditions where an unelected regime fielded an unrepresentative "national" side during a climate of foreign hostility and internal insurrection, the results of such contests have often developed a keenly political edge.

The international embattlement of white South Africans was amplified by their minority status within their own borders. Sport matches provided constant, vocal reminders of the "enemy within," with the black side of the stadium routinely cheering the Springboks' opponents. Evidently, patriotism was expected even from the disenfranchised: "unpatriotic" crowd behavior prompted one city, Bloemfontein, to ban all black spectators.[7] Divided loyalties in the stadium had to be suppressed, for they were discomfiting reminders of a nation at war with itself.

In many team sports, the form and idiom of the game are redolent of war, as the playing field becomes a projection of an imaginary map of adjacent, hostile national territories. The talk is of crossing borders and boundary lines, of opposing forces beating a retreat, mounting an assault, gaining or surrendering ground, launching rearguard actions, aerial assaults, and counter-attacks, piercing the opposition's defenses, and driving deep into its territory. When South Africa's white sporting establishment imported surrogate international teams during the 1980s in an effort to bust the boycott, the sportsmen were condemned through military metaphors—as "mercenaries" or "blood players" who participated in "rebel" or "pirate" tours.

At times, the analogies between military and sporting prowess become flagrant. In 1981, a Springbok rugby victory over arch rivals New Zealand coincided with a massive South African military assault on Angola. The South African Broadcasting Corporation's propagandists had no hesitation in bracketing these triumphs: "Just as, over the weekend, South Africans rejoiced at the splendid victory of the Springboks in New Zealand, others of the country's representatives were returning from the battlefield in Angola. Their mission, too, was splendidly accomplished...."[8] Yet such analogies are not a South African peculiarity. In 1982, immediately after Britain's victory in the Falklands/Malvinas War, the English tabloids exhorted the national football team to victory in that year's World Cup, on the grounds that two such virile triumphs would make a "perfect pair."[9] So, too, when the U.S. basketball team "massacred" Cuba by 79 points in the playoffs for the 1992 Olympics, one television commentator observed: "Those of you who loved Grenada will love this."[10]

If the design and argot of sport give weight to George Orwell's aphoristic depiction of it as "war minus the shooting," sport may on occasion become war *plus* the shooting. This was notoriously borne out by *la guerra futbol*—the conflagration sparked by the 1969 World Cup playoffs between Honduras and El Salvador. On each leg of the contest, home supporters subjected the visiting side to relentless harassment and psychological warfare, on the correct assumption (as the scoreline verifies) that a sleepless, mentally shattered side is more readily defeated. Amidst reciprocal cries of foul play, the two nations determined to transfer their unresolved differences from the playing to the battle field. In the ensuing football war, six thousand people were killed and twelve thousand wounded.[11]

The convergence of sporting and military agons as expressions of nationalism challenges the insistent perception of sport as a sovereign realm paradoxically both beneath and above politics. On this view, sport is a mere pastime, but a pastime of transcendent import. Indeed, sporting idiom is shot through with a religious register: fanatical fans adore their sporting idols or gods and the crowd mood builds towards a state of rapture, ecstasy, or frenzy. It is a tabloid cliché that a venerated stadium, like London's Wembley, is nothing other than a football shrine where sublime players tread the hallowed ground, later to be immortalized in the pantheon of the great. White South Africans were vulnerable to a boycott not because sport transcends politics, but because sport's quasi-theological rites are wholly integral to the politics of nationalism.[12] Great victories achieve a redemptive quality, allowing the nation to pass into Messianic time, in Walter Benjamin's sense of a state that instantaneously fulfils past and future.

For a citizen in a secularized or religiously eclectic society, devotion to the national side offers an alternative outlet for transcendental impulses, while simultaneously deepening his or her identification with a projected national community. On the other hand, in communities where a single religion dominates—as in Catholic Brazil or Calvinist Afrikanerdom—the national side's triumphs and defeats may readily be ascribed to divine intervention.[13] In South Africa, rugby—the religious home of the far right—has been unusually prone to such interpretations. When, in 1969, the British rugby team conquered the Springboks on the field and anti-apartheid protesters mortified them off the field, one commentator explained the double humiliation in these terms: "To us in South Africa, rugby is really our god with a small letter, and to be defeated like that—the mishaps, the players who were injured—it was abnormal. God spoke to us."[14]

BOYCOTT POWER

In a 1970 survey, white South Africans ranked the lack of international sport as one of the three most damaging consequences of apartheid—a melancholy statistic, but an index, nonetheless, of how deep the boycott cut.[15] Had black South Africans been polled, it is improbable that the loss of international sport would have ranked among their top grievances. However, the quite different issue of apartheid's disastrous impact on sport would almost certainly have ranked highly. These discrepant perspectives are encapsulated by the slogans to which opposing forces gravitated during the boycott era: "Keep Politics Out of Sport" for most whites and "No Normal Sport in an Abnormal Society" for the majority of blacks.

If white South Africans generally adhered to the conviction that sport should be quarantined from politics, the conditions in which black South African sportsmen and women played precluded such a perspective. Weather-ravaged, overextended, underequipped, underfunded, and understaffed facilities in black townships meant that sporting events promised not a flight from politics but full immersion in it.

Ever since 1894, when Krom Hendricks, a talented Malay bowler, was excluded from the South African national cricket team, a stream of top black sportsmen and women have been denied South African colors. Yet, for the overwhelmingly black organizations who advocated nonracial sport, matters could not be resolved simply through more equitable representation at the highly visible, celebrity level of international sport. Indeed, advocates of the boycott contended that changes in the glamorous upper echelons alone would prove counterproductive, distracting from the need to transform the institutional conditions of sport from the grassroots up. Thus, from early in the campaign, supporters of the ban insisted that racism in sport could only be redressed by rescinding the whole matrix of apartheid laws—the Population Registration

Act, the Group Areas Act, the Reservation of Separate Amenities Act, the Liquor Act, the Bantu Education Act—that governed the daily conditions in which sport was played.

By the mid-50s, anti-apartheid forces had begun to pinpoint sport as the Achilles heel of white national morale. Black journalists on the Johannesburg magazine, *Drum*, were the first to give the issue public exposure, with an intrepid special issue in 1955 that asked: "Why shouldn't our blacks be allowed in the SA team?" The following year, Trevor Huddleston anticipated that white South African teams would find themselves wholly isolated. He wagered that "because the Union is so good at sport, such isolation would shake its self-assurance very severely. Fantastic though it may sound, it might be an extraordinarily effective blow to the racialism which has brought it into being."[16] Shortly after this prediction, a nonracial sports organization was founded and began to campaign for merit selection of national teams.

As the base of the nonracial sports movement expanded, so too did the range of its demands. The 1960 Sharpeville massacre proved a watershed event. In the wake of the killings, the regime imposed a state of emergency and launched a draconian clampdown on activists, including "subversives" in the sporting arena. The ANC and PAC were banned, went underground, and called for armed struggle. These conditions hastened the radicalization of the resistance, not least among leading advocates of nonracial sport.

The Sharpeville massacre also provoked the first international outcries against apartheid sports teams at the 1960 Olympic Games and, that same year, against New Zealand rugby players departing for South Africa and South African cricketers arriving in England. These intimations of foreign support for a sports ban combined with the newfound militancy of the liberation movement to insure that when the South African Non-Racial Olympic Committee (SANROC) was formed in 1962 its demands were suitably more radical than those of its predecessors. SANROC targeted international sport as a locus of activism, but was insistent that merit selection of national teams was an untrustworthy index of the deracialization of South African sport. From then onwards, the racial composition of the national side was treated as subsidiary to the paramount concern with overturning apartheid laws in education, health, housing, voting, residential, and land rights, and in access to amenities, all of which prevented blacks from competing with whites on remotely equitable terms. SANROC and its successor organizations insisted that leverage gained from pressure at the most illustrious and conspicuous level of sport be used to transform the invisible grassroots of the games. Merit had to come into play not just at the moment of selection but in the distribution of opportunities.

SANROC scored its first major triumph with the expulsion of South Africa from the 1964 Olympics. The regime struck back at once, outlawing the organization. By the middle of 1964, SANROC's leaders were in prison, under house arrest, in exile, or underground—all in the name of a government policy of "keeping politics out of sport."[17]

Yet SANROC surfaced phoenix-like in London two years later. By driving it into exile, the regime had inadvertently aided the organization's cause. Turning adversity to advantage, SANROC enjoyed improved visibility and leverage, found itself better placed to lobby international sporting federations, and could lie in wait for visiting South African teams who became the targets of anti-apartheid mass actions. The passage into exile of South African sports activists like Dennis Brutus, Sam Ramsamy, Reg Hlongwane, Chris de Broglio, and Peter Hain proved indispensable for converting the sports boycott from a local fantasy into an international movement.

Brutus became a decisive figure, particularly during those early years. From the mid-1940s onwards, he had challenged the exclusion from South Africa's Olympic side of black athletes who were clocking record performances. In 1961 the state had issued him with a banning order that forbade him from writing. This was followed, in 1963, with a second ban prohibiting him from belonging to any organization, teaching, or attending any gathering of more than two people, including any sports event.[18] Later that year, he was charged with "the crime of attending a sports meeting" and released on bail.[19] Determined to testify at Baden-Baden, where the International Olympic Committee was preparing to debate South Africa's participation in the 1964 Olympics, Brutus escaped to Mozambique, where the Portuguese colonial police captured him and handed him over to the South Africans. On attempting a second escape, Brutus was shot in the stomach by the Security Police who left him bleeding on the pavement. Brutus served eighteen months on Robben Island before leaving South Africa on an exit visa that barred him from ever returning.

SANROC was refounded in 1966, soon after Brutus's arrival in London. The boycott movement received a further boost that year with the inauguration of the Supreme Council for Sport in Africa.[20] Ten years earlier, the Supreme Council would have possessed negligible clout in the arenas of world sport. Indeed, prior to Abebe Bikila's triumph in the 1960 Olympic marathon, no African athlete had ever won gold. But in the sixties, athletes like Bikila, Mohammed Gammoudi, Kip Keino, Amos Biwott, Mamo Wolde, and Naftali Temu began to reel off victories in the long distance events. The Supreme Council found itself in a position to convert athletic feats into political muscle: along with SANROC, it persuaded thirty-two African and eight other countries to pledge a boycott of the 1968 Mexico Olympics if South Africa participated. The tactic worked: South Africa was ousted from the games and, two years later, expelled from the Olympic movement.

These were central victories in their own right. But they also set a strategic precedent which was to be invoked effectively in the coming decades. From the 1968 Olympics onwards, African, Asian, and Caribbean nations extended the reach of the sports ban by producing a knockon or domino effect, refusing to play not just against apartheid teams but against nations who maintained ties with white South African sport. Ultimatums of this nature repeatedly jeopardized the Commonwealth Games, while the presence of a New Zealand squad at the 1976 Montreal Olympics—shortly after a New Zealand rugby tour of South Africa—led to a mass boycott by African nations.[21] In later domino effects, India and Guyana refused visas to English cricket teams that included players who had competed or coached in South Africa. The Indian government denied visas to eight English cricketers who maintained ties with South Africa; as a consequence, England's 1989 tour of India was cancelled. In the ultimate expression of this domino pressure, all Commonwealth governments signed the Gleneagles Agreement in 1977 which committed them to discouraging their sporting nationals from contact with South Africa.

The events of 1967 and 1968 vindicated years of anti-apartheid backroom labor, as white South Africans suffered successive political defeats in the sporting arenas in which they had the deepest white nationalist investment: the Olympics, rugby, and cricket. In 1967 the New Zealand rugby team cancelled their South African tour when the regime refused to admit Maori players. Smarting from this blow, Prime Minister Vorster hinted that Maoris might in future be "acceptable"—although he refused to relax any of the strictures against nonracial sport among South Africans. (The following New Zealand rugby tour of South Africa in 1970 exposed the hollowness of Vorster's "compromise." Capitulating to South African pressure, the New Zealand rugby board included only light skinned Maoris and Samoans who could "pass" for white). But Vorster's miniscule theoretical concession brought his far right regime under pressure from the doubly far right who were so outraged at the prospect of a smattering of "mixed" sport—even against foreign sportsmen—that they seceded to form the Herstigte Nasionale Party. This is not to say that multiracial sport was the sole cause of the breach: it became a focal symptom of deeper economic and political disputes. However, the birth of the Herstigtes surely marks the only instance of a "deviation" in sporting policy being cited as grounds for the creation of a secessionist political party.

That same year, a single incident catapulted the sports boycott out of obscurity, pitching the anti-apartheid cause with unprecedented force and regularity onto both the front and back pages of the British national press. The event came to be known as the D'Oliveira Affair. Basil D'Oliveira was a mercurial mixed race cricketer whose frustration with his blunted prospects led him to emigrate from Cape Town to England in 1960. Within six years, he had established himself as a full member of the English cricket team. During the runup to the selection of the English side due to tour South Africa in 1968, the prospect of D'Oliveira's inclusion so perturbed the Vorster regime that it sent an agent to try to buy him off with a sumptuous ten-year coaching contract, a house, and a car on condition that he declare himself unavailable for England.[22] D'Oliveira refused. The chance of flaunting his talents on the very playing fields from which

Fig. 2: Rugby riot during the Springbok tour of New Zealand. (AP/Wide World Photos)

he had been banished offered the priceless, sweet promise of revenge—the return of the oppressed.

Despite a blistering burst of form, D'Oliveira was excluded from the England team to tour South Africa in 1968. In an act of blatant complicity with apartheid, the English cricket authorities had contrived to drop D'Oliveira in the hopes of averting an "international incident." The alliance between politics and sport was exposed for all to see. The D'Oliveira Affair enraged citizens on whose mental maps apartheid had barely registered, helping ratchet the British anti-apartheid movement into a cause with populist dimensions. The English selectors were so roundly shamed that when an injured player withdrew from the team, D'Oliveira was reinstated. Vorster, however, promptly declared that D'Oliveira had been reduced to a "political football." Any team that included him "was not the team of the MCC, but the team of the Anti-Apartheid Movement and the team of SANROC" and was therefore unacceptable.[23] The English cricket selectors declined to budge and the tour collapsed.

Over the next eighteen months, the boycott movement gathered breadth and momentum: by 1970, the ruling bodies of over twenty sports had expelled South Africa.[24] Riled by these successes, the regime bore down heavily on internal advocates of nonracial sport, people like Morgan Naidoo, the president of the nonracial swimming union, who was served with a five-year banning order in retaliation for the expulsion of the white swimming union from international competition.[25]

By the 1980s, apartheid sport was becoming as sealed off as a faulty nuclear reactor encased in a concrete sarcophagus. The Springboks could no longer play abroad, and virtually the only teams entering South Africa were the rebel sides who received exorbitant sums to compete in pseudo-internationals. This was sport's version of the Sun City principle—an attempt to rupture the boycott by offering top prices for the consciences of celebrity players. But no less than at Sun City, the ruse failed. Few stars came. The West Indian, Australian, Sri Lankan, English, and New Zealand players who accepted such "blood money" were mostly embarrassingly mediocre performers who suffered banishment from international sport and ostracism at home. In the Caribbean, so great was the stigma of playing with apartheid that several West Indian cricket "rebels" were forced to emigrate.

It may seem surprising that football (soccer), much the most popular team sport in South Africa, was never on the frontline between the boycotters and boycott busters. This resulted partly from the international body's prescient, decisive expulsion of the white South African football federation as early as 1961. In addition, South African football players and fans are predominantly black and some of the leading footballers were active in anti-apartheid organizations in the 1970s and 80s. To a greater extent than any other sport, football began, in the 1980s, to be played and administered along nonracial lines. It could thus neither form a repository for white nationalism nor offer a promising environment for adversaries of the boycott.

The scale of funds lavished on the "rebel" cricketers, however, demonstrated that the problems in South African sport resulted less from a shortage of cash than a shortage of political will. Players' fees alone for the West Indian travesty came to $1.8 million. The regime awarded tax breaks covering 180 percent of expenses to white businesses sponsoring rebel tours and in 1982, one corporation alone, South African Breweries, expended $2 million on such ventures.[26] This was at a time when whites—15 percent of the population—owned 73 percent of all athletic tracks, 82 percent of rugby fields, and 83 percent of public pools. It has been estimated that the regime was spending, during this period, between nine and twenty-three times more per capita on white than on black sport.[27]

There was yet another side to the rebel tours—the harassment, detentions, and state-commissioned assaults on sports figures who spoke up for nonracialism and against such gross prodigality. Among these were the Watson brothers, who rocked the white rugby establishment by joining a hitherto all black club. Cheeky Watson, the most adroit of the trio, committed the cardinal affront of declining to play for the white "national" side in preference to nonracial club rugby. This simple act of principle, unheard of among white players at the time, was amply rewarded by Port Elizabeth's black community. When a black consumer boycott paralyzed the city's white businesses during the mid-80s, the Watsons' clothing store was granted sole exemption—indeed, thrived as a result. The Civil Co-operation Bureau, which launched hit squads against "enemies of the state," responded otherwise. A CCB arsonist razed the Watsons' home and a paid assassin broke into the hotel room of one brother, opening fire on him before being overpowered.

INTERVENTIONIST SPECTACLE

Sport's primetime profile renders it a particularly seductive sphere for the staging of interventionist spectacle. In seeking to catalyze opposition abroad and reach outside the ranks of the predictably progressive, the boycotters turned to their advantage the special relation that has arisen between sport and TV. Indeed, the successful conversion of the sports boycott into a populist cause offers a salient lesson in the politics of spectacle.

The increasing refraction of identities through TV suggests that the old styles of activism need to accommodate the politics of spectacle more fully. No social movement can rest its case on purely moral grounds: we have to take politics seriously enough to convert it into telegenic theater. International sporting coverage holds out particular possibilities in this regard, for it differs from other programs that draw high ratings—soaps, say, or game shows—by its ability to concentrate a vast, anonymous community around an event devised to arouse nationalist passions. While viewers may place themselves differently in relation to the image of the national team, any cause that can locate itself at those crossroads where people's loyalties to the rites of the box, to a specific sport, and to a particular nation converge can register considerable political gains.

Across a succession of "demo-tours" between 1969 and 1990, anti-apartheid demonstrators proved remarkably creative in their production of disruptive spectacle. This tactic resulted in the cancellation of a number of tours in advance and, failing that, of individual matches once a tour was underway. Prior to matches, buckets of glass and thousands of tacks and fish hooks were sometimes strewn across the rugby field; "commando squads" were sent to infiltrate the Springboks' hotels; Operation Wide Awake kept up a nighttime racket insuring sleepless nights. Cricket grounds proved especially vulnerable to preemptive strikes. Boycotters could infiltrate the grounds at night to dig up the cricket pitch—the sensitive, meticulously prepared grass strip at the heart of the field— or saturate it with oil. On the 1981 Springbok rugby tour of New Zealand, a World War II pilot forced the cancellation of one match by seizing a four-seater Cessna and threatening to dive kamikaze style into the packed grandstand.[28] On the same tour, arsonists gutted the clubhouses of teams that had agreed to play the Springboks. (Nor was this the first time that the disenfranchised and their supporters had used fire against discrimination in sport: in 1913 British suffragette arsonists attacked sports clubs whose patterns of exclusion mirrored those that barred women from voting).[29] If a match went ahead, demonstrators drew on backup tactics to insure that playing conditions were unendurable. They fired off smoke bombs, paint bombs, and flashed mirrors in players' eyes. Scores of whistle-blowing activists infiltrated the stands, causing pandemonium on the field and giving a whole new meaning to the idea of a whistle-stop tour.

Such measures turned sport against Springbok teams into an economic and symbolic liability. The policing costs became prohibitive, contributing to the cancellation of some series altogether, financial pressure succeeding where moral pressure had failed. On the symbolic front, the boycotters proved particularly adept at converting international sport into a law and order issue. They exploited sport's reliance on the maintenance of an equilibrium between the expression of violence on the one hand and, on the other, its containment by rules, group discipline, and the inviolable authority of the referee's whistle or the umpire's adjudications. Having carried the apartheid issue into a sphere ordinarily considered exempt from politics, the boycotters tilted the balance of the game towards lawlessness, so that on- and off-field violence began to blur. Instead of serving as a carefully monitored, socially sanctioned outlet for unruly impulses, sporting contests became emblematic of a violence that burst uncontrollably from the space-and-time frame of the game. In the middle of the Springboks' 1981 tour, the leader of the New Zealand opposition party warned that rugby was driving his entire nation to "the threshold of carnage."[30]

The aerial attack on the South African-New Zealand rugby match in Auckland in 1981 illustrates this convergence of sporting and nonsporting violence. An activist in a light aircraft made 60 low-level runs across the field, disrupting play with a barrage of flour bombs, leaflet bombs, and smoke cannisters. Such is the violence of rugby that it is not unusual for a player to be semi-concussed. However, when one of these bombs felled a New Zealand player, some of the country's politicians and media seized upon it as an image of an alien violence spilling over from the rugby field and engulfing New Zealand as a nation.

The perception of Springbok teams as conduits for social mayhem vexed the South African regime and white sports administrators. Dr. Danie Craven, the excitable president of the South African rugby board, raged: "We can't go abroad without causing chaos. It's not pleasant to feel as if we're suffering from a dis-

Fig. 3: More clashes, New Zealand. (AP/Wide World Photos)

ease....We live in a world of sick people, weaklings, so-called leaders, who are intimidated by boycotts."[31] But from an anti-apartheid perspective, the export trade in chaos drew invaluable media coverage. It recreated the spectacle and atmosphere of a police state in countries unaccustomed to such levels of public violence, providing a symbolic sample of "the South African way of life."[32] In England, Ireland, New Zealand, Scotland, Wales, France, and Australia, the sight of police massing behind barbed wire and armed with shields, batons, and snarling dogs made a mockery of claims that they were simply there to separate politics from sport. In a manner redolent of the Latin American dictatorial practice of converting sports stadiums into detention camps, the arrival of the Springboks turned what had hitherto been leisure facilities into fortresses. The repercussions of hosting the Barbed Wire Boks, as they were dubbed, helped solidify the association between apartheid, militarization, and the absence of democracy, as happened strikingly in Australia in 1971.[33] Such was the scale of the protest against the rugby tourists that the Governor of Queensland declared a state of emergency, suspended democratic process, and guaranteed the Springboks' safety by escorting them in army planes replete with military guards.[34]

At their most intense, the confrontations between protesters and police assumed apocalyptic dimensions: they did not merely simulate the atmosphere of a police state but, on occasion, enacted its overthrow. The match at Hamilton, New Zealand in 1981 offered just such an inspiring augury as thousands of demonstrators overran the barricades and overwhelmed the police.

THE BOYCOTT'S REPEAL

In a dramatic move in 1991, the ANC gave its imprimatur to the lifting of the sports moratorium. Sports organizations that met express conditions—unification, adherence to nonracialism, and the implementation of township development programs—began to gain admission into international competition. This process was dramatically sealed by South Africa's presence at the 1992 Cricket World Cup, at the 1992 Barcelona Olympics, and by the announcement that the country was to host the next Rugby World Cup. These were, after all, the three sports which activists had targeted to greatest effect.

The repeal was bound to be controversial. Some saw it as a defeat for the principle of "No normal sport in an abnormal society," while the ANC vindicated its decision as a preemptive strike that would express its determination to redistribute opportunity by transforming existing institutions along nonracial lines. Sport remained, after all, one of the few arenas where the ANC, in its jockeying for power with the National Party, was incontestably in control.

Since the summer of 1990, when Mike Gatting's rebel cricket tour had foundered on the twin reefs of a well-organized resistance movement and the unbanning of the ANC, establishment sporting bodies had begun to sue for peace. They had agreed to a moratorium on the divisive, squanderous rebel tours and, in some sports, had begun to cooperate in setting up sports development programs in the townships. The ANC judged that it could convert these promising developments to political gain by taking command of the pace and conditions of South Africa's admission into international sport.

The campaign to broker sporting unity in advance of political reconciliation involved a delicate wager with uncertain returns. But the two figures who emerged as the principal spokesmen for this position—Steve Tshwete and Sam Ramsamy—were well acquainted with risk. Tshwete won a name for himself as a rugby player and a saboteur of telephone pylons. During his fifteen years on

Robben Island for guerilla action, he ran the Island Rugby Board, a keenly disputed league of ten teams. Tshwete went on to help found the United Democratic Front and, in 1990, helped orchestrate resistance to the infamous Gatting tour.[35] Over the course of three decades, Ramsamy emerged alongside Dennis Brutus as the cardinal figure in the international drive to isolate apartheid teams. Like other leaders of the South African NonRacial Olympic Committee, Ramsamy was forced into exile in the early 60s when the Nationalist government slapped a ban on SANROC. At the height of his anti-apartheid campaigning, his London home was subjected to gunfire by agents of the South African state. Ramsamy was probably the sports administrator most reviled by the white establishment, which found itself in the early 90s dependent on his mediations while covertly striving to marginalize him.

In sport, as elsewhere in South African society, there is a pressing need for the swift democratization of institutions, rendering them answerable to the requirements and values of the oppressed. The ANC's gamble of revoking the boycott took shape as a response to this recognition. At a time when de Klerk was making most of the political running, sport was one circuit where the ANC found itself ideally placed to take the lead. By manipulating the white obsession with international participation, the liberation movement and its allies could begin to restructure sport from the grassroots up. In so doing, this alliance refused to use the racial composition of the national teams as the primary barometer of change. To have imposed the principle of racial "balance" on teams would have been to perpetuate race as a criterion for selection. It would have seemed disturbingly redolent of the kind of nominal, celebrity multiracialism advanced by the Nationalist regime since the early 70s in its efforts to distract attention from the profound segregation of sport at the local level.

If most whites salivated at the prospect of international "return," for most blacks the loss of international competition had always been indissociable from a far wider sense of deprivation. Thus they could not treat the "restitution" of international ties as their overriding objective. (In any case, South Africa was not, strictly speaking, renewing its sporting links with the outside world, but competing for the first time as a nation rather than as a race in national guise). Where the white camp was apt to view sport preeminently as an international matter, the black camp tended to place more stress on the local implications, on the dependence of sporting progress on changes in the whole fabric of the apartheid legacy—in education, health, transport, and housing.

Yet, it was felt, as an interim measure sporting unity might serve as a catalyst and harbinger of change. In the words of the leading football administrator, Styx Morewa, it could operate as an "emotional unifier."[36] In lifting the boycott, Ramsamy, Tshwete, Morewa, Thabo Mbeki and others in the ANC camp wagered that, under the altered conditions of the interregnum, the ban had more value as carrot than stick. Progressive sports administrators thus sought to capitalize on white self-interest in order to begin institutionalizing nonracialism in at least one sphere of society. It was more productive, they argued, to have pro-ANC figures strategically placed during the runup to elections than to persist with an obstructionist policy whose expiry date—in the light of changes in international perceptions of apartheid—was in any case beginning to show.

During the early 1990s, the central challenge facing progressive forces with proven oppositional skills began to redirect those energies toward the creation of affirmative, propositional policies. The National and Olympic Sports Congress was launched in June 1990 to answer these altered needs. Its brief was to unite black sports people and to admit such sectors of the white sporting establishment that embraced nonracialism and were prepared to work for its implementation at a local level.[37] As South Africa's largest and most politically forceful sporting organization, NOSC devised an alternative course to the once effective but superannuated policy of noncooperation while simultaneously rejecting the assumption prevalent in some white quarters that black sportsmen and women should simply be subsumed under existing white structures. NOSC resolved "to propose rather than perpetually oppose," but was leery of superficial assimilation which it recognized as a hindrance to sport's radical transformation.[38]

The Tshwete-Ramsamy wager could not be dismissed easily as a gesture of defeatist expediency. By insisting on the terms for South Africa's participation in international sport, the ANC-allied forces have begun to redirect the flow of funds—above all, corporate funds—away from pseudo-internationals and into a combination of official internationals and township development programs. This was consistent with the recognition that no undertaking in South African sports is more urgent or more daunting than the redistribution of resources, for under apartheid 90 percent of all sponsorship was lavished on white events.[39]

While the ban was conditionally lifted, sport's role in giving form to national identity remained as ferociously contested as ever. Stormy exchanges over the destiny of the Springbok insignia revealed the persistent volatility of the issue of national representation. The ANC-aligned forces determined unilaterally that the prancing antelope should be summarily dispatched. For the great majority of South Africans the issue was clear-cut: the buck stops here. NOSC launched a search for a substitute in which the conscientiously nonracial zebra emerged as an early front-runner, with the kudu, the rose, the rhino, the protea, and the fish eagle bringing up the rear.

For de Klerk, self-styled prototype of the New South African, this was pushing novelty to extremes. In one of his most bitter attacks on the ANC, he accused them of desecrating tradition and urged that the Springbok be preserved as the national emblem. Despite the pitch of his protests, when a South African team of cricketers traveled to India and engaged in international competition for the first time in twenty-two years, they were expressly not called the Springboks. There was something half-apt yet utterly bizarre about the scenario that unfolded. India had been the first country to break off all ties—including sporting connections—when apartheid was officially adopted in 1948. Nearly half a century later, Hindu extremists had pledged to burn down the Bombay cricket stadium if a scheduled tour by Pakistan went ahead. The secretary of the Indian Cricket Board decreed that the Pakistanis' safety could not be guaranteed, cancelled the series, and invited the South Africans as less controversial replacements. Thus a dazed set of cricketers arrived at very short notice to make their debut before a crowd of one hundred thousand jammed into Calcutta's Eden Gardens in a Marxist-ruled state. Garlanded in the streets, the South Africans were called upon to deliver syrupy speeches beneath banners flaunting hammers and sickles and the visages of Marx and Lenin. The only dissident noises seemed to come from West Bengal's Revolutionary Youth League who mounted a modest protest, and President de Klerk who mounted a rather more vocal one over the dumping of the national emblem.[40]

In July 1992, the South African Olympic squad traveled to Barcelona with all its insignia in suspension—as befits a nation in abeyance. Again, the name Springboks was dropped and a doctored Olympic flag substituted for the South African one. Moreover, it was determined that should any team member strike gold, the Olympic band would respond with neither that old neo-Nazi marching tune, "Die Stem," nor the ANC's "Nkosi Sikelel' iAfrika," but with Beethoven's "Ode to Joy." This melody, it was later realized, would render a South African victory indistinguishable from a Russian one, the ex-Soviets having arrived at an identical solution to their transitional condition.

The de Klerk regime had wanted South Africa to participate at Barcelona but had insisted on dictating the terms. As a result of the ructions over iconography and its distaste at seeing an adversary like Ramsamy command the proceedings, the regime refused to give a penny to the National Olympic Committee.[41] While this made Ramsamy's task of funding the team's trip immeasurably more difficult, it did, usefully, drive a wedge between the regime and its traditional allies, sport's corporate sponsors, who were keen to cash in on the Olympic connection.

But de Klerk has always had an eye for the main chance, as they say in South Africa. His uncooperative stance toward the Olympics did not prevent him from recognizing the mileage to be gained from sporting spectacle. With the opportunism that has characterized his political performance, de Klerk temporarily commandeered the boycott issue as an electoral weapon, wielding it against the extreme right, to whom he dealt a sport-aided trouncing in the all-white referendum in 1992.

To head off the far right threat and to consolidate his bargaining power at the negotiating table, de Klerk called a snap whites-only referendum on the future of reform. He announced the referendum just after South Africa, admitted into the World Cricket Cup for the first time, had scored an upset victory over the world champions, Australia. Capitalizing on the buoyant mood among South African whites, de Klerk leveled the threat of the sport boycott's return against his Conservative adversaries. Indeed, the success of his campaign depended centrally on his manipulation of two powerful white populist anxieties: that a NO to reform would result in the restitution of punitive sporting and economic sanctions.

Sports grounds in Australia were plastered with billboards urging "VOTE YES"—surely the first time ever that exhortations addressed to the electorate of one country have littered a second country half way around the globe. As South Africa's cricket captain later remarked "We were crucial to the National Party strategy."[42] In South Africa, a chorus of sportsmen and women were dragooned into advertisements urging a YES vote, backed by slogans like "Give South Africa a Sporting Chance."[43] Even Dr. Danie Craven, the most powerful figure in white rugby and an unconscionable racist if ever there was one, did his incoherent best to prove that he, too, was a New South African. "Any sportsman or woman voting NO," he warned, "will be raping his or her own conscience."[44]

The scale of ideological cross-dressing in contemporary South Africa defies belief. But even those accustomed to such mutations were astonished by the sight of the National Party—for almost half a century the aggrieved target of boycotts—adapting one of the liberation movement's most effective strategies by wielding the threat of sports and economic bans. De Klerk's eager commandeering of left wing tactics further evinces the political kudos to be gained from interventions in the emotionally charged, spectacular rituals of international sport.

By 1992, the ANC had achieved greater sway over South Africa's sporting future than the Nationalists. However, in his showdown against the ultraright Conservatives, de Klerk adapted the liberation movement's boycott strategy so adroitly that when the Conservative leader, Andries Treurnicht, comes to pen his autobiography, we can expect echoes of Harold Wilson's lament at his sport-induced defeat. It was Wilson, one recalls, who blamed his loss in the 1970

British elections on a downswing in national mood following England's defeat by Germany in the finals of the World Cup.

CONCLUSION

"South Africa cannot have both a Boipatong and a Barcelona."[45] Desmond Tutu's words rang out in the aftermath of the Boipatong massacres. Within a few days of the carnage at Boipatong, the ANC's shadow minister of sport, Steve Tshwete, declared: "The country is in a state of mourning. We will ask sporting bodies to reimpose the moratorium until the political situation is normalised."[46] The good faith wager of negotiations—let alone the prospect of sport serving as an emotional unifier—had faltered disastrously. Barcelona was to have offered a presentiment of political unity; from the depth of bloody machinations, it threatened to do no more than travesty such hopes.

Many South Africans made the emotional link between the carnage at Boipatong and the massacre, some thirty years earlier, at nearby Sharpeville. The Sharpeville killings had sparked the first international protest against apartheid sports teams at the Rome Olympics, and, for a time, it seemed as if Boipatong would cause South Africa's withdrawal from Barcelona. De Klerk's perfidious failure to rein in his security forces and bring Inkatha murderers to dock left a deeper rift between the Nationalists and the ANC than at any time since Mandela's release.

Yet the threatened reimposition of the boycott proved short-lived once the ANC realized how unpopular that decision would be. Sports administrators like Ramsamy, Mluleki George, and Styx Morewa expressed concern that a renewed ban would erode ANC support by undermining the morale of athletes and their supporters. Ensuing events vindicated their fears. A couple of weeks after Boipatong, the Cameroon football team was due to arrive in Johannesburg for a series of internationals that would mark South Africa's return to world football. When the ANC scuppered the Cameroon tour in protest over the killings, black fans jammed the organization's switchboards demanding to know why the preeminent black sport was being forced to atone for the crimes of others. Hadn't football, to a greater degree than any other sport, been played, administered, and watched along nonracial lines? Didn't football fans deserve some compensation for decades of compliance with the boycott while other, white-dominated sports, had been mounting rebel tours?

Mandela traveled to the Cameroon and had the series swiftly reinstated. On arrival in South Africa, the Cameroonians toured Boipatong in a massive, high profile expression of solidarity for that wracked community. The ANC resolved that outrage over the massacres would be expressed through channels other than sport: through the suspension of negotiations, a national strike, and related mass actions.

The South African team ventured to Barcelona more as a wager of hope than as a reflection of any existing, or even imminent, national unity. Their historic presence at the Olympics was a mark of the ANC's continuing leverage over South Africa's acceptance in the arenas of world sport; it was a mark, too, of the International Olympic Committee's determination to stage—after all the boycotts and banishments that had marred the Games since World War II—a healing Olympics, an event they could bill as the most universal Games ever. Juan Antonio Samaranch, President of the IOC, wished to unveil an Olympics that would be immortalized not just as the first post-Cold War Games but as the Games that finally drove politics out of sport.

Yet Catalonian, no less than South African history, warned against equating the absence of boycotts with the redemption of sport from politics. Didn't the line into the Olympic stadium pass *La Fossa de la Pedrera*, the vast graveyard for those fallen in the Spanish Civil War? And hadn't Samaranch himself once served as Franco's Minister of Sport? Yet for those who wished to reclaim it, Barcelona also offered a less dispiriting memory of sport's implication in politics. In 1936, four hundred athletes pledged to mount an alternative, People's Olympiad in protest against the Fuhrer's determination to stage-manage an orgy of Olympic Aryanism in Berlin. Barcelona was to be the chosen city of this counter-Olympic. The Civil War erupted before a race could be run, but the athletes' anti-fascist defiance nonetheless anticipated the possibilities, best embodied by the South African boycott, of reclaiming sport for the furtherance of social justice.

6

SUNSET ON SUN CITY
The Dilemmas of the Cultural Boycott

Bophuthatswana is far away
(Run-DMC)

But we know it's in South Africa no matter what they say
(Kurtis Blow & Afrika Bambaataa)

You can't buy me, I don't care what you pay
(Duke Bootee, Melle Mel & Afrika Bambaataa)

Don't ask me Sun City because I ain't gonna play
(Linton Kwesi Johnson & all rappers)

—Little Steven Van Zandt, et al, "Sun City"

A FEW YEARS BACK, Johannesburg commuters were hailed by the ubiquitous bumper sticker, "Boycott hell. Repent and Believe in the Lord Jesus Christ." The spirit of the exhortation may have been unbounded but the rhetoric was consummately of its time and place. For the 1980s saw the emergence in South Africa of a vast mesh of boycotts that helped snarl the regime and render the country virtually ungovernable. It was an era of consumer, commuter, and rent boycotts, boycotts of civic councils, schools, and elections and, on the international front, of revitalized efforts to sever South Africa's sporting, economic, and cultural bonds with the world at large.

Over the course of more than three decades, internal and international anti-apartheid forces collaborated to implement a cultural boycott of South Africa.[1] The historic attempts to vindicate apartheid by way of cultural argument made this a symbolically crucial sphere for disruption. Most whites granted preeminence to their own meagre cultural values, derogating and sidelining the imaginative resources of the black communities. But more than casual disdain was at stake: apartheid ideology was premised on a vision of culture as a divinely sanctioned marker of difference, thereby affording it a transcendental and neo-biological determinism. For the world to excommunicate South African cultural bodies meant thus a tangible, if symbolic, repudiation of all cultural rationales for segregation.

Over and above its subversive achievements, the cultural boycott left a legacy of affirmation. The challenge to institutionalized racism in the arts helped seed—particularly in the 1980s—a vision of culture as within the orbit of ordinary people's creative agency, not as something rarefied and distant. The spread of this spirit helped carry forward a sense, at once local and national, of grassroots involvement in conceiving a democratic role for the arts in advance of apartheid's decease.

The cultural boycott also generated its fair share of acrimony and, in its latter days, was marred by a tendency to self-immolate. It often proved difficult to back the ban's symbolic importance with strategic precision, not least because it was the most exacting boycott to define, monitor, and coordinate. Culture is pervasive, ordinary, and conflictual; this makes it an exasperatingly baggy and diffuse political target. Even if one considers culture in the limited sense of the arts, each artistic medium has distinctive forms of creation, distribution, and reception which, from the boycotters' standpoint, demand discrete strategies in reponse.

The tactical complexity of the cultural boycott contrasted markedly with the narrow focus and strategic clarity enjoyed by sports protesters. International rugby or cricket matches offered easily targeted events spanning a few hours or days in an enclosed arena.[2] Moreover, sports boycotters had merely to disrupt the traffic in players, while the cultural boycott also entailed the more taxing task of interrupting the flow of commodities. It proved incomparably easier to picket and harass a team of sportsmen visiting or leaving South Africa than it was to deny South Africans access to foreign books, plays, videos, or TV programs. And, of course, the merits of such a denial were far more open to case-by-case debate.[3]

The obstacles to delimiting and implementing the cultural boycott were legion. One of the cardinal difficulties flowed from the forms of representation involved. Unlike sport, the arts are not structured in a pyramid with the national team at its apex. Thus, musicians, writers, photographers, or painters could not be assailed as the official representatives of a racist nation-state. Furthermore, while a sports team could hardly argue that they should be allowed in or out of the country to articulate their anti-apartheid "message," the situation for artists was quite otherwise. Theater troupes, singers, poets, and film directors could and increasingly did claim exceptional status on the grounds that their art voiced opposition to apartheid.

For most of its duration, the cultural boycott was shaped and directed by exiles in league with foreign solidarity movements whose political metier was anti-racism. However, the democratic movement inside South Africa—thread-bare when the boycotts began, but powerful by the mid-80s—had a more complex project: it needed not only to overturn racism, but to reshape the society's cultural values and institutions in anticipation of its democratic metamorphosis. As this affirmative political impulse gained impetus in the mid-80s, the execution of the boycott became even more tortuous, with tensions arising between the internal needs of local cultural bodies and the external designs of solidarity movements abroad.

For these manifold reasons, the sports boycott was always the more probable sphere of success. The cultural ban remained symbolically powerful but strategically vexing, an area of sometimes striking but often erratic rewards. In so complex, so loosely bounded a realm of protest, the liberation movement could at best hope to narrow, not seal off, the channels of contact.

THE BOYCOTT'S INCEPTION

As far back as 1945, American Actors' Equity passed a resolution dissuading its members from performing in South Africa.[4] But it was Father Trevor Huddleston, of Sophiatown fame, who first won international coverage for the idea of an orchestrated moratorium on cultural contacts with apartheid. Writing in the British *Observer* in 1954, Huddleston called for

> a cultural boycott of South Africa. I am asking those who believe racialism to be sinful or wrong...to refuse to encourage it by accepting any engage-ment to act, to perform as a musical artist or as a ballet dancer—in short, to engage in any contacts which would provide entertainment for any one section of the community.[5]

Huddleston's wording reveals the modest ambitions of the boycott in its ear-liest days: the protest was principally an attempt to dissuade foreign artists from conniving at racially segregated performances. But within a few years, the vision of what the boycott might help achieve had grown exponentially. In the wake of the 1960 Sharpeville massacre, the outlawing of the liberation movement, and the state's decimation of alternative institutions, the cultural boycott was reconceived as one facet of a far broader assault on apartheid. The Nobel Peace Prize recipient and president of the ANC, Albert Luthuli, appealed in the early

1960s for United Nations backing for the total ostracism of South Africa. Luthuli invoked United Nations Article Seven, which permits the imposition of sanctions against any nation whose policies are adjudged to jeopardize world peace.[6] Luthuli envisaged the cultural ban as more than a protest against racism in the arts; it would become an integral facet of a global campaign to rid South Africa of apartheid.

Fig. 1: Poster in support of the cultural boycott. (Mayibuye Centre)

In the late 50s and 60s, as Connie Braam and Fons Geerlings have documented, a welter of artistic organizations acted upon Huddleston's and later Luthuli's appeal.[7] The impact of these decisions was most marked in the societies with which white South Africans enjoyed extensive cultural ties, viz. Britain, the United States, and the Netherlands.[8] In 1956 and '57, the British Actors' Union, Equity, and the British Musicians' Union forbade members from working in South Africa; forty leading British playwrights followed suit in 1963, withdrawing the rights for their plays to be performed under apartheid.[9]

The American protest gained visibility largely through the labors of prominent African Americans who helped draw in like-minded entertainers. When, in 1965, sixty-five performers and writers signed a *We Say No to Apartheid* pledge, the list boasted such stars as Sammy Davis Jr., Nina Simone, Arthur Miller, Leonard Bernstein, Harry Belafonte, and Sidney Poitier. The signatories were well placed to capitalize on the organizational impetus, black-Jewish alliances, and rhetoric of the civil rights movement. Davis's and Poitier's names carried a particular personal force. When the film *Oceans 11* traveled to South Africa, the official poster, which showed Davis accompanying two white actors was doctored to obliterate the African-American.[10] Poitier's films, too, had long rankled with apartheid's censors: some had been banned outright; in others, Poitier's image had been meticulously excised from interracial scenes, reducing his screen presence to a ghostly white void.

Belafonte was to prove the celebrity mainstay of the American anti-apartheid movement, binding the eras and worlds of Martin Luther King and Desmond Tutu, a lineage of protest from Birmingham and Sharpeville to Sun City. As Belafonte's, and later, Stevie Wonder's symbolic centrality to the American anti-apartheid campaign suggests, the boycott's force in the U.S. depended largely on its ability to rally musicians to the cause. This was not just due to African-Americans' visibility in that domain, but because music—unlike, theater, literature, the plastic arts, and photography—held out the seductive promise of stadium politics.

In Britain, the options were more flexible. There, as I argued in the previous chapter, the volatile, spectacular, telegenic anti-apartheid clashes in the country's sporting arenas dwarfed the cultural boycott. America's slender sporting ties with South Africa rendered music the best alternative conduit to crowd politics and a mass audience. Thus when Belafonte and Arthur Ashe founded Artists and Athletes Against Apartheid in America, it became manifest that artists would always constitute the more decisive wing of their paired venture.[11]

By 1969, a major portion of Luthuli's wish had been realized: in that year the United Nations General Assembly passed a resolution urging member states to suspend "cultural, educational, sports and other exchanges with the racist regime" and with all institutions "which practice apartheid."[12]

FOREIGN TACTICS, DOMESTIC CHANGE

The cultural boycott followed different courses on opposite sides of the Atlantic. If, in the U.S., musicians served as the boycott's mainstay, actresses provided the British with their most pronounced celebrity backing. Glenda Jackson's stand typified this spirit: "I've always felt that since I would not physically go to work in South Africa, my shadow, by virtue of a silver screen, should not be able to go either."[13]

The British anti-apartheid movement was able to draw on the radical mood that pervaded British theatre through the 60s and 70s. The AAM garnered support from stars who bridged stage and screen (Vanessa Redgrave, Julie Christie, Jackson, et al) along with a cluster of dissident playwrights (Harold Pinter, David Hare, and Edward Bond among them). But the boycott could not be built on stars alone; its strength came to depend, above all, on Equity's coordinated militancy.

The boycott took root more easily in theater than in film, not least because it is easier to monitor the destination of live performances than celluloid ones. Moreover, the dearth of a significant anti-apartheid lobby within Hollywood meant that protests like Glenda Jackson's remained symbolically bold but ultimately marginal affairs. The only notable disruptions in South Africans' access to movies were inflicted by the country's own censors.

The flaunted philistinism of white South African culture meant that some theatrical stands—like Pinter's and Jean Genet's refusal to permit South African productions of their work—remained principled but gestural protests. Television, however, is a majority taste. When British Equity interdicted the BBC and ITV from supplying South Africa with programs that featured its members, Equity struck one of the most forceful blows of the boycott campaign. The Equity ban was passed in 1975, a year before the regime's belated introduction of TV. This meant that aside from the odd documentary or sports footage, South Africa's state-run television has been comprehensively denied British programming for the entire duration of the country's exposure to the medium.[14] The support of the 38,000 strong British Musicians' Union gave the ban additional muscle, as a program could be withheld from South Africa on the grounds that BMU members had performed or composed the accompanying score. The preemptive withdrawal of British programming induced in South African TV a far greater reliance on American material than would otherwise have occurred. This dependence, in turn, has been the single greatest factor behind the accelerated Americanization of South African culture—for good and ill—since the mid-70s. Something of a Pretoria-Dallas cultural axis has emerged among many suburban Afrikaners, while township gangs and youth activists have turned to programs as varied as the *A-Team* and *V* for iconographic inspiration.

In the absence of a national union as progressive as British Equity, American TV performers and producers offered little organized support for the boycott during the 60s and 70s. Not until the 80s were American programs withheld from SATV and then only in small numbers. Bill Cosby withdrew his show (a hit in South Africa) at Desmond Tutu's prompting in 1987; Lorimar Production Company cancelled SATV's access to *Knots Landing* and a couple of other series, while the stars of *Cagney and Lacey* expressed their political disaffection by donating their South African earnings to the ANC.

Although the period from the early sixties to 1987 was nominally the era of the comprehensive boycott, anti-apartheid forces tacitly recognized that they could never aspire to place South Africa in total cultural quarantine. Equity's blocking of South African access to TV was more the exception than the rule, for cultural boycotters proved less successful in impeding the flow of commodities than in disrupting the traffic in performers. Some artists vocally opposed to apartheid gained easy exemption from the ban: the theatrical trio of Athol Fugard, John Kani, and Winston Ntshona, for instance, continued to put on plays like *Sizwe Bansi is Dead* and *The Island* in New York, New Haven, London, and Edinburgh. On balance, exemptions were more frequently conferred on South African artists traveling abroad than on foreigners seeking to perform inside the country.

In its blanket phase, the boycott did enjoy a certain tactical economy. However, the targeting of the ban would have been greatly simplified had there been a significant body of artists advocating apartheid. But white South Africans whose lyrics, fiction, photographic essays, or documentaries actively promoted apartheid values were exceedingly thin on the ground. In contrast to the white sporting fraternity, most artists held liberal or progressive views; few, particularly those courting foreign ties, inclined toward the regime.

White artists across the ideological spectrum, however, benefited from the regime's grossly inequitable distribution of resources. But the ANC, in keeping with its nonracial tenets and with its determination to draw whites into the liberation struggle, refused to use race as the decisive criterion in determining who should be barred from performing abroad. The difficulty of implementing the boycott along racial lines can be illustrated by the case of *Ipi Tombi*. On the surface, this was a black performance: a "traditional musical" celebrating Zulu life in a swirl of song and dance. However, the producer, Bertha Egnos was white and had, as David Coplan observes, "hired African talent at bargain rates, appropriated African performance culture, debased it for sale at a huge profit, claimed it as her own legal property, and prevented her performers from marketing their own talents and resources freely thereafter."[15] Yet the pickets that drove *Ipi Tombi* from Broadway in 1976 were protesting more than rank exploitation. New York anti-apartheid groups rightly adjudged that the show's tone rendered it promotional material for black joie de vivre under apartheid. Indeed, the Johannesburg program for this pseudo, mish-mash of "tribal" exuberance boasted that: "When it goes overseas *Ipi Tombi* may well become South Africa's most valuable export, and the cast our most exciting ambassadors. The commodity it sells is happiness, which surely must compare favorably with the export of our gold and our diamonds."[16]

From the regime's perspective, the timing of this musical emissary's departure for European and North American stages was fortuitous indeed. *Ipi Tombi* paraded throngs of joyous migrant workers and bare-bosomed brides amidst scenes of rustic ease at a time when the Nationalists were assiduously pursuing international recognition for the "homelands" which they had packaged as a system for preserving "authentic" ethnic cultures. Thus the successful picketing of *Ipi Tombi* in New York marked a clear instance where the cultural boycott had ramifications well beyond the sphere of the arts.

Nineteen seventy-six, the year of *Ipi Tombi*'s expulsion from New York, also witnessed the Soweto Revolt. The uprising by black schoolchildren was the highwater mark of a radical turn, during the mid-seventies, away from the demoralization of the previous decade. From 1972 to 1977 the country experienced a level of militancy among newly unionized workers and newly organized students that surpassed anything since the early the sixties.[17] These were the peak years of the influence of Black Consciousness, an ideology most forcefully articulated by Steve Biko. Although Black Consciousness waned somewhat after Biko's death in police custody in 1977 and the banning of eighteen organizations the same year, the movement had a sharp impact on the direction of the cultural boycott. It also anticipated the dilemmas that would dog boycott policy in the 1980s. Biko spoke powerfully of the need to break free from the strangling values and institutions of white culture; black cultural pride and self-affirmation lay at the heart of his political vision.

The sprouting of Black Consciousness groups in the early and mid-70s contrasted with the organizational drought that had blighted the 60s, the decade that had shaped boycott policy. The rise of this new ideology, with its emphasis on engendering cultural pride, afforded culture an unprecedented political centrality. It also marked a shift in strategic emphasis, from censure to affirmation. Could the cultural boycott, a tactic whose genesis had been fundamentally punitive, be reconceived to accommodate a more affirmative political role?

SUN CITY

The anti-apartheid movements abroad were well placed to oppose South African racism but, unlike South Africa's internal democratic movement, they did not bear a double responsibility. For in addition to white-anting the supports of a racist society, the internal forces had to lay the institutional foundations for an alternative South Africa. The emergence of two vast umbrella organizations—the United Democratic Front and the Congress of South African Trade Unions—marked a major advance in this direction. Within a year of its inception in 1983, the UDF had six hundred affiliate organizations with an aggregate membership of two million.[18] COSATU, founded two years later, brought nearly half a million workers into a single federation.[19] Between them, the UDF and COSATU became the principal bearers of the decade's radical democratic impulse. Both bodies adhered to nonracialism rather than to the separatist tenets of a declining Black Consciousness. However, many UDF and COSATU leaders had first entered politics in the Biko era and selectively carried forward

Black Consciousness precepts in adjusted form. Among these was the conviction that cultural organizations should be given their political due, by recognizing their potential for nurturing an alternative ethos.[20]

By 1985, the pitch of the resistance inside South Africa had helped rally international support for anti-apartheid boycotts on an unprecedented scale. In quick succession, two projects masterminded by American musicians, Little Steven Van Zandt's *Sun City* album and video and Paul Simon's *Graceland* tour, expanded popular awareness of the cultural boycott, ensuring that hundreds of millions worldwide were exposed to the issues at stake. Of all the arts, only music in an MTV age commanded the power to deliver such audiences.

The impact of these musical events cannot be apprehended in isolation: *Sun City* and *Graceland* emerged out of tectonic changes in the resistance to apartheid at home and abroad. Thatcher's ascent to power in 1979, and Reagan's the following year, had profoundly altered the political line on apartheid in Britain and the U.S.A. Reagan's advocacy of "constructive engagement" with the Botha regime gave an urgent, contrastive clarity to the message of those who had long maintained that only cultural and economic disengagement from South Africa would bring constructive results.

The UN Special Committee Against Apartheid seized the initiative in this polarized climate by issuing a list of entertainers who had breached the ban on performing in South Africa.[21] The ensuing adverse publicity persuaded droves of artists to support the ban in exchange for the deletion of their names from the register. The roll call of those who agreed never to return for an apartheid performance is impressively eclectic: Tina Turner, Elton John, Liza Minelli, Julio Iglesias, George Benson, Chicago, Barry Manilow, David Essex, Nana Mouskouri, Max Bygraves, Kenny Rogers, Shirley Bassey, and Rod Stewart. Even Frank Sinatra, having initially insisted on his right to play anywhere, eventually submitted to the pressure.[22] The UN register helped narrow to a trickle the cataract of performers that had poured into Sun City.

In 1985 and 1986, Artists United Against Apartheid in the U.S.A. and an allied body in Britain launched an even more damaging assault on Sun City.[23] The two organizations garnered support from a lustrous array of stars as well as from every corner of the industry—performers, producers, promoters, D.J.s, and songwriters. Sun City's publicists had duped many performers into playing in Bophuthatswana on the grounds that apartheid's pleasure dome was located not in South Africa but in a neighboring state; perhaps, from afar, artists couldn't be expected to tell their Bophuthatswanas from their Botswanas. However, with the appearance of the *Sun City* album and video from Artists United Against Apartheid in 1985, naivete ceased to be an excuse. This musical sortie against apartheid, involving fifty-four artists from six continents, became the unequivocal success story of the boycott: it upped the decibels of the anti-apartheid movement, blasting Sun City—the Las Vegas of the bantustan system—clear off the performance circuit.[24]

As Reebee Garofalo has argued, mega-events like *Sun City*

> involve the creation of a variety of cultural products—live performances, worldwide broadcasts, ensemble recordings, compilation LPs, home videos, and/or *The Making of...*documentaries—each of which can be produced and consumed in a variety of ways. It is now literally possible for hundreds of millions of people to "attend" the same concert simultaneously, be it at the "live" event, at a public broadcast, or in the privacy of their own living rooms.[25]

Audio and video recordings can be put to work in classrooms and community organizations. "A feedback loop is thus completed, as the consumption of the original event is used in the service of producing another."[26]

Sun City shared these proliferating forms of reinforcement with other contemporaneous mega events like *Live Aid, Band Aid, Farm Aid*, and *We Are The World*. However, *Sun City* differed from the others by calling not just for charity but for political action.[27] Moreover, it was not a one-off appeal but an integral facet of an already wide and well-established international campaign. Most importantly, *Sun City* connected the cultural boycott to the divestment movement that was surging across American campuses and plugged both into MTV culture.

This wider political impulse was evident from the album cover that provided rudimentary information about apartheid. The backup teaching guide became a signal success; schools across North America and Europe adopted the guide and the video.[28] The timing of the *Sun City* intervention proved critical, for reporting on South Africa had begun to wane as a result of Botha's 1985 ban on coverage of political uprisings. When the country's rulers had demonized the camera as an "insurrectionary instrument," the response of most mainstream American media had been prostrate and unimaginative; by contrast, the *Sun City* video and documentary helped keep alive images of state repression and popular revolt.[29]

THE *GRACELAND* CONTROVERSY

I have suggested that in the mid-80s both the UDF and the unions put a premium on "people's culture" and worked sedulously to foster alternative institutions answerable to grassroots needs. Ironically, the strengthening of these popular organizations posed the greatest threat yet to the cultural boycott in its blanket form. Because the ban was the brainchild of a defensive, reactive era, protest, not affirmation, was its metier. Thus the gains made by grassroots cultural groups in the mid-80s raised, with compounded urgency, the question first voiced in the Biko era. Could the boycott be converted from an obstructive to a constructive force?

The prospect of such a strategic shift raised tormenting problems, not least the difficulty of reconciling the tactical priorities of the internal and international resistance. This dilemma was brought to a head by the acrimonious *Graceland* affair. Paul Simon's nascent enthusiasm for South African music was prompted in the early 1980s by the Zulu a capella group, Ladysmith Black Mambazo and by a mystery tape—no label, no credits, no song titles—that a friend had passed on to him.[30] In February 1985, Simon travelled to Johannesburg and, together with Ladysmith Black Mambazo, the "mystery" group Juluka, and several others bands, recorded the bulk of what would become *Graceland*.

The *Sun City* and *Graceland* albums appeared in quick succession. This only heightened the awkwardness of Simon's project. *Sun City* had enjoyed an imaginative and strategic simplicity: at home and abroad, the casino complex came to incarnate racist profligacy in the midst of bantustan abjection. Alongside this politically translucent campaign, *Graceland* appeared, by contrast, altogether turbid.

At issue was the critical matter of authorization: Simon had sought approval for his visit from neither the ANC nor the UN Special Committee on Apartheid. Without discipline, these groups argued, the boycott would crumble. But the nature of this attack on Simon's venture only quickened differences between overseas and internal activists, above all, between UN bureaucrats and exiled politicians on the one hand and local artists on the other.

International anti-apartheid representatives maintained that Simon's unauthorized venture jeopardized the gains of the Sun City campaign; it blurred the boundaries of the boycott at a time when South Africa was being perceived, with growing clarity, as wholly off-limits. Condemnations—from the UN, the ANC, and anti-apartheid pickets in Europe and the US—rained down upon him. Ironically, Simon had twice refused lucrative offers to play Sun City. Other foreign artists had pocketed their bucks and run, then apologized and been granted official pardons. The *Graceland* project, by contrast, provided work and global visibility for a cluster of South African artists whom Simon paid three times American union rates. It helped reanimate the careers of Miriam Makeba and jazz trumpeter Hugh Masekela, while rocketing Juluka and, above all, Ladysmith Black Mambazo to world renown. Simon himself drew no income directly from the tour, as the proceeds were divided between the South African musicians and a fund to support children in detention.

For his initial visit to Johannesburg, Simon had achieved clearance of a sort—from the South African musicians who voted in favor of him coming.[31] He later garnered support for the tour from both African-American impresarios like Belafonte and Quincey Jones and anti-apartheid leaders like Desmond Tutu and Alan Boesak. Charges that Simon had fleeced South African artists came overwhelmingly from abroad not within: some foreign protesters traduced *Graceland* as if it were an exercise in exploitation of the order of *Ipi Tombi*.[32] By contrast, the mercurial South African guitarist, Ray Phiri, lauded *Graceland* as "the best thing that ever happened to South African music"; for Ladysmith Black Mambazo it became "our gateway to the world."[33]

But it was Masekela, a stalwart of the North American and European anti-apartheid scene, who emerged as the most vocal champion of *Graceland*. The terms in which he defended the album and tour—as an iconoclastic "development project for artists"—ramified well beyond the Simon affair, challenging both the priorities of the boycott and dutiful notions of what counts as political art.[34]

Masekela's choice of phrase suggested an emerging rift between foreign activists tactically obsessed with punishing the regime and internal activists who advocated showcasing the creative forces of black culture, enabling South Africans to project themselves as more than anonymous, pitiful victims. While the isolationist and affirmative impulses were not mutually exclusive, it was proving increasingly difficult to maintain an equilibrium between them.

Besides accusations that Simon had flouted the boycott and exploited black musicians, a third charge was leveled against him: that the *Graceland* lyrics were not expressly anti-apartheid. Simon's response was simple and impenitent: "my strength is not political writing."[35] However, many activists overseas found his attitude jarring; it seemed out of kilter with the musical mood of anti-apartheid militancy that prevailed in the mid-80s, a period that delivered Special AKA's "Free Nelson Mandela," Stevie Wonder's "Apartheid is Wrong," Peter Gabriel's "Biko," Labi Siffre's "So Strong," Youssou N'Dour's "Nelson Mandela," Sonny Okosuns's "Fire in Soweto," Nona Hendryx's "Winds of Change," "Sweat" by Sweat, Alpheus Blondy's "Apartheid is Nazism," Little Steven's "Pretoria," Miles Davis's "Tutu" and "Full Nelson," Peter, Paul and Mary's "No Easy Walk to Freedom," Mighty Sparrow's "Invade South Africa," Captain Blackburn's "Free South Africa," and a succession of other rousing protests.

But Masekela, for one, insisted that it would be a mistake to limit music to a declamatory role in the struggle.[36] He argued that the creativity of Duke Ellington, Count Basie, and Miles Davis had given the world access to the emotional texture of African Americans' experience through music that was not directly about racism. Masekela's contention was borne out by the fact that, throughout the *Graceland* world tour, Ladysmith Black Mambazo emerged as the most luminous and popular performers. The ten-man *a capella* choir sang mainly in what, from a Philadelphia or London standpoint, was inaccessible Zulu. Nor could their lyrics be classified as protests against apartheid. Joseph Shabalala, the group's songwriter and lead singer—and an ordained Pentecostal minister—insisted that he knew "nothing of politics."[37]

Yet Ladysmith's soaring harmonies gave the anti-apartheid movement abroad a dimension and a resonance it had previously lacked. The group brought to life, in all its anguish and majesty, a Zulu choral tradition that grew out of the travails of migrant workers exiled to the mines. To judge from their lyrics, Ladysmith Black Mambazo shied away from politics; yet their wrenching performances on tour released, as no protests could, a visceral sense of creative powers wrought from pain.

The concern that anti-apartheid typecasting might shrink the spectrum of South African music finds its literary equivalent in Njabulo Ndebele's lapidary essay, "Against Pamphleteering the Future."[38] Ndebele avers that the urgency of South Africa's political conflict compounds the temptation to reduce language to "a purely manipulative function."[39] He cautions writers to resist such reductive pressures and to ensure that no element of the life of the oppressed is dismissed as artistically off-limits.[40] In short, while slogans may be of assistance for mobilization, they cannot substitute for aesthetic forms—be they literary or musical—that offer a more demanding and flexible social understanding.

THE SELECTIVE BOYCOTT

One cannot grasp the tensions exposed by the *Graceland* affair without appreciating that the cultural boycott was a strategy fundamentally shaped by and for the climate of the 1960s, that most desperate of decades in the annals of the South African resistance. The state's clampdown had left alternative organizations within the country shattered, the remnants driven underground, into jail, or exile. Given the dearth of strong alternative cultural bodies inside South Africa, the cultural boycott had come to be controlled from abroad—by the exiled leadership of the liberation movement in league with the UN and the various national anti-apartheid movements that were emerging around the world. Thus through its formative era, the cultural boycott had taken shape as an essentially punitive tactic implemented from overseas.

The *Graceland* imbroglio, however, helped instigate a profound shift in the terms of the boycott. That it did so was partly a matter of timing, for it brought to the surface tensions that had been mounting during the mid-80s recrudescence of the culture of resistance. By the time the *Graceland* furor erupted in 1986, some local artists—increasingly assured and better organized—expressed disquiet at policy pronouncements descending on them *ex cathedra* from abroad.

In 1987, shortly after the *Graceland* tour, a conference of South African artists was convened in Amsterdam. The event signalled a decisive turn in the boycott's destiny. As the title intimated, "Culture in Another South Africa" had a prospective focus, concentrating as a matter of urgency on the values and institutions to be advanced in place of those promulgated by the apartheid order. Many of the three hundred participating artists maintained that world isolation of apartheid had to be complemented by international exposure to the creative energies of those South African artists who were giving imaginative form to an alternative order. In Amsterdam, the artists wrested three fundamental concessions from the politicians: the boycott would henceforth be applied selectively; there would be greater consultation with internal forces; and artists—as opposed to exiled party bureaucrats and foreign sympathisers— would assume a new centrality in the shaping of boycott policy.

Not everyone was happy with this outcome. In Amsterdam and at a UN conference convened in Athens the following year, "purists" called for the cessation of all ties with South Africa. Seasoned international campaigners warned the ANC that it risked fine-tuning the boycott right off the dial. British anti-apartheid leader, Mike Terry, urged the ANC to weigh the advantages of international cultural exposure against the dangers of international tactical confusion. He feared a domino effect: the collapse of the larger anti-apartheid campaign if the cultural ban were perceived to be caving in.[41] Stan Martin, of the British Musicians Union, warned that "boycotts are a rather crude weapon— once you start to make them sophisticated, you might as well forget it."[42] American solidarity groups argued that "to advocate a flexible boycott is like being half pregnant. There either is or there isn't a boycott."[43]

The mass appeal of the international anti-apartheid campaign had indeed relied on strategic simplicity, depending on a stark, almost timeless anti-racism. However, as Paul Gilroy has warned in the British context, "it may be easier to talk about racism than about black emancipation."[44] Solidarity groups overseas risked becoming trapped in a tactical time-warp and perhaps impeding the advance of a self-empowering culture within South Africa.[45] Thus, by 1987, the predominance of anti-racism in the international movement had threatened to become an encumbrance.

If the selective boycott proved more accommodating than its iron-cast predecessor, its plasticity created fresh difficulties of definition and adjudication. Who was to be exempt and on what grounds? In some official pronouncements "the culture of the oppressed" would be excluded from the boycott, in others, "alternative culture;" the first was by implication racially delimited, the second was not. The UN Special Committee Against Apartheid issued new directives, but these compounded the confusion. For they defined the boycott as targeting "those artists and musicians who represent the apartheid system."[46] As scarcely any artists represented apartheid, such guidelines, if implemented, would have nullified the boycott entirely.

Barbara Masekela, the ANC's Secretary for Culture, explained that "anti-apartheid culture produced in South Africa must be seen and heard world-wide." "Anti-apartheid," she added, "refers to those who have lent their talent to support the struggle, and who are recognized as the representatives of the genuine South African culture in the making by their compatriots."[47] But such explications resolved little. Given the ANC's insistence that such "representatives" could be black or white, and need not be ANC or Mass Democratic Movement members, the progressive cultural organizations were left facing a welter of individual judgment calls.

It quickly became evident that, despite its desirability in other regards, a selective ban would require more, not less, administering. The Mass Democratic Movement experimented with a succession of strategies, some byzantine, for vetting insiders wanting out and outsiders wanting in. The most notorious of these tactics was the ominously named, wisely abandoned "cultural desk" which foundered on the classic ills of bureaucratic life: party politicking, accusations of cronyism and caprice, a brittle insistence on protocol, and artists' exasperation at the slow hand that bears the rubber stamp.

Ironically, it was the easing of the boycott that brought the charge of censorship to the fore. Shortly after the "desk's" instigation in 1988, journalist Sefako Nyaka warned that people who had long fought state censorship were bridling at being censored by the Mass Democratic Movement.[48] The style of the "desk" was notoriously high-handed, the atmosphere inquisitorial; in its brief life, it became a resented embodiment of the predilection for trying to promulgate (in the words of one artist) "culture by decree."[49]

THE DISSOLUTION OF THE BOYCOTT

In 1989 and '90 a succession of writers appealed for the cultural ban to be rescinded. Such calls had long been issued from liberal, mainly white quarters, principally on the grounds that the boycott hampered creativity; what differed this time were the origins and motives of the appeal. Achmat Dangor, Junaid Ahmed, Mike van Graan and Frank Meintjies were all not only writers but organizational linchpins with impressive credentials in the anti-apartheid campaign.

Dangor suggested that the selective boycott had become a "blunt instrument" in a period of political struggle that required sharper initiatives.[50] Meintjies, a former publicity officer of the Congress of South African Trade Unions, maintained that in the political atmosphere of a transitional South Africa, the boycott that had once helped foster local culture risked stunting its growth. He urged activists to move away from a prophylactic toward an innovative mentality that might help shape the cultural institutions of the new order.[51]

In a joint paper issued in November 1990, Mike Van Graan and Junaid Ahmed, general secretary of the Congress of South African Writers—an organization representing 1600 authors, 80 percent of them black—called for the boycott's instant repeal. Ahmed and Van Graan maintained that tactics which had formerly worked under the State of Emergency had grown counterproductive.[52] They expressed concern, moreover, that progressive organizations might seem more preoccupied with censoring culture than with promoting it. Ahmed and Van Graan further argued that the preparation for democracy required that the left jettison mouldy tactics: "The Pretoria government is beginning to win increasing sympathy at home and abroad. The rules of the game and the nature of the struggle have changed significantly. The progressive movement can no longer rely for support on grounds of its former status as victim...."[53]

Ahmed and van Graan voiced particular concern that many alternative cultural bodies had "had their genesis in the need to monitor and implement the cultural boycott."[54] They feared that the legacy of these beginnings might be a reactive mentality that would hamper inventive, prospective creativity. As James Wood later observed, South Africa's future dispensation risked inheriting a milieu "crawling with advisers and committees and activists and 'cultural desks' and cultural workers, all of them producing a mound of prescriptive ash which may yet entirely obliterate a real creative culture."[55]

Some of the boycott's critics feared that if the movement continued to preoccupy itself with disabling the regime rather than attending to the more exacting business of preparing people for rule, South Africa would suffer a version of the Zimbabwean scenario.[56] Since independence in 1980, black Zimbabweans have found themselves so short of the necessary skills, experience, and financing that they have had little success in wresting art galleries, museums, publishing houses, and record companies from white control.

A year after the unbanning of the ANC and Nelson Mandela's release, not just outspoken writers but a crescendo of voices from across the arts chorused that the cultural boycott had outlived its usefulness. The progressive, nonracial South African Musicians' Alliance pressed for the ban to be lifted, a position echoed by many in the Congress of South African Writers. Growing numbers of writers and musicians felt that an obstructionist mentality risked becoming the boycott's most debilitating legacy. Yet unanimity remained elusive, and the increasingly porous boycott retained the ANC's official support.

In the four years since the boycott had gone selective, the trickle of artists crossing the country's borders had swollen considerably. While the ANC temporized in 1991 over the boycott's fate, the first Zairean band ever to play South Africa, Lubumbashi Stars, were performing to great acclaim in downtown Johannesburg. The reopening of the musical channels between South Africa and the continent sparked particularly excited debate, for the boycott had previously insured that even popular bands like the Bhundu Boys and Thomas Mapfumo from neighboring Zimbabwe had neither the permission nor the inclination to play in South Africa.

Nor were restless, anticipatory contacts restricted to music. During the closing months of the selective ban, COSAW invited Arthur Miller to Johannesburg for a spirited forum on literature and political responsibility; he was soon to be followed by Edward Said, Angela Davis, Sterling Plumpp, Alice Walker, and others. A shift toward positive tactics had become evident: for example, Walker, who had previously barred the sale of her books under apartheid, now allocated local royalties to a development program for women writers.[57]

CONCLUSION

By 1991, the principal challenge facing progressive forces with a demonstrable genius for opposing, negating, obstructing, resisting, and subverting, was how to devise regenerative and persuasive new policies. Crisp slogans like "Total Isolation" and "Free Nelson Mandela" had receded into the past. In the new mudfight for power, there was all the difference in the world between adhering to firm principles and clinging to ossified ones.

The categorical trade-off—that the cultural boycott remain until apartheid had ended—was becoming counter-productive. To end the boycott entailed less a recantation of past strategies than a recognition that what was once timely had grown superannuated. The ANC required fresh, creative tactics to wrest the initiative from de Klerk in an effort to shape the prevailing values of the democracy to come. There was a widespread recognition that the preparatory impulse was now more pressing than the punitive one; a recognition, too, that cultural values, unlike flags, cannot be hoisted or lowered on the stroke of midnight.

Energy expended on gatekeeping an unenforceable and increasingly ineffectual ban was sorely needed in more affirmative spheres of cultural activity. An erstwhile asset was becoming an encumbrance: progressive forces had either to administer the boycott's retirement or they would be embarrassed into admitting, ex post facto, its effective demise. Under pressure on myriad fronts, the cultural boycott was finally, at the end of 1991, repealed.

The strategic disarray of the boycott's final phase should not distract from its achievements—mostly under malign conditions that saw artists censored, detained, banned, imprisoned, tortured, driven into exile, and, on occasion, shot. While the cultural boycott may never have tormented the white establishment with the full force of the sports ban or economic sanctions, it did exert some significant subsidiary pressure. It helped, among other things, unsettle the country's oppressive cultural orthodoxies by assaulting the pretensions to normality of what was known, with chilling euphemism, as "the South African way of life." Some whites were pried loose from the institutions that had secured their privilege and shaped their crimped image of culture. Above all, activism around the boycott gave rise to nonracial organizations that were more fully grounded in the values and cultural priorities of the country's majority. In short, the boycott emerged as more than a strategy for driving apartheid society deeper into the laager of isolation there to be devoured by its own paranoias; for it became, in the process, an instrument of profound redefinition.

Njabulo Ndebele has spoken of "the challenge to free the entire social imagination of the oppressed from the laws of perception that have characterized apartheid society."[58] Whether this daunting ambition is realised will depend largely on the alacrity with which the circuits of knowledge are rendered more democratic. This, in turn, will require the swift reallocation of resources in a manner that deracializes the conditions of creativity. In all these areas, the impress of the boycott years will be felt, though whether negatively or positively remains as yet uncertain. The risk looms of conflict between artists, finally disencumbered of the pressures of apartheid, who fear asphyxiation by committee, and incoming politicians who, keen to secure their hegemony in every sphere, treat creativity as a kind of boycott in reverse, to be coordinated through high-toned party political directives.

However, at its best, the boycott did leave an alternative, inspirational legacy, one that could well prevail in the future. It exhorted people who had felt cowed by the very word culture to take command of their circumstances and amplified their understanding of their powers. It thereby imbued many black artists, in particular, with an expanded sense of agency. The boycott invigorated writers, sculptors, actors, photographers, and musicians who strove to counter the cultural malnutrition endured through decades of education for servitude. It emerged as an essential force in the wider drive, as Meintjies put it, to "decolonize our minds of passivity and fear."[59]

part three

SOUTH AFRICAN
CULTURE AND THE
AFTERMATH OF THE
COLD WAR

7

MANDELA, MESSIANISM, AND THE MEDIA

We're so troubled by racial conflict in New York that we desperately need some kind of Messiah.

—Rashida Ismaili on welcoming Nelson Mandela to the city, June 1990

He stands somewhere between earth and heaven, beyond the criteria reserved for politicians.

—European Community diplomat on Mandela, June 1993

FROM THE OUTSET, the South African state seemed to fear that Mandela possessed a talent for immortality. On trial for sabotage in 1964 and clearly aimed toward the gallows, Mandela had, through the force of his own defense, turned accuser into accused and successfully skipped the grave. The state countered by treating him as someone who threatened to become not just larger, but longer than life. The prison identity card that was pinned to his person read: "Nelson Mandela. Crime—sabotage. Sentence—life plus five years," as if those posthumous five years, like the stone rolled against the gospel tomb, could secure apartheid against the prospect of his resurrection.[1]

Mandela first won his reputation for uncanny powers of survival in 1961, when he vanished from public life and taunted the state by organizing bold underground actions. He traveled inside South Africa disguised as a chauffeur and popped up abroad under the name David Motsamayi on an Ethiopian passport granted him by Emperor Haile Selassie. For his elusiveness, the press dubbed Mandela the Black Pimpernel.[2] After seventeen months underground he was finally captured and put on trial.

At the time, I was a child growing up in the ANC stronghold of Port Elizabeth. I recall how within days of Mandela's arrest, the walls of the public library, government offices, and township shacks were daubed with the words FREE MANDELA, the first signs of what would become across the globe, the most durable of political graffiti. Nearly three decades later, on 11 February 1990, the world's newspapers would reverse that slogan in a gesture of momentous simplicity: MANDELA FREE.

Nadine Gordimer once observed of Mandela that "his people have never revered him as a figure of the past, but as the personification of the future."[3] During his years of incarceration, his relation to time, however, was even more ambiguous than that. Between 1964 and 1990 he was absented from the political present, yet remained a preeminent inhabitant of South Africa's past and future. He lived on the cusp of time, embodying a people's hope, yet monumentalized on a scale ordinarily reserved for the dead.

During his twenty-seven and a half years of imprisoned fame, Mandela accrued a reputation of near-Messianic dimensions. There were several reasons for this: the redoubtable convictions of the man himself; the scale and inventiveness of the international tributes enacted in his name; the peculiar progress of his relation to the media; and the sweeping power in South African history of the idiom and psychology of redemptive politics—replete with deliverance from bondage, covenants, chosen people, divine election, promised lands, apocalypse, chiliasm, and all manner of eschatology.

While these conditions accentuated the redemptive vision of Mandela, we should keep in view the man's efforts to repudiate the idolatry of Messianic politics which can ultimately invite autocracy. From the instant of his release, Mandela strove to dismantle the cult of personality constructed by the media and to subordinate his prestige to that of the ANC. We should concern ourselves therefore both with the cultural production of the Messianic Mandela and with the limitations of redemptive politics.

By the time he gained his liberty, Mandela had acquired an almost posthumous eminence. In 1973, when nuclear physicists made a scientific breakthrough at the University of Leeds, they christened their discovery the Mandela Particle.[4] In Lagos in 1989, Sudanese and Nigerian teams tussled in the final of Africa's premier soccer competition, the Nelson Mandela Cup.[5] When Roxbury and other predominantly African-American neighborhoods sought to secede from Boston, the proposed breakaway city was to have been known as Mandela.[6] On the occasion of his seventieth birthday, 170,000 letters and cards poured in from the Netherlands alone.[7]

Fig. 1: Youths in Soweto celebrate Nelson Mandela's release. (Phillipe Wojazer; Reuwters/Bettman)

Expelled as an undergraduate from South Africa's Fort Hare College for mounting a student protest, Mandela has since assembled, as if in fabulous compensation, honorary degrees from universities in New York, Lesotho, Havana, Zimbabwe, Brussels, Michigan, and Lancaster, and human rights awards from India, Venezuela, Malaysia, Austria, the GDR, West Germany, Spain, Libya, Sudan, and the NAACP.[8]

While locked up and disenfranchised in his native land, Mandela acquired keys and honorary citizenship in Florence, Sydney, Islwyn, Glasgow, Rome, Olympia, Wijnegen, Aberdeen and myriad other places.[9] So many Mandela statues sprang up around the world that, by the time he left prison, he had become a monumental leader in more than the usual dead metaphoric sense.

The protracted Rivonia trial of 1963-64, which saw nine ANC leaders sentenced to life for "sabotage," enabled black South Africans to stage their grievances under the spotlights of the international press. The pitch of the world outcry took the Verwoerd regime by surprise; *the New York Times*, for instance, hailed Mandela and his fellow accused as the new George Washingtons and Ben Franklins.[10] Mandela's jailers assumed that if media visibility opened the door to fame, invisibility would shut it. So they decreed that the man's words, as well as photos, even sketches of him, be whited out. Having acted against the past, they sought to shut down the future, hiding him (for life plus five years) from all cameras and keeping him mute, confident that he would wither from public memory.

Instead, the South African authorities had guaranteed the kind of scarcity that provokes media fascination by setting up a gigantic photo opportunity in reverse. Mandela became an off-camera phenomenon and his silence grew more eloquent than words. By January 1990, international agencies were offering $300,000 for the first shots of him.[11] At that very moment, Mandela, chuckling to himself, found he could saunter anonymously past the rows of zealous photographers who scanned the prison gardens for a long-gone man bearing his name. Once his guards took him shopping in the malls of Cape Town, a city pulsating with rumors of his release, yet he proved as invisible as Bruno Ganz on his angelic tour of Berlin in Wim Wenders's *Wings of Desire*.

So the South African regime helped station the idea of Nelson Mandela on the threshold between the dead and the living, between commemoration and expectation. They also unwittingly sheltered his image from the erosions of time and diversity. The ban on photographing Mandela allowed the same few images to keep circulating in a heraldic fashion perfect for the needs of an international political movement. By the late seventies, the image of Mandela of Robben Island had become such a unifying resource for apartheid's opponents that the regime sought to disencumber itself of its burdensome captive. The state's efforts to wash its hands of Mandela were conducted in the conditional: if he agreed to live abroad, they would release him…if he renounced violence…if he retired to a bantustan…if they could swap him for two Soviet dissidents.[12] Mandela waited. He foresaw that his unconditional moment would arrive. He must have garnered strength from knowing that the patience of captivity—quarrying stone, sewing mailbags, harvesting seaweed, shadowboxing with solitary time—was slowly turning into the patience of power.

De Klerk, according to a former Secret Service officer, believed that he had blundered in the runup to the Namibian elections by barring the guerrilla leader, Sam Nujoma, from entering the country until just a few weeks before polling day.[13] This, in de Klerk's view, had left too little time to demythologize him in the eyes of the populace and had contributed to his electoral triumph. Determined not to repeat this error in South Africa, de Klerk wagered that a long lag between Mandela's release and polling day would scale down the man's dimensions.

A few days before Mandela's fifty-yard walk to freedom, de Klerk issued the first recent photograph of the prisoner. He was conspicuously not alone but stood alongside the South African president—a last-ditch effort at image control that only succeeded in making de Klerk appear a provisional custodian beside the country's de facto leader.

In the myriad American interviews during those first weeks of freedom, Rather, Koppel, Brokaw, Donahue, and all the others could not decide whether Mandela was more intriguing as a maker or a misser of history. His bearing, his diction warped time. He would pluck carefully at the creases of his trousers before taking his seat; "Quite so," was his standard form of agreement. Asked what films he watched, he spoke movingly of Carmen Miranda and Cesar Romero as if their hits had premiered last Saturday around the corner at the Odeon.

Here was an international media colossus who, by 1990 and age 71, had given just one TV interview. Of the same vintage as Reagan, he emerged as a Great Communicator of the opposite sort—a statesman, not a media bite; stirring, in demeanor and rhetoric, memories of the high era of anti-colonialism, of the early Nkrumah and Kenyatta, of Nyerere, Nasser, Gandhi, Nehru, and King. His social manner brought together, in disarming union, the militancy of the populist hero with the civility of a mission school training. He proved brilliantly informed about world events, if evidently ignorant of the Reaganite dicta that facts impede communication and that one should meet a media question with a media answer, never with a conviction backed by ideas. Mandela spoke thoughtfully, unashamed of the pauses, the silences, that escort reflection. All this had the effect of reintroducing him to the world as someone who had leaped boldly across history instead of living through it, giving him a disconnected, time-machine aura.

CANAANITES AND REDEMPTION MYTHS

The week before Mandela's release, an unnamed Afrikaner told Ted Koppel on "Nightline": "We need a Messiah to lead us out of the wilderness. Maybe Nelson Mandela is that man."[14] In the object of his admiration, this may have been startling iconoclasm for an Afrikaner, but we should recognize the deep tradition-alism in the cast of thought.

During the countdown to February 11, "Waiting for Mandela" became a rou-tine headline, reinforcing a very South African preoccupation with imminent time. In their distinctive ways, the nation's black and white cultures have sought obsessively to command the future through metaphors of dawn, birth, and rev-olutionary redemption, or apocalypse and historical closure. For confirmation of this predilection, one need look no further than the titles of prominent works of South African literature: *To Every Birth Its Blood, Promised Land, The Late Bourgeois World, In the Fog at the Season's End, Time of the Butcherbird, Waiting for the Barbarians, Paradise is Closing Down.*

South Africa's is a psycho-political climate that nurtures Messianism. The Exodus narrative and its New Testament analogues have achieved a hold on the imaginings of Afrikaans and African nationalism alike. We are talking about a society in which a former ANC president, Albert Luthuli, could call his autobi-ography *Let My People Go* and an influential Afrikaans novel bears the title *Gelofte Land—Promised Land*.[15]

A few years back, in the pages of *Grand Street*, Edward Said offered a Canaanite reading of Michael Walzer's *Exodus and Revolution*. Where Walzer gleaned from Exodus an uplifting narrative of radical hope, Said found a more tormented story implicated in conquest, exclusion, national self-righteousness, and what he called "moral triumphalism."[16] Relations between apartheid and Exodus bear out Said's skepticism. Afrikaner nationalists have persistently rein-vented their past through the tropes of Exodus politics: in these terms, the 19th century Great Trek inland becomes a flight from Egyptian (aka British) tyrants. The Afrikaans Israelites were sorely tested by their God as they roamed the wilderness before signing a divine covenant that brought them victory over the Zulu Canaanites. To press the contradictions in this narrative, one need only recall that the trekkers' exodus was largely spurred by their outrage at the British abolition, in 1833, of slavery.

The principal exegetical tension between South African readings of the bibli-cal redemption myths lies in the sense, widespread among Afrikaners, that their deliverance occurred in the past, while blacks have tended to invest the same story line with a future force. If, for most South Africans, the sight of Mandela gaining his liberty flung open the gates of the future, the same event prompted far-right wingers to gather in Pretoria's Church Square and excoriate de Klerk for his betrayal of history. In their midst, they placed a small white coffin for the Afrikaans children killed in the civil war. They draped the coffin in a neo-Nazi flag, then scattered on top thirty pieces of silver.

The black nationalist rendition of the Exodus story is more accommodating of democratic aspirations. Revived in recent years by Desmond Tutu among others, it stresses how Moses will triumph over pharaoh and free blacks from the yoke of slavery, foregrounding liberation while avoiding the bigotry of divine election.[17] Nor is this version populated with Canaanites waiting to be vanquished. However, even this more benign application of the redemption myth builds on a disturbing prototype for nationalist leadership: that of the autocratic, solitary, prophetic figure who commands from on high, in short, precisely the kind of one-nation, one-leader model that Mandela has cited as a hindrance to democracy.

The allure of redemption myths in situations of advanced tyranny has been heightened in South Africa by the ruling Nationalists' relentless Antichristing of the Mandela name and the ANC. He was, they broadcast, a "known" terrorist and a minion of the godless Muscovites. At one point, the Special Branch burst into the house of his wife, Winnie, to arrest a bedspread quilted in the ANC's black, green, and gold.[18] In 1985, President P.W. Botha maintained that the state persisted in detaining Mandela for the same reason that the Allied powers had held Rudolf Hess.[19] Nobel Prize winner, Wole Soyinka, for one, drew inspiration from Botha's remark. A poem in his *Mandela's Earth* opens this way:

> Got you! Trust the Israelis
> I bet they flushed him out, raced him down
> from Auschwitz to Durban, and Robben Island.
> Mandela? Mandel...Mendel...Mengel...Mengele!
> It's he! Nazi superman in sneaky blackface![20]

THE MANTLE AND THE MAN

The major document of ANC principles, the 1955 Freedom Charter, declares that "our struggle is a struggle of memory against forgetting."[21] All these years, Mandela had been the trump card for the forces of remembrance. For the ANC, his reemergence was to be an exhilarating yet testing moment. The unbanning of the organization on 2 February 1990 and the release of Walter Sisulu et al. had produced a convergence of three branches of leadership with quite dissimilar experience and credentials: the exiled members (headed by Oliver Tambo), the ex-prisoners, and the leaders of sympathetic organizations prominent in the internal struggle, especially the United Democratic Front, the Congress of South African Trade Unions, and the Mass Democratic Movement. Matters might be further complicated by the ANC's ideological inclusiveness: its coalition embraced African nationalists, socialists, communists, and social democrats. Clearly, in releasing Mandela, the regime sought among other things to try the ANC's community of purpose.

At that point, Mandela's legendary repute remained the ANC's best resource. Yet if, after February 11, the cult of personality grew unchecked, it might equally turn into a liability. Frantz Fanon's *Wretched of the Earth* offers an uncanny anticipatory gloss on the dangers of Mandelamania. (The book first appeared in 1961, just months before Mandela embarked on his clandestine tour of newly and imminently independent African nations, where he was hosted by such Messianic figures as Ben Bella, Senghor, Kaunda, Nyerere, Selassie, and Nkrumah). Fanon saw with great prescience the pitfalls of emblematic leadership in Africa's era of independence.[22] He observed how under white domination the people had internalized an impoverished sense of their own potential. By investing hope and power in a single exceptional figure, each new order risked not only erecting an autocratic future, but extending, among the general populace, the stagnant attitude that they were bereft of political influence. The fledgling state ought rather, Fanon averred, to convince its citizens "that there is no such thing as a demiurge, that there is no famous man who will take the responsibility for everything, but that the demiurge is the people themselves and the magic hands are finally only the hands of the people."[23]

During Mandela's first public speech after his release—before a Cape Town crowd of perhaps one hundred thousand—it became evident that he, better than anyone, intuited the strategic necessity of deconsecrating himself. To do so would help reaffirm his democratic commitments and check the surging expectations coming from an impatient, overextended people. However, in forswearing demiurgic powers, Mandela had nonetheless to preserve enough prominence to keep South Africa in the media's eye and to maintain pressure on de Klerk, who clearly hoped the prisoner's mystique would tarnish in the open air. Mandela's first speech, therefore, would be a delicate affair to manage.

For the international media, February 11 developed into a day of waiting. Mandela's emergence from Victor Verster Prison had been delayed an hour-and-a-quarter, and he arrived several hours late for the speech on Cape Town's Grand Parade. These expanses of waiting tried the readiness of TV commentators—both South African and American in their distinctive ways—to transcend their unease about the ANC. South Africa's state-controlled network, accustomed to the certainties of stiff censorship, betrayed some initial difficulty feeling out the limits to its suddenly expanded license. The quandary of SATV's commentator was unenviable: he had to ensure that the event of Mandela's release redounded to the government's credit, while avoiding direct reflection on the person of Mandela, his qualities, or the injustice of his suffering. At one point, not fully able to keep the superlatives at bay, he resorted to praising Victor Verster as "the most beautiful prison in the world"—a serious case of displaced eulogy. Nonetheless, SATV coverage inadvertently paid homage to Mandela's stubborn foresight when it had a young anchorman, one Hendrik Verwoerd, break the news of his release. Twenty-six years earlier another Hendrik Verwoerd, the anchor's grandfather and the mastermind of apartheid, had vilified Mandela as a bloodthirsty communist and secured his imprisonment.

During the same drawn-out wait on Cape Town's Parade, one American channel's commentary team flew the colors of a distinctively U.S. paranoia. To while away the hours, they had been discussing activities on the City Hall balcony, which was to be Mandela's podium and from whence the anti-apartheid clerics, Rev. Frank Chicane and Rev. Allan Boesak, had been urging patience on a sweltering, raucous crowd. At one point, the consolingly familiar figure of Boesak descended into the gathering to persist in his efforts; in his absence a group unrecognizable to the Americans ascended to the balcony which they proceeded to bedeck in a South African Communist Party flag. Panic broke out in the commentary box. To judge from the blur of eruptions—"This is getting out of control, the balcony has been taken over by the radicals"—the quite predictable prominence of the SACP had startled the commentators, who seemed persuaded that a godless Red coup had intervened between Boesak's disappearance and Mandela's arrival.[24] Only when it became apparent that this was merely one among an array of symbolic gestures did the commentators repair their damaged equanimity and continue the job of rendering events accessible to their American viewers.

When Mandela finally arrived, the occasion turned into an oddly unmediated, un-American political event. Rather than using the crowd as a decoy for an address, via satellite, to the world, Mandela appeared indifferent to the cameras while speaking directly to those bodily present, as if spellbound, just hours out of solitude, by such physical evidence of his reunion with the mass of humanity. His oratorical style and the crowd's spirit brought to mind a rally from a pre-tech era. Mandela's public manner had been shaped by the live politics of the 50s, two decades before South Africa got television, and in an era when his pro-democracy speeches were too radical for the state-run radio. If their leader seemed above the pressures of media packaging, a sizeable proportion of his audience, even in 1990, would not have possessed TVs. And the minority who did would have mistrusted its fierce censorship of the news.

Mandela launched his first live speech in almost three decades by taking direct issue with the redemptive conception of him. "I stand before you," he declared, "not as a prophet, but as a humble servant of you, the people."[25] In casting off the lonely mantle of the prophet, he democratized responsibility for the future and subordinated his powers to popular authority. For much of that benchmark speech he was at pains to remind his audience that he was not an elected leader of the ANC and that, in any case, only "disciplined mass action," not individual genius, could assume the task of unifying the country. It is typical of the man that his appeal for collective responsibility harmonized the idiom of parliamentary democracy with the more radical register of Comrade Mandela, "loyal and disciplined member of the African National Congress," as he repeatedly portrayed himself.[26]

Fig. 2: Mandelamobile, New York, June 1990. (© 1990 David Vita, Impact Visuals)

But the surest index of his deference to grass-roots power was edited out of the press transcripts the next day. Early in his speech, Mandela launched into a roll of honor, commending by name the many organizations—women's groups, trade unions, community groups, guerrilla wings, popular fronts, the alternative press, anti-conscription organizations and so forth—that had brought the struggle to this pass. Few of them were known outside South Africa. It was a very African moment—full of the measured salutations and respect that reanimate community belonging. If the litany of thanks made for opaque international TV, it was a moment of constructive parochialism, a vital move toward promoting an alternative to the one-nation, one-leader brand of Messianic politics. In those ten minutes of greetings, Mandela walked away from the media trope of him as a one-man shadow government running the show from his fax machine in Victor Verster.

Any prisoner fashioned into marble and granite must face, on release, the excessive strain of reconciling the epic self with the person who reenters public

life. Yet this could not, in Mandela's case, involve a pristine transition from public myth to private man. In the glare of the media, control over his identity
would remain contested ground. "Dignified" became, on the American networks, the most overtaxed and abused adjective of the week. Some of it could be
put down to sigh-of-relief syndrome (no revolutionary fangs were showing).
The rest arose, in a twisted kind of way, from racial bigotry. Would reporters
have fussed with such boundless amazement over the dignity of a European or
American politician—Mitterand, say, or Bush—as if they had been expecting, all
along, Idi Amin to come crashing in?

Mandela's American interviewers clung to the spectacle of his heroism as a
martyr for the cause. Dan Rather: "What was the worst thing that happened to
you in prison?" "Did they beat you?" "Real bad?" "What was the best thing that
happened to you in prison?" Koppel, less clunkily, but to similar effect, asked:
"How does it feel to know you are one of the most admired men in the world?"

Mandela answered civilly, though sometimes with discomfort at the call to
strut with talk-show egotism. More than humility was at stake. He comes from
a society whose rulers had detained, over the previous five years, some fifty thousand activists. Organization after organization had had its leadership skimmed.
Under such conditions, to concentrate power, talent, and hope in a prestigious
few was simply to invite beheading. Trade unions grew faster in South Africa
during the second half of the 1980s than anywhere else on earth; this success,
together with that of the Mass Democratic Movement, depended on lateral
styles of organization that allowed resistance to regenerate itself, phoenix-like, ad
infinitum. This tactic was not without South African precedent: in 1953 a beleaguered ANC adopted a proposal to regroup into a complex lattice of street-based
cells. The strategy was code-named the M (for Mandela) Plan.[27] It is thus consistent with the genesis of Mandela's democratic vision that he would use his
media prominence to augment the struggle, but recoil on principle from glam-
or politics, an ill-starred approach, if ever there was one, to the pursuit of
democracy under apartheid.

NIGHTLINE MAKES HISTORY

There had been an American twist to Mandela's capture twenty-seven years, six
months, and six days before his release: a CIA agent had apparently alerted the
South Africans as to the whereabouts of their most wanted fugitive.[28] There was
an American involvement of a different sort in the days leading up to 4:16 PM,
Sunday 11 February 1990 for the networks were out in force. If the individual,
spectacular image of Mandela walking free threatened to usurp the gains of less
telegenic collective processes of social transformation, the American coverage
of the occasion sometimes jostled to make itself the primary story.

During the countdown to the release, ABC advertized Ted Koppel's series from Johannesburg as "Nightline' Makes History"—a description not without its possibilities, but, coming from ABC's mouth, little more than an ambush on historical agency. The Koppel series culminated in a "Town Hall Meeting" which brought together a spectrum of leading South Africans ranging from the far right Conservative Party's Koos van der Merwe and the Nationalists' Stoffel van der Merwe to Helen Suzman (doyenne of white parliamentary liberalism), a representative of Inkatha's youth wing, the UDF's Allan Boesak, and, beamed in by satellite from Lusaka, the ANC's Thabo Mbeki.

Koppel allowed the first hour to become wholly dominated by banter and polite needling between himself and the two van der Merwes. It was only during the second half, broadcast between 12:30 and 1:30 AM Eastern time (by which hour many viewers would have switched off), that probing questions from the audience finally put the regime's representative on the spot. That initial show-down between the Far Right and the right wing government might have been choreographed by President de Klerk himself, so perfectly did it accord with his efforts to abandon the growling, finger-wagging, menacing public demeanors of his two predecessors, P.W. (Crocodile) Botha and John Vorster, in favor of a pol-icy of conscientious charm. Alongside the uncompromising Koos (who, after a protracted bout of circusry, left for breakfast to protest the ANC presence on the program), the Nationalist Stoffel van der Merwe could project himself as a beacon of reasonableness and moderation.

This new readiness of the Nationalist leaders to jettison the body language of "total onslaught" as they strove to mimic the media manners of American politicians, exerted extra pressure on the emergent Mandela. For Koppel's Town Hall Meeting and allied coverage enabled the regime to showcase itself as fairly bursting with liberalish goodwill, asking for little more than the ANC's renunciation of violence and a bill of minority rights, instantly recog-nizable American-style issues, which of course figure quite differently in the two societies.

HERO HUNGER AND AMERICAN MESSIANISM

Within a day of Mandela's emergence from Victor Verster, African American and ANC leaders were hatching plans for an American tour. Mandela journeyed to the U.S.A. four months later, taking eight cities in eleven days by storm. The venture was devised primarily to caution the Bush administration, city and state governments against repealing sanctions, to campaign for funds, to raise the profile of the ANC, and to enhance the organization's leverage in its imminent negotiations with apartheid's *ancien régime.*

To secure these ambitions, Mandela had to engage with the Messianic traditions of black American culture without being subsumed by them; he had also to accommodate himself to the hyping impulses—the mythologizing and the merchandizing—in American culture at large. Indeed, the thunderous success of the tour resulted largely from Mandela's acute brinkmanship, above all, from his determination to use his mythic aura to cast light on the inspirational power of historical precedent. Through his commitment to remembrance and naming, Mandela ensured that he became a hero not of isolation but of continuation. He thereby broke with the American idiom of the schlock of the new—the insistently self-made, one-of-a-kind celebrity.

Mandela was the first African and only the third private citizen ever invited to address Congress. Afforded an opportunity that black American leaders had been denied, he enunciated, alongside the record and aspirations of South Africa's oppressed, a lineage of American heroes and martyrs whose names seldom echo in Congress: "We could not have heard of and admired John Brown, Sojourner Truth, Frederick Douglass, W.E.B. DuBois, Marcus Garvey, Martin Luther King, Jr. and others—we could not have heard of these and not be moved to act as they were moved to act."[29] In commemorating such figures in the same breath as Washington, Lincoln, and Jefferson, Mandela applied the weight of his own prestige to help reconceive the prevailing hierarchies of American history. So, too, before a predominantly white crowd in Boston, Mandela paid homage to that city both as the birthplace of the American independence struggle and as the site where a black man, Crispus Attucks, had sacrificed his life for the revolutionary cause.[30]

From his first day on American soil, Mandela found himself represented simultaneously as a visitor from the historical past, a guardian of future hopes, and a redeemer of mythic dimensions. David Dinkins likened Mandela to King before introducing him to New Yorkers as "a Modern day Moses leading the people of South Africa out of enslavement at the hands of the Pharaoh."[31] At an interfaith service in Riverside Church, Jesse Jackson implored that "as dramatically as the Red Sea opened, ...let the walls of apartheid come tumbling down."[32] The Messianism invested in Mandela's person was accentuated by the widespread sense that his arrival coincided with a particularly demoralized, leaderless juncture in black Americans' collective history. Figures as diverse as Harry Belafonte, Dizzy Gillespie, Roger Wilkins, and former Black Panther, Dhoruba Bin Wahad, voiced the sentiment that Mandela had stepped into an imaginative and emotional breach in the African-American community, giving direction and hope to an aimless, unled people.

In contrasting Mandela with the empty careerism of today's "cardboard celebrities," Wilkins and others cast him as an embodiment of politics as principle.[33] As one anonymous fan in D.C. put it:

> To have a living brother who is fine, upstanding, and straightforward in a
> time when many of our leaders are selling out, to see a brother who is actu-
> ally standing by his principles in the face of the President and the media,
> is to make us all very, very proud. Nelson Mandela seems almost like the
> one we've been waiting for.[34]

The stress here on a "living brother" goes to the heart of Mandela's African
American appeal. Throughout his tour, Mandela found himself relentlessly
likened to those dead brothers, King and Malcolm X, who represented an
extinguished style of leadership—resonant, defiant, and self-sacrificial.
Unlike say, Jesse Jackson, Mandela was not a would-be inheritor of King or
Malcolm's mantle. He stood, after all, not as their successor but as their contemporary. He had delivered his great speech from the dock a couple of
months prior to King's "I Have a Dream," and had disappeared from this
world before either man was assassinated, only to reemerge a living martyr
who embodied the spirit of those dead ones. Here was a voice from the past
that was also a voice on the ascendant.

Mandela's power to incarnate hope through remembrance achieved its most
forceful expression when he traveled to Atlanta to lay a wreath at King's tomb.
His moment before the crypt captured, in ceremonial form, the dynamic bonds
between the two men and the struggles they represented. Nor did it escape some
onlookers that that very week South African journalists had uncovered a plot
on Mandela's life.

Throughout the tour, Mandela insisted on carrying forward the memories of
both King and Malcolm, rather than upholding one at the cost of the other. He
spoke of black pride, but a pride that had to be reconciled with the principle of
nonracialism. Mandela began his address at Georgia Tech Stadium with the
words "I have a Dream"; shortly thereafter he embraced Betty Shabaz on stage.
When, at King's tomb, a journalist pressed him into taking sides—did his presence there mean that he embraced nonviolence?—Mandela responded that
King's was an honorable but circumstantial ideal. After decades of nonviolent
protest, the ANC had been compelled to counter the massacring of its people
by taking up arms. (In a 1964 radio interview, one recalls, Malcolm X had
argued that Mandela's and the ANC's recent turn to violence testified to the
untenability of King's nonviolent strategies).[35]

Mandela chose to launch his American tour in Bedford Stuyvesant, the
nation's largest black community. From his invocation of Marvyn Gaye to his
appearance alongside Rosa Parks and Smokin' Joe Frazier, the journey offered an
inspiring testament to the binding possibilities in black culture and politics.
Over the course of his travels, Mandela was careful to cast the relationship
between black South Africans and black Americans as reciprocal rather than

one of unilateral debt. When *Ebony* magazine asked him "To what extent has the freedom struggle of American Blacks influenced the [South African] freedom struggle and your own struggle?" Mandela answered with a polite but determined rephrasing: "You are correct, there are many similarities between us. We have learned a great deal from each other."[36]

If the most intense moments of the tour were animated by this sense of half-shared history, Mandela did not become a local hero for African-Americans alone. His presence magnetized the three quarters of a million people who lined the streets of New York, as well as stadium-sized audiences in Detroit, Atlanta, Oakland, Los Angeles, Boston, and D.C. From George Bush and Mario Cuomo to Ted Koppel and Dan Rather, eminent white Americans sought a piece of his reflected glory. "It's a nice feeling for people to talk of you as a hero," Mandela expostulated, "but this is not really directed at me. I am a peg on which to hang all the aspirations of the African National Congress." "I'm sorry if I am seen as a demigod....I submit to the collective leadership of the ANC."[37] Faced with the combined pressures of American individualism and African-American Messianism, Mandela was hard pressed to deflect attention from himself toward the organization that he represented. In the American context at least, the ANC was destined to linger in the shadow of Mandela's fame. But he did enjoy the satisfaction of witnessing tens of thousands of Americans waving ANC flags in one sports stadium after another, and of seeing the Empire State Building lit up in the ANC's black, green, and gold. Moreover, his monumental popularity abroad helped fortify Congress, strategically and financially, for its tough negotiations with the de Klerk administration.

CONCLUSION

Pretoriastroika—the thawing of apartheid—has begun its irreversible course, but the process remains beset by traumatic uncertainties. Already, however, it is clear that many of the rhetorical verities of the struggle have come to feel the pressure of the expectation of power. While scarcely straightforward, the endlessly oppositional task of rendering the country ungovernable was less taxing than the need to produce the kind of practical policy minutiae necessary for the ANC to govern. Its routine position on the nationalization of key mines and industries, for instance, has been subject to unprecedently animated debate over the need to redress inequality while reviving economic growth. The question of how to integrate the diverse command structures of the struggle—the exiled leaders, the Robben Islanders, key UDF and COSATU figures, and, most recently, Bantustan leaders who have converted to the ANC—proved difficult to resolve. The team compiled by the ANC to enter the opening "talks about talks" with the government was unevenly weighted: nine of its eleven delegates were over sixty years old. The group's composition held little reassurance for the youth and trade unionists, constituencies widely yet guardedly supportive of the ANC and reluctant to see their militant legacies bartered cheaply away.

The organization faces the unenviable task of weaving its way through the impacted language of resistance, negotiation, participation, compromise, collaboration, co-option, and plain selling out. Each term in this spectrum possesses its own bloody history. One of the UDF's most resilient slogans was, after all, "Long Live the Spirit of No Compromise"; the ANC sought to revise (without quite reversing) the slogan through a massive campaign of T-shirts and bumper stickers declaring "Negotiations Are Struggle."

The risk remains that the gulf may widen between the spectacular sphere of media politics, where Mandela and de Klerk loom large, and an obscured Lilliputian realm of mass politics. As the euphoria of release has dissipated and the easing of oppression has allowed long-buried differences within the liberation movement to surface in debate and feuding, Mandela has found himself hard pressed to sustain an aura as a national politician equal to his international prestige as elder statesman. Indubitably, of the two, his internal authority will continue to come under greater pressure as South Africa enters the tunnel at the end of the light.

Despite these threats, however, I would hesitate to join those purists who reduce the media concentration on Mandela to an unambiguous betrayal of grassroots social processes. Mandela's planetary visibility continues to engage people who would otherwise struggle to identify with and involve themselves in a far-off, faceless cause, however estimable. For instance, the crucial call to the European parliament to preserve sanctions gathered unique credibility from having Mandela issue it in person.

While Mandela's tremendous media presence has cemented ANC support internationally, the Congress's considerable domestic authority has proven more difficult to stabilize, not least because any organization banned for three decades needs time to establish itself, root and branch, at the local level. Even here, Mandela's prestige has improved the chances of easing grim divisions, for the PAC and Inkatha, bitter rivals of the ANC, have both shown greater respect for the man than for the organization he represents. Apartheid's success, however incomplete, in fostering a reactionary stripe of Zulu ethno-nationalism has left a divisive force at least as fearful as the Afrikaner nationalism that helped nurture it in the first place. Indeed, the timing, tone, and outcome of Mandela's rapprochement with Inkatha's Buthelezi should prove his most nerve-wracking challenge, given the pitch of popular loathing that Buthelezi elicits, especially from the radical youth and unions, who have suffered most at his hands. In these matters, so much depends on how the ANC deploys the time which

Mandela's lingering allure has bought them. In the months immediately following the unbannings and his release, the organization too often seemed caught off guard, retreating into reactive or rhetorical stances, poor substitutes for new initiatives.

The prospect remains that, in the aftermath of South Africa's first democratic elections, Mandela may be saddled with inhuman expectations which, being mortal in a deeply riven country, he cannot be asked to fulfil. There were shades of this in his effort, soon after his emergence, to stem the bloodshed in Natal—ranked in 1990-91 as the most violent spot in the world. Mandela urged all parties to hurl their *pangas* into the sea. But nothing happened—a response that exposed the limitations of individual appeals, no matter how charismatic, unsupported by resourceful policies.[38]

Winnie Mandela once recalled how living with Nelson she had to shelter her "extinct ego" from his towering authority: "You just fizzled into being his appendage, with no name and no individuality except Mandela's; Mandela's wife, Mandela's child, Mandela's niece."[39] As with Winnie so too, in a sense, with the ANC, for whom appendage politics has sometimes proved a debilitating side effect of the net asset of Mandela's gifted presence. Any organization wedded to one of the century's most commanding figures risks vanishing beneath the long shadow of his apostrophe.

The most remarkable development in South Africa during the 1980s was the deepening of the country's traditions of radical democratic process through the organizing efforts of bodies supportive of the ANC: the UDF, the Congress of South African Trade Unions, and the Mass Democratic Movement. It is therefore quite wrongheaded for Conor Cruise O'Brien to cast Mandela as a one-man Burkean buffer standing between the awfulness of the massing black Jacobins and the destruction of all prospects for democracy. O'Brien would have us believe that Mandela is hated and feared by the grass-roots left, which is peopled by "instinctively totalitarian minds."[40] There are indeed elements within the ANC who are bereft of democratic instincts. Yet one need neither trivialize the difficulties of ushering in democracy nor deny the tinderbox atmosphere in South Africa to recognize O'Brien's extravagant opposition between Mandela and the rest as profoundly false. More to the point is whether the returning ANC exiles build on or bypass—and thereby risk both squandering and frustrating—the structures of local democratic experience erected during the long years of embattled resistance. Against conceptions of the post apartheid order as a prefabricated edifice to be imposed from above or crated in from abroad, such indigenous traditions remain the country's principal, if vulnerable, resource of hope. With them, too, lies the hope that the anti-apartheid resistance will gain fortitude and publicity from Mandela's fame while warding off the alternative disposition, prevalent in the society and exacerbated by the media, toward a vision of the man as South Africa's anointed redeemer.

8

AN EVERYBODY CLAIM DEM DEMOCRATIC
Multiculturalism and the *New* South Africa

> An everybody claim dem democratic/but some a wolf an some a sheep/an dat is problematic/noh tings like dat yu woulda call dialectic?/…Kaydar/e ad to go/Zhikov/e ad to go/Honicka/e ad to go/Cauchescu/e ad to go/just like apartied soon gaan.
>
> —Linton Kwesi Johnson, "Me Revalueshanary Fren"

IN JANUARY 1991, Gordon van der Merwe, the Johannesburg editor of a magazine for military conscripts, shot his daughter, son, and wife in their sleep before turning the gun on himself. The incident was just one in a spate of killings misleadingly dubbed Afrikaans "family suicides." What distinguished this one was the lucidity of the man's motives. In a note tossed over the garden wall, his neighbor read the next morning that van der Merwe had followed this desperate course because he saw no future for himself or his family in "the New South Africa."[1]

Lesego Rampolokeng is a sensational young performer whose work fuses the traditions of Jamaican dub, American rap, and Sotho oral poetry. Had he been in the United States during the Gulf War, he might have rallied behind the protesters' ubiquitous incantation: "the New World Order has an Old World Odor."

For Rampolokeng dismisses the local variant of that new order as "New South Africa theatrics:" "To me, it's cobwebbed—there's absolutely nothing new about it."[2] Moreover, it has provoked great confusion: "Ask writers what they are going to write about—they don't know. Before, there was a clearcut line."[3]

Internationally, the onset of fin-de-millennium fever seems marked less by fantasies of apocalyptic consummation than by a passion for abandonment, a desire to be rid of the past. The 90s ring with announcements of a New World Order, a New Germany, a New Man, New Age thinking, and, in Britain, New Times. Nineteen ninety-three saw the creation of a New Europe and ritual "rediscoveries" of the New World. This deluge of the "New" has been further swollen by a flood of "posts." The terms postmodern and postcolonial throng the air; we hear, too, of post-Marxist, postfeminist, post-Cold War, postindustrial, post-Fordist, and postnuclear. We have seen, in addition, a profusion of big endings, most notoriously Fukayama's unapocalyptic end of history, neither quite banging nor whimpering.

Discourse about South Africa in the early 90s resonated with all these obsessive forms of the beyond: the New South Africa, the postapartheid era, the end of apartheid. Yet, with each phrase (and not only in the South African instance), excitement at some recognition of change was cast in terms that failed to do justice to the continuities.

On the sense of an ending so much depends. So many trade-offs, so many returns have hung on the conditional "only when apartheid has ended." In the minds of many, that will be the moment to lift sanctions and boycotts and to invite South Africa back into the community of nations. Among those dispossessed by apartheid and among their supporters abroad, many have looked to apartheid's death as the occasion when freedom will become official. One thinks, for instance, of "Art contre/against Apartheid," a traveling exhibition of work by eighty-five artists and sculptors established in Paris in 1983. The collection was conceived as "the basis of a future museum against apartheid," as a prospective institution destined to circulate in exile. But the organizers decreed that this nomadic exhibition would only come to rest in South Africa with the abolition of apartheid.[4]

However, other exiled institutions were quick to wend their way home. The International Aid and Defense Fund, the most durable and influential of foreign antiapartheid organizations, was unbanned by de Klrek in February 1990 along with the ANC. In June 1991, IDAF closed its London headquarters and dispatched its resources to the University of the Western Cape in Cape Town.[5] The move, while not exactly constituting recognition that apartheid had ended, at least signalled that one phase of the struggle was over.

Significantly, the IDAF material will provide the foundations for a Museum of

Apartheid. The University of the Western Cape is an imaginative, progressive institution that would not stage a kind of Chamber of Horrors without also dramatizing a history of the resistance. What intrigues me, however, is the timing of the sudden obsession, across the country, with collecting apartheid memorabilia, given that museums often serve to force a division between past and present.

By late 1990, images of despairing curators rummaging through garbage heaps for formal signs of apartheid dotted the pages of South Africa's conservative and neoliberal press. In interviews, museum personnel complained that just months after de Klerk had repealed the Separate Amenities Act, the pandemic signs partitioning municipal landscapes—Whites Only, Blacks Only,

Fig. 1: Turning apartheid into dust? Coco Zuzile chisels away at the surface signs of discrimination. (AP/Wide World Photos)

Malays Only, Coloureds Only, No Blacks Allowed—had vanished without a trace. Many such signs, one suspects, had been seized by the far right as inspirational reminders of a past to be restored; others had doubtless been destroyed by black South Africans who bore their psychological weals. Yet, in the press, the metaphoric implication of the etherized signs was unmistakable: apartheid had gone beyond the dustbin of history and had already passed through the incinerator.

One wishes the equation were so easy: that white supremacy could be curated into a realm of pure memory, and that the disappearance of public signs and the appearance of apartheid retro could together amount to the advent of a postapartheid era. The questions raised are huge and tormenting. What is the relationship between passing signs and lingering effects? How are we to seize the opportunities offered by this phase of the struggle, without, through our actions, giving off the suggestion that apartheid is dead? Such questions are of particular import for determining boycott policy and the pace of negotiations.

For Gordon van der Merwe, the New South Africa had already travelled too far, too fast; for Lesego Rampolokeng, it had produced a different kind of betrayal, a rush of chimerical changes. But in government and business circles there was no hesitation in capitalizing on the phrase. South African Airways, for one, blitzed European and North American newspapers with full-page ads that exhorted "Be There as the Sun Rises Over the New South Africa....The Sun Has Never Shone Brighter in South Africa Than It Is Shining Now."[6]

Among the neoliberal set who dominate the South African media, the New South Africa was considered in 1991 less a threat or a hollow promise than a largely achieved reality which, after the long years of revolutionary talk, seemed less disruptive, less unpleasant than they had imagined. And so, at Jan Smuts airport on the way in, I could pick up a copy of South African *Cosmo*, whose editors thrilled to the example of their model of the month. Glossy blonde Claire, they bugled, "sparkles with the spirit of the New South Africa—she's everything the New South Africa is meant to be—pretty, positive, and down-to-earth."[7]

The New South Africa: de Klerk himself coined the phrase that soon circulated with abandon. The occasion of its rhetorical birth was the celebrated speech of 2 February 1990, in which de Klerk hailed "the end of apartheid," unbanned the ANC and other resistance organizations, announced Mandela's imminent release, and promised the repeal of apartheid laws, thereby wresting the initiative from both his left and right wing adversaries.[8] The speech was accompanied by a widely distributed document entitled "A Manifesto for the New South Africa." Nothing then suggested that the New South Africa would become de Klerk's best-known coinage and an indispensable asset in the astute marketing of his regime as converts to decency and penitence, in a campaign that saw an instinct for political survival passed off as a species of righteousness. The regime's success in persuading Western media and governments that the NSA was becoming a virtual reality exacerbated their waning interest in the persistence of apartheid.

Soon after Mandela's triumphal parade through the streets of New York in June 1990, coverage of South Africa began to fall away dramatically in a manner more to the National Party's than to the ANC's advantage. Attention shifted elsewhere: to German unification, the disarray in the Soviet Union and Eastern Europe, the Gulf Crisis, the war, and the Kurdish exodus. South Africa was reduced to a two-note tune: the Winnie Mandela trial and the carnage wreaked by Inkatha-ANC feuding. Neither story redounded to the ANC's credit.

Amid the mayhem, the ANC leadership—still scrambling to organize itself after three decades of outlaw status—proved indecisive and lackluster. As is typically the case when revolutionary movements are confronted by their newfound legitimacy, a quick transformation was hampered by the Congress's tendency to confer senior positions on stalwarts of the struggle. More precisely, it initially favored veterans from exile or Robben Island over the local, generally younger figures who had developed profound community and institutional links through their leadership of the UDF, the Mass Democratic Movement, and COSATU under the States of Emergency. The ANC missed an early chance to integrate these considerable resources in a manner that would have extended the democratic impetus of the previous era.

In a country where over 40 percent lack jobs, the lumpen bands of unemployed and unemployable youths who throng every township do not always await directives from a leadership engaged in seesawing rhetorical exchanges about preconditions for endlessly postponed talks. Millions of militants, youths above all, had envisioned history delivering not a nuanced, drawn out *indaba* but something more spectacularly decisive, something closer, in Aime Cesaire's phrase, to a "rendezvous of victory."[9] Hence the ANC found itself facing the steep battle of exhorting its constituency to abandon a traditionally dramatic image of apartheid's decease while offering little immediate evidence that a change of tack would bring rewards. It soon became clear that civil war remained a fearful possibility, while revolution, in any form beneficial to the ANC, did not. However, if the lost youth felt themselves pushed beyond the margins of hope, and if nothing seemed forthcoming other than intensified Inkatha violence and a laboriously negotiated set of political adjustments, there was a danger that they would be tempted to invoke the seasoned register of revolution and fall back on their proficiency in the arts of disruption.

By late 1990, the raging violence had already given the lie, on a daily basis, to all the brouhaha about the arrival of a New South Africa. In the tribunals of the media, the complexity of the violence was being judged in simple terms. Sometimes a prefatory concession was included to the effect that the inequities of apartheid were the deep cause. But the coverage focused principally on the inability of the ANC to rein in its supporters and on the fierce divisions among blacks—an extension of the "black-on-black" reportage that took hold in the 80s.

As the anticipated winners of any election, the ANC soon became vulnerable to a version of their own past tactics. Inkatha, with the collusion of state security forces, have sought to discredit the projected government by rendering the situation ungovernable. The sometimes collaborative efforts of the regime and Inkatha to demonstrate that the ANC is unfit to govern have been conducted locally in the Transvaal townships and rural Natal as well as on the international front. That much became manifest when, in May 1991, the South African consul general in Norway, Willem Bosman, arranged, hosted, and bankrolled a Scandinavian tour for Inkatha central committee member Musa Myeni, who pronounced in Oslo: "Apartheid is dead. Today we are suffering under an emerging African National Congress dictatorship, backed by communists all over the world."[10]

Had they been successful, such tactics would effectively have produced a coup in advance of elections. Unfortunately, much of the media coverage of South Africa played along with this presumptive strategy, reporting the ANC's failure to curb the violence as if the Congress were already the ruling party. Yet the ANC commanded none of the institutions of state power. de Klerk, the man to whom the police and the military remained officially answerable, had his international reputation boosted by the violence—at least for the first two years after the ANC's unbanning. He was frequently painted as a lighthouse of moderation amid a sea of black homicidal intolerance. Yet month after month, the role of the police proved catastrophic. Their actions ranged from those of *agents provocateurs*—the so-called Third Force—to the age-old apartheid ploy of providing armed cover and logistical support for Inkatha. When not helping kindle the strife, the police often adopted a laissez faire approach to it, implicating them in a form of culpable strategic indolence.

TRADITIONAL CULTURAL WEAPONS

Nothing smacked more soundly of the Old South African way than de Klerk's protracted refusal to disarm Inkatha supporters. It was decreed that their spears, clubs, knives, machetes, battle-axes, and ultimately their guns did not constitute instruments of war, but were to be respected as "traditional cultural weapons." The language of distinctive ethnonationalist entities that guaranteed Inkatha its arms was not the brave new rhetoric of a post-apartheid South Africa but a revamped version of the language of Verwoerdian social engineering that produced the Hydra-headed bantustans. As Natal journalist, Khaba Mkhize, remarked, "only in South Africa is the emphasis so obsessively placed on race and skin colour that even weapons are categorised according to their culture. Assegais, knobkerries, pangas and bolted sticks are referred to by the South African Police as 'Zulu cultural weapons.' Yet an AK 47 has never been described as a 'Euro-Asian weapon.'"[11]

De Klerk demanded that the ANC renounce (as opposed to merely suspend-ing) its armed struggle, while permitting Inkatha members to take up weapons and assume battle formations. Both the ANC and the Inkatha Freedom Party are political parties, yet they have been judged by different criteria. The ANC, as a transethnic organization, has been denied all the perks of laying claim to a distinguishing ethnocultural lineage; Inkatha, on the other hand, has been treat-ed as if it were the guardian embodiment of Zulu cultural tradition. Thus Inkatha alone has been able to shelter behind arguments based on the sanctity of a past which has putatively bequeathed a unitary, unbroken culture.

This one-sided prerogative would have been less destabilizing were it not that the male warrior has been enshrined as the definitive icon of Zuluness and (through cooption) of Inkathaness. The strategic construction of an indissociable ethnicity and a culture of militancy has allowed Inkatha's lead-ers a reversible line of argument unavailable to rival organizations. Buthelezi, King Goodwill Zwelethini, and other Inkatha eminents routinely deflect political criticism of Inkatha's violence with a cultural retort about Zulu iden-tity. Thus Buthelezi can define his party's weaponry as purely "a sign and a token of the militancy of this ethnic group to defend its cultural and ethnic identity. They are a tool of self-identification and a reminder of their ethnic roots and history. Their primary purpose is not to cause injury to others."[12] And King Goodwill can dismiss "the call to ban the bearing of cultural weapons by Zulus [as] an insult to my manhood. It is an insult to the man-hood of every Zulu man."[13] Inkatha's insistence on framing the debate in terms of an ethnically specific culture of manliness occludes the central issues: the warriors' role in advancing party political power and in creating a semblance of "inter-ethnic" strife.

When, after several years of controversy, the regime eventually did outlaw "cultural weapons" it became instantly clear that the ban would not seal the cultural loophole. The very next day, Inkatha members, armed to the teeth, marched in protest; asked why they hadn't shut down the march, police responded that it had been no more than a cultural occasion. Once again, Inkatha's allies could invoke the reversible logic of violent provocation as an ethnic-cultural attribute.

Inkatha effectively claims not just the right to display specific weapons—the *de rigeur* knobkerries, shields, and sticks—but more sinisterly, to go about armed as an expression of a putatively innate warrior temperament that enjoys the imprimatur of history. Thus at Inkatha "cultural events" Buthelezi's men may brandish such prize exhibits of authenticity as ski-poles, hockey sticks, guns, and automobile parts torn from the junk heap.[14] (In a less lethal tinkering with the idea of tradition, some of Inkatha's lesser chiefs have taken to wearing cost-effective fake leopard skins).[15]

Those who decry the breaching of tradition frequently seek, through their protestations, to alter popular conceptions of what comprises "traditional culture"—and to do so in a manner that redounds to their political advantage.[16] That is, the most radical breaks with the past are often executed through invocations of the past. In Tom Nairn's shrewd metaphor, such enlistments of the past are Janus-faced—an insight that Shula Marks has profitably brought to bear on Natal history.[17] Buthelezi's political methods epitomize such inventive defensiveness: he has not shielded the "traditional" past against the deformations of modernity, but modernized his power base under cover of the retailored loincloths of the premodern.

Attempts to fob off Inkatha's blood-stained arsenal as the ornaments of pure

Fig. 2: Mangosuthu Buthelezi (center) leads 10,000 Inkatha members through Durban in October 1992 to protest a newly imposed ban on 'traditional cultural weapons.' Marchers flouted the ban, waving spears, clubs and sticks as police watched but did not intervene. (AP/Wide World Photos)

Zuluness are merely the latest update of a century-old effort by South Africa's rulers to invent and reinvent Zulu traditions to white hegemonic advantage.[18] This process has inevitably involved the uneven cooperation of a thin class stratum of Zulus. The collusion between whites who romanticize Zulu "nobility" and a reactionary Zulu ethnonationalism sank to a sorry new low on 26 May 1990 when, having completed his address to forty thousand subjects in Soweto, King Goodwill Zwelithini requested John Aspinall to deliver his bellicose exhortation. This crank British casino owner, zoo-keeper, devotee of H. Rider Haggard's fiction, and self-designated "white Zulu," brayed that he had come to repay

> the lifelong debt I owe your ancestors for giving me a model of how a life should be lived and also how somebody should die. Some of the other groupings in this country have made it their play to goad and taunt the Zulu nation, relying on their historic courteousness and forbearance…but these groupings now realize they have wakened the Zulu giant.[19]

Courteous, forbearing, restrained, peace-loving, nonviolent—these are the qualities that continue to dominate Inkatha's self-portrait and the image of it advanced by its white allies. Yet according to an independent survey conducted by the Community Agency for Social Enquiry, during the period from 22 July 1990 to 1 May 1991, Inkatha was the aggressor in 60 percent of all violent political conflicts in the Transvaal.[20] (Of the remainder, 18 percent were attributed to the South African Police and Defense Forces and 6 percent to the ANC.) Thus, the de Klerk regime's stance toward the nonviolence took a profoundly hypocritical turn. The ANC, as a nonracial, interethnic political party, could stake no claim to "traditional cultural weapons," yet the Inkatha Freedom Party could march about legitimately armed as if it were less a political party than the apolitical repository of venerable Zulu traditions. And so the aftermath of virtually every Inkatha peace or cultural rally saw killings in the immediate community, ensuring that the violent excesses on all sides continued spiralling upward.

Since the black consciousness era of the seventies, there has been a buoyant tradition on the South African left of contending that "culture is a weapon of struggle," a position most famously argued by Mafika Gwala in his essay, "Writing as a Cultural Weapon."[21] In 1990, Albie Sachs's charge that that particular rallying cry had outlived its usefulness became the center of a heated debate ranging across the arts.[22] But there is all the difference in the world between invoking the metaphor of culture as weaponry in an effort to infuse township theater, performance poetry, or music with a sense of urgent instrumentality, and Inkatha, during a period of supposedly suspended hostilities, rushing through the streets, brandishing literal spears, clubs, and axes in the name of cultural self-expression.

Inkatha's success in bludgeoning its way into the national and international headlines has set a disturbing precedent that could impede the achievement not just of universal suffrage but of stable democracy. As David Beresford warns, "it would be a mistake to confuse electoral support with power. Wars, unfortunately, are not decided at polling stations. With the help of the 'Third Force' Inkatha is far more of a match for the ANC than it would be on the hustings."[23]

Violence is always a media priority, and media priorities tend to affect, unduly, the shape of political agendas. (Coverage of South Africa during the 70s and 80s bore out the lure of bloodshed: the formation of the largest trade union in the country's history, for instance, did not receive equal media attention to the "necklacing" of one person.)

In the case of Inkatha, an organization that would draw, according to most polls, between two and five percent of the vote has managed to disseminate, through violence, the illusion of size.[24] Hence, on the basis of its media prominence, Inkatha is perceived abroad as the country's third significant constituency, whereas polls suggest that the Pan African Congress could pull in several times as many votes. Similarly, Buthelezi's claim to equal standing with Mandela—a man who represents a party with some ten times his following—is a media claim fobbed off as a constituency one.

Evidence suggests that the regime has sometimes encouraged Inkatha to serve as shock troops in a double strategy of urging peace while fomenting black unrest, so that de Klerk, rather than Mandela, could appear as the architect of realism and messenger of hope. The aim has been to fracture the ANC alliance sufficiently for a right-of-center grouping dominated by the Nationalists and Inkatha to acquire a more decisive influence over the future constitution. Even in 1993, when Inkatha began to boycott the ANC- and Nationalist- led negotiations and to court the white far right instead, the Nationalists have stood to gain more than the ANC from Inkatha's stance of non-cooperation.

On no account can the rise of Inkatha be wholly wished away as a state conspiracy. The disruptive power of Buthelezi's relatively small forces and the persistence of the clashes suggest the partial success of the apartheid strategy of divide-and-rule. But they are also indicative of certain limits to the ANC's constituency, particularly in rural Natal and among Zulu migrant workers. That, of course, does not undermine the ANC's unchallenged status as the only party with a majority of votes within its grasp. But those limits should be observed rather than, as sometimes happens, papered over with the argot of pamphlets. Mandela, for instance, remains the most esteemed leader, but speaks with nothing as reductive as the voice of the people. Nor can the ANC be said to express anything as romantically unified as the people's will. To imply otherwise is to court disillusionment.

STRATEGIC DUALISM AND THE TWILIGHT ZONE OF THE *NEW* SOUTH AFRICA

Apartheid's internal opponents, the anti-apartheid movements abroad, and the international media have all, in their different ways, struggled to find their bearings during the half-light of the 90s—neither the long night of apartheid nor the glorious day of liberation. The very success of the resistance in wresting concessions from de Klerk has diluted the sense of a common, mobilizing, unifying trauma, complicating, although scarcely exhausting, the *raison d'etre* for the struggle. Internally, amid a fierce recession, surging unemployment, and the jockeying that accompanies the prospect of power, it has become harder for anti-apartheid forces to keep their ranks cemented against an adversary who is now more equivocally the enemy. That equivocation is, of course, conditional. For the great majority who continue to suffer from apartheid's legacy, the trickle-down from de Klerk's changes and sundry statements of intention have brought almost no immediate advantage.

It is abroad, where media coverage and anti-apartheid activism have both lost impetus, that the neither-nor perception of South Africa has wrought the most damage. De Klerk has achieved remarkable victories in the PR battle to tone down his National Party's previously demonic international image. If, unavoidably, Mandela's performance has seemed somewhat tarnished after the Messianic expectations invested in him, de Klerk has faced the infinitely easier task of only having to appear more reasonable and attractive than predecessors like Hendrik Verwoerd, John Vorster, and P. W. Botha. After 1990, it quickly became apparent that any attempt to equate the superficially user-friendly de Klerk with the snarling, finger wagging Botha (him of "fortress South Africa" and "Total Onslaught") was a bankrupt tactic. And however self-interested de Klerk's motives, it would have been equally poor strategy to treat him as unaltered from the former self who, invoking classic apartheid-speak, had once announced that "the government has no intention of putting each race into a separate compartment. However, we would never accept integration."[25]

Why did de Klerk prove more successful than the ANC at damage control? The answers are numerous. His impeccable timing, for one. Under pressure from the internal resistance and the complementary success of international sanctions and boycotts, de Klerk recognized the moment of Eastern Communism's implosion as the chance for the National Party to be seen to dance to the melody of "democracy around the world," particularly if de Klerk released Mandela as assurance of his government's honorable intentions. Above all, de Klerk succeeded in making an inevitable decision appear like a magnanimous one. He continued, through crisp image management, to promote himself as the paradigmatic New South African. The ANC's ineptitude in the crucial task of moulding public perceptions certainly eased de Klerk's burden. But, in fairness, the ANC's difficulties were exacerbated by their lack of a strong base in the South African media and the rigid forms of public perception they inherited from the previous phase of the struggle.

This last point is crucial. The anti-apartheid cause became one of the epic crusades of this century by passing beyond politics onto a moral plane. By that, I do not mean that it became non-ideological, but that its appeal, particularly in the West, was reliant on invocations of conscience, standards of human decency, and justice. Thus gradually, during the neo-liberal era that followed World War II, apartheid emerged as the human rights issue par excellence. The successful conversion of the anti-apartheid cause into a world movement was in large part proportionate to the Manichean clarity of the issues at stake, as a showdown between good and evil, victims and villains, black and white, oppressed and oppressors, the masses and a racist minority. On a grand scale, apartheid (or the Afrikaner) became the lodestar of iniquity.

Tactical simplifications become inevitable if a social injustice is to be converted into an international cause. But the wager of conducting Occam's razor politics may exact long-term costs. The stark binaries that helped build the international pressures which, in league with domestic resistance, forced de Klerk's hand, have converted into pressures on the ANC. The foreign media and anti-apartheid movements, in particular, have coped poorly with the meltdown of the apparently cast-iron divides between heroism and villainy. The shortfall of explanation in the past means that, at the current juncture, more explanation is required.

Let me ground these comments with an example. In directing *Cry Freedom*, his film about Steve Biko and Donald Woods, Richard Attenborough spoke of trying to expand international awareness of apartheid, of reaching the unconverted, of avoiding the dumping ground of the art house circuit. With this in mind, Attenborough decided to omit the presence of black policemen in his recreation of the Soweto Uprising. His reasoning was that "to have had blacks firing at blacks would have been too confusing, unless the film had taken time to explain how blacks, as well as whites, have been caught up in defending the apartheid system."[26] Attenborough chose, for a practical reason, not to address black cooption as an integral component of white domination But that kind of short cut, repeated myriad times, wears a representational rut. And when events like the township strife and Winnie Mandela's fall no longer fit that morally motivated groove, confusion and disillusion are compounded.

I do not wish to imply that all anti-apartheid coverage or all international activism succumbed to what playwright Barbie Schreiner calls "the Captain Marvel view of the struggle."[27] Nor am I suggesting crudely that the regime was better than people thought or the popular resistance worse. But neither possessed simple, stable, unitary identities, free from contradictions or reducible, without political risk, to abstract good or evil.

The most pressing challenge, of course, has been less how to trace the subtleties in the political dynamics and more how to produce a sufficiently broad national and international front to ensure that a system of brutal legalized racism is eliminated. The other challenge has been how to render those two goals more compatible. For the conventions whereby a campaign has been advanced cannot be erased overnight simply because the political climate has altered. Mobilizing through strategic dualism, however expedient under a State of Emergency, sooner or later leads to costly mistakes on the ground. The current neither-nor status of apartheid—in which it is equally disastrous to strategize as if nothing has changed and as if everything has changed—requires new forms of political attention for which the old binary certitudes are poor preparation.

The lack of preparedness for the crisis of the 1990s has been heightened by the expectations born of dualistic traditions of reportage and mobilization. The mutable, contested diversity of South Africa never could be contained by those impossibly grand units—the people, the masses, the oppressed—however loosely valid and effective that vocabulary proved in applying pressure on the regime. In media terms, the epic moral clarity of the South Africa story was, along with the violence, its cardinal asset. Once the story line defeated such coherence, that former asset became a liability, saddling Mandela's forces with onerous, unrealistic expectations. Two dangers have arisen from this: that the blurring of the divides may give rise to the view that apartheid is over; and that the media may ultimately prove less interested in the fate of South Africa than in the black-and-white of apartheid.

MULTICULTURALISM AND THE *NEW* SOUTH AFRICA

The disturbance of the routine dualisms can be fruitfully considered in relation to the questions of identity and difference that preoccupy much current "postcolonial" theory. Let us take the case of a Sotho woman, a mother and grandmother, a commuting textile worker, a member of a conservative and pacifist African Zionist church, who was forcibly relocated to the Bophuthatswana bantustan and is married to a Tswana policeman. It is preposterous to insist, as an apartheid regime would, that a woman with such complex ties is a "natural" citizen, on biological and marital grounds, of the Bophuthatswana pseudostate. Yet equally, it would be a mistake to assume, in reaction against such imperious categorizing, that her deeply oppressed condition will ensure that she will automatically line up "on the side of the oppressed." For cutting across her suffering under apartheid are the tensions among the multiple, often contradictory sites that shape her identity. Even amid the extremities of the South African strife, individuals possess at best probable, never automatic political profiles. As Nelson Mandela, for one, is aware, constituencies have to be produced; they cannot be relied upon to emerge out of "natural" commitments, particularly during the countdown to a transfer of power. That much is manifest in Mandela's appeal to police to desist from providing cover for Inkatha: "you too," he declared, "can be heroes of the people."[28]

Yet "postcolonial" theorizing about the mutable, hybrid sites of identity and analyses of the South African struggle continue to pass each other like ships in the night. There is an immediate reason for this: talk of contradictory identities, ambivalence, and structured difference can seem luxuriously arcane and effete in the face of the more pressing question of how to overcome tyranny. Yet the two need not be mutually exclusive. Revolution (though not necessarily radical social change) is in decline as a primary frame of reference in South Africa. With this retreat, polar visions of the tangled forces have also lost ground. A recognition that the centers of struggle are more dispersed and mutable than that can only raise the political stakes of understanding the contingent, mobile possibilities contained within identities at every level.

Yet there is another, more formidable reason why talk of difference, diversity, and fragmented identities has percolated very slowly into progressive debate about social transformation. The difficulty is the more daunting for being uniquely South African. Since the late 1950s, difference (as opposed to unity) has been perceived—for sound historical reasons—as a government term. This is so because the South African brand of racial supremacy has been couched as a form of sensitivity to the special needs and cultural particularities of diverse "peoples." An attentiveness to difference is thus perceived as apartheid's business, a way of coating state racism with a democratic gloss.

Americans are often baffled by the steely commitment of key organizations—the ANC, the United Democratic Front, the Mass Democratic Movement, the Congress of South African Trade Unions, and the South African Communist Party—to the term *nonracial* rather than *multiracial* or *multiethnic*, which are the obvious choices from an American standpoint. The South African preference suggests unity through cancellation or transcendence, the American, unity through incorporation. The distinction in approach is symptomatic of a deeply felt need to counter the regime's sedulous accentuation, embellishment, and fabrication of different "nations" for the ends of divide-and-rule. No one who has lived through the rhetorical reinvention of the pariah term "apartheid" as separate development, democratic pluralism, a constellation of nations, multinational democracy, multicameralism, and so forth, can hear "multi-" as anything other than a kiss-of-death prefix.

At one stage, the regime even officially designated black South Africans as "plurals."[29] The hypocrisy of such an equation—that each language and culture indicates a self-defining people or nation that requires a territory to call its own—has, of course, been exposed by the official construction of whiteness, which is premised on a quite contrary formula, one admitting white speakers of Afrikaans, English, Portuguese, Greek, Hebrew, German, Hungarian, and so forth as members of a single cultural-national-territorial unit. On occasion, government spokesmen invoked these incompatible formulae to charge that South Africa was a white-majority country containing a myriad of black minorities. Thus, one cabinet minister maintained:

> As regards all the various nations we have here, the White Nation, the Coloured Nation, the Indian Nation, the various Bantu Nations, something to which we have given too little regard is the fact that numerically the White Nation is superior to all other nations in South Africa....This has a very wide implication for us all....Firstly, it demonstrates the utter folly of saying that a minority government is ruling others in South Africa. ...It demonstrates our duty as guardians.... Our policy is based on...the separateness and diversity of the various Bantu Nations and other nations in South Africa as separate national groups set on separate courses to separate destinies.[30]

This argument, even in the regime's own byzantine terms, fell away once the Zulus alone had outstripped the combined white population.

The contrast with North American traditions of imagining ethnicity helps account for the greater enthusiasm across the Atlantic for teasing out difference, whether in relation to the "melting pot" metaphor of the United States or the Canadian "mosaic." The South African-American contrast is not just academically instructive, for it reveals the problems of cross-cultural translation involved in trying to organize nonreductively against apartheid. The Stanford core curriculum battles that brought the debates on multiculturalism to a head provide a ready example: conservatives argued that multiculturalism's advance as an educational philosophy would replace the mom's-own-brew of melting-pot American nationalism with a smorgasbord of nutritionally-impoverished cultural identities. Thus, multiculturalism in the United States has become associated with liberal or progressive assaults, in the name of democracy, on established institutions of power.

But in South Africa, "multicultural" can only sound profoundly undemocratic, a cue for the denial, not the advancement, of rights. In 1987, South Africa's Minister of Constitutional Development, Chris Heunis, declared, in an utterance typical of the government position, that "South Africa is multicultural, and the constitution must reflect this."[31] His speech was entitled "The Peoples of South Africa: a Kaleidoscope of Cultures." Almost every word brings a shudder, despite the benign similarities of kaleidoscopes to mosaics and Standford-style multiculturalism. More recently, the devious history of "multi-" has been extended by the regime's appeal for a constitution to be drawn up by a multiparty conference as opposed to the ANC's call for a constitution devised by a nationally elected constituent assembly. Under the regime's proposal, "multi-" fronts for a bogus diversity that would deny the ANC, as the largest party, proportionate representation.

The issues of difference and multiculturalism bear directly on popular conceptions of apartheid's end. In South Africa, the language of multiplicity has been the language of false endings. Apartheid is an old hand at presiding over and surviving its own burial by clothing itself in a winding sheet embroidered from a patchwork of differences. In reaction, the resistance organizations have made cohesion a priority through their long decades of disenfranchisement. This goal has been invested with both strategic and symbolic urgency, as a voice of undivided outrage was essential to counter state theories of multiple, discrete black "national" cultures. While practice always fell short of such an ideal, the liberation movement and the popular fronts of the 1980s did produce large enough alliances to bring the nation to the brink of ungovernability and expose to ridicule the logic behind bantustan partitioning.

Yet, faced with the prospect of parliamentary power, no party can produce nuanced policy by reversing the terms of the previous dispensation. The ANC has long possessed detailed, elaborate policies of its own. But, that said, the organization exhibited a palpable tendency toward reactiveness in the early 90s. This was exacerbated, first, by the way a long exclusion from power tends to produce ossified or untested policies, and second, by the ANC's ill luck of having its rising star coincide with the falling reputation of socialism, to which many of its policies were tied.

The ANC and its allies, in moving beyond what had become a semipermanent role of obstructing, negating, boycotting, undoing, and generally making government impossible, are having to reconceive their political role. From being either vilified as terrorists or extolled as liberators of the people, the ANC now has to adjust to less Manichean perceptions of its political character.

Progressive inquiry into the complex, unstable identities of political subjects is of increasing relevance to the strategic challenges and prospects raised by the current historical turn. What is needed is an approach to differences—whether regional, religious, ethnic, gendered, class, generational, or differences of sexual preference—that breaks with smiling multiculturalism and its ugly mirror image, apartheid, by recognizing that inequalities in power slice across the sites of identity. Glorification of diversity per se, without attention to power, is always hazardous. The metaphor "constellation" often serves as a telltale sign of this approach: as if our differences were (to misappropriate George Bush) a thousand points of light all twinkling with perfectly democratic intensity.

POLITICAL BINARIES AND WINNIE'S TRIAL

Of the critical political events since the unbanning of the liberation organizations, the Winnie Mandela trial most dramatically defeats explanation in bald binary terms. In the international media, the legacy of hagiography and political binarism meant that responses swung between two extremes. Most reports were written in a spirit of zealous handrubbing at the sight of the mighty fallen. Justice had won the day and a ruthless woman had been suitably punished. For example, Beresford, the (British) *Guardian*'s ordinarily adroit correspondent in South Africa, argued that "there was a degree of reassurance to be found in watching Winnie Mandela standing to demure attention in the dock yesterday as sentence was handed down on her."[32] And that "the Winnie case has seen the judicial system survive a critical test." The opposing school of reportage portrayed Winnie as a casualty of white justice who, regardless of her actions, had been transported beyond the realm of guilt or innocence by her long history as a target of brutal state harassment.[33]

Both responses are perturbing, the first because it gives credence to the regime's authority to distinguish civic from political trials. The timing of the much-postponed hearing, the efforts to tarnish the Mandela name and the ANC by association, and the provocatively severe sentence were all political calculations. Less obviously, to imply the neutrality of the judicial system is to endorse the view that the New South Africa is already falling into place, that the society possesses a set of civic institutions that can be rendered effective through internal reform. And it suggests that judges appointed by an unelected government can dispense justice by adopting more enlightened attitudes. This is typical of New South African thinking: once the old personnel have changed their minds, little else need change, least of all the institutions of power.

But to counter such implications with a rearguard reverence for Winnie by resurrecting her unproblematically as a martyr is reactive politics at its weakest. Long before she appeared in the dock, Winnie's image had lost the clean iconographic lines of "Mother of the Nation," a figure who stood for the suffering and defiant resilience of all black women. In the townships, she had become an ambiguous, divisive figure, an impressive symbol of militancy to some, while others associated her with autocracy, hubris, nepotism, and "street justice" run amok. The ANC leadership's dissociation of itself from the trial could not have been more pointed. None of the executives served on the Winnie Mandela Support Ad Hoc Committee, and aside from her husband (and briefly, Chris Hani), none of them attended the trial.

The distressing feature of the proceedings was the persistence with which Winnie's defense team, in its efforts to represent Rev. Paul Verryn as a vile and threatening figure, used "child abuser" and "homosexual" synonymously. A banner brandished by a black, middle-aged, working-class woman outside the court captured the spirit of this tactic: "HOMOSEX IS NOT IN BLACK CULTURE."[34] Yet 1990 saw the first moves by the ANC to acknowledge sexual preference as a civil rights issue and also saw blacks and whites parade together through Johannesburg's streets in the country's first gay-pride march. Thus, despite the regressive dimensions to the Winnie case, there are positive signs that liberation politics is moving haltingly but irreversibly beyond Manichean formulations and that a strong ANC will have to recognize difference as a potential resource that cannot be swept aside as divisive.

The growing authority of the campaign for women's rights illustrates this process most explicitly. In a little-publicized event that took place concurrently with Winnie's trial, one thousand delegates of the ANC's Women's League met to elect their executive.[35] Winnie was one of the three candidates for the organization's top position, but it was the other two, Gertrude Shope and Albertina Sisulu, who were voted in as president and deputy president respectively. By opting for figures whose names did not resonate internationally but who possessed firmer track records than Winnie as campaigners for women's rights, the League indicated that it was moving beyond the kind of appendage politics that had seen Winnie appointed controversially in 1990 as the ANC's Head of Social Welfare ahead of other, better-qualified candidates.

When de Klerk first laid out his vision of a New South Africa in February 1990, he spoke freely of the need for reconciliation. To this end, all factions were to put old recriminations behind them. Yet the state's decision to proceed with Winnie's trial while burying other more egregious offenses committed prior to the February speech left de Klerk vulnerable to charges of partisan forgiveness and forgetfulness. One wishes that half the legal and media energy expended on Winnie had been directed at the regime's failure to bring to trial the hitmen employed by the state's assassination unit, the monstrously euphemistic Civil Co-operation Bureau. The CCB was officially disbanded in August 1990, but numerous assassinations in 1991—including those of the anti-Inkatha Zulu Chief Maphumulo and the lawyer Bheki Mlangeni—were linked to it. A former CCB agent has testified that the unsolved killings of a lengthy list of ANC personnel and anti-apartheid activists were all committed by this state-funded body. Among the scores of radical leaders thus assassinated were human rights lawyers, Griffiths and Victoria Mxenge; David Webster, anthropologist and UDF activist; Ruth First, ANC member and writer; Dulcie September, ANC chief representative in France; Anton Lubowski, lawyer; Joe Gqabi, ANC chief representative in Zimbabwe; and Richard Turner, academic.[36] ANC lawyer, Albie Sachs, mangled by a car bomb, is a rare survivor of a CCB assault. The ANC demanded the resignation of Defense Minister Magnus Malan, whose awareness of the CCB had been proven; it also insisted that those behind the death squads be called to account. As the ANC pointed out, "state funds…have been employed to terrorise, intimidate, maim and murder citizens of this country for voicing demands that the government today concedes are legitimate."[37] In select cases like Winnie's, the state showed no qualms about prosecuting a pre-February 1990 crime so as to cleanse the "New" South Africa. But where the crimes were its own, they were treated as occurring on the wrong side of the Old-New divide, and dismissed in a spirit of constructive amnesia.

CONCLUSION

De Klerk's New South Africa has proved part promise, part abomination, and part impacted confusion. The white president's proclamation that apartheid would be buried by June 1991 was indeed supported by a better ratio of action to rhetoric than any of the system's many previous, premature obituaries. Yet his assumption that apartheid could be eliminated prior to negotiations, a constituent assembly, and universal suffrage reinforced the deceptive image of him as a neutral broker already operating in a postapartheid power vacuum. De Klerk's claim to be ushering in a New South Africa rested principally on his repeal of key racist legislation. However, even when the last discriminatory law has been rescinded, we should be wary of confusing necessary with sufficient conditions for apartheid's demise. Laws are not just lifted, they are replaced. And the new Abolition of Racially Based Land Measures Bill—to take just one instance—makes no provision for returning land to blacks who suffered forced removal under apartheid.

Historically, South Africa was singled out as a uniquely offensive society not because of its discriminations, state brutality, injustices, or unequal opportunities, but because it enshrined racism in law. It has thus been all to easy in the early 90s to misconstrue the attenuation of legalized racism as the end of apartheid. If that perception prevails, once the laws have gone, South Africa will slide from the news and join the ranks of the myriad more or less anonymously unjust societies. Without the economic redress and swift institutional transformations that require international support and investment, privilege and dereliction will remain distributed almost entirely along racial lines. If we permit that to happen, the future will hold out little more than flag-independence from apartheid, which will continue to govern the society from the past.

9

THE RETREAT FROM COMMUNISM
AND ANTI-COMMUNISM

Why this sudden bewilderment, this confusion?
(How serious people's faces have become.)
Why are the streets and squares emptying so rapidly,
everyone going home lost in thought?

Because night has fallen and the barbarians haven't come.
And some of our men just in from the border say there are no barbarians
any longer.

Now what's going to happen to us without
barbarians?

They were, those people, a kind of solution.

—C.P. Cavafy, "Waiting for the Barbarians"

We are going to do something terrible to you—we are going to deprive you of
an enemy.

—Soviet envoy, Georgi Arbatov, in a statement to the U.S. Senate, 1988

THE DEMISE OF THE SOVIET UNION has had extraordinary repercussions for
South Africa's transformation. Efforts to dismantle apartheid have been substantially complicated by the depth of the unexpected discrediting of both
communism and anti-communism. Although only a minority among the anti-
apartheid forces are card-carrying communists, the dissolution of the Soviet
Union has weakened the appeal of revolutionary Marxism and to some extent of
socialism, ideologies that have inspired resistance to apartheid for over four
decades. The populist insurrections of 1976-77 and 1984-86, along with the
upsurge of radical trade unionism since the late 70s, appeared to turn South
Africa into a uniquely promising scenario for revolutionary triumph. Indeed,
socialism and revolution became so wedded to the idea of the anti-apartheid
struggle that South Africa emerged as a cause celebre of the left, a central exhib-

it in the broader arguments and campaigns for socialism. As recently as 1986, Paul Sweezy and Harry Magdoff could project a vision of South Africa as "the only country with a well-developed, modern capitalist structure which is not only 'objectively' ripe for revolution but has actually entered a stage of overt and seemingly irreversible revolutionary struggle."[1]

From such a vantage point, the current negotiations in South Africa are both a success and a failure. The revolutionary impetus did prove irreversible in so far as it rendered the country unmanageable, fulfilling the ANC's insurrectionary slogan: "Make apartheid unworkable and the country ungovernable." This helped force the de Klerk regime to submit to measures that contradicted fundamental precepts of National Party rule, not least the unbanning of the ANC and kindred radical organizations, the release of Mandela and other political prisoners, entry into negotiations with people previously deemed "terrorists" and "communists," the rescinding of the most heinous edicts sustaining racial domination, and—while resisting the notion of majority rule—the recognition of the inevitability of universal suffrage.

There are other ways of viewing these successes. We have heard much of late of the "short twentieth century" stretching from the October Revolution to the epochal events of 1989-91, a century marked by a vast, failed experiment with communism, a failure that has brought with it the demise of the polarized East-West hostilities. Yet this has also, crucially, been the century of decolonization. And the imminent, surely inevitable, rise to power of the ANC will contribute to our sense of the century's early closure. Founded in 1912, the ANC became, over the course of eight decades, the world's most venerable anti-colonial movement.[2] If, as the Palestinian struggle most explicitly illustrates, the battles to decolonize have hardly reached their terminus, the transformation of the ANC from an exiled, underground, guerilla movement into an elected national government will nonetheless mark a watershed moment in the global uprisings against European, American, and Russian domination.

The convergent declines of communism and apartheid have provoked widespread ideological disarray. Clearly, in these tumultuous times, disorientation and an accompanying climate of political improvisation are not unique to South Africa. But many South Africans have felt the need to adjust their bearings with distinctive force due to the country's extensive reliance on a highly polarized ideological grid. Suddenly, in unadjusted form, the dependable invocations—whether of communism, socialism, anticommunism, or apartheid—sound with an anachronistic ring to all but the most obdurate believers.

From this perspective, Magdoff and Sweezy's anticipation of "irreversible revolutionary struggle" seems off target. Whatever the electoral result, South Africa will assuredly not have a "revolutionary" government; it remains improbable that it will even acquire a socialist one. As we have seen in repeated anti-colonial struggles this century, the very success of a revolution often marks the erosion of the principles that sustained it. The prospect of imminent power places revolutionary guarantees under unprecedented pressure, transforming them—too often unrecognizably—into "practical" social policies. In the case of the ANC, this process has been complicated by the loss of an international context for many of its principles through the collapse of an international community of "socialist" nations, however ideologically diffuse that community may have been.

Fig. 1: Anti-Communism's last stand: the far right protest. (Phillipe Wojazer; Bettmann Visuals)

With good reason, apartheid has long been seen as a special case in world politics, a pestilential system warranting a unique level of opprobrium and isolation. However, the very distinctiveness of apartheid has often induced the left to view the issue in isolation from shifts in global politics. It is therefore not surprising that the full force of the links between the collapse of communism and the fate of South Africa was first intuited, not by the left, but by the right. On 2 February 1990, President de Klerk shifted the terms of the South African struggle with an inspired act of political opportunism that was also a mark of his embattlement: in a stroke, he unbanned the ANC, the South African Communist Party, the United Democratic Front, and allied progressive organizations. In announcing these unforeseen measures, de Klerk was quite explicit: they had been largely occasioned by the upheavals in Eastern Europe and the

Soviet Union.[3] Many Afrikaner nationalists railed against de Klerk's reforms as the suicide of apartheid, somewhat as Soviet Communist Party stalwarts charged Gorbachev with provoking communism's self-destruction. De Klerk saw things differently, arguing that his reforms were proportionate to the newly receding threat of Marxism. For, he contended, communism's demise and the disintegration of the Eastern bloc had weakened anti-apartheid organizations by denying them invaluable sources of ideological, financial, and military sustenance.

De Klerk's significant, if conditional break with the past was motivated neither by suicide nor philanthropy. It was a calculated wager at survival which broke the political deadlock. Over the course of the 1980s, the ANC and its allies had rendered South Africa ungovernable and, in tandem with international forces banked against South Africa, had thrown the economy into a parlous state. However, neither an October Revolution nor a Jericho was in the offing. While the anti-apartheid forces had proved expert at disruption, there was no prospect of them ever overthrowing the state by force. On both sides of the divide, there was little alternative but to negotiate.

During the years since de Klerk first voiced the entangled fates of apartheid and communism, the Soviet Union and South Africa have undergone the most far-reaching sea-changes in their post-World War II history. For both societies, 1990 and 1991 were years of intense promise and deep foreboding. They began the nemesis of two totalitarian systems—communism and apartheid—that had long served as shorthand for the two states themselves. In its distinctive way and to differing degrees, each system began to disintegrate through a combination of causes: economic crisis, popular pressure from below, dismantling from above, international isolation, the excessive costs of their war economies, and grossly authoritarian structural inefficiencies that inflicted brutal damage on the economy and populace alike. But communism's decomposition has been more precipitous than that of apartheid: as one commentator put it, "apartheid's not dead, it just smells funny."[4] The system is, nonetheless, gravely ill and has entered its terminal decline.

In both societies, the sudden waning of the old order unleashed a revolution of expectations. When the BBC organized a panel discussion of the documentary, "Russia Year Zero," a leading Yeltsin adviser named the exhaustion of social patience as the principal threat to the future of the former Soviet Union.[5] (He went on to predict—accurately as it turned out—that Yeltsin would meld democracy with "reasonably authoritarian" measures to contain the anticipated unrest.) Another panelist, a former Gorbachev adviser in his first week of early retirement, demurred: the principal threat was ethnic nationalism. Both fears possess a South African resonance: rising frustration over the failure of the reputedly "new" South Africa to deliver improvements in everyday life has fueled the country's strife, some of which has been represented in ethnic nationalist terms.

Heady talk of the advent of the post-Soviet and post-apartheid eras has exacerbated the lethal lag between the pace of legislative change and their conversion into tangible advances for ordinary people. Indeed, as improvements proliferated on paper and as the euphoric rhetoric of radical change soared, so vast swathes of each society continued to experience a downward spiral in the quality and availability of food, housing, jobs, and health care, and particularly in the purchasing power of their incomes.

To imply an already existing post-apartheid order at this stage of South Africa's transformation is both premature and incendiary. As the ANC keeps reiterating, the unelected de Klerk has enjoyed the privileges of player and referee. Nevertheless, the euphoria over Mandela's release—which acquired the aura of a victory parade—prompted the illusion that the ANC was taking over, or at least controlling the country in tandem with the National Party. Thus de Klerk could lumber the ANC with the weight of popular expectations while the organization still lacked control of the state apparatuses necessary to implement change. In a sense, the National Party's two track strategy of reform and persistent destabilization of its opponents turned the ANC's tactics on their head. Now it was the white minority regime who sought to render South Africa ungovernable in the hopes that this might provoke doubts—internally and internationally—over the ANC's fitness to rule.

The ploy met with only partial success. While discontent with the ANC has grown somewhat, the regime's complementary hope of forging a rival, electable Christian Democratic Front around Inkatha, the National Party, and the middle and lower middle classes in the Coloured and Indian communities has foundered badly. There is still no party within hailing distance of the ANC's mass appeal; nor, with the country's first elections in sight, is one likely to emerge. Polls late in 1991 gave the ANC 54 percent of the national vote. The National Party, on 17 percent, emerged as its closest rival, with no other organization clearing 10 percent.

Transitional South Africa, like the former Eastern bloc, has suffered regional explosions of violence as mounting expectations have combined with poverty, repression, inter-group vendettas, and the political manipulation of such tensions. Of the sanguinary post-communist conflicts—Romanian, Georgian, Armenian, Azerbaijani, and so forth—only the Yugoslavian civil war has exceeded the loss of life that has devastated rural Natal and the industrial heartland of the Transvaal. In the ten months from January to October 1991 alone, 2,161 South Africans died in political violence. For the period 1987 to 1994 fatalities exceeded fourteen thousand.[6] Thus the South African interregnum has witnessed far higher casualties than the peak periods of anti-apartheid resistance, during 1976-77 and 1984-87. Not since the Anglo-Boer War of 1899-1902 have so many people been killed in conflict on South African soil.

Advance analyses of the end of communism and of apartheid were typically couched in the language of exchange: liberation would replace totalitarianism, fallen tyrannies would give way to democratic dispensations. Yet as events have proved in the Eastern bloc and South Africa, such two-point equations—while integral to the politics of mass mobilization—could not account for the contorted transformations that would follow, the unsteady compromises between the legacies of the past and the projected values of alternative futures. Whether in Germany, Russia, or South Africa even the most decisive rejection of the past cannot tune the dial of history to year zero.

Across much of the Commonwealth of Independent States and Eastern Europe, hydra-headed ethnic nationalisms have become the principal destabilizing threat to the new and callow democracies. South Africa's feuding, however, has tended to be more inter-organizational than ethnic nationalist, despite the media cliche of a Zulu-Xhosa conflict. Most of South Africa's recent strife has developed between Inkatha and the ANC—COSATU—UDF alliance. Much, though by no means all of it, has been fueled by the police, the army, and the notorious Third Force. While ethnic nationalist animosities have so far remained relatively contained, there are signs that such tensions have begun to increase, particularly in urban townships.

If the threat of inter-ethnic strife is to be contained, the ANC, on assuming office, will have to quell social impatience through early delivery of the fruits of change. Although their constituencies and ideologies are utterly dissimilar, Mandela and Yeltsin do share two circumstances. Mandela, too, will be assuming power after an unstable interregnum when the collapse of the old has become irreversible, but the character of what will replace it remains ill-defined. The uncertainty and duration of such an interregnum—far longer in Mandela's case than Yeltsin's—serve to increase the burden of expectations shouldered by the incoming order. The trial period ordinarily granted to a new dispensation will be curtailed by the popular sense, however mistaken, that the transition itself constituted such a period of grace. This pressure will be particularly acute in Mandela's case because of the media trope of him as presiding in tandem with de Klerk over apartheid's decease.

The second similarity is this: Mandela will be taking over from a leader who has won international acclaim (however ambiguously deserved) as a daring broker between an authoritarian past and a democratic future, someone who has subjected his party to previously unthinkable reforms. Although Gorbachev was late to realize it, and de Klerk is resisting the inevitable, implicit in each process has been the certainty that the Communist and National parties were reforming themselves out of office. As each society approached its first ever democratic election, neither Gorbachev nor de Klerk could expect a popular mandate.

THE COLLAPSE OF COMMUNISM

There are four cardinal reasons why communism's subsidence has reverberated so powerfully in South and Southern Africa. First, because South Africa possesses one of the world's last commmunist parties with significant popular support. Second, because socialism and Marxism have been historically central to the anti-apartheid struggle well beyond the ranks of the South African Communist Party. Third, there is the question of timing—the fact that the ANC's ascent toward political power coincided with the decline, internationally, of the ideologies that have sustained it. Finally, communism's collapse has had such profound ramifications in South Africa because the region that it dominates contains four other countries—Angola, Mozambique, Zimbabwe, and Namibia—in which revolutionary socialist guerilla movements rose to power.

Fig. 2: Lenin prostrate. (Bettmann Visuals)

The South African Communist Party (SACP) can make an astonishing claim: in the sixteen month period from August 1990 to December 1991 its membership swelled fivefold, a boast that no other surviving communist party—whether in Italy, West Bengal, or the Philippines, for example—could possibly match. Yet statistics can mislead. August 1990 marked the official relaunching of the SACP after thirty years of outlaw status. The leadership and many of the party's five thousand members had recently returned from exile and the twenty thousand who joined in the ensuing months were not so much new and sudden converts to communism as old supporters at last free to sign up legally.

The absence of Soviet financial and ideological sustenance and the widespread discrediting of communism make an upsurge in the SACP's political fortunes improbable. However, the party is also unlikely to dissolve and it possesses a prominence disproportionate to its moderate numbers. The SACP has a long, creditable record of resisting apartheid and, on this front, has been far bolder and more effective than South African liberalism. Yet viewed from an international perspective, the SACP has revealed many of the dismal tendencies of communist parties ideologically and financially wedded to the Soviet Union, such as supporting the Red Army's bloody repression of reforms in Budapest (1956) and again in Prague (1968), as well as condoning the Red Army's invasion of Afghanistan. Any assessment of SACP's record should mark both the courageous and atrocious positions it has adopted in the past.

If the idea of communism retains a lingering prestige among sectors of South African society, this is due largely to the National Party's predilection, over the past forty years, for wielding the term against ideologically diverse opponents of apartheid. A broad swathe of South Africans have thus suffered under anti-communist measures, which has increased the allure of at least the term communism. So for many South Africans, the SACP retains an honorable reputation less for the precise values it upholds than for the values it has stood against.

But the imminent prospect of majority rule in South Africa has brought the SACP, like other resistance organizations, under sudden pressure to inject intricate policy content into the sweeping, often reactive rhetoric of the nonracial, anti-apartheid struggle. The need for greater precision has been immensely complicated by the simultaneously plummeting credibility of communism as a political system. The SACP has negotiated this double adjustment with a mixture of anachronism and disorientation, as the stands assumed by its leaders reveal. At one extreme, Harry Gwala applauded the Soviet generals' August putsch against Gorbachev's "betrayal of socialism." Govan Mbeki, on the other hand, rejected the appearance of the phrase "democratic socialism" in the party's redrafted constitution on the grounds that "according to Marx, socialism is necessarily democratic. It does not need an adjective."[7] This implies a quite different conception of socialism from Gwala's. Again, other party leaders like Joe Slovo have yoked the SACP to the word democracy at every turn, pledging to pursue socialist aims through parliamentary means. This latter tendency has earned the SACP the sobriquet the Sheepish About Communism Party.

The prominence of the SACP has been extended by its role in a three-pronged alliance with the ANC and the Congress of South African Trade Unions. As the ANC commands the support of some 58 percent of South Africans according to a 1993 poll, and COSATU boasts a well organized membership of 1.2 million, the tripartite alliance comprises by far the most significant grouping in South African politics.[8] The extensive cross-membership among the three organizations sometimes seems complementary, at times strained. The SACP and above all COSATU can serve as a brake on the ANC during a period when many fear that hasty negotiations with de Klerk's regime's will short-change the black working class. COSATU and—again, to a lesser extent—the SACP can offer accountable bases to the ANC whose sudden legitimacy in 1990 found it short of the grass roots structures necessary for democratic exchanges between the leadership and supporters on the ground. COSATU's democratic reputation and the depth of its organized base are vital to the ANC, particularly as during the first eighteen months after its unbanning the ANC drew frequent fire for its high-handedness and lack of consultation.

The majority of the ANC's executive also belongs to the SACP. This has perturbed some progressives, even within quarters of the ANC. Alan Boesak, who heads the ANC's Western Cape branch, has urged his organization to sever the alliance, arguing that the ANC's association with communism alienates would-be supporters, including many coloureds who predominate in the Cape, and many Christians in a country with a Christian majority. Certainly, in ideological terms, the bond between the ANC and the SACP has an air of unreality to it: despite the overlapping membership, the majority of top ANC positions are not held by people who would be ideologically identifiable as communists or Marxist-Leninists. But the ANC and SACP have cooperated since the 1950s and at least for the time being, the historical links and structural benefits are holding out internally, although internationally, the alliance has proved harder to vindicate.

The ANC itself has never been a communist organization but a broad coalition of African nationalists, Marxists, socialists, social democrats, and liberals. Under the banner of nonracialism, it has incorporated Africans, so-called coloureds, Indians, and whites across a spectrum of classes. The ANC's eclecticism has been a strength under some circumstances: its status as a congress, not a party, certainly helped broaden its appeal. But the organization's inclusiveness has also had its drawbacks. Since the ANC was unbanned, its policy recommendations have often suffered from a diffusion and instability that bear the combined marks of its history as an alliance, the collapse of communism, and the pressures of the give-and-take of prolonged negotiations. Thus, for example, the leadership includes those who continue to present themselves as socialists, and those who see the term as an encumbrance. On his emergence from prison, Mandela had reiterated his organization's adherence to socialism, only later to insist that "We won't follow socialism. We have our own programme."[9] Nothing illustrates this shift more limpidly than the ANC's draft Economic Manifesto. The document refrains not merely from mentioning communism, but socialism and capitalism as well.[10] Increasingly, the ANC's official statements side-step such bipolar schemes.

The ANC's edginess around the word socialism is indicative of the current difficulty of mobilizing around that term, even in societies where the values it should represent enjoy a broad appeal. This dilemma is a direct symptom of the collapse of the regimes who were wrongheadedly but persistently reputed to embody "actually existing socialism" or "state socialism." The democratic left should be elated that such regimes are no longer around to claim "socialism" for themselves, thereby muddying the issues at stake. Yet, ironically, among democratic socialists the most energetic labor of dissociation has been required since the "actually existing socialists" have ceased actually to exist. The leaders of the August putsch claimed to be rescuing socialism; Gorbachev went down reiterating his unshaken faith in socialism. Such claims only deepened the guilt by association between Soviet communism and socialism. Inside South Africa and internationally, we have seen a flurry of books and articles like *After the Fall*—subtitled *The Failure of Communism and the Future of Socialism*, and "The Downfall of Communism—Is it a Tragedy for Socialism?"[11] The work of dissociation—too often approached indifferently in the past—has acquired a fresh focus and intensity.

Within South Africa as well as globally, "democratic" has emerged as the hands down winner in the idiom stakes. It has become almost impossible to imagine political circumstances where "democratic"—unlike the terms "communist," "capitalist," "socialist," "nationalist," "federalist," and "internationalist"—could be uttered as an accusation. The term has become so available, so necessary, and so ethereal: its pandemic allure has not aided its precision. Organizations seeking to bask in the aura of democracy include the British Communist Party, which in November 1991 rechristened itself the Democratic Left; Democratic Forum, who were central to Hungary's anticommunist protests; the Foundation for the Restoration of Democracy (FORD), a Kenyan popular front who (despite their discomfitingly corporate acronym) have valiantly resisted Arap Moi's tyranny; and the right wing, racist, Sweden Democrats. Manifestly, the vogue for the appellation democratic has only increased the draughty, open-endedness of the term. To stress this is not to trivialize the one ineluctable criterion of democracy: multiparty elections. If, as a

South African, a Lithuanian, a Kenyan, a Pole, a Zambian, or a Ukrainian you have never voted with choice, the advent of such an opportunity—however circumscribed—marks a significant, emotional breakthrough.

By itself, however, a party's allegiance to democratic elections is no more than an initial step. It solves little apart from providing the breathing space afforded by respectability. Over the past few years, one after another, the major South African parties have clambered aboard the reputable raft of "democracy" in the hopes that it will ease their passage through the ideological turbulence of the times. Under the title, Convention for a Democratic South Africa, some twenty parties gathered in late 1991 to thrash out the policy implications of, among other things, their contrary perceptions of that term.

South Africa's "democrats" make an improbable crew. Where the ANC and its allies formerly went under the banner of "national liberation movement" now they increasingly present themselves as the "democratic national liberation movement." Also ranged in the ANC alliance on the left, we have seen the United Democratic Front and the Mass Democratic Movement. The all-white Democratic Party, which positions itself somewhere between the ANC and the National Party, extends the rightward range of the term. Still further to the right, de Klerk sought to shore up his power by engineering a Christian Democratic Alliance between the National Party, Inkatha, and a couple of smaller, right-of-center parties.

When apartheid was in full swing, the National Party president, P. W. Botha, insisted that "of course South Africa is a democracy—for those who have the vote." Botha's reformist successors are more subtle and less tautological. By mid-1991, President de Klerk was embracing the awfully progressive sounding "participatory democracy"—yet another symptom of the ideological cross-dressing than has become rampant in South Africa.[12] More recently, de Klerk has advocated the pursuit of "sustainable democracy," the kind of ominous qualification that we have come to associate with Boris Yeltsin.[13] Just as, from Romania and Bulgaria to the Ukraine and Azerbaijan, many of the newly vocal democrats in power are thinly retreaded communists, so too in South Africa the ranks of the new democrats are replete with remodeled apartheid apparatchiks.

The terminologically emphatic but ideologically confused march of "democracy" has been evident not just in South Africa but across the Southern African region—most recently, with the moves in Angola and Mozambique toward multiparty systems. The repercussions of communism's fall have been felt with a distinctive force across the region because Southern Africa has generated, over the past three decades, the world's largest concentration of national liberation movements identifying themselves either as Marxist-Leninist or revolutionary socialist: Frelimo (Mozambique), MPLA (Angola), SWAPO (Namibia), ZANU (Zimbabwe), and the ANC (South Africa). More remarkably, if (as is assumed) the ANC wins South Africa's first democratic elections, every one of these liberation movements will have risen to power. Yet none of these governments could now be described as socialist. The Zimbabwean economy remains dominated by white farmers, businessmen, and industrialists and plans to redistribute land, wealth, and opportunity have largely fallen by the wayside. Namibia, with a total population barely in excess of one million, was unlikely to embark on any radical experiments on South Africa's doorstep, particularly given South Africa's record of military occupation and regional destabilization.

In contrast to Namibia and Zimbabwe, independent Angola and Mozambique both set about implementing socialist policies. They thereby incurred the anticommunist wrath of South Africa and—in Angola's case—of the U.S.A. too. Thus one should speak less of the failure of socialism in Angola and Mozambique than of the success of South Africa and America's decade-and-a-half programs of destabilization. With the disappearance of Eastern bloc economic and political support, both these war-wrecked countries have been thrust into the hands of the World Bank and the IMF who, predictably, have imposed the kind of structural adjustment packages that have typically deepened the plight of nations throughout the South.

In fighting off the South African-American onslaught, Angola relied principally on Cuba which, once the Gorbachev dispensation began severing its global commitments, lacked the capacity and motivation to go it alone. Mozambique's closest ties, on the other hand, were with the erstwhile German Democratic Republic. Licinio Azevedo's affecting documentary, *Farewell GDR*, captures just one aspect of the Mozambican repercussions of communism's demise, focusing on the 15,000 Mozambicans stranded in the GDR. With the postcommunist collapse of the cooperative programs between the two countries and the rise of racist neo-Nazism in Germany, thousands of these Mozambicans were forced back to their war-shredded country. Tossed from the grim fringes of one tumultuous region to the far grimmer fringes of another, none of them, after six months back in Mozambique, had found employment. They were, to put it mildly, beneficiaries neither of the postcommunist "New" Europe nor of the "New" Southern Africa.

THE COLLAPSE OF ANTICOMMUNISM

It is one of the truisms of the 90s that we have now passed into the post-communist age. But it is less commonly remarked that we have entered, just as decisively, the age of post-anticommunism. Variants of communist rule persist—in China, Vietnam, North Korea, and Cuba—but the ideology's decease in Eastern European and the Soviet Union struck a blow from which the forces of anticommunism will not recover. Efforts to summon the old specter back

Fig. 3: Youth with imitation rifle celebrates Mandela's release by straddling the statue of former South African Prime Minister Jan Smuts. Cape Town, February 1990. (AP/Wide World Photos)

from the grave sound just that: merely necromantic. This was apparent, for instance, when in November 1991 Margaret Thatcher urged Europe to defend Croatia from the Serbian "communist onslaught," and when Inkatha executive, Musa Myeni, warned that South Africa was "suffering under an emerging African National Congress dictatorship, backed by communists all over the world."

The headlong retreat, arm in arm, of communism and anti-communism has had considerable consequences for Western Europe, the U.S.A., and South Africa, though for each in distinctive ways. Communism allowed Western Europe the illusion of being a continent. The fall of communism has produced an unbounded Europe, exposing the contradictions within the EC's economic, political, and military ambitions. At the very moment when a German-centered EC is seeking to consolidate itself as a world power, it seems an indeterminate entity unsure of how best to capitalize on the new world disorder raging along its borders and beyond. In his last annual report as UN Secretary General, Javier Perez de Cuellar, side-stepped the term Soviet Union, referring instead to something he called "the northern Eurasian land mass."[14] Given the porousness of its eastern borders in the post-Soviet era, perhaps the erstwhile "Europe" should provisionally submit to the designation of "western Eurasian land mass." Certainly, the days are gone when Western Europeans could speak of "Europe" automatically, arrogantly, and without risk of being misconstrued, when they merely meant the nations of the EC.

Resurgent anti-Muslim racism in France, Germany, Austria, Spain, Italy, and (in the wake of *The Satanic Verses*) in Britain, serves a grim reminder that after the historical interlude when the agon between communism and anticommunism moved centerstage, there are strong signs of a reversion to the more ancient conflict that pitted the lands and races of Christendom against those of Islam.[15] In Europe, as in the U.S.A. (though for quite different historical reasons), anti-Islam is emerging as a leading surrogate for anticommunism. The American military-industrial complex and the Bush administration have resorted to a roster of rotating enemies—sundry Muslims, Latin American drug-dealers, and Japanese protectionists—in an unsuccessful effort to generate an aura of external threat equal to that projected through anticommunism.

Along with the U.S.A., South Africa is arguably the country whose rulers have been left most bereft by the demise of anticommunism. Since its ascent to power in 1948, the National Party has relied upon anticommunism as its most versatile justification for all manner of domestic repression and regional imperialism. The Suppression of Communism Act of 1950—which inflicted four decades of unrelieved suffering on South Africans—gives some sense of the protean referents of the label "communist" under Nationalist rule. An organization could be banned or a person detained, imprisoned, or executed as a communist if they sought, in the eyes of the law, to bring about "any political, industrial, social, or economic changes within the Union by the promotion of disturbance or disorder, by unlawful acts of omission or by means which include the promotion of disturbance or disorder, or such acts or omissions of threat." A communist was further defined as anyone who "aims at the encouragement of feelings of hostility between the European and non-European races."[16]

The pretext of anticommunism thus allowed successive Nationalist regimes open season on their opponents. By the mid-70s, the National Party had phased out the overtly offensive language of racial supremacy, preferring to rationalize white domination and racial capitalism through the rhetoric of ethnic national differences and multiculturalism. The sidestepping of racist rhetoric (though not racist policies) increased the regime's reliance on anticommunism as the ideological cement binding its repressive policies. Anticommunist hysteria rose after the crisis of the mid-70s, precipitated by the radical guerilla victories in Mozambique and Angola and by the Soweto uprising. President P.W. Botha, who ruled South Africa from 1978 to 1989, declared that South Africa was besieged by communism. His foreign minister, Pik Botha—a man of inimitable flair in such matters—observed how "like creeping lava and suffocating gas...the menacing hegemony of Russia is spreading over this planet."[17] But it was P.W. Botha who gave voice to the battle cry of his era: South Africa needed a "total strategy" to meet this "total onslaught."

During the 1980s, the Botha doctrine of anticommunism dovetailed with the Reagan doctrine. The South African and American governments both routinely deployed military and economic imperialism to destabilize foreign governments in the name of anticommunism. Such measures were adopted to prevent nations from achieving levels of economic and political independence that would distance them from the South African and American spheres of influence. To this end, the Botha regime invaded seven countries militarily (Angola, Mozambique, Swaziland, Botswana, Lesotho, Zimbabwe, and Zambia), bankrolled, trained, and armed right wing dissidents in Mozambique and Angola, disrupted oil supplies, and sabotaged the railway networks on which the frontline states depended for imports and exports. Between 1980 and 1988 alone, South African "anticommunist" destabilization cost the nine neighboring states an estimated $60.5 billion.[18] During the same period, 1.3 million people died in Angola and Mozambique as a result of South African and (in Angola's case) American sponsored wars.

In South African government circles, at least as strongly as in their American equivalents, the "defeat" of communism has been experienced as a Pyrrhic victory and a kind of abandonment. No less than the left, the South African right has lost the security of its traditional bearings and has had to engage in rapid ideological and policy improvisation. The relative prominence of the SACP and its intimate ties with the ANC have enabled the National Party to revert, on occasion, to anticommunist vitriol. But in the post-Soviet era, communism has become a wholly implausible threat, especially now that South Africa's major political parties are committed to negotiations, not revolution, and the SACP's principal source of financial and ideological sustenance has evaporated.

The spirit of anticommunism still surfaces, at times, in the speeches of Buthelezi and de Klerk. But it is fundamentally associated with far right organizations like the Conservative Party, Afrikaanse Weerstandsbeweging (AWB), Order of the Boerevolk, and the White Wolves. The neo-Nazi appeal to anticommunism erupted catastrophically in April 1993 when a Polish immigrant, Janusz Waluz, assassinated SACP general secretary, Chris Hani. The outcry over Hani's death, which provoked 85 rallies nationwide, testified to the monumental popularity of the Communist Party leader. But it evidenced, too, the marginalization of anticommunism, the degree to which it had been forced from the mainstream of South African political life and into the tributaries of the extreme right; it was but a trickle of its former force.

So the much-heralded rollback of communism on the international front has robbed the apartheid order of a principal *raison d'etre*. Other enemies will be found and fabricated, but in its comprehensiveness and versatility, the red peril is irreplaceable. In reflecting on that loss, one recalls the sly words of the Irish writer, Flann O'Brien: "We must keep the wolf from the door—in case he gets out." Communism, that intimate enemy, has finally bolted.

CONCLUSION

The approach of majority rule in South Africa could scarcely have occurred in more uncertain, combustible times. When the ANC ascends to power, it will do so in an age of defeats without clear victors. Now more than ever, the binary, video-game simplicities of Cold War thinking do not hold: one system is dead, the other groaning in the sick bay. South Africa, faced with the possibility of the most profound metamorphosis in its twentieth century history, also faces a dearth of redeeming social and economic models. None of the sundry IMF, World Bank, and Group of Seven-style cures have narrowed the gulf between North and South. Indeed, during the 1980s IMF-approved structural adjustment programs ordinarily exacerbated the unequal distribution of wealth inside the countries of the South, while also increasing the South's poverty relative to the North.[19] Much of the South—above all, much of Africa, from Somalia and Ethiopia to Zaire, Angola, and Mozambique—now lies in the Cold War casualty ward, in no condition to derive whatever benefits may spring from that system's decease and with no immediate alternatives to that grim reaper, structural adjustment.

These world developments have a particular pertinence to South Africa because it contains within its borders the world's most inequitable distribution of wealth, a one-nation approximation of the North-South divide. Such is the economic stranglehold of the six largest monopolies—above all, the mining giant, Anglo American—that the former Communist Party leader, Joe Slovo, once quipped that the South African economy was less in need of nationalization than of privatization.

During its long tenure as a resistance movement, the ANC's principal economic guidelines were enshrined in the 1955 Freedom Charter, which committed the organization to "transferring the ownership," of mines, monopolies, and banks, "to the people as a whole." It no longer holds to a vision of comprehensive nationalization. In this regard, at least, the ANC has been fortunate in its timing: the collapse of communism has exposed, once and for all, the bankruptcy of the command economy model and spared South Africa that royal road to ruination. At the same time, the ANC will hopefully be better placed than the countries of Eastern Europe and the Soviet Union to resist the blandishments of the free market missionaries, should it ever have been so tempted. The dodgy state of the British and American economies has reduced the Thatcherite and Reaganite idolatry of free market capitalism to a superannuated set of incantations. By now it is quite apparent that Japan, Germany, Austria, and the other economically successful European nations have deviated from an ultra-free market course, placing greater emphasis on, among other things, public investment, social services, education, and worker participation.[20] South Korea and Taiwan, two other success stories, have done so through a mixture of corporate capitalism and significant state interference in the economy. While none of these models may be directly appropriate for South Africa, at least the country's new dispensation will be in a better position to adapt them to its own circumstances, rather than succumbing to the dictates either of the command economy or Reaganomics.

The post-Cold War world is congealing into three power blocs around the Pacific rim, Europe, and North America. Geopolitically peripheral, South Africa will need considerable ingenuity—and historical good fortune—if it is to avoid economic marginality. The internal and international uncertainties surrounding the country's economic future are increased by the fact that the West's interest in South Africa fixated on its significance for the "anticommunist defense perimeter" and its possession of strategic mineral deposits which were—in the mad argot of NATO—described as the richest "in the free world." South Africa remains the world's largest gold producer, although profitability and its proportion of global output have declined.[21] Moreover, the international significance of gold has dwindled with the waning of East-West hostilities. If the Gulf War was the first international conflict of the post-communist era, it also marked the first international crisis when the price of gold did not soar. Iraq's invasion of Kuwait, the Gulf War, the coup in the Soviet Union: in the past, comparable events—like the 1980 revolution in Iran—induced panicked buying of gold. The end of East-West hostilities has flattened the price of gold for the foreseeable future, reducing its significance as a hedge against threats of political and economic turbulence that are now perceived as more local than global.

Since the early 70s, South Africa has slipped from being an upper-middle-income to a lower-middle-income nation. Yet compared to most Southern nations, it retains an abundance of mineral, agricultural, and industrial advantages, as well as a fine transport infrastructure. The advent of a democratic dispensation should release the greatest external brake on South Africa's economic growth, the international ban, since 1985, on loans to the apartheid regime. The resultant balance of payment crisis and lack of foreign capital has severely inhibited the economy's productive capacity.[22] Any movement away from racial capitalism should also bring considerable savings as South Africa sheds the cumbrous inefficiencies of apartheid. By the late 80s, for example, military expenditure amounted to 15 percent of the national budget; as a proportion of the GDP it exceeded even Soviet levels. Further wastage resulted from the bureaucratic enforcement of apartheid's labyrinthine racist regulations. When the system was at its height, the state employed one in three economically active whites. Such administrative shelters for white labor were complemented by job reservation laws that barred blacks from moving into skilled positions. These expectations, in turn, were built into the Bantu Education system—aptly described as education for servitude. Consequently, although South African unemployment exceeds 40 percent, the economy remains desperately short of skilled labor which, most recently, has been imported from Eastern Europe.[23]

South Africa's captains of industry and the ANC at least agree that the inefficiencies of the old system have to be eradicated. They also concur that, without an end to the violence, desperately needed foreign capital will not materialize, the already damaging level of capital flight will increase, and the pool of skilled labor will shrink further through emigration, all exacerbating the economy's downward momentum. Where the country's industrial leaders and the ANC differ most is on the pace and depth of change. It is all very well urging stability, but that will only materialize if the incoming dispensation begins to remedy the black majority's unmet needs—in housing, jobs, healthcare, and education—which have been explosively pent up under decades of apartheid. Economic growth will be inseparable from the pursuit of social justice and economic democracy.

South Africa's prospects, like those of the former Soviet Union, will be irreparably damaged if the idea of democratization becomes firmly associated with falling living standards. The result would be a crisis without beneficiaries. Under the circumstances, it would prove impossible to resuscitate organized revolution by simply resuming the struggle where it left off in 1990. De Klerk's reforms, the legalizing and demystifying of the liberation movement, the new alliances generated by negotiations, and the decline of the communist-anti-communist divide have collectively produced a complex configuration of forces that cannot be returned to the largely bipolar model that characterized the high era of anti-apartheid revolt. If negotiations flounder, or if an incoming ANC dispensation fails to deliver rapid and deepcutting social changes, the result will not be revived revolution but chaos, the Lebanonization, not the liberation, of South Africa.

10

OF BALKANS AND BANTUSTANS
Ethnic Cleansing and the Crisis in National Legitimation

> Let me say something briefly about the so-called black-on-black violence in our country....What we are confronted with here is a problem of violent resistance to democratic change, and not a situation of ethnic conflicts that are supposedly inherent in African societies. South Africa is not Bosnia-Herzegovina.
>
> —Nelson Mandela, Speech to NAACP Convention, Indianapolis, 1993

> The word pollution is often on the lips of the violent.
>
> — Natalie Z. Davis, *Society and Culture in Early Modern France*

AN ACADEMIC PROPHECY can seldom have been so instantly superannuated as the closing words to Eric Hobsbawm's book, *Nations and Nationalism Since 1780*. For Hobsbawm, writing in 1989, progress in the analysis of nationalism signalled that "the phenomenon is past its peak. The owl of Minerva which brings wisdom, said Hegel, flies out at dusk. It is a good sign that it is now circling round nations and nationalism."[1] Hobsbawm's owl seems to have been lured out less by the twilight of nationalism than by its bloody new dawn.

Eminent theorists of nationalism like Hobsbawm, Benedict Anderson, Ernest Gellner, and Tom Nairn, who established their reputations on the subject in the late 1970s or 80s, could not have anticipated the unprecedented proliferation of nation-states since 1990. In the past few years, more new states have arisen in Eastern Europe and Eurasia than during those high eras of European national birthing, 1848 and 1917 to 1921. German reunion, the fracturing of the Soviet Union, the splitting of Czechoslovakia, and Yugoslavia's sanguinary disintegration have all signalled an upsurge in ethnic nationalisms bent on redrawing the boundaries of nation-states—whether through irredentism or, more commonly, by carving large states into more ethnically homogeneous polities.

These developments have sharply raised the stakes of ethnic nationalism by creating, through the power of immediate precedent, a land-grabbing atmosphere in which national boundaries appear to be more elastic. Only a smattering of recognized states can claim ethnic homogeneity, yet the belief that a state should bring in train a unitary lineage of culture, tradition, ethnicity, and nation retains a lingering international prestige. In the current climate of border changes, this residual prejudice in favor of "sameness" encourages the destabilizing pursuit of that *ignis fatuus*, ethnic consistency. This point has been demonstrated with brutal force by the assault on Bosnia-Herzegovina: amidst a resurgent view that people who are the "same" deserve and require ethnic self-rule, a history of multi-cultural tolerance can be transformed into a liability.

During the early 1990s, the combination of imperial collapse, state proliferation, and ascendant ethnic nationalism has brought on a crisis in the procedures for national legitimation. If national claims resting on ethnic foundations appear destabilizing, how else are aspirant states to mount their appeals? Arguments based on historical occupation resolve little in the myriad cases of layered possession; only a minority of states display linguistic unity; and economic viability carries little weight in a world of micro-states like Andorra, Gambia, and St. Vincent. Other than simply freezing the status quo—which would be catastrophic for the Palestinians, among others—there appear to be inadequate internationally sanctioned counters to the redrawing of national boundaries along ethnic lines.

The train of logic that idealizes the alignment of culture, ethnicity, and the nation-state provides a powerful means of staking a territorial claim; read in the opposite direction, the same logic explains violence as a "natural" explosion of primordial ethnic differences—the revenge of the past, in the purported manner of Yugoslavia. The Balkan conflicts have, in many quarters, given weight to this perilous assumption that ethnic differences "naturally" produce conflict, and conversely, that ethnicity offers a "natural" basis for national community.[2] This reversible argument threatens to become an axiom of nationalist politics in the 1990s. It has found favor with advocates of "immigrant" expulsion, population "transfer," ethnic segregation, "ethnic cleansing," and/or ethnic secession in societies as varied as Israel, France, Zaire, Azerbaijan, South Africa, Bosnia-Hercegovina, India, Iraq, Kuwait, Israel, and Germany.

The revival of ethnic nationalism has given focus not just to the unstable procedures for national legitimation but also to the equivocal character of the term of ethnicity. If ethnicity is conventionally associated with cultural attributes as opposed to the biological constructs of race, it would seem to be the more accommodating of the two categories—admitting a looser, more conditional image of identity achieved through socialization not genes. Yet, particularly in the context of nationalism, the cultural markers of ethnicity may become invested with a surrogate determinism that achieves a neo-biological intensity.

The efforts to sanctify ethnicity as an impermeable, inescapable identity have been intensified during the transitional crises in South Africa and the former Yugoslavia. The assumption that ethnic difference is the fount of South Africa's violence reinforces suggestions that the conflict is the predictable outcome of mixing incompatible "ethnic nations." This belief can in turn be used to brace arguments for a federal constitution that reinforces the old racially ordered inequities. And, as in Bosnia-Herzegovina, the view that the conflict is at heart an inter-ethnic blood feud weakens the case for decisive international involvement—an issue of pressing importance with regard to the monitoring of South Africa's first democratic elections.[3]

To those whose economic and political calculations cannot accommodate symbiosis, cosmopolitanism—be it in Sophiatown or Sarajevo—stands as a symbolic provocation to a system premised on inviolable ethnic difference. The project of "cleansing" such places may be vindicated by the contention, among others, that "improving" a community's ethnic consistency requires short-term violence for the ends of long-term peace. But the claim that ethnic homogeneity enhances the prospects of social stability remains wholly unsubstantiated. Moreover, in both South Africa and the former Yugoslavia, this misguided assumption has produced an inverted account of a violence which has its source less in ethnic incompatibility than in the futile, infinite, and bloodstained labor of seeking to divide the indivisible. Ethnic difference is not the wellspring of "ethnic violence" which flows instead from (among other things) historical efforts to impose categorical ethnic identities. Thus a symptom of the violence— the defensive production of brittle ethnicities—is readily misconstrued as its cause.

THE AMPLIFICATION OF ETHNIC NATIONALISM

Over one hundred new states have emerged during the post-World War II era, the majority of them in the *soi-disant* "Third World" following the breakup of the European empires. But almost all of these states—barring a handful of exceptions like India, Pakistan, Lebanon, and the Cameroon—have remained circumscribed by territorial boundaries inherited from the colonial epoch. Since then, secessionist movements representing the Palestinians, Kurds, Kashmiris,

Western Saharans and others have campaigned for the redrawing of international borders. But rarely have their efforts met with success.

However, the perception that the early 1990s offer a uniquely propitious moment for publicizing minority nationalist causes has spread westward and southward from the former communist bloc. In Western Europe, events to the east didn't so much catalyze new claims as enhance the visibility of old ones by representing them as part of an international drive. Thus, Breton, Walloon, Scottish, Basque, Catalan, Sardinian, Gibraltan, and Tyrol nationalisms all sought to capitalize on the political atmosphere, particularly in 1991, when the (now wavering) prospect of European unity held out the promise of an autobahn running from regional to EC polities and bypassing centralized states.

Fig. 1: Forced removals. (AP/Wide World Photos)

While these European developments have drawn extensive comment, there has been little discussion of the reverberations of the newly fortified idiom of ethnic nationalism beyond Europe and Eurasia's borders. Dissidents in Zaire, for instance, have sought to advance their secessionist campaign against Mobutu's kleptocracy by calling for the birth of "the Baltic states of Zaire: Katanga, Kasai, and Kivu."[4] And Jacques Parizeau, leader of Parti Quebecois, has invoked the fall of the Soviet empire as proof that Quebec's separatists had been "visionaries, nearly prophets all along."[5]

The amplification of ethnic nationalist discourse has set up dangerous echoes in South Africa where right wing forces ranged against the ANC have alighted, with dismaying speed, on the political kudos to be gained from Soviet and Yugoslavian analogies. The European-led resurgence of the ethnic nationalist idiom has coincided with two developments which will have a critical impact on the longterm character of South Africa's transformation. These are the upswing in violence and negotiations towards a democratic constitution.

Over the past seven years, more South Africans have died in conflict than in any comparable period this century—since what Gerhard Mare sardonically calls the "white-on-white violence" of the Anglo-Boer War.[6] Ironically, it is European conflicts that have fortified ethnic interpretations of South Africa's violence; yet such explanations can be conveniently fused to the colonial charge that "tribal" warfare is an immanent, atavistic African failing.[7] If the towering issue of violence in South Africa is projected as the result of "natural" hostilities between innately different ethnic nations, this strengthens the hand of those who maintain that ethnic faultlines are "natural" divides which ought to play a leading role in the reorganization of the South African state. This in turn would retard efforts to redress apartheid's central legacy, the racial imbalances in access to resources and institutional power.

APARTHEID AND THE DISMEMBERMENT OF YUGOSLAVIA

Just four years ago, Leroy Vail could begin a book on *The Creation of Tribalism in Southern Africa* by questioning whether socialism could furnish African states with a transcendent "pan-ethnic class consciousness." It was, in his view, improbable that "Africa would be a continent of new Yugoslavias."[8]

This past year, the specter of Yugoslavia has returned to haunt South African politics. But how differently it appears. Yugoslavia has metamorphosed from a symbol of a pan-ethnic socialism ostensibly beyond African emulation into a reminder of what might lie ahead for South Africa if it spurns a federal model of government responsive to "ethnic awakenings." This fashionable analogy has found particular favor among conservatives partial to Inkatha Freedom Party and hostile to the ANC. It has been upheld by, among others, Chief Mangosuthu Gatsha Buthelezi, Andries Treurnicht (leader of the Conservative Party), and the Oxford political scientist, R. W. Johnson. Writing in *The Times*, Johnson has warned that "without federalism, South Africa might simply split apart like a huge African Yugoslavia.... As Yugoslavia has shown, once the dominoes begin to fall it is a matter of *sauve qui peut*."[9]

But how salient is this comparison? And what is the political cost of accepting it?

The views of Treurnicht, a die-hard ring-winger, reveal some of the unsettling implications of brisk analogies between South Africa and Eastern Europe. Treurnicht has hailed the secessionist aftermath of communism's fall as a belated vindication of "separate development." "The ethnic awakening and demand for self-determination in Eastern Europe," he opined,

> has been political practice in South Africa for the past four decades, but is now being betrayed [by the pressure to democratize according to majority rule].... South Africa has a deeply divided population—along racial, ethnic, cultural, language and religious lines.... To force together such largely disparate people, cultures and races, will amount to a form of tyranny, the very opposite of democratic freedom. ... [Instead we must promote] the development of separate freedoms for the various peoples, ethnic groups, in their own territories, or homelands.[10]

This is back to the future with a vengeance: the bantustan system as the fin-de-siecle's fast lane to democracy.

However, it is Buthelezi who has most energetically worked the possibilities of Eastern European and Balkan analogies. Although he represents only a minority of Zulus, Buthelezi has become the torch-bearer of an at times neo-biological vision of the "Zulu nation" as a primordially vindicated, historically sanctified, ethnic community. Through a sleight of hand, he has then equated his political organization, Inkatha, with this inviolable ethnic nation. Buthelezi is also South Africa's most vocal advocate of a federal "solution" with ethnic nationalist overtones. For these reasons, he stands to gain symbolically from the upheavals in the former Eastern bloc. He has, for instance, threatened to "lead his homeland of KwaZulu to secession," thereby taking what he calls the "Yugoslavia option."[11] Buthelezi develops this threat in a document that he calls (in an echo of Ian Smith's UDI) his Unilateral Declaration of Autonomy.

As the antagonists in the Bosnian war argued over ethnically charged plans for regional autonomy and states-within-a-state, so too, in South Africa, opponents of the ANC's vision of a unitary, nonracial state aired schemes that would produce an ethnic carve-up. Buthelezi's declining fortunes, together with the secessionist mood in Eastern Europe, have emboldened him in his longstanding efforts to establish Natal/KwaZulu as an embryonic state. Buthelezi has proposed that this "state" draw up its own autonomous constitution—replete with opt-out clauses—*prior* to negotiating membership of a federal South African state. The Inkatha leader posits an Afrikaner homeland and the parlous homelands of the Ciskei and Bophuthatswana as "potential states", along parallel lines—a *de facto* cementing of apartheid's bantustan legacy.[12]

In one of his wilder posturings, Buthelezi has maintained that the ANC and the National Party are jointly prosecuting a policy of "ethnic cleansing" against his "Zulu nation."[13] This is a risible claim: as the Inkathagate Scandal proved in 1992, Buthelezi's forces have enjoyed the financial and logistical support of the country's police and military elite.[14] Moreover, the majority of political killings in recent years have resulted from inter-Zulu violence—between Zulu supporters of the ANC and its allies, and Zulu supporters of Inkatha.[15] Polls consistently show that more Zulus back the ANC than Inkatha, yet Buthelezi persists in projecting his organization and the Zulu nation as isomorphic. The ANC possesses a deep history of Zulu support, particularly, though not exclusively, among urban workers. The eminent Zulu chief, Albert Luthuli, stands as one of Mandela's most honored precursors, both as president of the ANC and as a fellow recipient of the Nobel Peace Prize. Yet Buthelezi papers over such complexities in his efforts to portray his political party, alias the "Zulu nation," as the target of "ethnic cleansings."

Conservatives like Buthelezi and Johnson who read Yugoslavia's disintegration as an omen for South Africa flatter the country's secessionist potential. The appeal of their contention rests partly on its graphic and topical simplification: the South African violence becomes instantly more intelligible if it is recast as an intimation of a Balkan scenario. But more than simplification is at stake. To predict successive ethnic and regional secessions is to inflate Inkatha's importance by projecting it as a bellwether of future defections from South Africa.

To cast Inkatha in this role requires that Buthelezi, Johnson et al maintain a symptomatic silence about the dissimilar histories of ethnic engineering in Yugoslavia and South Africa. Very stark differences pertain. Yugoslavia's socialist rulers saw the containment of ethnic nationalist claims as a condition of the state's survival, while in South Africa the central order sought to safeguard its authority by deepening ethnic divides and fostering multiple ethnic nationalisms. The apartheid regime's efforts to kickstart ten bantustans was, for several decades, a defining feature of the centralized apartheid state.

Ethnic nationalism thus became firmly associated with apartheid's paradoxical attempts to consolidate power through the illusion of dispersing it. The appeal of ethnic secession in South Africa remains muted by its association with cynical state efforts to impose ersatz "independent ethnic nation-states" in the absence of popular impulses sustaining such constructs from below. Resistance to the bantustan legacy of *divide et impera* does not guarantee the unity of those whom it oppressed; nor can the raw memories of that system halt the violence per se. However, apartheid's calamitous attempts to fabricate ethnic "homelands" has shrouded ethnic nationalist politics in suspicion for the foreseeable future, thus curbing its centrifugal power.

That much is manifest from South Africa and Yugoslavia's contrasting experiences of "ethnic cleansing." In the former Yugoslavia, this policy was prosecuted by Radovan Karadzic's forces *after* the central state had unravelled. The Serbian clampdown in Kosovo notwithstanding, "ethnic cleansing" was a post-Yugoslavian phenomenon.[16] In South Africa, however, "ethnic cleansing" was a hallmark of the old order. While that repellent phrase never featured in apartheid's lexicon, the process was systematic and longstanding. How else is one to interpret the notorious pronouncement by Connie Mulder, Minister of Bantu Administration and Development, in 1978: "If our policy is taken to its logical conclusion as far as the black people are concerned, there will not be one black man(sic) with South African citizenship."[17] The perception of this policy as a kind of "cleansing" became explicit in references to the need to eradicate "black spots" from "white" South Africa—an image that drew on the discourses of epidemiology and domestic labor for a project of ethnic engineering.[18]

Black South Africans may not have endured the precise equivalent of the Bosnian camps, but they suffered over several decades all the other brutalities that comprise "ethnic cleansing": collective expulsion; forced migration; the bulldozing, gutting, or seizure of homes; the mandatory carrying of "passes" detailing the holder's putative ethnicity and movements; and the corralling into rural ghettos of people decreed to be "illegal squatters," "surplus," "idle," "alien," or "unassimilable." These removals, in the South African case, were conducted under the guise of a spurious repatriation.[19]

The apartheid version of "ethnic cleansing" was cynically and transparently packaged as the fruition of ethnic self-determination. The regime sought—with almost no internal or international success—to present its actions as a species of decolonization. It argued that "separate development" was "not a policy of discrimination on the ground of race or colour, but a policy of differentiation on the ground of nationhood...granting to each self-determination within the borders of their homelands."[20] The completion of this argument required several legerdemains, exemplified by the utterances of another Nationalist MP, Louis Nel. Nel declared that "while no umbrella nationalism exists among the black people, there are strongly rooted ethnic nationalisms."[21] Not only does this utterance gainsay the history of black resistance, but it posits ethnic nationalisms that are largely the conceptual offspring of the regime's reinvention of ethnic difference.

Nel's second vindication of the "bantustan" policy, although voiced in 1977, achieves a grim resonance in the 1990s:

> The more heterogeneous a society the greater the potential for conflict and even bloodshed. The reverse of this argument is also true, namely that the more homogeneous a society the greater the potential for conflict and even bloodshed.[22]

This unfounded, indeed incendiary, assumption now echoes across Europe and beyond. Just as South Africa's Nationalists could forcibly drive 3.5 million people from their homes under the guise of creating harmonious pockets of homogeneity, a similarly circular argument is being popularized by Karadzic and his cohorts—that violent "cleansings" serve as a prophylactic against violence.

When the bantustan policy was most ruthlessly implemented in the 1960s and 70s, the South African regime sought to link its actions imaginatively not just to a decolonizing Africa but to European precedents as well. A contest over analogies took shape: the regime sought to assimilate the bantustans to the idea of "cantonisation," while the liberation movement condemned them as attempts to "balkanise" African nationalism.[23] For those who lived through this shootout between analogies, Western euphemisms for Bosnia's dismemberment have acquired a macabre familiarity. While the Serbs carved up the internationally recognized state of Bosnia-Herzegovina and the Croats opportunistically grabbed bits for themselves, Lord Carrington urged that this particular Balkan conflict be resolved through "cantonisation." [24] Not for the first time were territorial plunder and ethnic "purification" graced with a Swiss name.[25]

POLLUTION AND BIOLOGICAL NATIONALISM

Karadzic, together with his allies in Belgrade and the Yugoslav People's Army, adopted a genocidal policy toward Bosnia's Muslims that exposed the lurking biologism in the very ideal of the "healthy" nation. For the intelligibility of the noxious metaphor of "ethnic cleansing" depends on the prior, seemingly innocent figure of the nation as body politic. Karadzic's forces have pursued this idiom with a bloody literalness, reminding us of the insidious danger of representing nations as healthy or ailing. Such an idiom readily serves, in economic and ideological crises, as a bridge to the discourse of national pathologies. The "ailments" or "degeneration" of the national body can then be readily ascribed to the presence of "alien bodies" and "parasites" the antidote for which is cleansing, purification, or a *cordon sanitaire* to prevent further "contamination"—all on the assumption that "disinfecting" the nation is a precondition for its "convalescence" or "recovery."[26]

On the cultural front, the baleful consequences of the tyranny of cleanliness were not restricted to Serbian nationalism. The Croatian writer, Dubravka Ugresic, recounts how in the euphoric aftermath of Croatia's independence empty cans bearing Croatia's red and white coat of arms and the label "Clean Croatian Air" became all the rage. The popularity of such nationalist kitsch was a stimulus to and a symptom of a broad campaign to purify school curricula, genealogies, libraries, and towns of "Serbo-Byzantine" history, blood, books, and houses.[27]

The glaring offensiveness of the idiom of national sanitation has, by now, been repeatedly remarked upon. However, the "cleansing" may serve as a decoy for our outrage, distracting us from questioning its "ethnic" designation. Plainly, the goal of "ethnic cleansing" can only proceed on the basis of ethnic definition and recognition, yet much of the media has acquiesced in the assumption that categorical ethnic differences predated, indeed, detonated the Bosnian conflict. Even those with only a passing knowledge of the former Yugoslavia can recognize an asymmetry in the naming of the principal antagonists: Serbs, Croats, and Muslims. Yet, in most reporting on the conflict, "Muslim" has come to serve as an ersatz ethnic category. It ought to have signalled that, while Bosnia-Herzegovina is crossed-hatched with religious and cultural differences, it requires a sleight of hand to classify these as firm ethnic divides. Muslims, Serbs, and Croats are, after all, all Slavs who speak mutually intelligible variants of Serbo-Croatian.[28] Lejla Somum, formerly of Sarajevo, has argued that prior to the war, most of the city's Bosnian Serbs did not believe in their ethnic difference and even during the siege many continued to refuse that designation.[29] However, the idea of ethnic incompatibilities has been institutionalized through a dialectic between the military enforcement of difference on the one hand, and, on the other, the West's accession to the notion of this as an ethnic war.

The unquestioned assumption that the target of the "cleansing" is a discrete ethnicity reinforces the link between an essentialist theory of ethnicity and the notion of "natural" conflicts. Such reasoning has proved catastrophic for Bosnia-Herzegovina, reducing a politically complex war to a force of nature—a conflagration or a tornado, best left to burn or blow itself out. This obscures the political calculations at stake along with the moral distinctions between territorial aggressors and defenders. Ethnicity serves as an ethical leveler. Thus the apparently mitigating ethnic factor in Bosnia has helped excuse the temporizing and virtual quietism of Western leaders. In short, the combustible "nature" of ethnic difference and the geopolitical "nature" of the Balkans have allowed the West what Mark Thompson has aptly called "the comforts of fatalism."[30]

A version of this process is evident in representations of the South African conflict. Nelson Mandela has complained that by failing to marshal its military resources to contain the violence, the de Klerk regime treats black lives as cheap. If the conflict can be designated as "ethnic"—as a blood-feud between "*the* Zulus" and "*the* Xhosas"—it can be smoothly dismissed as "natural," thereby cheapening the lives at stake.

The currently ascendant assumption that there are "natural" national communities—and by extension "natural" conflicts between them—rests on a crucial ambiguity in the very idea of ethnicity. The term wavers between the poles of culture and biology, between the contingencies of socialization and the fixity of genetic determinism. In the liberal aftermath of World War II, it became less acceptable to enunciate racism in racial terms. Yet, as Paul Gilroy and Stuart Hall have observed in Britain and Etienne Balibar in France, the retreat of articulated racism did not diminish the power of what Balibar calls "racism without race."[31] While the rhetoric of racial determinism—the idiom of blood lines, degeneration, genetic purity, and physical stigmata—declined, racism was readily admitted through the open fanlight of ethnic culturalism.

Thus the distinction between a paradigm foregrounding physical features and one emphasizing cultural contingencies is by no means absolute. That much was manifest in the South African regime's representations of the bantustans as, by turns, "ethnic nation-states" and "biologically demarcated tribal states."[32] This latter conceptual omelette is indicative of the tendency, common among ethnic nationalists, to inflate the authority of the nation-state by straining to portray it as a genetic rather than a merely cultural institution.

However, the biological assumptions underpinning the nation-state are seldom so self-defeatingly explicit. What one witnesses instead is biology by other means, most often through the surrogacy of ethnic cultural or primordial claims. Ethnicity, as one among many aspects of our identity, lacks the uncompromising closure of a genetic pedigree: for those who would raise mere ethnic consciousness to the pitch of ethnic nationalism, the porousness of cultural identity becomes a liability. If ethnicity is to be mobilized on behalf of national destiny, cultural differences must be internalized as inbred and inviolate.

Hence, among nationalists, the cultural instability of ethnicity often gives way to the kind of ethnogeneticism that suffuses the official pronouncements of Karadzic in Bosnia and Buthelezi in KwaZulu. That much is apparent from Buthelezi's insistence that Zuluness is genetic and membership of Inkatha determined at birth (notwithstanding the fact that only a minority of Zulus have joined his organization).[33] Thus Buthelezi has decreed that "all members of the Zulu nation are automatically members of Inkatha if they are Zulus. There may be people who are inactive members, but no one escapes being a member as long as he or she is a member of the Zulu nation."[34] In keeping with this sentiment, Buthelezi and Karadzic have condemned Zulu and Serbian members of rival political parties as blood-traitors. Both men have sought to seal off the exits from *Blud und Boten* nationalism by insisting that their political parties are primordially vindicated—a neo-genetic attempt at shielding their ethnic organizations against the complicating claims of historical identities.

As Deniz Kandiyoti and Anne McClintock have observed, in nationalist quests for air-tight, invariant identities, women are often assigned symbolically crucial roles as reproducers of the nation and as upholders of its innermost values.[35] Women may thus serve in a double sense as the bearers of the nation, carrying in their wombs the hope of perpetuity while also incarnating national values. Moreover, women are ordinarily institutionalized as male property; they come to mark the borders between ethnicities. Thus ethnic biology, ethnic culture, and ethnic territory converge in their beings.

During a war of dispossession, this symbolic freight can become costly indeed—as evidenced by the Serbian enlistment of rape as a strategy for "ethnic cleansing."[36] Caught in the crossfire of a male war, women find themselves unenviably cast as first-class icons but second-class citizens. They are denied the arms to defend themselves while weighed down with symbolic responsibilities as guarantors of homeland, ethnos, and lineage.

The mapping of the ideas of ethnic continuity, purity, and territory onto women makes such militarized rape brutally overdetermined. Rape is commonly coded by law as a crime, not against a woman's person, but against male property. If women are projected as the inner sanctum of the patriarchal homeland, for Serbian men to invade them is symbolically and legally continuous with the gutting, looting, and seizure of Muslim property. Such defilement becomes the mark of a homeland that, in every sense, is no longer impregnable.

Mass rape is, among other things, organized insemination, men's way of interfering with the lineage of the enemy. In their campaign of "ethnic cleansing" the Bosnian Serbs have deployed rape obstructively to prevent the "mothers of the nation" from reproducing a "pure" Muslim "nation." Any ensuing children will be vulnerable to rejection as the living embodiments of personal and national violations. Thus the Serbian strategy threatens not just to seed unwanted children but to implant, as well, a mentality of ethnic purity among people who have previously had little reason to think in such constricting terms.

THE MULTIPLE ORIGINS OF VIOLENCE

Most academic, as opposed to media, analysts of South Africa's violence resist the view that the country is experiencing the tectonic rumblings of buried ethnic nationalisms. There is no "Yugoslavian" scenario in the offing. Instead, studies by Shula Marks, Lauren Segal, Mike Morris, and Doug Hindson suggest that any limited, reactive retreat into ethnicity must be viewed alongside the effects of chaotic urbanization, epidemic unemployment, economic recession, generational conflict, the legacy of migrant labor, and the attendant crises in masculinity.[37]

Since the abolition of apartheid's influx control laws in 1986, the growth-rate of South African cities has ranked among the highest in the world. Yet the regime has not even attempted to provide the civic structures or housing to accommodate these changes. These pressures have been exacerbated by the discrepancy between the four hundred thousand new workers who are entering the labor force annually, of whom only forty thousand are finding work in the formal sector.[38] In such conditions, new class tensions arise between a relatively elite working class who possess housing and a swelling ring of squatters vulnerable to the brutal, exploitative patronage of warlords.

To refute the view that the South African conflict is at heart ethnic-nationalist is not to gainsay the power of ethnic consciousness as one facet of social identity. Nor is it to deny that violently affirmed identities readily provoke equally powerful counter-identities. In circumstances where Zulu speaking migrant workers have been killed on the sometimes unwarranted supposition that they are Inkatha members, this can stir non-Inkatha Zulus into embracing the allegiance wrongly ascribed to them.[39] A similar spiral of action and reaction has dogged the Yugoslavian crisis. If you risk being raped, tortured, or killed for being a Muslim on ascriptive grounds of accent, appearance, or belief, you might as well—in circumstances that deny you the option of upholding multi-culturalism or cosmopolitanism—avail yourself of the resources of Muslim solidarity.

However, to acknowledge the reactive hardening of exclusive identities amidst a crisis is not in the least synonymous with designating ethnicity as the overweening, most "natural" of identities, and therefore as a fundamental factor in the remapping of a country and its constitution. As Marks points out, ethnic interpretations of South Africa's violence fail to address the fact that the majority of the six thousand people killed in political violence during the late 80s and early 90s died in feuds between Zulus. It was only latterly, when the violence was carried into the ethnically symbiotic heartland of the Transvaal, that ethnicity could even be posited—by those who found such explanations politically expedient—as the wellspring of the problem.[40]

To insist on a farrago of causes may be intellectually unwieldy and journalistically inconveniencing, but it is a necessary acknowledgement of tensions between South Africa's residual and emergent orders. Those who see ethnic incompatibility as the source of clashes between hostel-dwellers and surrounding urban communities tend to bypass apartheid's disabling institutional legacy—not least the congested barracks for male migrant workers.

Ironically, the evidence suggests that the violent feuding in the Transvaal resulted more from a shortage than an excess of inter-ethnic contact. Apartheid's self-enclosed hostels for migrants inserted into the cities vast enclaves of men who retained predominantly rural allegiances. These workers often remained on the periphery of the processes of urban synthesis—cultural transfer, polylingualism, inter-marriage, and civic organization—that encourage more elastic conceptions of ethnicity. Among hostel-dwellers, recession, political uncertainty, and the lifting of constraints on urbanization, have triggered desperate male competition over jobs, women, and territory. The violence should thus be seen not as expressive of primordial ethnic differences, but as a response to unstable historical conditions that catalyze essentialist identities—be they ethnic, generational, gender, class, or urban-rural ones.

Ethnically slanted explanations obscure a further critical factor: the security forces' zealous funding, fuelling, and fanning of violence in a manner that has invented an ethnic aspect in some circumstances, exaggerated it in others.[41] By December 1992, reports by the Goldstone Commission and others had pressured de Klerk into sacking some of his highest officers whom the press, military defectors, and the ANC have long accused of fomenting "Third Force" violence (whether with or without de Klerk's knowledge). Far from being the work of rogue wild men, this campaign has been meticulously orchestrated from within the Directorate of Military Intelligence. Strategies have included hit squad assassinations, the staging of train massacres, disinformation against the ANC, the hiring of RENAMO "contras" from Mozambique, the secret training of Inkatha police, and the bankrolling of Inkatha rallies and trade unions. After February 1990, the "Third Force" devised contingency plans for a military coup, a fact that crystallizes de Klerk's dilemma—how to weaken the ANC's support but in a manner that does not simultaneously increase the political leverage of the Conservative Party which, according to one estimate, holds the allegiances of 90 percent of the police and the military.[42]

To stress the scale of this conspiracy is not to imply that it accounts directly for all or even most of the violence. This is unnecessary. Under the tinder-dry conditions of 1990s South Africa, it is far easier to spark a conflict than to douse it. And those who stand to gain most from the violence—Inkatha, the Nationalist regime, and the security forces—have had little motive for controlling it. All these forces, in their diverse ways, have reason to discredit the ANC's vision of a unitary, nonracial state. There is, moreover, a partial but significant community of interest between the security forces and the Inkatha leadership, both of whom have benefited materially from the apartheid legacy of neo-federal, neo-ethnic politics. Government support for the KwaZulu bantustan as a bulwark against the ANC has given Buthelezi access to state slush funds, the support of the ruthless KwaZulu Police, and the administrative authority and financial means to dispense patronage—jobs, housing, and the like. Hence the leaders of Inkatha and of South Africa's security forces are equally fearful of their power atrophying under a new, democratic order.

Whatever limited comparisons can be made between the Balkan and South African conflicts are best sought not in ethnic nationalism but elsewhere: in the contest over dwindling resources amidst local and global recessions; in ideological bewilderment following the implosion of old certitudes (be they apartheid, socialist, communist, or anti-communist); and in the uncertain promise of the elusive, often rhetorical idea of democracy.

Perhaps most significantly of all, both the former Yugoslavia and South Africa face the labor of emerging from beneath decades of inflated militarization which, as a proportion of GNP, has dwarfed the spending of even heavily militarized Western countries like Britain and the U.S.A. As a result of these buildups, both the former Yugoslavia and Southern Africa are saturated with arms and military personnel who have every motive for forestalling their own obsolescence. The dissipation of the enemy constructs that secured their employment and the waning of the old regimes has rendered many professional soldiers violently insecure, as they ponder fates ranging from tribunals and prison to unemployment and evaporating pensions.

In seeking to shore up their precarious power, the military relics of the decaying orders in ex-Yugoslavia and South Africa have found the discourse of ethnic nationalism highly serviceable. The ethnic nationalist adventurism of the Bosnian Serbs would have stalled without the considerable backing of the Yugoslavian National Army. And in South Africa, the campaign for an ethnically slanted federalism would have achieved little resonance without, on the one hand, support from the South African Defense Force and the KwaZulu Police and, on the other, politically contrived analogies to the campaigns for greater ethnic autonomy in the former Yugoslavia and the Commonwealth of Independent States.

MILITARIZED MEMORY

"I am always fascinated," the Scottish historian, Neal Ascherson, once observed, "when people talk about 'the forging of a nation.' Most nations are forgeries, perpetrated in the last century or so. Some nationalisms relied on literal forgeries: the epics of Ossian in Scotland, the phoney 'Libuse' manuscripts supposed to date from the Czech past, the ancient Welsh literature which was actually written by Iolo Morganwg in the King Lud pub at the bottom of Fleet Street."[43] Ascherson's exposé of national forgeries is consistent with the current trend toward theorizing the nation through the idiom of artifice—inventing, crafting, imagining. This tendency marks a decided advance over theories of natural nations, but it does harbor dangers of its own. For the ethereal idiom of national imaginings can distract us from the institutional solidity of their effects. Perhaps even more insidious is the temptation to assume that all nations or aspirant-nations have available to them a past that is equally susceptible to effective reinvention.

For ethnic nationalist politicians, the decisive challenge is not whether they can generate random reimaginings but whether they can reconceive the past in a manner that guarantees it a popular purchase. The invention of an illustrious ethnic patrimony is of nugatory political value unless it rallies prospective adherents to the ethnic nationalist cause. That much is manifest from the divergent fates of Zulu nationalism under Buthelezi and Ciskeian nationalism under "President" Lennox Sebe. When South Africa goaded the Ciskeian bantustan to "independence" in 1982, Sebe faced a critical difficulty. How was he to manufacture even superficially plausible myths of ethno-genesis in circumstances where there were no cultural, linguistic, or historical grounds for distinguishing Ciskeian Xhosas from their Xhosa neighbors in the Transkei? Despite the ministrations of government ethnologists, and the erection of a National Shrine (inspired by a visit to Israel's Mount Massad), all Sebe's ethno-genetic flights of fancy pranged on take-off. There was no concealing the fact that the idea of "Ciskeiness" as an ethnic nationality lacked any imaginative resonance prior to the 1970s. Sebe's reimaginings were risibly transparent as top-down impositions; he was thus incapable of rousing in his subjects any ethnic nationalist sense of felt antiquity.[44]

Fig. 2: Militarism and Beyond? (Juda Ngwenya; Reuters/Bettmann)

Buthelezi faced no such obstacles in seeking to mobilize ethno-history for political gain. The quest for hegemony over the idea of Zuluness has been bitterly contested since the mid-nineteenth century by forces within Zulu society and by settler interests.[45] Buthelezi has been tirelessly inventive in straightening the vagaries of Zulu history, in suppressing the contingencies of Zulu identity and, above all, in enshrining his political party, Inkatha, as the sole repository of Zulu nationhood.[46] While Buthelezi's methods have often been coercive, he could not have established a following through coercion alone.

Inkatha's militant ethnic nationalism has been mounted not just for the purposes of territorial control but for control over a past that is particularly susceptible to reinvention in epic heroic terms. In the bitter contest over the idea of "Zuluness," the preeminent sanctities are military battles and military leaders, above all, the towering figure of Shaka, arguably the most renowned and mythologized of all nineteenth century African leaders.

The iconography and history that Inkatha has sought to commandeer are relentlessly male and militaristic. The insistence on a warrior blood-lineage and a history narrated through battlefield victories and defeats has meant that Buthelezi repeatedly characterizes the state of "his" Zulu nation in terms of virility or emasculation. Thus, for instance, he and other Inkatha leaders have consistently portrayed the ANC's criticisms of Inkatha's so-called "traditional cultural weapons" as an attempt to impugn Zulu manhood and thereby, the essence of Zulu identity.[47] To be Zulu, in these terms, is to exhibit a martial, "manly" pride that is at once an expression and a defense of the past, an attitude that fuels South Africa's violence.

Buthelezi has obsessively advanced the idea of an indivisible Zulu nation seamlessly descended from Shaka the imperial warrior king. To this end, he (and his cheerleaders in the right wing media) have been party to all kinds of genetic chicanery and gestures of fake primordialism. Typically, one South African newspaper depicts Buthelezi as "Chief Minister of KwaZulu—a position filled by his family since the days of Shaka."[48] Such an illustrious military pedigree is the fruit of some fantastically inventive topiary on Buthelezi's family tree. Moreover, it overlooks the fact that KwaZulu—as opposed to the differently circumscribed Zululand—did not exist prior to the early 1970s. Sometimes, not content with 19th century beginnings, Buthelezi lays claim to a prehistoric ethnic cohesion. "We were a people," he affirms, "long before those who snipe at us had any identity. We were a people since the beginning of time."[49]

Yet the very terms in which Buthelezi defines "Zuluness" testify to the instability of the claimed ethnic nationalist identity. That much is apparent from his startling plunge into the debates over the invention of tradition. Buthelezi chose to enter the intellectual fray not in some fusty, smoke-filled seminar room, but in an open-air stadium where he could vent his theories before tens of thousands of assembled warriors whom, we can assume, were not au courant with the niceties of Hobsbawm and Ranger, Anderson, Mudimbe, Appiah, and Marks.

On this occasion—the 1991 Shaka Day celebrations—Buthelezi set aside one third of his speech to assail Shula Marks for having the temerity to suggest that "we actually reinvented history so that we could paint a picture of Zulu unity" and that the warfare in Natal "has been between Zulus over what it means to be a Zulu."[50] Buthelezi had acquired a video of a Channel 4 documentary, "Age to Age," in which Marks expatiated on the politically charged reinventions of Zulu authenticity. The chief proceeded to regale his forces with a catalog of Marks's "errors," which he condemned as syptoms of

> a campaign to scale down Zulus as Zulus, and a concerted effort to re-invent Zulu history.... Nothing on God's earth is powerful enough to destroy the identity of the Zulu people. We are here because history brought us here.[51]

Yet what kind of historical deliverance is this? Buthelezi spends the bulk of his speech detailing Shaka's military conquests—"We know this because we have learnt it from our grandparents who learnt it from their grandparents who learnt it from those who were alive when King Shaka conquered and united and established his empire."[52] Buthelezi's Shaka Day speech constructs a version of Zuluness wherein the violent incorporation of others stands as a fundamental, historically vindicated expression of the national character. Thus, paradoxically, for Zulu nationalism to stay the same it must remain faithful to Shaka's putative legacy of conquest.

Buthelezi's most powerful ally, King Goodwill Zwelethini, adopts a related logic in goading Inkatha to attack the considerable numbers of Zulus who have identified with the ANC, the United Democratic Front, and the Congress of South African Trade Unions: "I command you to eliminate from your midst all those disgusting usurpers of our dignity.... Rout them out only to make them one of us. Thrash them, if necessary, only to purge them into becoming better Zulus."[53] King Goodwill thus sanctions violence for enforcing an unconditional equation between Inkatha as a political party and Zuluness as an ethnically pure blood-line. His call for purgation is the language not of "ethnic cleansing" but of "ethnic self-cleansing."

Inkatha's monopoly over the vernacular repertoire of Zulu culture has been amply contested, as *Black Mamba Rising*, an anthology of trade union performance poetry, and Liz Gunner and Mafika Gwala's fine collection, *Musho! Zulu Popular Praises*, both testify.[54] As Gunner, Gwala, and Ari Sitas document, Zulu poets aligned with the progressive Congress of South African Trade Unions have moulded Zulu poetic and historical material into something more plastic, more accommodating of an inclusive, non-ethnic vision of national belonging. Sitas distinguishes between the way Zulu traditions of poetic praise have been taken up by Inkatha's chauvinist "authoritarian populism" and by a broader "popular democratic culture." Yet even inclusive adaptations of Zuluness struggle to extricate themselves from a patriarchal ethno-history that has been conventionally narrated through male warrior triumphs and defeats, the aggrandizement of warrior values, and the founding presence of an imperial warrior-king.

The dangers of a nationalist iconography whose dominant images are those of men at war become equally manifest in the quite different context of Serbian history. A BBC documentary by Paul Palinowski gave focus to the epic-heroic verse of Karadzic, self-proclaimed President of the Serbian Republic of Bosnia and Herzegovina and self-styled warrior-poet.[55] Karadzic's compositions and performances on the *gusle* invoke a nationalist history of lost grandeur, returning above all to the Serbs' conquest by the Ottomans in the 14th Century Battle of Kosovo. Idiosyncratically, the crucible of Serbian ethno-genesis is not a martial victory but a cataclysmic battlefield defeat; all the same, the legacy of that founding moment—compounded by massive Serbian casualties in World War II—is a tradition of militant remembrance which easily tilts into ethno-fabulism. (One symptom of this resurgent martial imagination has been the sudden proliferation of Battle of Kosovo kitsch, what one critic has called "papier-mache medievalism."[56]) The bellicose, patriarchal, epic-heroic impulse behind Serbian nationalism has found particularly forceful expression in the novels of Dobrica Cosic, president of rump Yugoslavia. Cosic's romantic portraits of the Serbs' epic sufferings have been seized upon as a primary inspiration by that predatory wing of Serbian nationalism responsible for "ethnic cleansing."[57]

The violence in South Africa and Bosnia suggests that, in periods of economic and ideological crisis, distinctive dangers may arise when an ethnic nationalist political party possesses an obsessive military mythology backed by contemporary military might. Leaders in both instances rely, for their popular support, on an avalanche of inventive remembrance. The Serbs, backed by the Yugoslav National Army, are egged on to reprisal for slaughters fifty or six hundred years deferred. On a smaller scale, Buthelezi's *impis*, bolstered by the KwaZulu Police and the South African Defense Force, are emboldened by the fantasy that Shaka the Great—he who defeated the British army and a host of African societies—sired Inkatha.[58]

The role of militarized memory in the brutal chauvinisms of Buthelezi's and Karadzic's forces complicate efforts, such as Etienne Balibar's, to discriminate categorically between legitimate and illegitimate nationalisms. Balibar has sought to make the issue of power decisive: "We have no right," he maintains, "to equate the nationalism of the dominant with that of the dominated, the nationalism of liberation with the nationalism of conquest."[59] Yet this assumes an absolute divide. What of those many circumstances where an ethnic nationalist ideology is constructed from layered memories of subjection and dominance?

What, for instance, of the Palestinian predicament? The Palestinians stand, in Edward Said's lapidary phrase, as "the victims of the victims," oppressed by people who can mobilize in their defense memories of their own persecution.

Thus the power of ethnic memory enables presently oppressive ethnic nationalisms—be they Israeli, Afrikaner, or Serbian—to continue to fixate on past sufferings, whether at the hands of Germany, or the British or Ottoman empires. Sometimes power relations among nationalisms are triangulated—the Quebecois, for instance, can be projected as colonized and colonizing in relation to Anglo-Canadians and indigenous Canadian peoples. Afrikaners, while busy subjugating black South Africans, elaborated an ethnic nationalist narrative that centered on their own territorial dispossession and sufferings at British hands, including the death of twenty-eight thousand of their people in British concentration camps during the Anglo-Boer War.[60] When Italy occupied Ethiopia, the dominant Amhara viewed them as European oppressors while many other Ethiopian ethnicities—themselves conquered by the Amharic empire in the nineteenth century—embraced the Italians as liberators.[61]

These impacted narratives of ethnic nationalist self-perception admit a broader perspective on the power struggles waged by the Serbian and Inkatha ethnic nationalist leadership. Both groups were relative beneficiaries of the old, now declining orders. Yet the Serbs' current concentration of military and political might have not allayed their fears of Ottoman and Papal tyrannies revisited. And in striving to monopolize the idea of Zuluness, the Inkatha leadership has reanimated the Zulus' ambiguous status as a colonized empire, a people subjugated by white settlers but also—as their grand history putatively testifies—the "natural" overlords of other African peoples. Thus, from the perspective of ethnic nationalists, the question of domination or subjection is often unanswerable on the basis of present power alone and becomes instead subject to the militant, manipulative politics of ethnic remembrance.

South Africa enjoys two decisive advantages over the former Yugoslavia in the effort to keep pseudo-commemorative ethnic nationalisms at bay. For most South Africans, such political practices have been discredited in advance by apartheid efforts to mobilize ethnicity through the bantustans. Moreover, much the strongest current of nationalism in South Africa—that represented by the ANC—is inclusive, non-racial, and premised on a conciliatory unity not an enforced ethnic homogeneity.

The ANC has a far from unblemished record, as has been confirmed by the torture and summary executions in the Quatro guerilla camp and the organization's implication in the ongoing violence. Yet, mercifully, of the myriad forms of corruption open to it, ethnic absolutism does not rank among them. For the ANC is a broad church whose ethnic and ideological ecumenicism is of incalculable worth in the current epoch. Indeed, of the decisive political contestants in South Africa—the ANC, the National Party, Inkatha, and the Pan-Africanist Congress—the ANC alone can claim a durable record of ethnic inclusion: for more than a quarter of a century, the organization has accepted members from every South African ethnicity. As the visceral zealotries of ethnic nationalism threaten to become *the* malaise of the 1990s on a sweeping international front, South Africans should find solace in the fact that their most powerful nationalist party has long defined itself in terms that preclude any recourse to an ethnic pedigree. It is a party that offers no joy whatsoever to the purveyors of ethnic "authenticity," the crafters of primordial memory, and all the other ethno-antiquarians.

CONCLUSION

These past few years have brought to crisis point the profound international confusion in the procedures for national legitimation. A major factor in this crisis has been the persistent assumption that ideally nationalisms should correspond to ethnic cultures. This view is implicit, for instance, in Ernest Gellner's portrait of nationalism as "the striving to make culture and polity congruent, to endow culture with its own political roof, and not more than one roof at that."[62] Even if one set aside the always approximate character of ethnic identity, only a few micro-nation-states could meet this exacting criterion. However, the rift between principle and practice does not appear to have weakened the incentives for invoking a putatively cohesive ethnicity as primary evidence in claiming statehood.

How can the world "community" arrest this potentially regressive process without implicitly favoring the historical status quo? The blood-and-soil arguments that have fortified France or Sweden as nation-states are no more logical than those later mounted in favor of statehood for Palestine or East Timor or Croatia. Such appeals all resort in one way or another to the idiom of antiquity, tradition, cultural authenticity, linguistic uniqueness, ethnicity, and territorial integrity. Thus the division lies not between authentic and inauthentic nation-states, but between nations whose statehood achieved early international recognition and those from whom statehood was withheld.

Thus aspirant nation-states find themselves in a Catch-22: despite the rarity of ethnically homogeneous states, prospective states find themselves held to an archaic and potentially destabilizing vision of what constitutes a nation. Yet in seeking to reinvent themselves as singular and homogeneous they cannot legitimately resort to the conquests and "cleansings" that countries like France, Britain, Germany, Turkey, and Spain once used to secure the internationally sanctified statehood they now enjoy.

The bloody consequences of this unresolved procedural dilemma were exemplified by Germany's hasty recognition of Slovenia and Croatia's—but not Bosnia's—claims to independence. While Germany's decision may have helped check the Serbian onslaught against Croatia, it simultaneously precipitated the dismembering of Bosnia-Herzegovina on the altar of blood-and-soil nationalism. Complex historical allegiances lay behind the German decision, but it was prompted partly by a prejudice in favor of would-be-states that purport to ethnic homogeneity. Thus, the lingering prestige of sameness in the execution of such claims becomes an incentive for the violent measures required to produce a facade of uniformity.

That canny nineteenth century philosopher of nationalism, Ernest Renan, recognized this temptation: "Unity," he remarked, "is always effected by means of brutality."[63] While this may not be wholly true of "unity," it certainly holds for homogeneity. In the current world climate, the rewards for the pursuit of homogeneity remain explosively high. Far from resolving minority-majority tensions the pursuit of homogeneity is liable to provoke ever smaller micro-ethnic claims in a spiral of action and reaction, destroying, in the process, precious legacies of inter-communal forbearance.

NOTES

INTRODUCTION

1. Quoted, *Frontline: South Africa*, Programme 2, PBS, 26 August 1986.
2. Alan Pifer, "South Africa in the American Mind," *Commemoration Day Lecture*, University of the Witwatersrand, South Africa, 14 Oct. 1981. (Johannesburg: University of Witwatersrand, 1981), p. 10.
3. Ronald Reagan, "Interview with the President: Question-and-Answer Session with Walter Cronkite of CBS News, 3 March 1981," *Weekly Compilation of Presidential Documents* 17, 10, p. 235.
4. June Jordan, "South Africa: Bringing It All Back Home," in *Moving Towards Home* (London: Virago, 1989), pp. 116-17.
5. Hazel Carby remarks on black Americans' use of the Johannesburg analogy in her "Multicultural Wars," in *Black Popular Culture*, (ed.) Gina Dent (Seattle: Bay Press, 1992), p. 195. For South African invocations of Harlem and Chicago as analogies to Sophiatown, see for example, Ezekiel Mphahlele, *Voices in the Whirlwind* (New York: Hill & Wang, 1972), p. 98 and anon, "Inside Johannesburg's Underworld:

the New Chicago," *African Drum*, October 1951, pp. 5-7.

6. Paul Gilroy, "One Nation Under a Groove: The Cultural Politics of 'Race' and Racism in Britain," in David Goldberg (ed.), *Anatomy of Racism* (Minneapolis: University of Minnesota Press, 1990), p. 280.

7. Cornel West, Guest Lecture, Columbia University, 29 March 1993.

8. Neal Ascherson, *Games With Shadows* (London: Radius, 1988), p.13.

9. June Jordan, "Living Room," *Notes Towards Home* (Boston: Thunders Mouth Press, 1985), p. 87.

10. Unnamed National Party Member of Parliament speaking in the 1960s. Quoted David M. Smith, *Apartheid in South Africa* (Cambridge, England: Cambridge University Press, 1990), p. 39.

11. These popular perceptions, of course, belie the complex instability of official conceptions of ethnicity and race, as apartheid's ideologues sought to adjust the system—usually more in rhetoric than practice—to the waxing and waning of local and global pressures. On the subject of these changes, see Anne McClintock and Rob Nixon, "No Names Apart: The Separation of Word and History in Derrida's 'Le Dernier Mot du Racisme,'" in Henry Louis Gates (ed.), *"Race," Writing, and Difference* (Chicago: University of Chicago Press, 1986), pp. 339-53. See also Dan O'Meara's insistence that South African "racial policy is open to a sequence of somersaults, deviations, and permutations which endlessly confuse those who regard it as the product of a monolithic racial ideology." "The 1946 African Mine Workers' Strike and the Political Economy of South Africa," in Martin J. Murray (ed.), *South African Capitalism and Black Political Opposition* (Cambridge, Mass., 1982) p. 363.

12. Quoted, Rob Nixon, "Culture Heroes," *Voice Literary Supplement*, October, 1989, p. 15.

13. Miroslav Hroch, *Social Preconditions of National Revival in Europe: A Comparative Analysis of the Social Composition of Patriotic Groups among the Smaller European Nations*, trans. Ben Fowkes (Cambridge, England: Cambridge University Press, 1985), p. 132.

14. Njabulo Ndebele, *Rediscovery of the Ordinary: Essays on South African Literature and Culture* (Johannesburg: Congress of South African Writers, 1991), p. 8.

15. Njabulo Ndebele, "South African Literature and the Construction of Nationhood," *Staffrider*, 10, no. 4, 1992, p. 25.

CHAPTER ONE / Harlem, Hollywood

1. Bloke Modisane, *Blame Me On History* (1963; rpt. New York: Simon & Schuster, 1986), p. 16.

2. On the popularity of American labels in clothing, see especially Modisane, p. 50; on Sophiatown's taste in movie stars, see *Sophiatown*, the program to the musical (Johannesburg: Market Theatre, 1986), pp. 11-12 and Mattera's remarks in Pippa Stein and Ruth Jacobson (ed.), *Sophiatown Speaks* (Johannesburg: Junction Avenue Press, 1986), p. 10.

3. Can Themba, *The Will To Die* (1972; rpt. London: Heinemann, 1983), p. 110;

Anthony Sampson, *Drum: An African Adventure* (1956; rpt. London: Hodder and Stoughton, 1983), p. 26; Stein and Jacobson, p. 22; Paul Gready, "The Sophiatown Writers of the Fifties: the Unreal Reality of their World," *Journal of Southern African Studies*, 16, 1, March 1990, p. 154.

4. Mike Nicol, *A Good-Looking Corpse* (London: Secker and Warburg, 1990), p. 89.
5. David B. Coplan, *In Township Tonight! South African's Black City Music and Theatre* (London: Longman, 1985).
6. Lewis Nkosi, "The Fabulous Decade," *Home and Exile and other Selections* (London: Longman, 1983), pp. 3-24.
7. Dougmore Boetie, *Familiarity is the Kingdom of the Lost* (London: Barrie & Rockliff-Cresset Press, 1969), p. 19.
8. Themba, p. 104. As an index of the widespread hardship in Sophia, much of the community had just one tap for every forty people.
9. Themba, p. 107. Writers who have likened Sophiatown to Harlem include Mphahlele, Nakasa, and Mark Mathabane. See Ezekiel Mphahlele, *Voices in the Whirlwind* (New York: Hill and Wang, 1972), p. 98; Nakasa, in Essop Patel (ed.), *The World of Nat Nakasa* (1975; rpt. Johannesburg: Ravan, 1985), p. 188; and Mathabane, Introduction to Modisane, vii.

   Modikwe Dikobe has portrayed Sophia as the "Chicago of South Africa" in his story "Sophiatown Kayalam" (quoted Andre Proctor, "Class Struggle, Segregation and the City: a History of Sophiatown 1905-40, in Belinda Bozzoli (ed.), *Labour, Townships and Protests* (Johannesburg: Ravan, 1979), p. 49. For the Chicago analogy, see also Nicol, p. 41; Stein and Jacobson (eds.), p. 1; and anon, "Inside Johannesburg's Underworld: the New Chicago," *African Drum*, Oct. 1951, pp. 5-7.
10. "Little Harlem" was another of Sophia's popular names. On this score, see Coplan, p. 179. Arna Bontemps, "Harlem the Beautiful," *Negro Digest*, 15, no. 3 (Jan. 1965), p. 62. Bontemps's phrase referred to Harlem in the summer of 1924.
11. Ralph Ellison, *Shadow and Act* (New York: Random House, 1964), p. 78.
12. As is often the case with literary or artistic flowerings, the retrospective designation of them as movements tends to flatter their historical and geographical coherence. Defining the parameters of the Sophiatown Renaissance poses some particular difficulties: for example, much of the best writing about the period was published by exiled writers in the 1960s after Sophiatown had been destroyed and its artistic community dispersed.
13. Nakasa, p. 173.
14. David Levering Lewis comments on the urban reverberations of the natural disasters that struck the South's economy in 1915 and 1916. See Lewis, *When Harlem Was in Vogue* (1979; Oxford: Oxford University Press, 1989), p. 21. Tom Lodge observes how "between 1939 and 1952 the African urban population [of South Africa] nearly doubled"; this migration was principally prompted by wartime industrial demand, worsening conditions on white farms, and the droughts that struck during World War II. See, Lodge, *Black Politics in South Africa since 1945* (London: Longman, 1983), pp. 11-12.
15. Arnold Rampersad, "Langston Hughes and Approaches to Modernism in the Harlem Renaissance," in Amrijit Singh et al., *The Harlem Renaissance: Revaluations* (New York: Garland, 1989), p. 52.
16. See, for example, Lewis, pp. 3-24.

17. Nkosi, p. 3. Modisane recalls that large numbers of black South Africans sided emotionally with Germany during the war, partly because South Africans of British descent were their immediate oppressors but also because "the disillusionment of the Africans who fought in the First World War was still green in our memories." (Modisane, p. 78).

18. Nkosi, p. 8.

19. J.U. Jacobs, "The Blues: An Afro-American Matrix for Black South African Writing," *English in Africa* 16, 2 (Oct. 1989), pp. 3-17.

20. See Chapman, p. 213 and Mphahlele, *Afrika My Music: An Autobiography 1957-83* (Johannesburg: Ravan, 1983), p. 19. Mphahlele also records his debt to the Richard Wright of *Uncle Tom's Children* and his admiration for W.E.B. Du Bois (ibid, pp. 18 and 24). Hughes's generosity towards and impact on South African writers was not restricted to Mphahlele and Abrahams. Hughes sent autographed copies of *The Weary Blues, Laughing to Keep From Crying*, and *The Big Sea* to Richard Rive, another prominent contributor to *Drum* who, however, lived in Cape Town's District Six. For Rive's account of Hughes's inspiration and of their friendship, see *Contrast* 4, 2 (1966), pp. 33-39.

21. Motsitsi's prose was also influenced, as Tim Couzens first suggested, by Damon Runyon. See Couzens, *The New African: A Study of the Life and Work of H.I.E. Dhlomo* (Johannesburg: Ravan, 1985), p. 107. Among black South African writers prior to the Sophiatown era, Couzens observes Hughes's influence on both Peter Abrahams and H.I.E. Dhlomo.

22. Alain Locke (ed.), *The New Negro* (1925; rpt. New York: Atheneum, 1992).

23. Couzens, p. 110. For an analysis of the beginnings of the idea of the New African in South Africa during the inter-war era, see especially Couzens's invaluable third chapter (pp. 82-124). Couzens's focus is on the transatlantic ties between African-American and black South African political and cultural thought prior to Sophia's cultural heyday.

24. Abrahams also records his excitement at reading Du Bois's *The Souls of Black Folks* and Weldon Johnson's *Along This Way*. See Abrahams, *Tell Freedom* (London: Faber, 1954), p. 194. Although Abrahams had gone into exile before the height of the Sophiatown era, he revisited Sophia in the early 50s and established with the younger generation of writers there.

25. Locke, p. 15.

26. Ezekiel Mphahlele, quoted in Nicol, p. 2.

27. Themba, p. 105.

28. Miriam Tlali, *Muriel at Metropolitan* (Johannesburg: Ravan, 1975), p. 70.

29. The historic events covered by *Drum* included the Congress of the People in 1955, the 1957 Treason Trial, and the commitment in 1959 by both the ANC and the rival Pan-Africanist Congress to campaigns of non-violent resistance.

30. Nkosi, p. 17. Here Nkosi is speaking specifically of the wave of optimism unleashed by the 1956 musical, *Township Jazz*.

31. Modisane, p. 254.

32. James Weldon Johnson, "Race Prejudice and the Negro Artist," *Harper's*, 157 (Nov. 1928), p. 776; Locke, p. 9. For an account of Fauset's related optimism, see especially Lewis, p. 123.

33. Charles Johnson, quoted Lewis, p. 97.

34. See Mphahlele, *Down Second Avenue* (1959; rpt. London: Faber and Faber, 1984), p. 188.
35. Lewis, p. 117.
36. Lewis, p. 305.
37. On this score, see especially Nick Visser, "South Africa: The Renaissance that Failed," *Journal of Commonwealth Literature* 9, 1 (1976), pp. 42-57; Kelwyn Sole, "Class, Continuity and Change in Black South African Literature 1948-60," in Bozzoli (ed.), pp. 143-82; and David Maughan-Brown, "The Anthology as Reliquary?" *Ten Years of Staffrider* and *The Drum Decade, Current Writing* (Durban, South Africa), 1, 1 (1989), pp. 3-21.
38. See, for example, Mphahlele's criticism of the ANC leadership's indifference to cultural politics in *Down Second Avenue*, pp. 191-92.
39. Gready, p. 141.
40. Sampson, p. 55.
41. Cf. Maimane's insistence that "we [at *Drum*] created a new class of black person" who simultaneously earned the admiration of *tsotsis* (gangsters) and "respectable people." "We could talk to them[the tsotsis] on their level. We were nearer to them than the average black professional person." (Stein and Jacobson, p. 50).
42. As Dorothy Driver observes, "only two black South African women published books written in English in the 1960s—Noni Jabavu and Bessie Head—and both did so from outside the country." ("Urban/Rural Spaces: *Drum* magazine (1951-1959) and the Representation of the Female Body," p. 1. Unpublished paper presented at School of African and Oriental Studies, London, 6th June, 1993).
43. Ibid, pp. 2-10. As Driver observes, successful public women, like the political leader, Lilian Ngoyi, tended to be portrayed with a mixture of "idealization, anxiety and contempt."
44. See, on this score, Mphahele interview, p. 138.
45. Sampson p. 22. The phrase "jungle track" was picked up from Countee Cullen's poem "Heritage" which was republished in the first issue of *African Drum*, 1, 1 (1951). The Sophiatown set's rejection of the disparaged "jungle track" and their determined sense of urban belonging calls to mind Harlem's distaste for the primitivizing impulse that permeated works like Eugene O'Neill's *The Emperor Jones*. According to Langston Hughes, when *The Emperor Jones* played at Harlem's Lincoln Theatre, the audience "didn't know what to make of the Emperor Jones. ...And when the Emperor started running naked through the forest hearing the Little Frightened X, naturally they howled with laughter." They bellowed at Jones to "come on out o' that jungle—back to Harlem where you belong." Hughes, *The Big Sea* (New York: Knopf, 1940), p. 325.
46. Mphahlele, in Nicol, p. 212.
47. See Phillip Stein's remarks, in Pippa Stein and Jacobson (eds.), p. 62.
48. Phillip Stein, in Pippa Stein and Jacobson, p. 63; Nadine Gordimer, "Notes of an Expropriator," *The Times Literary Supplement*, 4 June, 1964, p. 7. The closing pages of Gordimer's *A World of Strangers* do, however, bear the clear imprint of Forster's skeptical, open-ended resolution of *A Passage to India*. See *A World of Strangers*, (1958; rpt. London: Penguin, 1988), pp. 265-66.
49. Modisane, p. 291.
50. Quoted Coplan, p. 174.

51. Harry Bloom, *King Kong: An African Jazz Opera* (London: Collins, 1961) , p. 19.
52. Ibid, p. 7.
53. Gordimer, *A World of Strangers*, p. 201. One observes, in passing, that white-directed musicals about Harlem life played a substantial role in spreading the white vogue for Harlem from the mid-20s onwards.
54. Rampersad, Introduction to *The New Negro*, xvi.
55. *Down Second Avenue*, p. 217.
56. Quoted Chapman, p. 192.
57. Modisane, p. 87.
58. In a shift of metaphor, Modisane also speaks of the likelihood of being crushed if you take up residence on the "fly-over" between the contending cultures. (Ibid, p. 254). Coplan observes a similar kind of brinkmanship among Sophiatown musicians who "made it" in white productions and clubs. Within the community, they were simultaneously revered for their talents and sometimes criticized for capitulating to the white entertainment industry. See Coplan, pp. 176-77.
59. Modisane, p. 94.
60. See "Crepuscule," in *The Will to Die*, pp. 2-11.
61. Ibid, p. 159.
62. As a vivid instance of this process, see Lewis's portrait of relations between Locke and the wealthy white dowager, Charlotte Mason: "Locke's bondage to Charlotte Mason…was more apparent than real. He walked a tightrope between obsequious accommodation to the old lady and nervous fidelity to his own beliefs, dissembling masterfully and taking the cash. His stratagem was to use Mason's money to prove how like well-bred, intelligent whites well-bred, intelligent Afro-Americans were. Mason's expectations of her chamberlain were quite different…to 'slough off white culture.'" (Lewis, p. 154).
63. Shula Marks, *The Ambiguities of Dependence in South Africa* (Baltimore: Johns Hopkins University Press, 1986), p. 2.
64. Baker, p. 17.
65. Modisane, p. 91.
66. Modisane, p. 90.
67. Ibid, p. 73.
68. Ibid, p. 75.
69. Nkosi, "Bloke Modisane," *Southern African Review of Books* (Feb/May 1990), p. 11.
70. Many African-Americans with advanced education were, of course, drawn into the political campaigns of the day; my point is merely that compared to Sophiatown, proportionately more were active as cultural brokers and artists.
71. At that stage, only one journalist, Henry Nxumalo, was black. On this point, see Chapman, p.188.
72. *The African Drum*, 1, 1 (March 1951), pp. 5-9.
73. "Opinion," *The African Drum* 1, 2 (April 1951), p. 1.
74. Alan Paton, *Cry, the Beloved Country* (1948; rpt. London: Penguin, 1987), p. 25.
75. I am not, of course, suggesting that this was Cullen's express intention, merely indicating how the appearance of his poem in *African Drum* can be read in terms of the vectors of South African cultural and political life.
76. The film version, directed by Zoltan Korda, appeared in 1951. See also, *Cry, the*

Beloved Country: a Verse Drama adapted by Felicia Komai (New York: Friendship Press, 1955); "Paton and His Beloved Country," *Life*, 27: 149, Nov. 14, 1949; Kurt Weill and Maxwell Anderson, *Lost in the Stars: A Musical Tragedy Based on Alan Paton's Novel, Cry, the Beloved Country* (1949; rpt. New York: Chappell, 1952).

77. The Sophiatown set's distaste for Stephen Kumalo is given dramatic form in Lionel Rogosin's film, *Come, Back Africa*. In a scene set in a local *shebeen*, Rogosin has Modisane, Themba et al. expound on the inadequacy of Paton's account of urban African life.

78. Nkosi, "The Fabulous Decade," *Tasks and Masks*, pp. 4-5. Nkosi expounds further on his resistance to *Cry, the Beloved Country* in an unpublished interview with Peter Davis (London, Dec. 1989, pp. 19-22). There Nkosi suggests that young male African viewers identified with John Kumalo, the priest's activist, irremediably urban brother, despite Paton's negative portrayal of him.

79. Mphahlele, quoted Nakasa, p. 192.

80. Paton himself was fully aware of the impact of this coincidence. He declared in his autobiography that the publication of *Cry, the Beloved Country* "could justly be called one of the two decisive events in my life. The extraordinary thing is that the second decisive event happened soon after.... [T]he event of May 26, 1948, brought my intention to nothing, and condemned me to a struggle between literature and politics." *Towards the Mountain*, (New York: Scribner, 1980, pp. 303-04).

81. Themba in Nakasa, xviii.

82. Ironically, after *African Drum* mutated into *Drum*, its African readership climbed, while most of its white readers fell away.

83. Quoted Sampson, p. 21.

84. The mission schools' bias toward male education, together with the patriarchal character of most black families, ensured that the New Africans were overwhelmingly men.

85. Lewis, p. 98.

86. Quoted Nicol, p. 29.

87. Quoted, ibid. In the music industry, Matshikiza observed the workings of a grasping "white claw" that was far more debilitating and exploitative than the white handclasp at *Drum*. See Robert Mshengu Kavanagh, *Theatre and Cultural Struggle in South Africa* (London: 1985), p. 59.

88. Zora Neale Hurston, "What White Publishers Won't Print," in Alice Walker (ed.), *I Love Myself When I'm Laughing. A Zora Neal Hurston Reader* (New York: The Feminist Press, 1979), pp. 169-73. I am grateful to Priscilla Wald for drawing my attention to the significance of this essay.

89. Hendrik F. Verwoerd, 7 June 1954, in A.N. Pelzer (ed.), *Verwoerd Speaks: Speeches 1948-1966*, (Johannesburg: APB Publishers, 1966), p. 73.

90. As Modisane mordantly observed, "a law-abiding African is as black as a lawless Native." (Modisane, p. 49.) Cf. Steve Biko's observation a generation later that: "No average black man[sic] can ever at any moment be absolutely sure that he is not breaking a law. There are so many laws governing the lives and behavior of black people that sometimes one feels that the police only need to page at random through their statute book to be able to get a law under which to charge a victim." (*I Write What I Like* (San Francisco: Harper & Row, 1978), p. 75.)

91. Modisane, p. 153.

92. For an account of Nakasa and Themba's endorsement of the outlaw image, see Nkosi in Themba, vii.
93. Nicol, 114.
94. Modisane, p. 63.
95. Sampson, p. 82. See also, *Sophiatown*, pp. 12-13, and Nkosi interview with Davis, p.5.
96. Sampson, p. 82.
97. Nicol, p. 70. Kort Boy's direct inspiration appears to have been the short gangster who knives a night watchman in *Street With No Name*. See, on this score, Sampson, p. 82.
98. Stein and Jacobson, p. 67-70.
99. Clive Glaser, "Anti-Social Bandits: Culture, Resistance and the *Tsotsi* Subculture on the Witwatersrand During the 1940s and 1950s," unpublished paper presented at the African Studies Institute, University of Witwatersrand, 17 Sept. 1990, pp. 1-2.
100. Ibid, p. 8.
101. On this score, see for example, Modisane, p. 64.
102. Ibid, p. 227.
103. Huddleston, p. 65.
104. Ibid, p. 63.
105. The first cult quote is from *Street With No Name*, the second from *Background to Danger*. See Sampson, pp. 78-82. See also, Mattera's comments re. tsotsis' appropriation of movie lines in Stein and Jacobson, p. 10.
106. Mattera, in Stein and Jacobson, p. 12.
107. Nkosi in Themba, x.
108. Modisane on occasion voiced doubts about the ethical impact of the movies: he felt that his retreat into Hollywood's world of technicolor gangsters had exacerbated his "repressed violence" and "tinsel morality." (Modisane, p. 172).
109. *Cape Times* (Cape Town), June 20, 1956,
110. *The Star*, 15 Jan. 1954; quoted Glaser, p. 17.
111. Ibid.
112. Sampson, p. 82.
113. Robert Stam and Louise Spence, "Colonialism, Racism, and Representation," *Screen* 24, 2 (1983), pp. 16-17. I am grateful to Cassandra Ellis for drawing my attention to the relevance of Stam and Spence's work to Modisane's autobiography in her insightful, unpublished Master's thesis, "Blame Me on Hollywood." (Columbia University, 1990).
114. Manthia Diawara, "Black Spectatorship: Problems of Identification and Resistance," in *Screen* 29, 4 (1988), p. 66.
115. In addition to Sampson, op cit., see Mattera in Stein and Jacobson, p. 16, and Nkosi's unpublished interview with Davis, pp. 1, 5-6.
116. Modisane, p. 168.
117. Nkosi interview with Davis, p. 2.
118. Ibid, p. 17.
119. South Africa's prohibition laws applied to blacks only. Thus *shebeen* queens had to organize runners who were prepared to operate between legal white and illegal black liquor outlets. In this critical dimension of the trade, a significant role was played by "coloreds" who were sufficiently light-skinned to be capable of passing.

120. Here I favor the original South African title to Mattera's autobiography—*Memory is the Weapon*—over the blander American version, *Sophiatown, Coming of Age in South Africa* (Boston: Beacon Press, 1989).
121. Ibid, p. 13.
122. Mattera, quoted Stein and Jacobson, p. 10
123. This did, however, vary somewhat from writer to writer. Mattera avers that Matshikiza only spoke patois on assignments for *Drum*, whereas Modisane was more steeped in the language because of his local, shebeen upbringing.
124. Modisane, p. 139.
125. *Memory is the Weapon*, p. 28.
126. Ibid, p. 23; p. 30.
127. Nakasa, p. 159.
128. For a fuller account of the riots, see Lewis, pp. 306-07.
129. In the post-Sharpeville years, many of the literary exiles, Modisane, Mphahlele, and Nkosi among them, aligned themselves more squarely with the liberation movements than they had while inside the country. The Publications and Entertainment Act (1963) and the Amendment of the Suppression of Communism Act (1966) both radically curtailed freedom of expression in South Africa.
130. Mphahlele, "South African Writers Talking," *English in Africa* 6, 2 (1979), p. 3.
131. Nakasa, xii.
132. Themba, pp. 8-9.
133. The imprint of Biko's example endures, in adjusted form, in the ANC. Notwithstanding the ANC's nonracialism, many of its prominent leaders emerged from the ranks of the Black Consciousness movement. While they came to reject Biko's separatism, they tended to carry forward other elements of this thought, like the importance of black leadership and the need for cultural regeneration and self-esteem. (Black Consciousness, one should add, went no further than the Sophiatown Renaissance in accommodating or fostering the creative talents of women writers. The cultural atmosphere of the 70s was as unrelievedly macho as that of the 50s).
134. Steve Biko, "Black Consciousness and the Quest for a True Humanity," in *Black Theology: the South African Voice*, (ed.) Basil Moore (London, 1973), p. 43.
135. See, for example, this remark from Serote in 1975: "When I started writing, it was as if there had never been writers before in my country. By the time I learned to write many people…had left the country and were living in exile. We could not read what they had written, so it was as if we were starting from the beginning." Quoted Mbulelo Vizikhungo Mzamane, "An Unhistorical Will into past Times," *Current Writing* 1 (1989), p. 37. In a similar vein, Miriam Tlali laments the unavailability of earlier black writing: "They say writers learn from their predecessors. When I searched frantically for mine there was nothing but a void. What had happened to all the writings my mother had talked about?" ("In Search of Books," *Star*, 30 July 1980.)
136. Mongane Wally Serote, "The Nakasa World," in *The World of Nat Nakasa*, xxxi, xxix. Cf. the statement by another of the Black Consciousness writers, Mafika Gwala, that "Nat Nakasa died on the side of whiteness." Quoted in Abraham H. de Vries, "An Interview with Richard Rive," *Current Writing* 1 (1989), p. 47.

137. Richard Wright, "Blueprint for Negro Writing," *New Challenge* 2 (Fall 1937), p. 53.

138. Zora Neale Hurston, "Characteristics of Negro Expression," in Nancy Cunard (ed.), *Negro Anthology* (New York: Ungar Press, 1934), p. 43.

139. Hughes, "The Negro Artist and the Racial Mountain," *The Nation* (June, 23, 1926), p. 692.

140. The revived interest in Sophiatown during the 80s manifested itself most strikingly in Junction Avenue Theatre's hit production, *Sophiatown* (1986), William Kentridge's film, *Freedom Square and Back of the Moon*, Jurgen Schadeberg's film *Have You Seen 'Drum' Lately?* (1989), as well as in an upsurge of oral histories and academic inquiry concerning the period. The impetus for this burgeoning interest came both from a sense of the 50s and 80s as politically kindred decades and from the long awaited unbanning, between 1982 and 1986, of most of the Sophiatown literature.

141. Houston A. Baker, Jr., xvi.

142. A. P. Mda, "African Youth and the Pictorials," *The Africanist*, May-June, 1955. Quoted Chapman, p. 199.

143. Couzens et al., "Looking in: Interviews with Es'kia Mphahlele," p. 125. Cf. Ndebele's judgment regarding this period that "where people are breaking out of a history of silence…it may seem more important for them initially to express themselves in any manner they can, than for them to postpone their speech while attempting to master the art of rhetoric." Ndebele, "The Ethics of Intellectual Combat," *Current Writing* 1, 1 (1989), p. 23.

144. Quoted Nicol, p. 230.

CHAPTER TWO / The Devil in the Black Box

1. Benedict Anderson, *Imagined Communities: Reflections on the Origin and Spread of Nationalism* (1983; rpt. London: Verso, 1985), p. 122.

2. Philip Schlesinger, *Media, State and Nation: Political Violence and Collective Identities* (London: Sage, 1991), p.123.

3. Anderson, p. 123.

4. Piet Meyer, *Report of the Commission of Inquiry into Matters Relating to Television* (Pretoria: Government Printer, 1971), p. 2.

5. Ibid.

6. *Republic of South Africa. House of Assembly Debates (Hansard)* (Pretoria: Government Printers, 1960), 9 March 1960, 3086.

7. Dr. G.C.F. Weisacker, quoted by Engelbrecht, *Hansard*, 9 Feb. 1970, cols. 533-35; and *Hansard*, 2 May 1967, col. 5278.

8. Hertzog, *Hansard*, 2 May 1967 col. 5287.

9. *Hansard*, 2 May 1967, col. 5275; *Hansard*, 19 Sept. 1966, cols. 2406-408. Cf. Hertzog's remark that "Television will destroy the salvation of the South African and the white man in South Africa." *Hansard*, 11 Feb. 1970, columns 830-32.

10. *Hansard*, 2 Sept., 1966, col. 2482.

11. Verwoerd, *Hansard*, 9 March 1960, col. 3003.

12. Dr. Kellerman, "Hy is Ons Vyand—Nie Bondgenoot" ["It is Our Enemy—Not Friend"], *Dagbreek en Sondagnuus*, 14 May 1967; W.W.B. Eiselen, quoted, T.

Dunbar Moodie, *The Rise of Afrikanerdom: Power, Apartheid, and the Afrikaner Civil Religion* (Berkeley: Univ. of California Press, 1975), p. 272.

13. Such sentiments persisted in some quarters of the far right after TV's introduction. Cf. the identical fears about denationalization and Americanization voiced by the Conservative Party MP, Tom Langley, in 1986 ("Langley Thumbs His Nose at SABC," *Daily Dispatch*, 27 Oct. 1986).

14. Quoted Basil Bunting, *The Rise of the South African Reich* (1969; rpt. London: International Defence and Aid Fund, 1986), p. 326.

15. On the genesis of Afrikaner nationalist anti-Semitism, see especially, Patrick J. Furlong, *Between Crown and Swastika: The Impact of the Radical Right on the Afrikaner Nationalist Movement in the Fascist Era* (Johannesburg: University of Witwatersrand Press, 1991), pp. 46-69.

    The Nationalists mounted some subsidiary objections: for instance, that South Africa had too many mountains to make it suitable TV terrain. But hadn't Switzerland and Peru overcome more severe versions of that problem? The country was too large and sparsely inhabited. What of other, more thinly populated nations—Canada, Sudan, Australia, Mongolia? Well, then, South Africa had too many languages. Weren't Ethiopia, Nigeria and Ghana, all of which admitted television before South Africa, more linguistically diverse?

16. One of the few media critics to take up this issue has been John Tomlinson. See especially, his *Cultural Imperialism* (London: Pinter, 1991), pp. 68 ff.

17. See, J. A. Marais, "Ruimte-TV sal vyand in ons huise bring" ["Satellite-TV will bring the enemy into our houses"], *Hoofstad*, 8 Sept. 1969, as well as "Ons Kan TV Nie Bekostig Nie" ["We Can't Affford TV"], *Hoofstad*, 9 Sept. 1969, and his comments in *Hansard* (South Africa), 19 March 1969, col. 2858. Herbert I. Schiller, "Fast Food, Fast Cars, Fast Political Rhetoric." *Intermedia* 20, 4-5 (Aug-Sept. 1992), p. 21. See, too Schiller's earlier work, such as *Mass Communications and American Empire* (New York: Kelley, 1970).

18. Stuart Hall, "Our Mongrel Selves," *New Statesman and Society*, 19 June 1992, p. 8.

19. See, for example, Kellerman, "Hy is Ons Vyand—Nie Bondgenoot." Such thinking was by no means restricted to Nationalist parliamentarians. See, for example, the letter from Mrs. C. Mathews "You Can Keep TV Ads. and Socialism," *Sunday Express*, 13 April 1969.

20. Dr. Kellerman, "Hy is Ons Vyand—Nie Bondgenoot."

21. P. J. Meyer, *Trek Verder: Die Afrikaner in Afrika* [*Trek Further: the Afrikaner in Africa*] (HAUM, Cape Town, 1959), p. 25. My translation.

22. On the subject of such deferential, submerged racism, see Balibar in Etienne Balibar and Immanuel Wallerstein, *Race, Nation, Class: Ambiguous Identities* (1988; London: Verso, 1991), pp. 23, 43.

23. Hertzog, *Hansard*, 24 March 1961, col. 3656.

24. For a discussion of "nationalist internationalism," see Wilhelm Reich, *Les Hommes dans l'Etat* (Paris: Payot, 1978), pp. 23-27. This type of reasoning was deployed, for example, by Meyer. See, *The Spiritual Crisis of the West* (Johannesburg: South African Broadcasting Corporation, 1966), p. 15.

25. Trevor Philpott, "The End of an Innocent Age?" *The Listener*, July 1976, p. 5.

26. Quoted Reginald Pound, "Orson Welles," *The Listener*, 29 Sept. 1955. Such depic-

tions of TV as the wrecker of home and national life continue into the present. British novelist, Fay Weldon, recently railed against TV for having "destroyed domestic conversation...driven our children to violence and crime...made the ugly self-conscious...and the poor discontented." (Quoted Cosmo Landesman, "Zeitguest," *Weekend Guardian*, 7-8 Dec. 1991).

27. Hertzog's official portfolio was Minister of Posts and Telegraphs. Hertzog's warning, issued in 1959, is quoted in "Its Here—Two Decades Later," *Rand Daily Mail*, 28 April 1971.

28. Ibid.

29. Lynn Spigel, "Television in the Family Circle: The Popular Reception of a New Medium," *Logics of Television: Essays in Cultural Criticism* (Bloomington: Indiana University Press, 1990), pp. 73-97.

30. Ibid.

31. Mr. Moore, *Hansard*, 2 May 1961, col. 5731.

32. Hertzog, *Hansard*, 24 Jan. 1964.

33. Mrs. Tienie Rutherford from Rustenburg writes in support of the moral watchdogs who would keep TV at bay: "...if your watchdogs no longer bark, evil descends unhindered on your house? Let us rather thank the lord that there are still priests who bark against evil and that our government stands by them." ("Bewaar Ons Kindes Van TV Se Onheil," *Hoofstad*, 23 April 1969).

34. *Eastern Province Herald*, 10 July 1971.

35. A. J. van Niekerk, *Hansard*, 11 Sept. 1953, col. 3340.

36. J.J.Engelbrecht, *Hansard*, 9 Feb 1970, col. 554

37. J.E. Potgieter, *Hansard*, 7 March 1960, col. 3003. According to Verwoerd, under pressure from the box "families disintegrate—they become slaves to television." (ibid). Cf. Hertzog's comments on TV slavery, *Hansard* 24 March 1961, col. 3646.

38. "Kophou," "Ons Moet Die Implikasies Van Beeldradio Ken," *Hoofstad*, 23 April 1969. My translation.

39. Hertzog, quoted in "The Other Vast Wasteland," *Time*, 20 Nov. 1964, p. 40.

40. Hertzog expressed concern that "the effect of the wrong pictures on children, the less developed and other races (sic) can be destructive." October, 1959, quoted, "Its Here—Two Decades Later," *Rand Daily Mail*, 28 April 1971. Prof. Coetzee voiced his alarm at the prospect of overly literal readings of TV, given "the immediacy and obvious concreteness of its images which give the illusion of reality," "Beheer Dit Met Oorleg" ["Control it With Care,"], *Dagbreek en Sondagnuus*, 14 May 1967.

41. See, "Ongeduld oor Beeldradio" ["Impatience About TV"], *Die Vaderland*, 10 May 1969.

42. Stuart Cloete, quoted by J.A. Marais, *Hansard*, 19 March. See Hertzog's similar comments in *Hansard*, 24 March 1961, col. 3659. Anti-TV sectors of the Afrikaans press also made much of an incident in Holland in which a woman was "inspired" by a play she had seen on TV to poison her husband. See "Gevare van Beeldradio" [The Dangers of TV"], *Transvaler*, 15 April 1969.

43. J.J. Engelbrecht, *Hansard*, 9 Feb. 1970, col. 554.

44. Hertzog, *Hansard*, 24 March 1961, col. 3661.

45. J.C. Otto, *Hansard*, 19 Sept. 1966, col. 2407.

46. See, for example, the Minister of Posts and Telegraphs hostility to the American

system, *Hansard*, 19 March 1969, col. 2889.

47. W.C.du Plessis, *Hansard*, 11 Sept. 1953. Du Plessis was protesting against the presence of advertising both in radio and TV.

48. Hertzog, *Hansard*, 24 March 1961, col. 3660.

49. See, for example, "TV: End of White Race," *Rand Daily Mail*, 30 June 1969.

50. I borrow this phrase from Harlan Ellison, *The Glass Teat: Essays of Opinion on the Subject of Television* (New York: Ace Books, 1970).

51. Elsabe Brink, in Cheryl Walker (ed.), *Women and Gender in Southern Africa to 1945* (London: James Currey, 1990), pp. 273-92; Isobel Hofmeyr, "Building a Nation from Words: Afrikaans Language, Literature and Ethnic Identity, 1902-1924," in Shula Marks and Stanley Trapido (eds.), *The Politics of Class and Nationalism in Twentieth Century South Africa* (New York: Longman, 1987), pp. 95-123.

52. W. Postma, *Die Boervrouw, Moeder van Haar Volk*, [*The Boer Woman, Mother of Her People*] (Bloemfontein: Nasionale Pers, 1918) p. 179. Quoted and trans. by Brink, p. 281.

53. An insert into *Die Huisgenoot*, July 1919, advertising *Die Burger Leeskring*. Quoted and trans. by Hofmeyr, ibid, p. 110.

54. Ibid.

55. Professor E. C. Pienaar, *Die Burger*, 19 Dec. 1929. Quoted Dunbar Moodie, *The Rise of Afrikanerdom: Power, Apartheid, and the Afrikaner Civil Religion* (Berkeley: University of California Press, 1975), p. 109.

56. Quoted Leroy Vail, in Vail (ed.), *The Creation of Tribalism in Southern Africa* (University of California Press: Berkeley, 1989), p. 11.

57. On the disreputability of the Afrikaans language, see Isabel Hofmeyr's fine article, "Building a Nation from Words: Afrikaans Language, Literature, and Ethnic Identity, 1902-1924," in Shula Marks and Stanley Trapido, eds., *The Politics of Race, Class and Nationalism in Twentieth Century South Africa* (London: Longman, 1987), especially pp. 97-98.

58. Ibid., pp. 95-123.

59. For an excellent account of this process, see Hofmeyr, pp. 95-123.

60. For the fullest account of the forging of Afrikaner nationalism, in its economic and, to a lesser degree, its cultural aspects, see Dan O'Meara, *Volkskapitalisme: Class, Capital and Ideology in the Development of Afrikaner Nationalism, 1934-1948* (Cambridge: Cambridge University Press, 1983).

61. Hofmeyr, p. 97.

62. Moodie, p. 286. Meyer issued this warning to the Broederbond shortly after Verwoerd's assassination in 1966.

63. *South African Broadcasting Corporation Annual Report.* (Johannesburg: S.A.B.C., 1968), p. 7. Cf. Meyer's insistence, a decade earlier, that "of all communications media…the warm, human spoken word is and remains the most powerful and influential. Whatever is carried in the other media, and however these media do it, the influence and effect depends in the last instance on whether the substance is taken up in human conversation, and how it is passed, processed and spread in living conversation." Unpublished address to a leadership course, Stellenbosch, SABC archives. Quoted Ruth Tomaselli et al., *Broadcasting in South Africa* (London: James Currey, 1989), p.71.

64. On the projected ill effects of TV on the Afrikaans language, see, for example, "Fynoor," "Wat Gaan Gebeur Met Beeldradio en Afrikaans," *Hoofstad*, 12 May, 1969; J.G. Truter, "TV Sal Net Onnidige Las Bring," *Die Transvaler*, 27 April 1968; J. A. Marais, "Ons Kan TV Nie Bekostig Nie," *Hoofstad*, 9 Sept. 1969. The one language-one channel argument is also advanced by Dirk Richard, in "TV Kom Dalk Gouer as Wat Ons Dink," ["TV May Be Coming Sooner Than We Think"], *Dagbreek en Landstem* 11 May 1969 and in the editorial, "Wie Arrogant is Oor TV?" ["Who is Presumptuous About TV?"], *Vaderland*, 31 July 1969.

Across the African continent, by 1973, there were radio broadcasts in 239 languages. In this regard only, the Nationalists were correct: nothing like that range could have been achieved through TV, given the relatively small audiences concerned. See Sydney Head (ed.), *Broadcasting in Africa. A Continental Survey of Radio and Television* (Philadelphia: Temple Univ. Press, 1974), pp. 406-11.

65. Pelzer, *Verwoerd Speaks*, p. 180.

66. I am not, of course, implying that their political philosophies went unadjusted from the 1940s to the 1960s. There were, however, some strong if selective continuities that the TV debates exposed in acute form.

67. *Hansard* , 24 Mar. 1961, col. 3646; ibid., 19 Mar. 1969, col. 2839; ibid., 19 Sept. 1966, col. 2409.

68. Meyer cofounded the Afrikaanse Nasionale Studentebond in 1933, and retired as chair of the South African Broadcasting Corporation in 1981. Over and above his leadership of the SABC and the Broederbond, Meyer held office at one time or another in (amongst others) the Afrikaanse Nasionale Studentebond, Afrikaner Nasionale Kultuurraad, the Economic Institute of the Federasie van Afrikaner Kultuurverenegings, and the Nasionale Raad van Trustees. He edited *Volkshandel* and a clutch of other Afrikaner nationalist publications and in 1938 helped found the militantly pro-Nazi Ossewa Brandwag (OB). He went on to lead the organization's labor front, the Arbeidsfront, and emerged as one of the OB's principal strategists and demagogues. In the mid-1940s, he campaigned alongside Hertzog in the Mine Workers Union in an effort to win over Afrikaans workers to the Christian National Unions. By the late 1950s he had become the second most powerful figure in the Broederbond. He went on to become the rector of the Rand Afrikaans University and to chair the Dutch Reformed Church's Inter-Church Anti-Communist Action Committee. Between 1969 and 1971 Meyer chaired the Commission of Inquiry into Matters Relating to TV and in 1976 he oversaw the introduction of the medium he had so long opposed.

De Klerk suggests that Meyer remained, even after the Nationalist Party victory, the most important interpreter of apartheid philosophy into apartheid policy. (*The Puritans in Africa*, p. 214); O'Meara portrays Meyer's influence as "ubiquitous." (*Volkskapitalisme*, p. 143).

69. Meyer was head of the South African Broadcasting Corporation(SABC) from 1959 to 1981 and of the Broederbond from 1960 to 1972.

70. Moodie, pp. 154-55. In an important essay, Andre du Toit stresses the limits of the neo-Fichtean formulation, especially when applied as if Afrikaner nationalism were a unitary, not an internally riven, phenomenon. While traces of neo-Fichteanism are present in the thinking of Meyer in particular, even in the 1960s, I do not mean to imply this was a general tendency among Afrikaner intel-

lectuals. See Du Toit, "Neo-Fichtean Nationalists" and/or Organic Intellectuals? Revisiting the Ideological Entrepreneurs of Modern Afrikaner Nationalism," unpublished paper, presented at the Institute of Commonwealth Studies, London, 6 Feb. 1990.

71. *Nasionalisme as Lewensbeskouing en Sy Verhouding tot Internasionalisme* (Bloemfontein: Nasionale Pers, 1936).

72. For Meyer's defense of Diederichs against Kuyperian Calvinist criticisms that he deified the nation, see Moodie, p. 161.

73. Diederichs, pp. 23-24. Quoted and translated Moodie, p. 159.

74. Diederichs initially represented race, as opposed to ethnic culture, as an unreliable, indeed irrelevant, guide to the demarcation of nations. By the early 1940s, however, he was decreeing that race as well as ethnic culture was an index of fundamental, divinely imbued national differences.

75. Quoted, T. Reagan, "Ideology and Language Policy in Education: the Case of Afrikaans," in H. Du Plessis and T. Du Plessis, *Afrikaans en Taalpolitiek [Afrikaans and the Politics of Language]* (Pretoria: HAUM, 1987), p. 135.

76. Nicolaas Diederichs, *Nasionalisme as Lewensbeskouing en sy verhouding tot Internationsionalisme.* (Bloemfontein: Nasionale Pers, 1935), pp. 23-24.

77. After South Africa became a republic in 1961, Verwoerd was more ambiguous on this score. He saw the need to forge a white alliance and was less concerned than Meyer, Hertzog, and Marais that such an alliance would once again subject Afrikaner cultural, political, and economic interests to English domination.

78. See Johan van der Spuy, "Die Feite Getuig Teen TV" ["The Facts Argue Against TV"], *Transvaler*, 21 February 1968; and Dr. J.C. Otto, *Hansard*, 19 Sept. 1966, cols. 2406-08.

79. *Hansard*, 19 Sept. 1966, cols. 2406-408. Cf. Senator Frey's view that TV "offers the opportunity for the spreading of liberalistic, and where necessary, covert Communist ideologies. The whole of the Western world is today holding particularly liberalistic ideas which are nothing less than the agenda, the preparers of the way for Communism which is behind these things." *Hansard*, 22 May 1961, cols. 4756-757. "Kophou," writing in *Hoofstad*, carried the argument somewhat further: U.S. liberalism had gone so soft on communism that American TV channels were clogged with "anti-Nazi propaganda like The Sound of Music." ("Ons Moet Die Implikasies Van Beeldradio Ken" ["We Must Recognise the Implications of TV"], *Hoofstad*, 23 March 1969).

80. Editorial, *Washington Post*, 28 August 1969. J.A. Marais, "Afrikaner sal TV nie voordelig kan aanwend" [The Afrikaner Won't Be Able to Employ TV Advantageously"], *Hoofstad*, 10 Sept. 1969.

81. See especially O'Meara, *Volkskapitalisme*.

82. Ibid.

83. See P. J. Meyer, *Demokrasie of Volkstaat?* ["Democracy or Volkstaat?"] (Stellenbosch: Wapenskou, 1942); *Arbeidsordening Binne die Volksbeweging en Volkstaat* (Stellenbosch: Wapenskou, 1943); *Die Stryd van die Afrikanerwerker: Die Vooraand Van Ons Sosiale Vrywording* ["The Struggle of the Afrikaans Worker: The Eve of Our Social Liberation"] (Johannesburg: Arbeider en Arbeid, 1944).

84. Cf. the kindred remarks by Dr. J.C. Otto, *Hansard*, 19 Sept. 1966, cols. 2406-408.

85. See, "Gevare van Beeldradio" ["The Dangers of TV"], *Transvaler*, 15 March 1969.

86. In verkrampte, Conservative Party circles such arguments persisted well after TV's introduction. In 1986, CP member of parliament Tom Langley accused SATV of trying to "denationalize" white South Africans and Americanize them: "Nowadays you only find American film material…and it is for one very obvious reason—they all have at least one black in them and its is all aimed at conditioning us and our children. If we allow our children to watch these programmes uncensored, they are going to lose their identity in the end." "Langley Thumbs His Nose at SABC," *Daily Dispatch*, 27 October 1986. Cf. the objection by another Conservative Party MP, Chris Jacobs, to the showing of *The Imposters*—a black-white love affair—which he cites as an instance of "integration propaganda." For the threat which American TV's allegedly "heroic" treatment of the civil rights threat would pose to white South Africans, see J.C. Otto, *Hansard*, 19 Sept. 1966, col. 2407.

87. Verwoerd, *Hansard*, 9 March 1960, col. 3004; Mr. J.E. Potgieter, *Hansard*, 7 March 1960, col. 2892.

88. Hendrik Verwoerd, *Hansard*, 9 March 1960, col. 3004. J.C.Otto, *Hansard*, 19 Sept. 1966, col. 2407. In the course of this particular outburst, Verwoerd suggests that TV could even be meteorologically damaging: "People from overseas who have come here have told me personally that if South Africa wants to retain her attractiveness, including her wonderful climate, the initiative and originality of her people and her progressiveness, the government must keep TV away as long as possible. Some of the immigrants who have come to our country even describe it as a pestilence and a plague."

89. Albert Hertzog, *Hansard*, 20 Sept. 1966, col. 2482.

90. P.J. Meyer, *The Spiritual Crisis of the West* (Johannesburg: South African Broadcasting Corporation, 1966), p. 15.

91. *Hansard*, 24 Mar. 1961, cols. 3665-666.

92. *The Times*, 26 Oct. 1970.

93. Beaumont Schoeman, "Beeldradio: Magtige Integrasiemiddel" ["TV a Powerful Medium of Integration"], *Hoofstad*, 23 April 1968. My translation.

94. Ibid.

95. Marshall McLuhan, *Understanding Media: the Extensions of Man* (1964; rpt. New York: Ark, 1987).

96. See, for example, Meyer's alarm at the way "the emergence of an extensive communications network and a world culture…have encircled and increasingly integrated the entire globe." *The Spiritual Crisis of the West*, p. 10. See, also, Kellerman, "Hy Is Ons Vyand—Nie Bondgenoot," and Prof. Dreyer, "TV Sal Kom, Maar Hou Hom Tog Lank Weg," *Dagbreek en Sondagnuus*, 14 May 1967.

97. M.D.C. de Wet Nel, *Hansard*, 18 May 1959, col. 6007.

98. Hertzog's phrase. Quoted, Philpott, p. 5.

99. Lebonia, Mosia, Don Pinnock, and Charles Riddle, "Warring in the Ether," *Rhodes Journalism Review*, July 1992, p. 41.

100. Ibid, p. 40.

101. "Hertzog Says He's Not Stubborn over TV," *Rand Daily Mail*, 20 May 1961. Cf. Mr. B. Coetzee's remark that "there are more and more broadcast from Africa to our border areas. We have Radio Accra, we have Radio Leopoldville, we have Radio Cairo and I understand there is a host of others who are continually inundating

the Bantu of South Africa with propaganda from outside." *Hansard*, 2 May 1961, col. 5734.

102. See, Rob Davies, Dan O'Meara, and Sipho Dlamini, *The Struggle for South Africa, Vol. 2* (London: Zed, 1984), pp. 288-89.

103. "Hertzog Says He's Not Stubborn Over TV;" *Hansard*, 2 May 1961, cols. 5734-35.

104. Ibid.

105. Douglas Fuchs, "Die Radio en die Gesproke Woord" ["The Radio and the Spoken Word"], *Tydskrif vir Geesteswetenskappe*, vol. 9, 1969, p. 241. Cf. The SABC's portrait of Radio Bantu as an effort to "bring home to the Bantu population that separate development is, in the first place, self-development through the medium of their own language." *SABC Annual Report* (Johannesburg: SABC, 1967), p. 10.

106. For concern over the cosmopolitan bias of TV, see Kellerman, "Hy is Ons Vyand—Nie Bondgenoot."

107. *Hansard*, 7 June 1962, col. 7363. Cf. Hertzog's warning that "if you want someone to buy something, you must make him dissatisfied with what he already has." (Quoted Bunting, p. 326).

108. Quoted in "All your ever wanted to know about TV but were afraid to ask...." *Financial Mail*, special supplement, 14 March 1975, p. 36.

109. Ironically, when the Botha regime sought (and failed) to create a materialistic black middle class as a buffer between white privilege and black revolution in the late 70s and 80s, it sought to harness TV as an ally in the construction of an anti-revolutionary black elite.

110. James Burnham, "Howdy Neigbor," *National Review*, 4 Oct. 1966, p. 976.

111. Ibid.

112. *Hansard*, 10 June 1957, col. 7709.

113. Mr. S.J.M. Steyn, *Hansard*, 9 March 1960, col. 3062.Cf. allied remarks by Helen Suzman, *Hansard*, 19 March 1969, col. 2875 and by E. G. Malan, *Hansard*, 9 March 1960, col. 3087.

114. Diederichs, *Die Burger*, 12 April 1936; quoted Moodie, p. 161.

115. On United Party political policy, see Rob Davies et al. *The Struggle for South Africa*, vol. 1 (1984; rpt. London: Zed, 1988), pp. 157-58.

116. "TV or not TV?" *Star*, 8 June 1962.

117. Mr. Weiss, *Hansard*, 7 June 1962, col. 7361; Mr. H. Miller, *Hansard*, 10 August 1970, col. 1398. Cf. the similar lament issuing from the United Party's Mr. Moore: "We are practically the only civilised country in the world which has not got television.... Television has come to stay in all civilised countries." (*Hansard*, 2 May, 1961, col. 5730)

118. "Out of this World," *Rand Daily Mail*, 21 July 1969. The *Rand Daily Mail*, one should point out, was more supportive of the minute, white Progressive Party than the United Party. However, Progressive Party support for television largely followed UP in its appeal to the discourses of civilization and modernity.

119. E.G. Malan, *Hansard*, 9 March 1960, col. 3087; cf. Malan's use of a similar metaphor in "The Age of the TV Tokoloshe," *Rand Daily Mail*, 27 Sept. 1964.

120. Head, p. 27.

121. *Hansard*, 7 June 1962, col. 7313; cf. Hansard 24 March 1961, col. 3646.

122. *Hansard*, 7 March 1969, col. 517.

123. Mr. E.G. Malan, *Hansard,* 11 Feb. 1970, col. 822.
124. "Out of This World," *Rand Daily Mail,* 21 July 1969.
125. *Hansard,* 19 Sept. 1966, col. 2406.
126. Mr. E.G. Malan, *Hansard,* 9 March 1960, col. 3087.
127. Meyer, *Report of the Commission of Inquiry into Matters Relating to Television* (Pretoria: Government Printers, 1971).
128. William Minter, *King Solomon's Mines Revisited: Western Interests and the Burdened History of Southern Africa* (New York: Basic Books, 1986).
129. Vorster himself was a staunchly authoritarian anti-Communist and had been interned during World War II for pro-Nazi activities. However, unlike Verwoerd, Meyer, and Hertzog, he had not come through the ranks of ethnically exclusive Afrikaner organizations during the 30s and 40s. This reduced his scepticism toward English-Afrikaner alliances on the basis of race rather than ethnicity. Cf. Moodie, p. 292.
130. Prof. Marius Swart, Rector of the University of Port Elizabeth, *Sunday Times,* 7 July 1968.
131. "Trade Body Wants TV," *Natal Witness,* 8 May 1969; "TV Call," *Daily Mail,* 24 October 1969.
132. *Volkskapitalisme,* p. 254.
133. *Rand Daily Mail,* 21 July 1969.
134. Douglas Alexander, "TV Ban Was Not Mine Alone—Hertzog," *Sunday Express,* 11 February 1968.
135. "Public's first taste of TV-viewing," *Sunday Times* 27 July 1969.
136. Mr. D. J. Marais, *Hansard,* 19 March 1969, col. 2853
137. "Dagbreek Editor Backs Clamor for TV," *Rand Daily Mail,* 28 July 1969.
138. *SABC: Annual Report.* (Johannesburg: SABC, 1968), p. 7.
139. Ibid.
140. *SABC: Annual Report.* (Johannesburg: SABC, 1969), p. 8.
141. Ibid, pp. 8-9.
142. Advance notice of this development appeared in "TV—Yes or No," *Sunday Express,* 18 May 1969. For parliamentary discussion of satellite technology, see *Hansard,* 9 Feb. 1970, col. 591 and 11 Feb. 1970, col. 829.
143. J. A. Marais, "Afrikaner Sal TV Nie Voordelig Kan Aanwend" ["The Afrikaner Won't be Able to Employ TV to Advantage"], *Hoofstad,* 10 September 1969.
144. Ibid.
145. Ibid
146. Ibid.
147. "TV End of White Race—Hertzog," *Rand Daily Mail,* 30 June 1969.
148. See the comments by Minister of National of Education, Senator J. P. van der Spuy, "Minister Explains the TV Delay," *Rand Daily Mail,* 28 April 1971.
149. Mr. Nissen, quoted in "TV Vital in National Defence," *Star* 13 April 1972.

CHAPTER THREE / Cry White Season

1. For instance, Euzhan Palcy speaks of film as "the perfect medium for enlightening people about apartheid," while Attenborough perceives Cry Freedom as an effort "to reach the unknowing and the uncaring." See Donna Britt, "'Season' of Euzhan

Palcy's Discontent," *Washington Post*, 26 Sept. 1989, p. D4; Andrew Yarrow, "Richard Attenborough On Art and the World," *New York Times*, 28 Nov. 1987, p. 27.

2. Clearly, I do not mean South African electoral politics, from which blacks are barred.

3. Jeffrey Butler, Richard Elphick, and David Welsh, eds., *Democratic Liberalism in South Africa: Its History and Prospect* (Middleton Connecticut: Wesleyan University Press, 1987).

4. Quoted in Mary Benson, *Chief Albert Lutuli of South Africa* (Cape Town: O.U.P., 1963), p. 31.

5. For a fine critique of the rhetoric of extended rights, see Njabulo Ndebele, "The English Language and Social Change in South Africa," *English Academy Review*, pp. 1-16.

6. E. M. Forster, *A Passage to India* (New York: The Modern Library, 1924), p. 63.

7. Nelson Mandela, *No Easy Walk To Freedom* (London: Heinemann: 1965), p. 170.

8. Alan Paton, *Contact*, 23 Oct. 1964.

9. An essay of this scope cannot, of course, provide a detailed account of the relations among liberalism, apartheid, and black resistance. For a fuller reading of the vicissitudes and ideological lineaments of South African liberalism see Paul B. Rich, *White Power and the Liberal Conscience: Racial Segregation and South African Liberalism 1921-1960* (Johannesburg: Ravan Press, 1984).

10. Andrew Young, *Sevendays*, 20 June 1977, p. 10. Quoted Kevin Danaher, *In Whose Interest? A Guide to U.S.-South African Relations* (Washington, D.C.: Institute for Policy Studies, 1984), p. 42. For one persuasive account of the limited appeal of capitalist rhetoric in South Africa, see Allister Sparks, *The Mind of South Africa* (New York: Knopf, 1990).

11. Sparks, pp. 374; 386.

12. From the proclamations issued by the State President of the Republic of South Africa, 11 December 1986. See Rob Nixon, "The Camera Eye," *The Nation*, 2 May 1987, pp. 578-580.

13. On the difficulty of "selling" black South African stories in another context, see Carolyn Hamilton's fine article on the South African television miniseries, "Shaka Zulu," and its marketing and reception in the U.S.A.: "A Positional Gambit: 'Shaka Zulu' and the Conflict in South Africa," *Radical History Review*, 44, p. 11.

14. This tendency repeats itself in Woods's self-admiring book, *Filming with Attenborough: the Making of Cry Freedom* (New York: Henry Holt, 1987). In the introduction, Attenborough observes: "if I had met Donald Woods without knowing anything about his life, I doubt if I would have thought he possessed a more than passing share of heroism," and hails him as "one of the most unlikely heroes of our time." (pp. vii-viii).

15. See, for example, Armond White, "Apartheid Chic," *Film Comment*, Nov/Dec 1987, pp. 11-16; Christopher Hitchens, "White Wash," *American Film*, Jan/Feb 1988, pp. 62-68; Rob Nixon, "Cry Freedom," *Cineaste* 26, no. 3, 1988, pp. 38-39; Pauline Kael, *The New Yorker*, Nov. 30, 1987, pp. 101-04.

16. Steve Biko, "White Racism and Black Consciousness," *I Write What I Like* (San Francisco: Harper & Row, 1986). The essay was first published in South Africa in 1972. See also Biko's contention that: "For the liberals, the thesis is apartheid, the

anti-thesis is non-racialism, but the synthesis is very feebly defined.... Black Consciousness defines the situation differently. The thesis is in fact a strong white racism and therefore, the antithesis to this must, ipso facto, be a strong solidarity amongst the blacks on whom this white racism seeks to prey. Out of these two situations we can therefore hope to reach some kind of balance—a true humanity...." (Ibid, p. 90.) For further criticisms of liberalism, see ibid, pp. 22-25; 66; 91; and 124.

17. Ibid, p. 91.

18. Quoted Gail Gerhardt, *Black Power in South Africa* (Berkeley: University of California Press, 1978), p. 267.

19. In its angle of vision and its treatment of the clash between familial and political devotions, *A World Apart* is surely also indebted to *Burger's Daughter* (Harmondsworth, England: Penguin, 1979), the most radical and self-questioning of Nadine Gordimer's novels. The titular Burger is a fictional version of Bram Fischer. First and Fischer were both white South African Marxists who rose to prominence in the anti-apartheid struggles of the 50s and early 60s and became celebrated as martyrs. Fischer was sentenced to life imprisonment in 1966 and died in jail. Like Shawn Slovo, Gordimer is less interested in the heroically activist parent than in the perspective of the daughter who labors beneath the consequences of such political single-mindedness. Gordimer's focus is on a daughter-father rather than a daughter-mother relationship. But for the rest, the novel's example remains too compelling to be accidental. Tensions between familial and political commitments also receive intense treatment in a recent book by Shawn Slovo's sister, Gillian Slovo, *Ties of Blood* (New York: William Morrow, 1990).

20. See Shawn Slovo, *A World Apart* (London: Faber and Faber, 1988).

21. For an instructive introduction to First's life, see Tom Lodge's afterword to Ruth First, *117 Days* (1965; rpt. New York: Monthly Review Press, 1989), pp. 153-68.

22. I am grateful to Michael Sprinker for drawing my attention to the parallel suppression of communism in *Daniel.*

23. This is particularly true of the draconian era of the sixties. Writing in 1966, three years after the historical setting of *A World Apart*, Nadine Gordimer conveys the contemporary scope of the Suppression of Communism Act succinctly: "[T]his Act is the much-extended one under which all extra-parliamentary opposition to apartheid, whether inspired by socialism, capitalism, religious principles, a sense of justice or just plain human feeling, is at least under suspicion in South Africa." In "Why Did Bram Fischer Choose Jail?" rpt. Gordimer, *The Essential Gesture*, (ed.) Stephen Clingman (New York: Viking Penguin, 1989), p. 68.

24. Herb Boyd, "A Tale of Two Worlds in One Country," *Guardian* (U.S.A.), 11 Oct. 1989, p. 24.

25. Ibid, p. 8. Sachs, like First, was a victim of a South African bomb delivered to Mozambique. He was severely maimed by a bomb placed in his car.

26. Ibid, p. 122.

27. While *A World Apart* is a British, not a Hollywood, production, Slovo's diary suggests how alert Menges was of the pressure to win over an American audience. The casting of Barbara Herschey as "Roth" represents one effort to broaden the film's appeal to Americans.

28. Slovo, p. 9.
29. Michael Bronski, "Reel Politick," *Z Magazine*, Nov. 1989, p. 76.
30. Ingrid de Kok, "Poetry and Society in South Africa," *Writers from South Africa* (Evanston, Ill.: Northwestern University, 1989), p. 60.
31. Alistair Brown, "Which World Apart?" *Southern African Review of Books*, Dec. 1988/Jan. 1989, pp. 3-4. Brown alludes to the moment when "Roth's interrogator berates her thus: "Your family is suffering because of your delusions....All this hand wringing and playing Joan of Arc is nothing but an excuse for being a terrible mother." Challenging Brown, the radical South African exile Hilda Bernstein testifies to the strategic forgetfulness toward her children which she found necessary during her own detention in a South African prison. ("Letters," *Southern African Review of Books*, Feb./March 1989, p. 22.) South African women interviewed in Diana Russell's recent *Lives of Courage* (New York: Basic Books, 1989) furnish similar testaments.
32. Quoted Glenn Collins, "A Black Director Views Apartheid," *New York Times*, 25 Sept. 1989, p. C20.
33. Quoted in Herb Boyd, "A Tale of Two Worlds in One Country," *Guardian* (U.S.A.), 11 Oct. 1989, p. 24.
34. Frantz Fanon, *The Wretched of the Earth*, (1961; rpt. New York: Grove Press, 1968), p. 51.
35. Andre Brink, *Writing in a State of Siege* (New York: Summit Books, 1983) p. 53.
36. While *A Dry White Season* stages the destruction of two families, one black, the other white, the black family remains pretty anonymous, while the camera lingers intimately over the breakup of Du Toit's family. Similarly and quite implausibly, the police hound and torment Du Toit more persistently than they do his black partner.
37. Bell Hooks, "A Call for Militant Resistance," *Z Magazine*, Jan. 1990, p. 53.
38. Quoted in Donna Britt, "'Season' of Euzhan Palcy's Discontent," *Washington Post*, 26 Sept. 1989, p. C-1.
39. *Cry Freedom*, *A World Apart*, and *A Dry White Season* were all shot in Zimbabwe.
40. One observes certain parallel developments in liberal Israeli film. Ella Shohat, in her important volume, *Israeli Cinema: East/West and the Politics of Representation*, questions the inverted stereotyping in Uri Barabash's *Beyond the Walls* on the grounds that "The positive, saint-like image of the Palestinian, which, in some ways, balances within Israeli culture the Kahane demonization of the Arab, enacts at the same time a kind of compensation mechanism." *Israeli Cinema* (Austin: University Texas Press, 1989), p. 271.
41. Don Pinnock, "Stone's Boys and the Making of a Cape Flats Mafia," in Belinda Bozzoli (ed.), *Class, Community and Conflict: South African Perspectives* (Johannesburg: Ravan Press, 1987), pp. 418-35.
42. The most incisive writer about lumpen life under apartheid remains Alex La Guma, most notably in *A Walk in the Night*, which traces the disturbingly porous division between legality and illegality experienced by that sector of the population. La Guma is particularly instructive on what he calls the "transferral of rage" which occurs under apartheid, a process directly relevant to the action of Mapantsula. See *A Walk in the Night* (Evanston: Northwestern University Press, 1967), p. 36.

43. *Blame Me on History* (1963; rpt. Johannesburg: A. D. Donker, 1986), pp. 63-4.

44. See Nicholas Haysom, *Mabangalala: the Rise of Right-Wing Vigilantes in South Africa* (London: Catholic Institute of International Relations, 1986).

45. Heribert Adam, "Engaging Joe Slovo," *Southern African Review of Books*, June/July 1990, p. 13.

46. James Leahy, "Taking Apart A World Apart," *FAWO News* (Johannesburg), April 1990, p. 20.

47. Biko, *I Write What I Like*, p. 63.

48. For one incisive account of the bankruptcy of Manichean authentic/inauthentic splits, see Jonathan Dollimore, "The Dominant and the Deviant: a Violent Dialectic," *Critical Quarterly*, 28, 1 & 2 (Spring/Summer, 1986).

49. *Weekly Mail*, 2-8 December 1988, p. 11. Quoted in Harriet Gavshon, "Bearing Witness": Ten Years Towards an Opposition Film Movement in South Africa," *Radical History Review*, 46/7, 1990, pp. 331-45.

50. Ibid, pp. 342-43.

51. Ndebele, "The English Language and Social Change in South Africa," p. 324.

52. Ndebele, "Liberation and the Crisis of Culture," *Southern African Review of Books*, February/May 1990, p. 23. Cf. Ndebele, "Redefining Relevance," *Pretexts* 1, 1 (Winter 1989), p. 42-43.

53. Ndebele, ibid, p. 42.

54. Alan Hirsch, "No New Sanctions, But The Old Ones Hurt," *Weekly Mail*, 21 Dec. 1989 to 18 Jan. 1990, p. 26.

55. The principal forces for the dismantling of apartheid have, I would insist, been internal: the unions, the UDF, the Mass Democratic Movement, the ANC, and the organizations associated with Black Consciousness. However, the international flank has applied indispensable pressure, often working dialectically with internal forces. For example, the refusal of American banks to renew loans to the South African government—a more economically decisive measure than sanctions—can be traced in part to the symbolic role sanctions played in stigmatizing South Africa in the U.S.A. But this in turn depended on the internal opposition's success at transforming South Africa into an ungovernable, economically unstable environment for loans and investment.

56. Butler et al., p. 16.

57. Ndebele, "The English Language and Social Change in South Africa," *The English Academy Review*, 1987, p. 8.

CHAPTER FOUR / Border Country

1. Bessie Head, quoted Susan Gardner, "'Don't Ask for the True Story': A Memoir of Bessie Head," *Hecate* 12 (1986), p. 114. Cf. also, Bessie Head, "Biographical Notes: A Search for Historical Continuity and Roots," in Ernest N. Emenyonu (ed.), *Literature and Society: Selected Essays on African Literature* (Calabar, Nigeria: Zim Pan-African Publishers, 1986), p. 95.

2. Letter dated 31 October 1968, in Randolph Vigne (ed.), *A Gesture of Belonging. Letters from Bessie Head, 1965-1979* (London: S A Writers, 1991), p. 65.

3. Quoted Gardner, "'Don't Ask for the True Story,'" p. 114.

4. Letter dated 4 June 1972., *A Gesture of Belonging*, p. 164.

5. Caroline Rooney, "'Dangerous Knowledge' and the Poetics of Survival: A Reading of *Our Sister Killjoy* and *A Question of Power*," in *Motherlands: Black Women's Writing from Africa, the Caribbean and South Asia*, (ed.) Susheila Nasta (London: The Women's Press, 1991), p. 118.

6. "Biographical Notes," p. 95.

7. Letter dated 31 October 1968, *A Gesture of Belonging*, p. 65.

8. Quoted, Etienne Balibar and Immanuel Wallerstein, *Race, Nation, Class: Ambiguous Identities*. London: Verso, 1991, p. 74.

9. Vernon February, *Mind Your Colour* (1981; rpt. London: Kegan Paul, 1991), vi-viii.

10. *Sechaba*, June 1984, p. 13.

11. Sarah Gertrude Millin, *God's Step-Children* (London: Constable, 1924).

12. One of the most notorious casualties of apartheid's rites of reclassification was Sandra Laing. Born of parents designated white, she was removed from school at the age of eleven because she "looked colored." The courts reclassified her as "colored"—a decision that was finally reversed after a protracted legal battle. By the time Laing had been officially redefined as white, she was in love with an African man and had to apply for further reclassification as African in order to gain legal sanction for that relationship. See *Rand Daily Mail*, 23 July 1983, p. 7.

13. Lewis Nkosi, *Tasks and Masks* (Harlow, England: Longman, 1981), p. 99; *Mind Your Colour*, p. 188.

14. For reasons of gender and geography, it was not easy for Head to build on the male traditions of mixed race writing that emanated from the Cape (e.g. Alex La Guma, Richard Rive, Dennis Brutus) and Johannesburg (e.g. Peter Abrahams).

15. Unpublished interview with Cecil Abrahams, quoted in Cecil A. Abrahams (ed.), *The Tragic Life of Bessie Head* (Trenton, New Jersey: Africa World Press, 1990), p. 4.

16. See Anne McClintock, "No Longer in a Future Heaven: Women and Nationalism in South Africa," *Transition*, 51 (1991), pp. 150 ff.; Elleke Boehmer, "Stories of Women and Mothers: Gender and Nationalism in the Early Fiction of Flora Nwapa," in Nasta (ed.), pp. 3-11; Floya Anthias and Nira Yuval-Davis, "Introduction," in Anthias and Yuval-Davis (eds.), *Woman-Nation-State* (London: MacMillan, 1989), pp. 1-15; and Andrew Parker et al., "Introduction," in *Nationalisms and Sexualities*, (ed.) Andrew Parker et al. (New York: Routledge, 1992), pp. 1-18.

17. This is not to imply that Head was herself politically active. "A very peripheral involvement in politics resulted in a refusal of a passport and I left South Africa on an exit permit." Quoted in *A Woman Alone: Autobiographical Writings*, (ed.) Craig MacKenzie (Oxford, England: Heinemann), p. 85.)

18. *Contemporary Authors*, (ed.) Ann Evory, vol. 29-32 (Detroit: Gale Research Co., 1978), p. 288.

19. Philip Schlesinger, *Media, State and Nation* (London: Sage, 1991), p. 174.

20. Don Mattera, *Sophiatown. Coming of Age in South Africa* (Boston: Beacon Press, 1989), p. 150.

21. This terrain is a terminological minefield. There is no indigenous "San" term covering the many formerly nomadic groups whom other Africans and Europeans have variously gathered together under the umbrella terms "Masarwa," "San," and "Bushman." "Masarwa" is unacceptable as it is the term of abuse dished out by

the Batswana who have historically dispossessed and enslaved the "San." Although "San" has achieved a certain anthropological respectability (if that is not a contradiction in terms), it, too, is derogatory in origin and has been flatly rejected by the people themselves. A number of commentators have observed that, despite its origins in colonial racism, "Bushman" is the term most commonly embraced from within the culture. (See Megan Biesele and Paul Weinberg, *Shaken Roots: the Bushmen of Namibia* [Marshalltown, South Africa: EDA Publications, 1990, p. 72]; Casey Kelso, "The Inconvenient Nomads Deep Inside the Deep," [*Weekly Mail*, July 24 to 30, 1992, p. 12]). Is this endorsement from within a defiant appropriation of a previously abusive term? Or has it been adopted in Botswana as an alternative to "Masarwa" which is associated with the people's principal contemporary source of oppression and dispossession, namely the Botswanan state? Even if the racist connotations of "Bushman" can be overturned, the problem of the term's gender specificity is insurmountable.

22. Quoted Rooney, p. 227.

23. A largely autobiographical version of the projection of Head as sexually "loose" on grounds of ethnicity and marital status is to be found in *A Question of Power* (1974; rpt. London: Heinemann, 1986).

24. In some remarkable research into the discourse of madness in Rhodesian mental hospitals between 1932 and 1957, Jackson observes how African women who appeared single in public spaces were sometimes apprehended by the authorities and institutionalized as mad on the grounds that they were, in the medical argot, found "stray" at the "crossroads." (Jackson, "Gendered Disorder in Colonial Zimbabwe: Case Analyses of African Female Inmates at the Ingutsheni Mental Hospital, 1932 to 1957, in Shula Marks (ed.), *The Societies of Southern Africa in the 19th and 20th Centuries*, Vol. 19. (University of London: Instit. of Commonwealth Studies, 1993), pp. 71-79. As recently as the first half of this century, certain British women were locked away in mental asylums on the grounds that giving birth out of wedlock was a mark of insanity. (See Steve Humphries, *A Secret World of Sex: Forbidden Fruit, the British Experience 1900-1950*. London: Sidgwick & Jackson, 1988).

Strictly speaking, Head was not an unmarried but a single mother, as she was estranged from her husband who had remained behind in South Africa. However, this distinction appears not to have made much difference to Botswanan perceptions of her as a woman with a child but no husband in train.

25. *Maru* (London: Victor Gollancz, 1971).

26. Letter dated 14 January 1969, *A Gesture of Belonging*, p. 71.

27. Letter dated 9 June 1970. Ibid, 125. See also, letter dated 12 October 1970, ibid, 132 and Bessie Head, "Social and Political Pressures that Shape Writing in Southern Africa," *A Woman Alone*, p. 68.

28. Letter dated 9 June 1970. *A Gesture of Belonging*, pp. 124-25. A terminologoical clarification is in order here. The Batswana (Motswana, sing.) constitute the majority of the inhabitants of the country Botswana. Those whom the Batswana have disparagingly dubbed the Basarwa (Masarwa, sing.)—otherwise known as the "San" or "Bushmen"—constitute a small minority of Botswana's population. If, at times, Head appears to use the terms Botswanan and Mostswanan interchangeably, this is a reflection of the numerical and political predominance of the

Batswana in the nation's affairs.

29. Letter dated 2 May 1969, ibid, pp. 85-85.

30. Letter dated 9 June 1970, ibid, pp. 125.

31. Bessie Head, "Dreamer and Storyteller," in *Tales of Tenderness and Power* (Oxford, England: Heinemann, 1989), pp. 141-42.

32. See ibid, p. 143.

33. See Head's short piece on Sobukwe, "The Coming of the Christ-Child," *Tales of Tenderness and Power*, pp. 131-40. Also, "Writing Out of Southern Africa," *A Woman Alone*, pp. 97-98.

34. See *A Gesture of Belonging*, p. 77.

35. Cf. Head's letter dated 9 August 1966: "it's been Batswana people I've been fighting with, so God help me, and that does not endear me to anyone, especially as I'm some kind of half-caste. You've no idea how frightened I really am because I thought Africa was my home and now I don't know what to do." (*A Gesture of Belonging*, p. 37). For other accounts of her rejection as a "half-caste," see ibid, pp. 68, 89, 121. And for a largely autobiographical version of her racial rejection in Botswana, see *A Question of Power* (1974; rpt. London: Heinemann, 1986). In "God and the Underdog," Head takes offense at being accused of being inauthentically African by an upper middle class African American woman. (*A Woman Alone*, p. 47.)

36. "Preface to Witchcraft," *A Woman Alone*, p. 27.

37. Letter dated 27 November 1965, *A Gesture of Belonging*, p. 14.

38. Letter dated 22 August 1969, ibid, p. 96.

39. Walter Benjamin, *Illuminations*, trans. Harry Zohn. (1970; rpt. London: Fontana-Collins, 1973), p. 258.

40. "Social and Political Pressures that Shape Writing in Southern Africa," *A Woman Alone*, p. 66.

41. See, for example, "Foreword to Sol Plaatje's *Native Life in South Africa*," "Social and Political Pressures that Shape Writing in Southern Africa," ibid, pp. 79-82 and 65-72

42. "Preface to Witchcraft," ibid, p. 30.

43. Bessie Head, *Serowe: Village of the Rain Wind* (London: Heinemann, 1981), p. 67.

44. Ibid.

45. Ibid, xii.

46. Serowe is the capital of the Bamangwato people, who have traditionally inhabited the northeast of Botswana. The Bamangwato are a subgroup of the Batswana.

47. Ibid, p. 68. This raises, of course, the thorny issue of why she resisted learning Setswana, which must have placed a fundamental limit on her assimilation. Was Head's resistance to linguistic assimilation a lingering response to her original rejection?

48. Ibid, p. 70.

49. "Social and Political pressures that Shape Writing in Southern Africa," *A Woman Alone*, p. 70.

50. See, for example, Walker's insistence that Head's work warrants more attention in the U.S.A. and her presentation of Head as one of "my favorite uncelebrated foreign writers." ("Let us now praise unsung writers," *Mother Jones*, January 1986, p. 27.) A character closely modeled on Head earns a cameo appearance in *The*

Temple of My Familiar and Walker acknoweldged her debt to Head in *You Can't Keep A Good Woman Down.*

51. Alice Walker, "From an Interview," *In Search of Our Mothers' Gardens* (London: Women's Press, 1984), p. 259.

52. Cf. Elizabeth's account of why she left South Africa in *A Question of Power*: "there wasn't any kind of social evolution beyond that [hatred], there wasn't any lift to the heart, just this vehement vicious struggle between two sets of people with different looks…" *A Question of Power*, p. 19.

53. James Baldwin, *Notes of a Native Son* (1955; rpt. London: Pluto Press, 1985), pp. 22, 14.

54. Njabulo S. Ndebele, *Rediscovery of the Ordinary: Essays on South African Literature and Culture* (Johannesburg: COSAW, 1991). From among these essays, see in particular, "Redefining Relevance," "The Rediscovery of the Ordinary," "Turkish Tales: Some Thoughts on South African Fiction," "Liberation and the Crisis of Culture," and "Against Pamphleteering the Future."

55. "Turkish Tales," ibid, p. 23.

56. "Redefining Relevance," ibid, p. 65.

57. See, for example, Lewis Nkosi's insistence that Head "is not a political novelist in any sense that we can recognise." (*Tasks and Masks* [Harlow, England: Longman, 1981], p. 100.) Two valuable exceptions to this tendency to conceive of Head as apolitical are Ketu Katrak, "From Pauline to Dikeledi: the Philosophical and Political Vision of Bessie Head's Protagonists," *Ba-Shiru* 12 (1985), pp. 26-35, and Neil Lazarus, *Resistance in Postcolonial African Fiction* (New Haven: Yale University Press, 1990), pp. 210-11.

58. "Writing Out of Southern Africa," *A Woman Alone*, p. 99.

59. "Social and Political Pressures that Shape Writing in Southern Africa," ibid, p. 67.

60. Cherry Clayton, *Women and Writing in South Africa* (Johannesburg: Heinemann, 1989), p. 1. On the subject of the economic and social obstacles facing black women writing in South Africa, see Ellen Kuzwayo and and Miriam Tlali's remarks in *Between the Lines*, Craig MacKenzie and Cherry Clayton (eds.), (Grahamstown, South Africa: National English Literary Museum, 1989), pp. 59 and 71.

61. Head once portrayed *The Collector of Treasures* as her "resume of 13 years of living entirely in village life." Quoted Charlotte Bruner, "Bessie Head: Shock and Loss," *African Literature Association Bulletin*, 12, (Spring 1986), p. 42.

62. "Social and Political Pressures That Shape Writing in Southern Africa," *A Woman Alone*, p. 67. Head's fascination with threshold figures surfaces in one of earliest autobiographical essays, "Woman from America," in which she admires a visiting African American woman's bold insistence on taking what she wants from Africa and America. See "The Woman from America," *A Woman Alone*, p. 36.

63. "Epilogue: An African Story," *A Woman Alone*, pp. 101-2.

64. For two incisive critiques of the implications of post-colonialism," see Anne McClintock "The Angel of Progress: Pitfalls of the Term 'Post-Colonialism,'" and Ella Shohat, "Notes on the 'Post-Colonial,'" both in *Social Text* 31/32, 1992.

65. "Property," *Tales of Tenderness and Power*, pp. 65-71; "The Lovers," ibid, pp. 84-101; "The Collector of Treasures," *The Collector of Treasures* (London: Heinemann, 1977), pp. 87-103; "The Special One," ibid, pp. 81-86; "Despite Broken Bondage," pp. 54-57.

66. See *A Woman Alone*, p. 95.

67. Susan Gardner, "Introduction," in *Bessie Head: A Bibliography*, (eds.) Susan Gardner and Patricia E. Scott (Grahamstown, South Africa: National English Literary Museum, 1986), p. 11.

68. Bessie Head, *When Rain Clouds Gather* (New York: Simon and Schuster, 1969).

69. The project was implemented by the exiled South African, Patrick van Rensburg, although Head emphasises that it built on indigenous traditions of volunteerism and self-help established under Tshekedi Khama. Ibid, p. 90.

70. "Preface to Witchcraft," *A Woman Alone*, p. 28.

71. Foreword to Sol Plaatje's *Native Life in South Africa*, in *A Woman Alone*, p.79.

72. Ndebele, *The Rediscovery of the Ordinary* and Mbulelo Mzamane, "Cultivating a People's Voice in the Criticism of South African Literature," *Staffrider* 9 (1991), pp. 59-70.

73. Solomon Tshekisho Plaatje, *Native Life in South Africa* (1916; rpt. Harlow, Essex: Longman, 1987), p. 6.

74. Serowe, xv.

75. Head "A Bewitched Crossroad," *The Bloody Horse*, 3 (1981), p. 5.

76. *Serowe*, p. 47.

77. See "Social and Political Pressures that Shape Writing in Southern Africa," *A Woman Alone*, pp. 71-72.

78. Among Head's numerous discussions of Khama the Great's innovations, see, for example, Michelle Adler et al., "An Interview with Bessie Head," in Craig MacKenzie and Cherry Clayton (eds.), *Between the Lines* (Grahamstown, South Africa: National English Literary Museum, 1989), p. 16; *Serowe: Village of the Rain Wind*, pp. 3-9 and 187-98; and "A Search for Historical Continuity and Roots," *A Woman Alone*, p. 87.

79. See Adler et al., "A Interview with Bessie Head," p. 16.

80. Theodor Adorno, *Aesthetic Theory* (New York: Routledge, 1987), p. 196.

81. Ibid, p. 16.

82. Bessie Head, The Cardinals, introduced by M.J. Daymond (Cape Town: David Philip, 1993).

83. *Serowe*, p. 5.

84. My principal supplementary sources are: Mary Benson, *Tshekedi Khama* (London: Faber and Faber, 1960); John Redfern, *Ruth and Seretse: A Very Disreputable Transaction* (London: Unwin Hyman, 1955); Michael Dutfield, *A Marriage of Inconvenience: The Persecution of Ruth and Seretse Khama* (London: Unwin Human, 1990); Paul Landau, "The Persecution of Ruth and Seretse Khama," *Southern African Review of Books*, Jan., Feb. 1991, pp. 18-19.

85. See, for example, *Serowe*, xiii, pp. 75 ff., and 96-98.

86. Quoted Landau, p. 19.

87. Ibid, p. 19.

88. *Serowe: Village of the Rain Wind*, p. 98.

89. "Biographical Notes," p. 95.

90. Paul Gilroy and Stuart Hall's critiques of Raymond Williams are salient to Head's ambiguous experience of settled community. Gilroy and Hall point out the racial and ethnic nationalist implications of Williams's unquestioning affirmation of the value of "rooted settlements." See Gilroy, *There Ain't No Black in the Union*

Jack: The Cultural Politics of Race and Nation (London: Unwin Hyman, 1987), pp. 49-50; Hall, "Our Mongrel Selves," *New Statesman and Society*, 19 June, 1992, pp. 6-8.

91. Letter dated 2 April 1968, *A Gesture of Belonging*, p. 58.
92. "Preface to Witchcraft," p. 27.
93. See "Biographical Notes," p. 95, and letter dated 4 June 1984, *A Gesture of Belonging*, 164.
94. Letted dated 31 October 1968, *A Gesture of Belonging*, p. 65.
95. *A Woman Alone*, p. 28.
96. Salman Rushdie, "Minority Literatures in a Multi-Cultural Society," *Displaced Persons*, (eds.) Kirsten Holst Petersen and Anna Rutherford, (Sydney: Dangaroo Press, 1988), p. 35.

CHAPTER FIVE / Apartheid on the Run

1. John Woodcock, "Plan to Disrupt Cricket Tour With Locusts," in Marcus Williams (ed.), *Double Century—Cricket in The Times, Vol. 2: 1935-1990* (London: Pavilion Library, 1990), p. 199.
2. Neil Macfarlane, *Sport and Politics: A World Divided* (London: Willow Books, 1986), p. 155.
3. Benedict Anderson, *Imagined Communities* (London: Verso, 1983), p. 19.
4. Figures like the golfer Gary Player who became celebrities in the elite, individualistic sports that were least affected by the boycott, were routinely billed by the regime as "ambassadors" or "emissaries of goodwill." The choice of metaphor suggests the sporting representatives' ability to deputize for political representatives, particularly under conditions where South African embassies had been shut down or tirelessly picketed.
5. On homosocial panic, see Eve Kosofsky Sedgwick, *Between Men: English Literature and Male Homosocial Desire* (New York: Columbia University Press, 1985), pp. 83ff.
6. Even military ceremonies, the only other events to parade a similar blend of uniformed nationalism and masculinity, are neither as sexually nor racially exclusive.
7. Richard Lapchick, *The Politics of Race and International Sport: The Case of South Africa* (Westport: Greenwood Press, 1975), p. 9.
8. Transcript, *Africa Survery*, SABC English for Abroad, Johannesburg, August 31, 1981, at 4pm GMT.
9. Gary Whannel, *Blowing the Whistle: The Politics of Sport* (London: Pluto, 1983), p. 23. In this context, one might also note how the territorial disputes and religious animosities that have dogged relations between India and Pakistan—both massively militarized societies—have resulted in an explosive atmosphere when the two nations confront each other on the cricket field. Some such matches have sparked social unrest and resulted in fatalities. Indeed, Indian and Pakistani cricket captains have on occasion been accused of fixing their contests to insure an inconclusive outcome, for fear that a victory for either side would spark religious or ethnic uprisings.
10. Patrick Harverson, "The Selling of an American Dream," *Financial Times Weekend*, 4 July 1992, p. 10.

11. The most memorable account of this extraordinary debacle is Ryszard Kapuscinski's, *The Soccer War* (New York: Alfred A. Knopf, 1991).

12. Historically, Western nationalisms came into being partly through the weakening of sacred communities—as Benedict Anderson reminds us. See, Anderson, p. 19.

13. When Brazil won the World Cup in Mexico, it defeated England en route to the finals. After that match, the Brazilian goalkeeper's spectacular efforts were portrayed as, in the fullest sense, supernatural saves. The Rio paper, *Jornal dos Sportes*, ran the headline "Jesus Defends Brazil," explaining that "whenever the ball flew towards our goal and a score seemed inevitable, Jesus reached his foot out of the clouds and cleared the ball." See Kapuscinski, p. 159.

14. Gert Yssel, *Sunday Times* (Johannesburg), 14 June 1970.

15. An *Argus* poll taken in 1970. Quoted in Robert Archer and Antoine Bouillon, *The South African Game: Sport and Racism* (London: Zed, 1982), p. 218.

16. Trevor Huddleston, *Naught for Your Comfort* (London: Collins, 1956), pp. 201-202.

17. J.D. Omer-Cooper, *New Zealand, South Africa and Sport: Background Papers* (Aukland: New Zealand Institute of International Affairs, 1976), p. 22.

18. Dennis Brutus, "Dennis Brutus," *World Authors 1980-85*, (ed.) Vineta Colby (New York: H.W. Wilson Co., 1991), pp. 120-23.

19. Ibid.

20. See Richard Lapchick, *The Politics of Race and International Sport: The Case of South Africa* (Westport: Greenwood Press, 1975), p. 80.

21. See Andrew Langley, *Sport and Politics* (London, 1989), p. 26, and Archer and Bouillon, p. 300.

22. Basil D'Oliveira, *Time to Declare* (London: W. H. Allen, 1982), p. 60.

23. Quoted in Lapchick, p. 128.

24. Archer and Bouillon, p. 206. Between 1980 and 1991, the United Nations published an annual list of sportsmen and women who had contravened the boycott. The list covered 46 sports.

25. Joan Brickhill, *Race Against Race* (London: International Aid and Defense Fund, 1976, p. 74).

26. By June 1986, South African businesses sponsoring rebel tours had submitted applications for rebates totalling $80 million. See Douglas Booth, "South Africa's 'Autonomous Sport' Strategy: Desegregation Apartheid Style," *Sporting Traditions* 6 (1990), p. 162.

27. *House of Assembly Debates* (South Africa), 2 May 1983, columns 6115-6128. Quoted Colin Tatz, "Race, Politics, and Sport," *Sporting Traditions* 1, 1 (1984), p. 17. See also, Cheryl Roberts, *Challenges Facing South African Sport* (Cape Town: Township Publishing Co-operative, 1990), p. 41.

28. "Anarchy Reigns in New Zealand after Halt to Match," The Times (London) 27 July 1981, p. 5.

29. Whannel, p. 6. The suffragettes' anticipation of anti-apartheid tactics went beyond arson: they also ripped up cricket pitches, football grounds, and golf courses.

30. "Mr. Muldoon Kicks for Goal," *The Guardian*, 28 July 1981, p. 19.

31. Dr. Danie Craven, "SARB R20,000 to Sporting Body," *Cape Times*, 7 December 1981.

32. Such levels of public violence are rare in contemporary England, Wales, and Scotland, though not, of course, in Northern Ireland.
33. *Barbed Wire Boks* is the title of a well known book about the 1981 tour of New Zealand.
34. Tatz, p. 25.
35. See "Tshwete at the Crease," *Financial Times*, 11 July 1991, and Denis Herbstein, "The State of Play," *The Observer*, 23 June 1991, p. 28.
36. "A Rare Case of Sport Influencing the Politicians," *The Times*(London), 11 July 1991, p. 34.
37. Tshwete's inaugural address at the launch of NOSC, quoted in Roberts, p.16.
38. Anon, quoted ibid., p. 9.
39. Ibid., p. 49.
40. Mathew Engel, "Calcutta says it with flowers for ex-Springboks," *The Guardian*, 9 Nov. 1991.
41. *Return to Olympia*, documentary shown on Britain's Channel 4, 29 April 1992.
42. "PW's plan to vote No," *Eastern Province Herald*, 9 March 1992.
43. The full text of this advertisement, which appeared in newspapers, magazines, and on TV, reads: "Without reform, South Africa hasn't got a sporting chance. Right now, a team of talented cricketers are representing South Africa for the first time in 22 years. If we say NO to reform on March 17, chances are, this will be the final innings for South Africa. So please, vote YES on March 17, and help keep South Africa batting. Vote YES on March 17 and keep South Africa in the game." The small print discloses that the ad was placed "in the interests of a better South Africa by the Private Sector Referendum Fund—a non-political initiative." *Eastern Province Herald*, 9 March 1992.
44. "PW's plan to vote No."
45. "De Klerk Flies Home from Spain for Crisis Meeting," *The Guardian*, 23 June 1992, p. 1.
46. Gavin Evans, "Back to the Starting Line," *Weekly Mail* (Johannesburg) 26 June – 2 July 1992, p. 6.

CHAPTER SIX / Sunset on Sun City

1. This collaboration was, for much of the boycott's duration, uneven, and tilted toward the external forces. In the later years of the boycott, the strategic needs of apartheid's internal and external adversaries sometimes proved divergent and strained.
2. Although the sport and cultural boycotts developed independent tactical trajectories, sport is clearly a subcategory of culture, the one in which white South Africans institutions proved most sensitive to attack.
3. As an instance of a controversial disruption in the flow of commodities, one can cite the decision by Alice Walker and the exiled Cape Town writer, Zoe Wicomb, to bar the sale of their fiction in South Africa. In anti-apartheid circles, this move provoked considerable disagreement. Who, it was argued, other than opponents of apartheid, would read such books in the first place? For one prominent black writer's concern over the consequences of a book ban, see Hein Willemse's remarks in Pallo Jordan, "The Cultural and Academic Boycott," in *Crossing the*

Borders: Writers Meet the ANC, (eds.) Ampie Coetzee and James Polley (Cape Town: Taurus, 1990).

4. "US Artists to Boycott South Africa," *Daily News*, 16 Oct. 1981.

5. Quoted Hein Willemse, "Sensuur of Strategie?" ["Censorship or Strategy?"] *Die Suid-Afrikaan*, 23, Oct. 1989, p. 19. In keeping with the spirit of Huddleston's appeal, the South African women's organization, Black Sash, picketed Dame Margot Fonteyn for "dancing to separate audiences." (Denis Herbstein, "The Hazards of Cultural Deprivation," *Africa Report*, July-Aug. 1987, p. 34.)

6. Jordan, p. 160.

7. Conny Braam and Fons Geerlings, "Toward New Cultural Relations: A Reflection on the Cultural Boycott," in *Culture in Another South Africa*, (eds.) Willem Campschreur and Joost Divendal (London: Zed, 1989), p. 174.

8. The full force of the cultural boycott was felt rather later—in the 1970s—in the Netherlands than in Britain and the U.S.A.

9. The Equity ban took effect in 1956, the one by the Musicians Union in 1957.

10. See Roger Omond, The Apartheid Handbook (London: Penguin, 1985), p. 209.

11. Artists and Athletes Against Apartheid was formed in 1983.

12. Quoted Braam and Geerlings, p. 175.

13. "Tighter Cultural Boycott Urged," *Citizen*, 6 Sept. 1989.

14. SATV did on occasion have access to programs that involved neither Equity members nor members of the British Musicians' Union. Understandably, these tended to be documentaries like *The World at War* rather than features or soaps.

15. David Coplan, *In Township Tonight! South Africa's Black City Music and Theatre* (London: Longman, 1985), p. 219.

16. P. F. Larlam, *Black Performance in South Africa*, unpublished Ph.D. dissertation, New York University, 1981, pp. 166-7.

17. Benchmark events include the formation of the Black People's Convention, an umbrella body for Black Consciousness organizations in 1972, and the strikes in Durban in 1972-73.

18. Robert Davies, et al., *The Struggle for South Africa: A Reference Guide.* (London: Zed, 1985), p. 1.

19. Dougie Oakes (ed.), *Illustrated History of South Africa*, second edition. (Cape Town: Reader's Digest, 1992), p. 455.

20. A crucial event in this regard was the founding in 1984 of the Durban Cultural Workers Local.

21. This list of cultural boycott busters appeared in 1983. It was a response to the highly effective register of sportsmen and women who had contravened the bansports boycott. The UN Special Committee Against Apartheid had introduced the sports' register in 1981.

22. "Facing up to the Culture Crunch," *Business Day*, 16 July 1986.

23. The British equivalent was called Artists Against Apartheid.

24. For an account of the project's genesis and success, see Dave Marsh, Sun City: the Making of the Record (New York: Penguin, 1985).

25. Reebee Garofalo, "Understanding Mega-Events: If We Are the World, Then How Do We Change It?" in *Technoculture*, (eds.) Constance Penley and Andrew Ross, (Minneapolis: University of Minnesota Press, 1991), p. 257.

26. Ibid.

27. "Sun City" did, of course, have a fund-raising dimension. Proceeds were distributed by the Africa Fund to "political prisoners and their families...in South Africa;
...to the educational centers and college set up by the ANC in Tanzania and
Zambia; ...and to grassroots educational outreach by the anti-apartheid movement in the U.S." (Correspondence from Jennifer Davis, executive secretary of the
Africa Fund, to Artists United Against Apartheid, 10 Sept. 1985.)

28. On the subject of the educational value of "Sun City", see Danny Schechter, "Artists
United Against Apartheid," *Africa Report*, July-August 1987, pp. 42-45.

29. For an analysis of the photographic ban and the resistance to it within South
Africa, see Paul Weinberg and Rob Nixon, "Taking Sides in South Africa: Afrapix'
Democratic Documentary," *Our Times*, August 1986, pp. 22-27.

30. David Friche, "African Odyssey: A Conversation with Paul Simon," *Rolling Stone*,
23 Oct. 1986, pp. 77.

31. Ibid.

32. Among Simon's most outspoken critics were Amer Araim, senior political affairs
officer at the UN Centre Against Apartheid and Dali Tambo, son of ANC president
Oliver Tambo and a founding member of Artists Against Apartheid.

33. Mxolisi Mgxashe, "A Conversation with Ray Phiri," *Africa Report*, July-Aug. 1987,
p. 31; Margaret A. Novicki and Ameen Akhalwaya, "Interview With Hugh
Masekela," *Africa Report* July-Aug. 1987, p. 27.

34. Novicki and Akhalwaya, p. 27.

35. David Friche, "African Odyssey," p. 78.

36. Novicki and Akhalwaya, p. 27.

37. David Friche, "Paul Simon's Amazing Graceland Tour," *Rolling Stone* 2 July 1987,
pp. 43.

38. Njabulo Ndebele, *The Rediscovery of the Ordinary: Essays on South African
Literature and Culture* (Johannesburg: Congress of South African Writers), pp.
133-44.

39. Ibid, p. 143.

40. Ibid.

41. "Why the British are So Unhappy With That Word Selective," *Weekly Mail*, 2–8
Sept. 1988.

42. Charlotte Bauer, "This is the Pulling Power," *Weekly Mail*, 2–8 Sept. 1988.

43. "South Africa as Hub of New Tour Circuit," *Weekly Mail*, 5–11 Apr. 1991.

44. Paul Gilroy, "Cruciality and the Frog's Perspective," *Third Text* 5, Winter 1988/89,
p. 43.

45. Bauer, *Weekly Mail*, 2–8 Sept. 1988.

46. Quoted Mxolisi Mgxashe, *Weekly Mail*, 12–19 Nov. 1987.

47. Barbara Masekela, "The ANC and the Cultural Boycott," *Africa Report*, July-
August 1987, p. 21.

48. Thabiso Leshoai, "Culture Boycott," *City Press*, 14 May 1989.

49. Graham Younge, quoted in James Wood, "Bringing Culture Out of Bondage,"
Guardian, 9 Jan. 1993, p. 32.

50. Achmat Dangor, "Cultural Boycott Comes Under Fire," *Business Day*, 13 Feb. 1989.
See also, Dangor, "Is It Time for the Boycott To Go," *New Nation*, 21–27 Sept.
1990.

51. Frank Meintjies, interview with the author, Johannesburg, 11 March 1991.

52. Ahmed and van Graan, "The Cultural Boycott: A Case for Its Immediate Lifting." Unpublished roneo, November 1990. See also, Ahmed and Van Graan, "Time to Move Beyond Cultural Boycott," *Weekly Mail*, 23–29 Nov. 1990.
53. Ibid.
54. Ahmed and van Graan, p.2.
55. Wood, p. 32.
56. Frank Meintjies, "Wanted: A Vision for Culture," Ingolovane no. 2, 1990, pp. 41-42.
57. "Boycott Continues," *New Nation*, 3–9 May 1991.
58. Quoted Wood, p. 32.
59. Meintjies, p. 41.

CHAPTER SEVEN / Mandela, Messianism, and the Media

1. Anon., "Mandela's Freedom the Last Chance for South Africa," *Manchester Guardian Weekly*, 18 Feb. 1990.
2. Phil Molefe, "Black Pimpernel Mandela Ducks Police for Months," Supplement to *Weekly Mail*, 16–22 Feb. 1990.
3. Nadine Gordimer, quoted in introduction to Jacques Derrida and Mustapha Tlili, eds., *For Nelson Mandela* (New York: Seaver Books, 1987), p.3.
4. Nelson Mandela, *The Struggle is My Life* (London: International Defence and Aid Fund, 1986), p. 241.
5. Anon., "A Lagos Soccer Cup in Honour of Mandela," *Weekly Mail*, 8–14 Dec. 1989.
6. Roger House, "Blacks in Boston Seek to Secede," *Nation*, 7 Nov. 1988, pp. 452-53.
7. *New Nation*, 27 July 1988.
8. Anon., *Nelson Mandela: His Life in the Struggle* (London: International Defence and Aid Fund, 1988), pp. 30-31.
9. Ibid.
10. Quoted Mary Benson, *Nelson Mandela: The Man and the Movement* (New York: W. W. Norton, 1986), p. 252.
11. John F. Burns, "Mandela, Faceless Man With a Fax," *New York Times*, 30 Jan 1990.
12. Tom Mathews, "The Leader No One Knows," *Newsweek*, 19 Feb. 1990, p. 50.
13. These are the views of former Secret Service office Major Nico Basson as reported in *The Observer*, 28 July 1991.
14. "Nightline," 4 Feb. 1990.
15. Karel Schoeman, *Gelofte Land* (1972); trans. Marion V. Friedmann as *Promised Land* (London: Futura, 1978); Albert Luthuli, *Let My People Go* (London: Collins, 1962).
16. Edward Said, "Michael Walzer's 'Exodus and Revolution': A Canaanite Reading," *Grand Street*, Winter 1986, p. 100.
17. Desmond Tutu, *Crying in the Wilderness* (Cape Town: Mowbray, 1981).
18. Fatima Meer, *Higher Than Hope: The Authorized Biography of Nelson Mandela* (New York: Harper and Row, 1990), p. 309.
19. Benson, p. 252.
20. Soyinka, *Mandela's Earth* (London: Deutsch, 1989), p. 3.
21. For a full version of the Freedom Charter, see Mandela, *The Struggle is My Life*, pp. 50-54.

22. Frantz Fanon, *The Wretched of the Earth*, trans. Constance Farrington (1961; rpt. London: Penguin, 1990), pp. 119-65.
23. Ibid, p. 136.
24. Channel 5, New York, 11 Feb. 1990.
25. "Mandela's Speech," Special Edition of *Weekly Mail*, 12 Feb 1990.
26. Ibid.
27. Mandela, *The Struggle is My Life*, p. 4.
28. David Beresford, "Patience, People, Patience," *Weekly Mail*, 16–22 Feb 1990, p. 8.
29. Nelson Mandela, "Address to the U.S. Congress, 26 June 1990," *Nelson Mandela Speaks* (New York: Pathfinder, 1993), p. 42.
30. Kenneth J. Cooper, "In Boston, Mandela Hails State's Leadership in the Anti-Apartheid Cause," *Washington Post*, 24 June 1990.
31. *Mandela in America. A Commemorative Video*, directed by Danny Schechter, 1990. Cf. the words of an anonymous admirer of Mandela in Los Angeles: "Nelson Mandela the father force, he's been our Moses, 27 years in jail, suffering for us." Ibid. Also, "A Modern Day Moses," a special edition of ABC's World News Tonight, 12 Nov. 1990.
32. Ibid.
33. Roger Wilkins, "With Mandela," *Mother Jones*, Nov./Dec. 1990, p. 19.
34. Nelson Mandela in America.
35. See George M. Fredrickson, "African Americans and African Africans," *New York Review of Books*, 26 Sept. 1991, p. 31.
36. D. Michael Cheers, "Nelson Mandela: A Special Message to Black Americans," *Ebony*, May 1990, p. 180.
37. *Nelson Mandela in America*.
38. Christopher Wren, "Mandela Urges Blacks of Natal to End Deadly Rivalry," *New York Times*, 26 Feb 1990.
39. Meer, p. 131.
40. Conor Cruise O'Brien, "A Linchpin of Democracy," *Times Literary Supplement*, 23 Feb.–March 1 1990, p. 190. Between the lines, one detects traces of a vengeful animosity in O'Brien's determination to reinvent Mandela as an embattled lone man of principle fighting off the undemocratic black masses. Is this O'Brien's riposte to black students for preventing him from speaking at the University of Cape Town in 1985 after he had announced, on apartheid TV, an ill-considered, presumptuous one-man campaign to breach the international academic boycott?

CHAPTER EIGHT / An Everybody Claim Dem Democratic

1. *Weekly Mail* (Johannesburg), 15 March 1991.
2. *Weekly Mail*, 26 April 1991.
3. Ibid.
4. See Jacques Derrida, "Racism's Last Word." Trans. Peggy Kamuf. *Critical Inquiry* 12 (Aug. 1985), pp. 290-99.
5. "Museum vir Apartheid Kom"["Museum of Apartheid Is On Its Way"], *Vrye Weekblad* (Johannesburg), 15 Feb. 1991.
6. See, for example, *Guardian* (London), 14 June 1991.
7. *Cosmo* (South Africa), February, 1991.

8. "Address By the State President FW de Klerk, DMS, At the Opening of the Second Session of the Ninth Parliament of the Republic of South Africa in Cape Town, Friday, 2 February 1990." Press Release, 1/90, The Permanent Mission of South Africa to the United Nations.

9. Aime Cesaire, "Notebook of a Return to Native Land," in *Collected Poetry*, trans. Clayton Eshelman and Annette Smith (Berkeley: University of California Press, 1983), p. 77.

10. *Weekly Mail*, 21 May 1991.

11. Khaba Mkhize, "Ways of Seeing: Ethnicity and Violence," *Indicator SA* vol 8, no. 1 (Sum. 1990), p. 13.

12. Anon, "Mangosuthu Buthelezi: Message of the Drums," *Financial Mail* (Johannesburg), 23 Oct. 1992, p. 26.

13. "Address to the Zulu Nation and to all South Africans" (First National Bank Stadium, Johannesburg.) Quoted Gerhard Mare, *Brothers Born of Warrior Blood: Politics and Ethnicity in South Africa* (Johannesburg: Ravan, 1992), p. 68.

14. David Beresford, *Guardian*, 22 Aug. 1992.

15. Ibid.

16. The most celebrated exploration of these issues is Eric Hobsbawm and Terence Ranger, eds., *The Invention of Tradition* (Cambridge: Cambridge University Press, 1983).

17. Shula Marks, *The Ambiguities of Dependence. State, Class and Nationalism in Early Twentieth Century Natal* (Johns Hopkins: Baltimore, 1987); and Marks, "Patriotism, Patriarchy and Purity: Natal and the Politics of Zulu Ethnic Consciousness," in Leroy Vail, *The Creation of Tribalism in Southern Africa* (Berkeley: Univ. of California Press, 1989).

18. See especially Marks, *The Ambiguities of Dependence*.

19. "Zulu King in New Attack on Mandela," *Guardian* 27 May 1991; and "White Warrior Dances to the Zulu Drumbeat," *Sunday Times* (London), 2 June 1991.

20. David Everatt,"Who is murdering the peace? CASE Research Statistics," (Johannesburg: Community Agency for Social Enquiry, 1991), pp. 1-2.

21. Mafika Gwala, "Writing as a Cultural Weapon," in *Momentum*, (eds.) M.J. Daymond, J.U. Jacobs, and Margaret Lenta (Pietermaritzburg, 1984), pp. 37 ff.

22. Albie Sachs, "Preparing Ourselves for Freedom," in Ingrid de Kok and Karen Press (eds.), *Spring is Rebellious: Arguments about Cultural Freedom by Albie Sachs and Respondents* (Cape Town: Buchu Books, 1990), pp. 19-29.

23. David Beresford, "With Fire and Fury," Guardian 7 August 1993.

24. "Who's Who in the 'All Party Conference,'" *Anti-Apartheid News* (London), April, 1991.

25. F. W. de Klerk, July 1975. Quoted in the *Weekly Mail*, 8 August 1989.

26. Quoted Nicholas Wellington, op cit.

27. "A Tale of Two Sisters," *Weekly Mail*, 8–14 June 1990.

28. Guardian, 11 May 1993.

29. For an analysis of this shifting political discourse, see Anne McClintock and Rob Nixon, "No Names Apart: The Separation of Word and History in Derrida's 'Le Dernier Mot du Racisme,'" *Critical Inquiry* 13, 1 (Fall 1986), pp. 140-51 and John Sharp, "Ethnic Group and Nation: the Apartheid Vision in South Africa," in Emile Boonzaier and John Sharp (eds.), *South African Keywords: the Uses and Abuses of*

Political Concepts (Cape Town: David Philip, 1988), pp. 79-99.

30. M.C. Botha, *Hansard*, 1966, cols. 4131-17.

31. Chris Heunis, "The Peoples of South Africa: A Kaleidoscope of Cultures," *South African Digest*, 17 July 1987.

32. David Beresford, "The Blind Eye of Nelson," *Guardian*, 15 May 1991.

33. For an example of this logic, see Chitre Gyan-Chand Okah, "Winnie is Victim of Repression," *Guardian*, 15 May 1991.

34. *Weekly Mail*, 15 March 1991.

35. See Mark Gevisser, "The Koeksuster Tannies of the ANC?" *Weekly Mail*, 19 April 1991.

36. "CC Death Squads Still Operating," *Anti-Apartheid News*, April, 1991.

37. Weekly Mail, 27 March 1991.

CHAPTER NINE / The Retreat from Communism and Anti-Communism

1. Paul Sweezy and Harry Magdoff, "The Stakes in South Africa," *Monthly Review*, 37, 6 (April 1986), p. 5.

2. This is not to imply that the ANC were revolutionary from the outset. For an account of the ANC's radicalization during the 1960s, see Tom Lodge, *Black Politics in South Africa Since 1945* (London: Longman, 1983).

3. "Address by the State President F. W. de Klerk, DMS, at the Opening of the Second Session of the Ninth Parliament of the Republic of South Africa in Cape Town, Friday, 2 February 1990." Press Release from the Permanent Mission of South Africa to the United Nations, 2 February 1990, pp. 2 and 10.

4. David Niddrie, "Apartheid's Not Dead, it Just Smells Funny," *Work in Progress*, 72, Jan-Feb, 1991.

5. "Russia Year Zero," directed by David Dimbleby, BBC1, 31 Dec. 1991.

6. Antoinette Louw, "Conflict Trends: January to September 91," *Indicator South Africa* 9, 1 (Summer 1991), p. 41.

7. Quoted in Anon., "Where the Party's Still in Full Swing," *New Statesman & Society*, Dec. 1991, p. 6.

8. "Mandela Tops," *Weekly Mail and Guardian*, 17–22 Dec. 1993. The survey was conducted by Integrated marketing Research in November and December, 1993.

9. Quoted in R. W. Johnson, "The Past and Future of the South African Communist Party," *London Review of Books*, 24 October 1991, p. 11.

10. See Patrick Bond, "Can It Satisfy the Majority's Basic Need?" *Work in Progress*, 75 (1991), p. 16.

11. Robin Blackburn, *After the Fall: The Failure of Communism and the Future of Socialism* (London: Verso, 1991). *Work in Progress*, 77 (1991), p. 3.

12. Patrick Laurence, "ANC Rejects Constitution Plan as Favoring Whites," *Guardian*, 5 Sept. 1991.

13. John Carlin, "South Africa Must Dilute its Witches' Brew," *Independent*, 28 Dec. 1991.

14. "USSR Renamed," *The Independent*, 18 Dec. 1991.

15. For a fine, suggestive account of the place of ethnicity in the warmup to the New Europe, see Scott Malcomson, "Heart of Whiteness: Europe Goes for the Globe,"

Voice Literary Supplement, March 1991, pp. 10-14.

16. Quoted, Roger Omond, *The Apartheid Handbook* (Harmondsworth, England: Penguin, 1985), p. 175.

17. Quoted, Joseph Hanlon, *Beggar Your Neighbours. Apartheid Power in Southern Africa* (Bloomington: Indiana University Press, 1987), p. 9.

18. UNICEF, *Children on the Frontline: the Impact of Apartheid Destabilization and Warfare on Children in Southern and South Africa* (Third Edition), UNICEF, 1989, pp. 24-25.

19. For a detailed account of this process, see Giovanni Arrighi, "World Income Inequalities and the Future of Socialism," *New Left Review*, 189 (Sept/Oct 1991), pp. 39-66.

20. For a useful analysis of the achievements of "impure" capitalism, see Robin Blackburn, "Fin de Siecle: Socialism after the Crash," *After the Fall*, pp. 78-109. See also, Mary Kaldor, "After the Cold War," *New Left Review*, March/April 1990, pp. 26-27.

21. South Africa possesses 47 percent of the world's gold reserves, 82 percent of manganese, 69 percent of platinum, 55 percent of chrome ore, 33 percent of vanadium, 24 percent of diamonds. Quoted, Robert Davies, "Post-Apartheid Scenarios for the Southern African Region," *Transformation*, 11 1990.

22. Jonathan Leape offers an incisive account of this issue in his unpublished paper, "South Africa's Foreign Debt: Implications of the Debt Crisis of 1985 and Prospects for the 1990s," presented at the Institute of Commonwealth Studies, London, on 23 Nov. 1991.

23. According to Leslie Maasdorp, four hundred thousand new workers are now entering South Africa's labor force annually, while only forty thousand of them are finding employment in the formal sector. "South Africa's Internal Economic Situation," unpublished paper presented at the Institute of Commonwealth Studies, London, on 23 Nov. 1991.

CHAPTER TEN / Of Balkans and Bantustans

1. E. J. Hobsbawm, *Nations and Nationalism Since 1780: Programme, Myth, Reality* (Cambridge: Cambridge University Press, 1990), p. 183.

2. If Hitler personifies the horrors of "ethnic cleansing," it is less often remembered that Churchill and Roosevelt embraced to a weak version of one of his assumptions, namely that homogeneous nation-states are more desirable and stable than heterogeneous ones. To this end the Allies oversaw the forced removal of millions of Europeans after WWII.

3. Indeed, Buthelezi and his allies have maintained that, on account of the persistent violence, democratic elections should be ruled out. Meanwhile, a constitution ought to be drawn up which partitions South Africa into strongly autonomous regions with ethnic majorities of Zulus, Afrikaners, Tswanas, Xhosas and so forth, each possessing the right of secession. Such a scheme would defer indefinitely the advent of democracy and exacerbate the bloodshed.

4. "Expatriates' Sun Sinks with Zaire," *Guardian*, 8 October 1991.

5. Patrick Wright, "Quebec's Tainted Separatist Dream," *Guardian*, 3rd September, 1992.

6. Gerhard Mare, "History and Dimension of the Violence in Natal: Inkatha's Role in Negotiating Political Peace," *Social Justice* 18, nos. 1-2 (Spring-Sum. 1991), p. 187. The portrait of the Anglo-Boer War as "white-on-white" could only be ironic, otherwise it would occlude the considerable numbers of black soldiers and civilians killed during that war.

7. Rupert Taylor gives an excellent account of such atavistic interpretations of South Africa's violence. He cites, for example, *Time* magazine's ascription of the conflict to "tribal-based animosities [between Zulus and Xhosas] that date back centuries." This despite the fact that a clash in 1827 is the solitary record of such a Zulu-Xhosa conflict. See Taylor, "The Myth of Ethnic Division: Township Conflict on the Reef," *Race & Class* 33, 2 (1991), pp. 3-5.

8. Leroy Vail (ed.), *The Creation of Tribalism in Southern Africa* (London: James Currey, 1989), p. 2.

9. R. W. Johnson, "The Danger of Majority Rule," *The Times* 4 Sept. 1992, p. 10. See his related views in "What Buthelezi Wants," *London Review of Books*, 19 December, 1991 pp. 14-15. Johnson's prophetic zeal seems undented by his spectacular failures in this sphere in the past, as in the final chapter of *How Long Will South Africa Survive?*

10. Andries Treurnicht, *International Herald Tribune*, 2 March 1990. I am grateful to Preben Kaarsholm for drawing my attention to this utterance in his paper "The Ethnicisation of Politics and the Politicisation of Ethnicity: Culture and Political Development in South Africa," presented at the Institute of Commonwealth Studies, 13 November 1992.

11. Radio 4 (Britain), 6 o'clock news, 6 October 1992. See also, *The Guardian*, 28 Sept. 1992.

12. Anon., "'Governor' Buthelezi's Tail Wags a National Party Dog," *Southern Africa Report*, 4 December 1992, p. 2.

13. Anon., "Mangosuthu Buthelezi: Message of the Drums," *Financial Mail* (Johannesburg), 23 October 1992, p. 26.

14. See "Pretoria and Inkatha: Evidence of a Conspiracy," *Independent on Sunday*, 28 July 1991, and "Pretoria Admits Giving Inkatha Financial Help," *Independent*, 20 July 1991.

15. On this point, see especially Shula Marks's incisive article, "The Origins of Ethnic Violence in South Africa," in Norman Etherington (ed.), *Peace, Politics and Violence in the New South Africa* (London: Hans Zell, 1992).

16. Despite the Serbs' draconian measures against Albanians in Kosovo during the late 1980s, "ethnic cleansing" was not instituted there.

17. Connie Mulder, *Hansard* (South Africa), 7 February 1978, col. 579.

18. On the subject of "black spots," see, for example, Verwoerd's speeches of 5 Dec. 1950 and 14 April 1961 in A.N. Pelzer (ed.), *Verwoerd Speaks: Speeches 1948-1966* (Johannesburg: APB Publishers, 1966), pp. 27 and 591.

19. See Lauren Platsky and Cheryl Walker, *The Surplus People—Forced Removals in South Africa* (Johannesburg: Ravan, 1985) and Elaine Unterhalter, *Forced Removal: the Division, Segregation and Control of the People of South Africa* (London: International Defence and Aid Fund, 1987).

20. Mr. G. F. van L. Froneman, chairman of the Bantu Affairs Commission, speaking in 1968. Quoted J. D. Omer-Cooper, *History of Southern Africa* (London:

Heinemann, 1987), p. 213.

21. Louis Nel, in a letter to the *Sunday Times* (Johannesburg), 10 July 1977.
22. Ibid.
23. See, for example, No Sizwe, *One Azania, One Nation: The National Question in South Africa* (London: Zed, 1979), p. 1; Colin Bundy, Re-Making the Past (Cape Town: University of Cape Town, 1986), p. 54.
24. For one account of Carrington's recommendations, see Christopher Hitchens, "Why Bosnia Matters," *London Review of Books*, 10 September, 1992, pp. 6-7.
25. "Balkanization," one should add, is also an unfortunate term, for it perpetuates the reductive image of the Balkans as a barbarous place that gives rise to small, vicious nationalist animosities.
26. For one brief but suggestive reflection on this metaphor, see Neal Ascherson, "The Tragically Easy Path to "Ethnic Cleansing,"" *Independent on Sunday*, 9 August 1991, p. 23.
27. Dubravka Ugresic, "Dirty Tyranny of Mr. Clean," *Independent on Sunday*, 6 Dec. 1992, p. 22.
28. For some emphatic arguments against the view that the Serbs, Croats, and Muslims constitute discrete ethnicities, see Robert Fisk, "The Lie That Leaves Bosnia in the Lurch," *The Independent on Sunday*, 6 December 1992, p. 13; Hitchens, pp. 6-7; and Thompson, p. 327.
29. Lejla Somum, "Fifth Column," a documentary shown on BBC2, 16 Dec. 1992.
30. Mark Thompson, "Comforts of Fatalism," *Guardian*, 13 November 1992.
31. Paul Gilroy, *There Ain't No Black in the Union Jack* (London: Unwin Hyman, 1987); Stuart Hall, "New Ethnicities," *"Race," Culture and Difference*, edited by James Donald and Ali Rattansi (London: Sage, 1992), pp. 252-59; Etienne Balibar and Immanuel Wallerstein, *Race, Nation, Class: Ambiguous Identities* (1988; London: Verso, 1991), p. 23.
32. J.A. Coetzee, *Nasieskap en Politieke Groepering in Suid-Afrika (1652-1968)* (Pretoria: Transvaalse Uitgewersmaatskappy, 1969), pp. 322-23.
33. With an eye to forthcoming national elections, Buthelezi has found himself in a dilemma. Regionally, his political trumpcard is his claim that Inkatha represents the Zulu nation; nationally, this same claim is a liability. Thus, particularly since 1990, Buthelezi has tended to vacillate between incompatible visions of Inkatha as embodying an exclusive ethnic nationalism and as accommodating the kind of inclusive, multi-ethnic nationalism that would be a prerequisite if he hopes to build a constituency in South Africa at large.
34. Quoted Gerhard Mare, *Brothers Born of Warrior Blood* (Johannesburg: Ravan, 1992), p. 75-6.
35. Anne McClintock, "Family Feuds: Gender, Nation, and the Family," *Feminist Review*, Spring 1993 and Deniz Kandiyoti, "Identity and its Discontents: Women and the Nation," *Millennium: Journal of International Studies* 20, 3(1991), pp. 429-443. See also, Cynthia Enloe, *Bananas, Beaches and Bases: Making Feminist Sense of International Politics* (1989; rpt. Berkeley: University of California Press, 1990), pp. 42-64.
36. For an account of the rape camps, see Maggie O'Kane, "Forgotten Women of Serb Rape Camps," *Guardian*, 19 December 1992. See also, Catherine Bennett's discussion of masculinity and rape in "Ordinary Madness," *Guardian*, 20 January

1993.

37. For some incisive commentary on this issue, see Catherine Campbell, "Learning to Kill? Masculinity, the Family and Violence in Natal," *Journal of Southern African Studies*, 18, 3 (Sept. 1992), pp. 614-22.

38. Leslie Maasdorp, "The Internal Economic Situation in South Africa," unpublished paper presented at the Institute of Commonwealth Studies, London, ICS 23rd Nov. 1991.

39. For an excellent account of these complex, compound tensions, see Lauren Segal, "The Human Face of Violence. Hostel Dwellers Speak," *Journal of Southern African Studies*, 18, 3 (Sept. 1992).

40. Marks, p. 25.

41. On this subject, see Kaarsholm p. 9 and Mike Morris and Doug Hindson, "The Disintegration of Apartheid: From Violence to Reconstruction," in Glenn Moss and Ingrid Obery (eds.), *South African Review 6* (Johannesburg: Ravan, 1992), pp. 152-70.

42. *Africa Confidential* 33, 4 (21 February 1992).

43. Neal Ascherson, *Games With Shadows* (London: Radius Books, 1988), p. 281.

44. For an instructive account of Ciskei's problems see Anonymous, "Ethnicity and Pseudo-ethnicity in the Ciskei," in Vail, pp. 395-413.

45. For a detailed analysis of these rivalries, see especially Shula Marks, *The Ambiguities of Dependence: Race, Class and Nationalism in Twentieth Century South Africa* (Baltimore: John Hopkins, 1986).

46. For a suggestive account of Buthelezi's efforts, see Mare, *Brothers Born of Warrior Blood.*

47. In a speech in 1991, Buthelezi argued that "The call to ban the bearing of cultural weapons by Zulus is an insult to my manhood. It is an insult to the manhood of every Zulu man." (Quoted, Mare, *Brothers Born of Warrior Blood,* p. 68.) Cf. King Goodwill Zwelithini's insistence that "The ANC seeks to deprive Zulu men of their manhood by taking away their cultural weapons." (*Weekly Mail,* 31 May 1991.) For a very suggestive analysis of the Inkatha premium on manliness against the backdrop of changes in the family, see Catherine Campbell, "Learning to Kill? Masculinity, the Family and Violence in Natal," *Journal of Southern African Studies* 18, 3 (Sept. 1992), pp. 614 ff.

48. "Mangosuthu Buthelezi: Message of the Drums," *Financial Mail,* 23 October 1992.

49. Speech delivered on 23 September 1990. Quoted Gerhard Mare, "History and Dimension of the Violence in Natal: Inkatha's Role in Negotiating Political Peace," *Social Justice* 18, 1-2 (1991), p. 190.

50. Mangosuthu Buthelezi, "Inkatha, 'Zuluness' and the Historians," *Passages: Newsletter of the Program for African Studies at Northwestern University,* 4 (1992), p. 9.

51. Ibid.

52. Ibid.

53. Quoted Mare, pp. 72-3.

54. *Musho! Zulu Popular Praises.* Trans. and edited by Liz Gunner and Mafika Gwala (East Lansing: Michigan State University Press, 1991); Ari Sitas, "Class, Nation, Ethnicity in Natal's Black Working Class," in Shula Marks (ed.), *The Societies of Southern Africa in the 19th and 20th Centuries,* vol. 15 (London: Instit. of

Commonwealth Studies, 1990), pp. 257-78.

55. Paul Palinowski, *Serbian Epics*, BBC2, 16 December 1992.

56. Thompson, p. 145.

57. See T.D. Allman, "Serbia's Blood War," *Vanity Fair*, March 1993, p. 34.

58. There has, of late, been considerable revisionist debate over the rise of the Zulu empire. See Carolyn Hamilton, "The Character and Objects of Chaka: a Reconsideration of the Making of Shaka as Mfecane "motor," and Julian Cobbing, "The Mfecane: a Rejoinder," both in *Journal of African History* (1992). See also, Hamilton and John Wright, "The Beginnings of Zulu Identity," *Indicator South Africa* 10, 3 (Winter, 1993), pp. 43-46; and Mary de Haas and Paulus Zulu, "Ethnic Mobilisation: KwaZulu's Politics of Secession," ibid., pp. 47-52.

59. Etienne Balibar, "Racism and Nationalism," in Balibar and Immanuel Wallerstein, *Race, Nation, and Class: Ambiguous Identities* (London: Verso, 1991), p. 45.

60. The memory of Afrikaners' territorial dispossession and of the 28,000 who died in British concentration camps during the Anglo-Boer War, became psychologically crucial to the Afrikaners elaboration of an ethnic nationalist narrative of themselves as a suffering, colonized people. But it was not only Afrikaners who died in those camps: there were 14,000 recorded concentration camp deaths among Afrikaners' African workers—predominantly tenant farmers—who were interned in large numbers. See Dougie Oakes (ed.), *Illustrated History of South Africa* (Cape Town: Reader's Digest, 1992), p. 256.

61. For the non-Amharas had themselves been conquered by the Ethiopian empire in the late 19th century and had suffered beneath the Amhara's policy of Christianization and coercive assimilation. I am indebted to the Ethiopian anthropologist, Alex Naty, for drawing my attention to the complexity of Ethiopia's layered imperialisms.

62. Ernest Gellner, *Nations and Nationalism* (Oxford: Basil Blackwell, 1983), p. 32. If the U.S.A., Australia, and some Caribbean states stand as exceptions to this generalization, even their eclecticism may become insitutionalized as a decisive trait of *the* national culture.

63. Ernest Renan, "What is a Nation?" trans. Martin Thom, in Homi K. Bhabha (ed.), *Nation and Narration* (London: Routledge, 1990), p. 11.

INDEX